# Fodor's

## BAHAMAS

# WELCOME TO THE BAHAMAS

Made up of 700 islands—some busy and bustling, some isolated and inhabited by no one but hermit crabs and seagulls—the Bahamas offers an alluring mix of land and sea activities. From Nassau to Eleuthera, you can play golf on a seaside fairway, dive dramatic wrecks and reefs, and sail in crystal clear water. Accommodations run the gamut from simple inns to sophisticated retreats, from practical fishing lodges to romantic honeymoon hideaways. And for those who look a little closer, there's a fascinating and diverse culture to be explored.

## TOP REASONS TO GO

★ **Beaches.** The powdery, soft sand creates some of the world's best strands.

★ **Boating.** Ideal conditions draw small dinghies, serious sailboats, and luxury yachts.

★ **Family Fun.** From sprawling water parks to horseback rides along the beach.

★ **Out Islands.** Quiet and uncrowded, these islands are hard to reach but worth the trip.

★ **Fishing.** From fly-casting for tarpon and bonefish to fighting with a giant marlin.

# Fodor's BAHAMAS

**Publisher:** Amanda D'Acierno, *Senior Vice President*

**Editorial:** Arabella Bowen, *Executive Editorial Director*; Linda Cabasin, *Editorial Director*

**Design:** Fabrizio La Rocca, *Vice President, Creative Director*; Tina Malaney, *Associate Art Director*; Chie Ushio, *Senior Designer*; Ann McBride, *Production Designer*

**Photography:** Melanie Marin, *Associate Director of Photography*; Jessica Parkhill and Jennifer Romains, *Researchers*

**Maps:** Rebecca Baer, *Senior Map Editor*; Mark Stroud and Henry Colomb (Moon Street Cartography), David Lindroth, *Cartographers*

**Production:** Linda Schmidt, *Managing Editor*; Evangelos Vasilakis, *Associate Managing Editor*; Angela L. McLean, *Senior Production Manager*

**Sales:** Jacqueline Lebow, *Sales Director*

**Marketing & Publicity:** Heather Dalton, *Marketing Director*; Katherine Fleming, *Senior Publicist*

**Business & Operations:** Susan Livingston, *Vice President, Strategic Business Planning*; Sue Daulton, *Vice President, Operations*

**Fodors.com:** Megan Bell, *Executive Director, Revenue & Business Development*; Yasmin Marinaro, *Senior Director, Marketing & Partnerships*

Copyright © 2014 by Fodor's Travel, a division of Random House LLC.

**Editor:** Douglas Stallings

**Writers:** Julianne Hoell, Jessica Robertson, Paul Rubio, Jamie Werner

**Production Editor:** Evangelos Vasilakis

29th Edition

ISBN 978-0-7704-3262-1

ISSN 1524-7945

## SPECIAL SALES

This book is available at special discounts for bulk purchases for sales promotions or premiums. For more information, e-mail specialmarkets@randomhouse.com

PRINTED IN COLOMBIA

10 9 8 7 6 5 4 3 2 1

# CONTENTS

## MAPS

# ABOUT
# THIS GUIDE

## Fodor's Recommendations

Everything in this guide is worth doing—we don't cover what isn't—but exceptional sights, hotels, and restaurants are recognized with additional accolades. **Fodor'sChoice★** indicates our top recommendations. Care to nominate a new place? Visit Fodors.com/contact-us.

## Trip Costs

We list prices wherever possible to help you budget well. Hotel and restaurant price categories from $ to $$$$ are noted alongside each recommendation. For hotels, we include the lowest cost of a standard double room in high season. For restaurants, we cite the average price of a main course at dinner or, if dinner isn't served, at lunch. For attractions, we always list adult admission fees; discounts are usually available for children, students, and senior citizens.

## Hotels

Our local writers vet every hotel to recommend the best overnights in each price category, from budget to expensive. Unless otherwise specified, you can expect private bath, phone, and TV in your room. For expanded hotel reviews, facilities, and deals visit Fodors.com.

## Restaurants

Unless we state otherwise, restaurants are open for lunch and dinner daily. We mention dress code only when there's a specific requirement and reservations only when they're essential or not accepted. To make restaurant reservations, visit Fodors.com.

## Credit Cards

The hotels and restaurants in this guide typically accept credit cards. If not, we'll say so.

### Top Picks
★ **Fodor'sChoice**

### Listings
- ✉ Address
- ✉ Branch address
- ☎ Telephone
- 🖷 Fax
- ⊕ Website
- ✎ E-mail
- ✒ Admission fee
- ☻ Open/closed times
- Ⓜ Subway
- ✛ Directions or Map coordinates

### Hotels & Restaurants
- 🏨 Hotel
- ↵ Number of rooms
- ✝◎✝ Meal plans
- ✗ Restaurant
- ✍ Reservations
- 🏛 Dress code
- ▭ No credit cards
- Ⓢ Price

### Other
- ⇨ See also
- ☞ Take note
- 𝍩 Golf facilities

# EXPERIENCE THE BAHAMAS

# WHAT'S WHERE

*Numbers refer to chapter numbers.*

**2 New Providence and Paradise Islands.** Nassau and nearby Paradise Island are the most action-packed places in the Bahamas. From flashy megaresort Atlantis to fine dining and high-end shopping, development here is unrivaled on any of the other islands.

**3 Grand Bahama Island.** Urban and deserted vibes mix to create a quieter alternative to fast-paced Nassau. Lucaya has great shopping, gambling, golfing, and beach parties, but old-island fishing settlements and vast expanses of untouched nature appeal to adventurous travelers.

**4 The Abacos.** Shallow, translucent waters, top-notch marinas, and idyllic, historic settlements spread over 120 miles of cays (some uninhabited) give the Abacos the apt title of "Sailing Capital of the Bahamas."

**5 Andros, Bimini, and the Berry Islands.** In the northwest corner of the Bahamas, these islands share many characteristics, most notably their reputation for excellent fishing and diving. Each exudes a casual, old-island atmosphere and abundant natural beauty.

Walker's Cay
Grand Cay
Strangers Cay
LITTLE BAHAMA BANK
GRAND BAHAMA ISLAND
Spanish Cay
Green Turtle Cay
Little Abaco I.
**3**
Freeport/ Lucaya
**4**
Marsh Harbor
*Northwest Providence Channel*
GREAT ABACO ISLAND
*Northeast Providence Channel*
Bimini Islands
Berry Islands
Harbour I.
Paradise Island
Eleuthera Island
**2**
**5**
**6**
Nassau
NEW PROVIDENCE I.
ANDROS ISLAND
*Santaren Channel*
GREAT BAHAMA BANK
*Tongue of the Ocean*
*Barrier Reef*
THE EXUMAS
*Exuma*
**7**
Great Exuma Island
Ragged Island Range
← TO HAVANA
CUBA

**0** |_____| 50 miles
**0** |_____| 75 km

*Atlantic Ocean*

Cat
and
▲ Mt. Alvernia
○
Port Howe
San
Salvador

nd
○ Rum Cay
Long
Island [8]
Samana Cay
Clarence
Town
*Crooked Island Passage*
Crooked
Island
Acklins
Islands
*Mayaguana Passage*
Mayaguana
Island
*Caicos Passage*
Providenciales
Little Inagua Island
Great Inagua
Island
Lake
Rose

**6** **Eleuthera and Harbour Island.** The Nantucket of the Bahamas, Harbour Island—rimmed by its legendary pink-sand beach—is the most chic Out Island. Eleuthera is the opposite, with historic churches and pretty fishing villages, unpretentious inns, and a few upscale, intimate beach resorts.

**7** **The Exumas.** Hundreds of islands skip like stones across the Tropic of Cancer, all with gorgeous white beaches and the most beautiful water in the Bahamas. Mainland Great Exuma has friendly locals and great beach parties.

**8** **The Southern Out Islands.** The Bahamas' southernmost islands have so few visitors and so many natural wonders. These islands are also known as the Family Islands, since many Bahamians have roots on these smaller and less populated cays.

# BAHAMAS TODAY

Like much of the world, the Bahamas has had to put big development plans on the back burner as the country rides out the economic recession. The largest project, the Baha Mar overhaul of the Cable Beach strip, is finally underway, but is years behind schedule. Bahamians have used this situation as an opportunity to spruce up existing properties and improve an infrastructure that was starting to show signs of age and neglect. Once the tide turns and tourism picks back up, the Bahamas will be better than ever.

## Today's Bahamas

**. . . is still very British.** From driving on the left side of the road (albeit mostly in left-hand drive cars) to tea parties to wig-wearing lawyers strolling into court, the Bahamas still has a decidedly British air about it. The country gained independence from England in 1973, but old colonial habits die hard. Bahamians learn British spelling in school, and the country still uses the Westminster style of government. That said, a constant diet of American media has had an impact on the country. Bahamians measure temperature in Fahrenheit instead of Celsius, and although the English gentleman's cricket is the national sport, you'll be hard-pressed to find a local who understands the game, much less plays it.

**. . . is a playground for the rich and famous.** With its near-perfect year-round weather, modern infrastructure and amenities, and proximity to the United States, it's no wonder that the Bahamas is a home away from Hollywood for many celebrities. Sean Connery lives behind the gates of the exclusive Lyford Cay community on New Providence Island. Johnny Depp owns his own private island in the Exumas, as do Tim McGraw and Faith Hill, David Copperfield, and Nicolas Cage, who also owns a home on Paradise Island. Mariah Carey and Nick Cannon got hitched on the grounds of her private Eleuthera estate; the island is also home to Lenny Kravitz, whose mother, actress Roxie Roker, grew up there.

**. . . is many different destinations.** The majority of the 4 million tourists who visit the Bahamas each year experience only Nassau, Paradise Island, or perhaps Grand Bahama. But with more than 700 islands, there's so much more to see and do. Each island offers a different flavor and none of them have the hustle and bustle of big-city life experienced in the capital. The farther south you venture, the slower the pace.

## WHAT WE'RE TALKING ABOUT

Bahamians are passionate about their politics. Despite elections only every five years, everyone is continually vocal about which party will win and which scandals will and will not sway voters.

The Bahamas has a parliamentary system, much like England's. As elsewhere in the British Commonwealth, there is a governor general who serves as the Queen's representative. A prime minister leads the government and bicameral legislature. The upper chamber is called the Senate, whose members are appointed by the prime minister in consultation with the opposition. Members of the lower chamber, the House of Assembly, are elected directly. Perry Christie and the Progressive Liberal Party unseated Hubert Ingraham and the Free National Movement Party for a second time in

Locals have distinct looks, dialects, and surnames on each island. White Americans and British settled in the Abacos and north Eleuthera, and their strong accents—putting an *h* where there isn't one and omitting one where there should be—help tell them apart from expats. Long Island is home to a large "conchy joe" population, white Bahamians who might have had a black great grandpa. Tell someone you're a Knowles and they'll want to know if you're a Long Island Knowles or an Eleuthera Knowles.

**. . . is getting spruced up.** After 10 years of temporary tent quarters, the Nassau straw market's magnificent $11 million new home opened in 2011. Bay Street, once Nassau's Madison Avenue, is on the road to recovery after years of neglect. The Lynden Pindling International Airport is now a modern gateway that truly welcomes visitors. And following a number of false starts, the multibillion-dollar Baha Mar transformation of the Cable Beach strip is well underway. As Nassau continues to develop, the Out Islands remain untouched, preserving the quaint nature that attracts adventure travelers each year.

**. . . is not part of the Caribbean.** Even though the country gets lumped in with the Caribbean in glossy travel brochures and on cruise itineraries, it is not geographically a part of it. Rather than being situated in the Caribbean Sea, the islands of the Bahamas are in the Atlantic Ocean. In fact, more Bahamians have traveled to nearby South Florida than to the Caribbean. But from a cultural and political point of view, the Bahamas is aligned with the neighboring islands. The country is a full member of the Caribbean Community (CARICOM) and Bahamians will cheer on their Caribbean brothers and sisters in any sporting match.

**. . . is worried about the environment.** Thankfully, the 2010 Deepwater Horizon oil spill did not affect the Bahamas, but Bahamians now have become much more aware of the need to protect the "sun, sand, and sea" that puts food on so many tables. The government works closely with the Bahamas National Trust to identify and develop protected green spaces, and any developer interested in putting up a sizeable or potentially environmentally sensitive project anywhere in the country is required to pay for and submit an Environmental Impact Assessment before consideration is granted.

2012. The Democratic National Alliance, led by a former FNM cabinet minister, was the first fringe party to run a full slate of candidates in 2012.

Even the most patriotic Bahamian will admit that the country's jewel—downtown Nassau—had lost its luster.

With the recent global economic slump, once spectacular stores had given way to tacky T-shirt shops or have been left vacant, and sidewalks and building facades had suffered. Since its formation in 2009 the Downtown Nassau Partnership has made

steady strides towards revitalization. The straw market destroyed by fire in September 2001 has been rebuilt, and Pompey Square, a vibrant open space that attracts locals and visitors to the area, has opened. Other clean-up is still underway.

# BAHAMAS TOP ATTRACTIONS

### Junkanoo

(A) The Bahamas' answer to Rio de Janeiro's Carnaval and New Orleans' Mardi Gras, Junkanoo is a festival of parades and parties held on Boxing Day (the day after Christmas) and New Year's Day. Groups compete with elaborate, colorful costumes and choreographed routines to distinctly Bahamian music created by goatskin drums, clanging cowbells, conch-shell horns, shrieking whistles, and brass bands.

### Pink Sand

(B) Head to Eleuthera, Harbour Island, or Cat Island to experience pink-sand beaches. The pink hue comes from the shell of a microscopic sea creature living on the coral reefs offshore. Waves crush the pink and red shells and wash them onto the beach. The most famous pink beach is on the northern side of Harbour Island.

### Coral Reefs

(C) The Bahamas is home to the world's third-largest barrier reef. If diving along the Andros Barrier Reef is too advanced for you, no worries, there are many opportunities to explore the magnificent undersea world surrounding the Bahamas. Colorful coral, sea fans, and marine creatures abound; take an underwater camera, since the only things you're allowed to bring back to the surface are photographs and memories.

### Fish Fry

No matter which island you're visiting, there's bound to be a fish fry in full swing at least one night of the week. Clusters of wooden shacks and stalls fry up snapper, goggle eye, or jack fish, served with fries or a thick chunk of sweet island bread. Each stall plays its own music, creating a cacophony of sound; groups gather around wooden tables to play dominoes or to catch up on the local sip-sip (gossip).

The fish fry at Arawak Cay in Nassau is open daily, but on the other islands they can be a once-a-week occurrence.

### Conch

(D) Conch, pronounced "konk," is popular for more than just its distinctive, spiral-shape shells; this sea creature, essentially a giant snail, is one of the mainstays of Bahamian cuisine. Firm white conch meat is tenderized, then turned into a variety of dishes. There's cracked conch, conch salad, conch chowder, and the popular appetizer, conch fritters. Islanders often claim that conch has two other magical powers—as a hangover cure (when eaten straight from the shell with hot peppers, salt, and lime) and as an especially tasty aphrodisiac.

### Rake 'n' Scrape

(E) Generations ago, many Bahamians didn't have the money to buy instruments, so they made music using whatever was at hand. Someone played a saw, someone else made a bass out of string and a tin tub, and another musician kept the beat by shaking a plastic jug filled with rocks or dried beans, or beating a goatskin drum. Today the best place to hear authentic Rake 'n' Scrape is on Cat Island, where the style is said to have been born.

### Rum Drinks

(F) The Bahamas has a long history with rum, dating back to the days of bootlegging during the United States Prohibition. Rum consumption is perfectly legal nowadays, and Bahamian bartenders have mixed up some rum-infused concoctions that have become synonymous with tropical vacations: Bahama Mama, Yellow Bird, and the Hurricane. If you're in Green Turtle Cay in Abaco, pop into Miss Emily's Blue Bee Bar, where the Goombay Smash was born.

# ISLAND FINDER

| | NEW PROVIDENCE AND PARADISE ISLANDS | GRAND BAHAMA ISLAND | THE ABACOS | ELEUTHERA | HARBOUR ISLAND | THE EXUMAS | THE OTHER OUT ISLANDS |
|---|---|---|---|---|---|---|---|
| **BEACHES** | | | | | | | |
| Activities and Sports | ● | ● | ● | ◐ | ◐ | ◐ | ◐ |
| Deserted | ○ | ◐ | ◐ | ● | ○ | ◐ | ● |
| Party Scene | ● | ◐ | ◐ | ○ | ● | ◐ | ○ |
| Pink Sand | ○ | ○ | ○ | ● | ● | ○ | ◐ |
| **CITY LIFE** | | | | | | | |
| Crowds | ● | ◐ | ○ | ○ | ◐ | ○ | ○ |
| Urban Development | ● | ◐ | ◐ | ○ | ○ | ○ | ○ |
| **ENTERTAINMENT** | | | | | | | |
| Bahamian Cultural Events and Sights | ● | ◐ | ◐ | ○ | ◐ | ○ | ◐ |
| Hot Restaurant Scene | ● | ◐ | ○ | ○ | ● | ○ | ○ |
| Nightlife | ● | ◐ | ○ | ○ | ◐ | ○ | ○ |
| Shopping | ● | ● | ◐ | ○ | ◐ | ◐ | ○ |
| Spas | ● | ◐ | ○ | ○ | ○ | ◐ | ○ |
| Casinos | ● | ◐ | ○ | ○ | ○ | ○ | ○ |
| **LODGING** | | | | | | | |
| Luxury Hotels and Resorts | ● | ● | ◐ | ◐ | ● | ◐ | ◐ |
| Condos | ● | ◐ | ◐ | ◐ | ◐ | ◐ | ◐ |
| **NATURE** | | | | | | | |
| Wildlife | ◐ | ● | ● | ◐ | ○ | ● | ● |
| Ecotourism | ◐ | ● | ● | ◐ | ○ | ● | ● |
| **SPORTS** | | | | | | | |
| Golf | ● | ● | ◐ | ○ | ○ | ● | ○ |
| Scuba and Snorkeling | ● | ● | ● | ● | ● | ● | ● |
| Fishing | ● | ● | ● | ● | ● | ● | ● |

●: noteworthy; ◐ some; ○: little or none

# THE BAHAMAS' BEST BEACHES

by Jessica Robertson

There's no feeling as invigorating as putting the first footprints on a powdery sand beach. With 800 miles of beachfront across the Bahamas, you could be the first to leave your mark even if you head out at sunset. But if your idea of a perfect beach day includes tropical drinks, water sports, and pulsating music, most islands have those, too.

pictured: Gold Rock Beach, Grand Bahama

# BEACH PLANNING

With so many spectacular stretches of sand in the Bahamas, how do you increase your odds of stumbling upon the best ones?

**Decide whether you want a deserted island experience or a beach with lots of amenities.** For beaches with bathrooms, water sport activities, and pick-up volleyball games, you'll find the most options on New Providence, Paradise Island, and Grand Bahama. The Exumas, Harbour Island, Bimini, and the Abacos have a good mix of secluded sand and beach parties. The farther south you travel, the more deserted the beaches become. You might have the sand entirely to yourself on Eleuthera or any of the southern Out Islands.

**Waters in the Bahamas are calm, for the most part.** But when weather picks up, so do the waves. That said, most of the Atlantic-side beaches are protected by coral reefs offshore, so waves are broken up before they reach you. More good news: these natural barriers break up shells, creating powder-fine white—and in some cases pink—sand. Most of the noteworthy beaches that don't face the Atlantic are in bays and coves where you'll rarely find a ripple in the water. These are the beaches to visit with small children and if you're a serious shell seeker.

**If you're traveling with children, shade is a must.** When you venture away from the hotel, head for a beach lined with tall casuarinas trees. Although considered invasive nuisances by locals because the carpet of needles they shed prevent any other native foliage to grow, they do provide the best shade from the relentless Bahamian sunshine.

Pink Sands Beach, Harbour Island

## PINK SAND

❶ **Club Med Beach, Eleuthera.** The island's less famous (and less crowded) pink sand beach got its name from the European resort that once overlooked it. The Atlantic-side beach has baby's-bottom-soft pink sand and lots of shady casuarinas pines.

❷ **Fine Beach, Cat Island.** Twelve miles of fine, powdery pink sand lie just north of Greenwood Beach. Despite the pristine beauty of this Atlantic-side beach, you'll likely be the only one here on any given day.

❸ **Greenwood Beach, Cat Island.** Eight miles of pink sand stretch along the Atlantic Ocean at the southeast tip of Cat Island. This remote beach is never crowded, so even on a busy beach day you'll find your own spot for swimming, strolling, or sunbathing.

❹ **Lighthouse Beach, Eleuthera.** Ask any Eleutheran to point you to his or her favorite beach, and you'll probably end up on a long drive south to Bannerman Town on roads with more potholes than asphalt. But when you get to Lighthouse Beach, you'll know you weren't led astray. Caves, cliffs, and a long-abandoned, centuries-old lighthouse make for fun exploring on the 3 mi of pink sand that curve around the island's southern point.

❺ **Pink Sands Beach, Harbour Island.** Finely crushed shells give this 3-mi stretch of sand its spectacular hue, and the wide, flat topography is ideal for sunbathing or galloping along on horseback.

Chat 'N' Chill, Stocking Island, the Exumas

Great Exuma

## BEACH PARTIES

❶ **Cabbage Beach, Paradise Island.** The fun and activities from the Bahamas' largest resort, Atlantis, spill over onto 3-mi Cabbage Beach. This is the best spot on Paradise Island for Jet Skis, banana boats, or parasailing. Dreadlocked men carrying cardboard boxes of fresh coconuts will crack one open and create your very own intoxicating concoction. If you're not staying at one of the resorts lining the beach, you can access it just east of the Riu Palace.

❷ **Guana Cay Beach, the Abacos.** On Sunday afternoon, head to Nippers, on the north side of the beach, and wonder at all the people. Locals and tourists alike come out for the legendary all-day pig roast. Grab a drink and find a perch at the bar, beach, or bi-level pool.

❸ **Lucaya Beach, Grand Bahama.** If you're looking for water sports, tropical music, and drinks served beachside, this 7.5-mi stretch of white sand is a good place to lay your towel. The most action is right in front of the Our Lucaya resort, but if you head west, you can barhop at the hotels, restaurants, and beach bars lining the strip.

❹ **Stocking Island, the Exumas.** On Sunday, everyone heads to Stocking Island for the pig roast at Chat 'N' Chill. The music is good, the food is spectacular, and the drinks flow. Play volleyball, go snorkeling just offshore, or sit under a tree with a fresh bowl of conch salad and an infamous Goombay Smash.

## WORTH THE TREK

❶ **Gold Rock Beach, Grand Bahama.** This seemingly endless stretch of sand near the Lucayan National Park is extraordinarily peaceful. As the tide goes out, wide, rippled sand banks pop out of the water, giving the illusion that you could walk out to the horizon. To access the beach, leave your car at the park and walk about a half hour over a low bridge crossing the mangrove swamps. Note, however, that there are planks missing in some parts of the bridge.

❷ **Sandy Cay, the Exumas.** The southernmost Exuma cay only gets more spectacular as the tide goes out. The main beach is exquisite, but it's the sand bar that emerges at low tide that makes this location well worth the short boat ride from William's Town, the southernmost settlement on Little Exuma. Starfish, sand dollars, and shells usually dot the tidal beach, and the kaleidoscopic crystal-clear water surrounding it is breathtaking. It's no wonder scenes from *Pirates of the Caribbean* were filmed here.

❸ **Surfer's Beach, Eleuthera.** The Bahamas aren't known as a surfer's paradise, but Surfer's Beach near Gregory Town, Eleuthera, is one of the sport's best-kept secrets. Even if you don't hang ten, this beautiful beach makes the treacherous journey worthwhile. Unless you're in an off-road vehicle, you'll probably have to abandon your car halfway down rough-and-bumpy Ocean Boulevard and walk nearly a mile up and over cliffs to the beach.

# FODOR'S CHOICE BEST BEACHES

**❶ Fernandez Bay Beach, Cat Island**

**Why:** The odds of being the only one on this sparsely populated island's most amazing beach are definitely stacked in your favor, even though it's home to a small resort. White sand lines the crescent-shaped cove from end to end.

**Claim to fame:** Nothing yet. It's just waiting for you to come and discover beach perfection.

**Don't miss:** The beach faces west, so sundown here is spectacular.

**❷ Cape Santa Maria Beach, Long Island**

**Why:** The sand on Cape Santa Maria Beach is shimmering white and powder fine, and goes on for more than 4 mi. Lined with swaying palms, this flat beach on the northwest coast of Long Island is postcard-perfect.

**Claim to fame:** Christopher Columbus named this cape after one of three ships he used to sail from Spain.

**Don't miss:** The chance to catch dinner when the tidal flats rise out of the turquoise water at low tide.

**❸ Pink Sands Beach, Harbour Island**

**Why:** The vibrant 3-mi pink sand beach and extraordinary palette of blues and aquamarines in the ocean make a stunning backdrop for a sunrise or sunset stroll.

**Claim to fame:** Martha Stewart, Nicole Kidman, and Brooke Shields have stayed at the beach's posh Pink Sands resort.

**Don't miss:** A chance for a seaside canter. Just look for the dreadlocked man with the horses, and pick your mount.

**❹ Treasure Cay Beach, the Abacos**

**Why:** One of the widest stretches of powdery white sand in the Bahamas, the beach at Treasure Cay is 3½ mi long and borders a shallow aquamarine bay that's perfect for swimming. Activities and a restaurant are on one end, and a deserted oasis on the other.

**Claim to fame:** Voted the Best Beach in the Caribbean in 2004 by readers of *Caribbean Travel and Life* magazine.

**Don't miss:** The sand dollars that line the sand as the tide gently rolls out.

# LIKE A LOCAL

If you want to experience more of the Bahamas than just the sand at your resort's beach, make like a local and try one of the following.

## Enjoy a Boil' Fish Breakfast

Pass on the eggs and pancakes and try a real Bahamian breakfast of boil' fish. Fillets of grouper, turbot, or muttonfish are cooked up in a delicious peppery lime-based broth with onions and potatoes. It's served with grits or a chunk of johnnycake. Alternatives on the Bahamian breakfast menu include stew' fish or conch—similar to boil' fish but cooked in thick brown gravy—chicken, pig-feet, or sheep-tongue souse.

## Worship at a Jumper Church

Religion plays a central role in the lives of many Bahamians, and there's a church on just about every corner of every island. While there is an array of traditional Anglican, Catholic, Presbyterian, and Lutheran churches, the Jumper Baptist services are often the liveliest and most unusual. Think fire-and-brimstone sermons, boisterous singing and dancing, and choruses of "hallelujah" and "amen." Congregations welcome out-of-town guests, but expect to stand up and introduce yourself. Bahamians put on their Sunday best for church, but won't turn away a visitor who isn't dressed the part; please be respectful.

## Speak Bahamian

To the untrained ear fresh off a cruise ship or plane, it could seem as if Bahamians are speaking a foreign language. English is the native tongue, but get a group of locals engaged in hot debate and you won't be able to keep up. Words are strung together, the letter g is dropped from the ends of most words, and quite a few slang words are thrown in for good measure. If a club is too crowded, a Bahamian might leave, saying "it's too jam up in dere"; your taxi driver might warn you that he needs to "back back" the car; a rude child might get a "cut hip" from his mother; the word "dead" is used to intensify any adjective as in "dead ugly"; and ask someone when they're going to do something or go somewhere, and they'll likely respond "terreckly," which means soon. Despite what you may see printed on T-shirts, Bahamians don't say "Hey mon!" If you don't understand, just ask the Bahamian to slow down and they'll quickly start speaking the Queen's English.

## Play Dominoes

Just about anywhere you see a group of men gathered around a makeshift table, you'll find a dominoes game in progress. Usually games are played for bragging rights and not money, and matches can get loud and raucous, as it's customary for anyone making a big play to slam the plastic tile down on the table. Ask if you can get in on a game (the same rules as American dominoes apply), but don't expect any mercy.

## Eat a Fish Top to Tail

Order a fried, grilled, or steamed snapper at any local restaurant or fish fry and be prepared to have your meal looking up at you from the plate. In the Bahamas, this tasty dish is served up whole, from head to tail. Take a look at a Bahamian's plate at the end of his meal and you'll never guess it once held a fish; all that's left is a pile of sucked-clean bones. If you don't think you can stomach the whole fish, ask your waiter to remove the head before bringing it to the table. Just be warned, the sweetest meat is found in the cheeks.

# KIDS AND FAMILIES

It might not be an exaggeration to say that the Bahamas is a playground for children—or anyone else who likes building castles in the sand, searching for the perfect seashell, and playing tag with ocean waves.

While water-related activities are the most obvious enticements, these relaxed and friendly islands also offer a variety of land-based options, particularly in Nassau and on adjacent Paradise Island. For tales of the high seas, **Pirates of Nassau** has artifacts and interactive exhibits of the original pirates of the Caribbean.

The **Ardastra Gardens, Zoo and Conservation Center** is home to a variety of animals. Some you'd expect to find in the Bahamas—like the world-famous marching flamingos—and others are endangered creatures from faraway places like the pair of jaguars and Madagascar lemurs.

Let the kids pick out their favorite straw-hat-wearing pony at the **Surrey Horse Pavilion** on Prince George Wharf and take a leisurely clip-clopping ride through the old city of Nassau. For a few extra dollars, most guides will extend your tour beyond the typical route to include other sites. Keep your guidebook handy to verify facts; guides are trained but often add their own twist on history, which can be entertaining to say the least.

Of course, megaresort **Atlantis** is always a crowd pleaser, with everything from pottery painting to remote-control car making and racing, to an 8,000-square-foot, state-of-the-art kids camp and the Bahamas' and Caribbean's largest casino and water park.

Both Nassau and Freeport, on Grand Bahama Island, offer the chance to have close encounters of the dolphin kind. **Blue Lagoon Island Dolphin Encounter,** off Paradise Island, lets you stand waist deep in a protected pool of water and interact with trained dolphins, or put on snorkeling gear and swim with them. In Freeport, **UNEXSO** (one of whose founders was Jacques Cousteau) has a similar program at Sanctuary Bay, a refuge for dolphins. After a performance of backflips and other tricks, these intelligent creatures literally snuggle up to be petted. Older children and adults also can spend a day learning how these remarkable creatures are trained.

For water-sports enthusiasts, snorkeling, parasailing, and boating opportunities abound. In the Exumas, rent a powerboat and take the kids to Big Major's Cay to see the famous **swimming pigs.** Don't forget some scraps! Kids will also get a kick out of the hundreds of **iguanas** on nearby Allan's Cay and the **giant starfish** near mainland Great Exuma.

Much of the Bahamas' most incredible scenery is underwater, but kids of all ages can enjoy the scenes beneath the sea without even getting wet. At **Stuart Cove's Dive Bahamas** in Nassau, kids 12 and up can go 15 feet under with a SUB (Scenic Underwater Bubble) and zoom around the reefs. **Seaworld Tours'** semisubmarine explores Nassau Harbour and Paradise Island for an hour and a half with sightseeing above and below water.

# WEDDINGS AND HONEYMOONS

With easy access from the United States and plenty of secluded beaches to make your own, the Bahamas is a no-brainer destination wedding location. Follow in Mariah Carey's footsteps and start planning your dream ceremony or celebration.

## The Big Day

**Find a Wedding Planner.** Contact the **Ministry of Tourism's Weddings and Honeymoon Unit** (☎ *888/NUPTIAL or 242/356–0435* ✐ *romance@bahamas.com*) for recommended planners or the **Bahamas Bridal Association** (☎ *305/767–4171* ✐ *info@bahamas-bridal-association.com*). If you choose to get married at one of the larger resorts, most have their own planners in-house.

**Get Your License.** The only government requirement to get married in the Bahamas is that the couple must be in the country at least 24 hours before they apply for a license. Licenses will be processed in two days although exceptions can be made for cruise passengers to get them the same day and cost $120. No blood test is required.

**Scout the Perfect Backdrop.** The obvious choice for a Bahamas destination wedding is right on the beach, with waves rolling in, guests wiggling their toes in powdery white sand, and the sun setting over the turquoise ocean. Many hotels have gazebos on the beachfront to make ceremonies more private. One of the most beautiful settings for a Bahamas wedding is the **Cloisters** on Paradise Island. The stone remnants of a 14th-century French monastery and steps leading down to the water's edge create a truly magical location.

**What to Wear.** Bahamian weddings tend to be formal affairs, but a simple dress with no shoes is a popular choice for out-of-town brides, and most grooms tend to shun the jacket and tie in lieu of white linen shirts and khakis. Classy sundresses for ladies and linen or cotton shirts and pants for men are acceptable wear for guests. If you plan on having a church wedding, respect local culture and dress a bit more conservatively (no bare shoulders).

## The Honeymoon

Many resorts offer honeymoon suites and special packages for newlyweds, so be sure to inquire when booking your stay. The following hotels are our top honeymoon picks.

**Cape Santa Maria, Long Island.** The resort has a special honeymoon package for newlyweds (which includes massages), and a beautiful beachfront gazebo makes the perfect wedding backdrop.

**Hope Town Harbour Lodge, the Abacos.** Secluded cottage-style rooms overlook the beach at the edge of town. This is where the TV show *Scrubs* filmed the janitor's wedding episode.

**Kamalame Cay, Andros.** This 96-acre all-inclusive resort sits on a private cay laced with white-sand beaches and coconut palms. Ask for a beachfront cottage or villa.

**One & Only Ocean Club, Paradise Island.** This exclusive resort on magnificent Cabbage Beach's quietest stretch also has the romantic Versailles Gardens, including 35 acres of terraced serenity and an imported French cloister.

**Pink Sands, Harbour Island.** Harbour Island's famed beachfront resort has long been praised by honeymooners for its 25 private cottages scattered over 20 secluded acres, including the renowned Pink Sands Beach.

# ECOTOURISM IN THE BAHAMAS

The word ecotourism is believed to have been coined by Mexican environmentalist Héctor Ceballos-Lascuráin in 1983. According to Ceballos-Lascuráin, ecotourism "involves traveling to relatively undisturbed natural areas with the specific object of studying, admiring, and enjoying the scenery and its wild plants and animals." His original definition seemed a bit too general, so in 1993 he amended it with a line that stressed that "ecotourism is environmentally responsible travel."

Natural beauty abounds in the Bahamas, so ecofriendly tourists will have no problem finding national parks to explore, birds to watch, or virgin reefs to snorkel, especially in the Out Islands. There's a concerted effort to make development more sustainable here, too. Time and money are being spent to ensure that as the more remote islands develop, it is done responsibly. The Bahamian government now requires that an independent **Environmental Impact Assessment** be conducted before approval is given for any major development project on any islands. Inagua was also selected for a pilot program sponsored by the **Inter-American Development Bank** to design a regional plan for sustainable development.

## Accommodations

Although there's certainly a long way to go before most properties can call themselves ecofriendly, many of the small resorts, particularly those on the Out Islands, are independently doing what they can to reduce their footprint and impact on the environment. Some have installed their own reverse osmosis systems to generate potable water, solar energy is becoming more popular, restaurants use local fishermen and farmers for food sourcing, and ecotour options have increased due to visitor demand.

The **Tiamo Resort** in Andros sets the standard for ecoresorts in the Bahamas and the Caribbean. The cottages were built of sustainable local pine and thatch. While many developers completely clear their properties in order to build, Tiamo cut down as few mature trees as possible. Energy on property is generated by solar panels, and hot showers come courtesy of the sun. An organic garden ensures meals are made from the freshest fruits and vegetables. Guests can indulge in a plethora of ecoactivities including bonefishing, snorkeling, biologist-led nature walks, and ocean kayaking.

**Hotel Higgins Landing** on Stocking Island in the Exumas is completely solar powered, uses cisterns that collect rainwater, and has a renowned biological composting toilet system. No cars are allowed on the island.

Few large Bahamas resorts are considered eco-friendly, but the mega **Atlantis** has coined its own phrase and concept: Blue Tourism. In addition to working with a number of environmental NGO's on coral reef protection efforts, they've teamed up with local dive operator Stuart Cove's to provide marine-based activities, and a portion of revenue from these Blue Adventure programs help fund their coral reef conservation projects.

## Bird-Watching

With birds migrating north and south for warmer or cooler climates, there's good bird-watching all year-round. More than 300 bird species live in the Bahamas, 28 of them found only here and in the Caribbean.

The endangered Bahama parrot is found only on Abaco and Inagua, and conservation efforts are underway to reverse the population decline. Inagua is also home to the West Indian pink flamingo. Other unique bird species include the Bahamas swallow, the Bahama woodstar hummingbird, and the Bahama yellowthroat.

**Grand Bahama Nature Tours** (☎ 242/373–2485) offers single or multiday birding tours. **Bahamas Outdoors Ltd** (☎ 242/362–1574) offers daily expeditions in Nassau starting early morning or midday and also organizes multiday trips to Andros, Eleuthera, Cat, San Salvador, Crooked and Acklins, and Inagua. Bird enthusiasts should not miss the unique opportunity to tour **Inagua National Park** (☎ 242/393–1317), home to the world's largest breeding colony of West Indian flamingos. Birding guides are certified by the Ministry of Tourism; contact them for more options.

## National Parks

The Bahamas boasts 25 national parks spanning more than 700,000 protected acres. *We've highlighted four exceptional parks at the start of Chapters 3, 4, 7, and 8.* For more information on visiting parks, contact the **Bahamas National Trust** (☎ 242/393–1317 ⊕ *www.bnt.bs*).

## Resources

The **Bahamas Ministry of Tourism's Cultural Heritage Unit** (☎ 242/302–2000 ⊕ *www. bahamas.com*) is developing eco-friendly programs for visitors. Visit their website for information on green travel and ecotours.

The **International Ecotourism Society** (⊕ *www.ecotourism.org*) has a database of tour companies, hotels, and other travel services that are committed to sustainable practices.

# CRUISING TO THE BAHAMAS

More tourists cruise into Nassau and Freeport than anywhere else in the Caribbean region. The islands are just a couple of hundred miles off the coast of Florida, so cruise lines are able to schedule short excursions over, or make it the first or last port of call on longer trips venturing into the eastern or western Caribbean. In 2009 the Bahamian government completed an extensive dredging project to make Nassau Harbour deep enough to accommodate the new supersize cruise ships. The first to hit the high seas, Royal Caribbean's *Oasis of the Seas*, made its inaugural voyage to the Bahamas in December 2009.

With Bay Street and historic sights just steps away from the cruise docks, Nassau is a great place to disembark for even just a few hours. Your first stop is **Festival Place**, a vibrant marketplace right on the wharf, complete with live Bahamian music and a variety of small shops designed to look like clapboard houses. You can get around downtown on foot or you can take a taxi, scooter, or horse-drawn surrey. If you have a full day, buy an **Atlantis** day pass and enjoy the waterslides, casino, walk-through aquarium, and beaches.

Freeport's cruise-ship port is a bit farther from town and the beaches, so you'll need to take a taxi or tour bus to explore. **Port Lucaya** is the no-brainer stop for shopping and a bite to eat. If you have a longer stopover, book an organized tour or take a taxi to **Lucayan National Park** and explore caves and Gold Rock Creek beach across the road.

Your cruise ship will likely offer tours and excursions that can be booked in advance. Unless you're dead set on doing something in particular and are concerned there might not be space, you might consider waiting until you disembark to book something with a local operator. Many times this is a cheaper option.

In addition to Nassau and Freeport, some cruise lines have leased private islands in the Bahamas. All have stunning beaches lined with lounge chairs and umbrellas, motorized and nonmotorized water sports, casual waterfront bars and restaurants, live entertainment, nature trails, and pricey souvenir shops. Disney Cruise Line stops off at **Castaway Cay** in the Abacos, Holland America visits the 45-acre **Half Moon Cay** between Cat Island and Eleuthera, Norwegian Cruise Lines has **Great Stirrup Cay** in the Berry Islands, and Royal Caribbean stops off at **Coco Cay** between Nassau and Freeport.

Most cruise ships offer just one or two stops within the Bahamas as part of a wider Caribbean itinerary, but there are a few smaller lines that offer cruises through the Bahamas chain. **Pearl Seas Cruises'** (☎ *800/983–7462* ⊕ *www.pearlseascruises.com*) eight-day Bahamas cruise on board a 335-foot, 210-passenger ship stops in Grand Bahama, the Abacos, Harbour Island, the Exumas, and San Salvador. The **American Canadian Caribbean Line's** (☎ *800/556–7450* ⊕ *www.blountsmallshipadventures.com*) 183-foot, 100-passenger *Grande Caribe* has a 12-night tour through the Bahamas, stopping in Nassau, north Eleuthera, and the Exuma Cays.

# LODGING PRIMER

With almost 16,000 hotel rooms across the country, you're bound to find a home away from home in the Bahamas. Unfortunately this is not an inexpensive destination, but almost all islands offer a mix of low-key lodges and sparkling resorts. Room prices come down significantly in the off season (mid-April through mid-December), and many hotels and resorts offer special deals on their room rates or throw in extras during peak hurricane season, late August and early September.

## Splashy Resorts

Mostly in Nassau, Paradise Island, and on Grand Bahama, these resorts are big enough and fancy enough to rival the major resorts found anywhere in the world. Casinos, amazing swimming pools, countless dining options, and rooms that make you wish you didn't have to go home are what set these properties apart. The downside—with thousands of rooms, the staff will provide top service, but aren't likely to remember your name. ⇨ *Atlantis, Paradise Island; Our Lucaya, Grand Bahama.*

## All-Inclusives

For the budget-conscious traveler, an all-inclusive resort is a good option. Rates cover the room, all meals, most activities, and usually your bar tab. Most guests tend to spend most of their vacation on property, since it's been paid for up front, so there are lots of activities to keep you entertained. Be sure to do your homework, as these resorts vary in terms of quality. ⇨ *Club Med, San Salvador; Breezes Bahamas, Nassau; Sandals Emerald Bay, the Exumas.*

## Boutique Resorts

These properties are small and don't often have a lot of amenities, but they've created a high-end luxury experience that makes that irrelevant. There may be just one restaurant on property, but it's guaranteed to be top of the line. Staff-to-guest ratios are higher than at any other property type and they are there to cater to your every whim and fancy. Of course, be prepared to pay for such special treatment. ⇨ *Firefly Sunset Resort, Elbow Cay; The Cove, Gregory Town Eleuthera; Rock House, Harbour Island; Sammy T's Beach Resort, Cat Island.*

## Budget Hotels

The Bahamas is not known for being a cheap destination, but throughout the country there are no-frills budget hotels if you're really just looking for a clean safe place to get a shower and grab a good night's sleep. If you plan on spending full days exploring the islands or lounging on a beach and are happy to do without extras like pay-per-view TV, in room minibars, room service, and high-thread-count sheets, this accommodation type is for you. ⇨ *Castaways Resort and Suites, Grand Bahama; Tingum Village, Harbour Island.*

## Homey Guesthouses and Cottages

Out Island accommodations tend to be more like a home away from home. Small, and often family owned and operated, these guesthouses and cottages are usually simply decorated, but have all you need to make your stay comfortable. Guests often gather in common areas for drinks, meals, and conversation, and the staff take a personal interest in making your stay perfect. On-site activities and amenities will likely be basic, but you'll feel right at home. ⇨ *Fernandez Bay Village, Cat Island; Orange Hill Beach Inn, New Providence; Seascape Inn, Andros.*

# FLAVORS OF THE BAHAMAS

You'll find food from all over the world in Nassau and Freeport restaurants, but you'll be missing out if you don't try the local cuisine. There's nothing fancy about Bahamian food, just fresh ingredients and peppery spices you'll remember long after your trip is over.

Breakfasts include hearty eggs, bacon, and pancakes, or Bahamian favorites such as chicken souse, boil' fish, or stew' fish, served with grits and johnnycake. At lunch you'll likely find variations on a few standards: fresh fish, conch, or chicken sandwiches, or hamburgers sided with french fries, coleslaw, or local favorites like peas 'n' rice or baked macaroni and cheese with jalapeño peppers. At dinner you'll find fish, fried chicken, and pasta.

"Steamed" fish means cooked with tomatoes, peppers, and onions. Order any fish "Bahamian style" and it will be baked and smothered in tomatoes and spices.

## Conch

(A) You'll find conch, the unofficial dish of the Bahamas, prepared in a variety of ways, on nearly every menu. The sea snail has a mild flavor and taste and texture similar to calamari. The safest way to ease into conch is conch fritters, tasty fried dough balls packed with chunks of conch. Conch chowder is tomato based; cracked conch is battered and fried; grilled conch is wrapped in a foil packet with lime juice, pepper, onion, tomato, and a bit of butter and cooked on top of the barbecue; and, perhaps the most popular entrée, conch salad is akin to ceviche. Fresh-caught conch is diced and mixed with chopped onions and red or green bell peppers. The mix is drizzled with fresh lime and sour orange juices, and spiced with either homemade hot sauce or finely minced local hot peppers.

## Guava Duff

**This** local favorite is similar to English pudding. A guava fruit compote is folded into a sweet dough and wrapped up in aluminum foil, and then steamed or boiled for as long as three hours. It's topped with a sweet rum or brandy sauce.

## Johnnycake

**(B)** Despite its name, johnnycake is not actually a dessert but a thick, heavy, slightly sweet bread that's typically served alongside souses, soups, and stews.

## Mac 'n' Cheese

**If** you order a side of macaroni, don't expect anything resembling Kraft mac and cheese. Bahamians bake their macaroni noodles in a mixture of cream, daisy cheese, and butter.

## Peas 'n' Rice

This popular side dish is made of white rice cooked with salt pork, thyme, a dab of tomato paste, and fresh or canned pigeon peas.

## Rum Cake

**(C)** Given Bahamians' long-standing love affair with rum, it's no surprise that rum cake is an all-time favorite in the islands. Rum is mixed into the batter and then poured in a syrupy glaze over the fresh-out-of-the-oven cake. Don't worry about getting drunk; the alcohol cooks off when it bakes.

## Souse, Boil', or Stew'

**(D)** A peppery bowl of chicken souse or boil' fish—the clear broth has a lime-and-goat-pepper base with pieces of chicken or meaty fish, onions, and potatoes—is an authentic breakfast dish. Variations include pig-feet and sheep-tongue souse, which are more of an acquired taste. You'll also find stew' fish or conch on most menus. The soup in bowls of stew is a Bahamian variation on the traditional French roux made with flour, water, and browning sauce, and seasoned with pepper and fresh thyme.

# IT'S 5 O'CLOCK SOMEWHERE

Drinking is an important of many Bahamas vacations. Rum, in particular, has played an interesting part in Bahamian history since the days of the U.S. Prohibition. Entrepreneurial Bahamians got rich smuggling liquor across the Atlantic from Britain; when the U.S. government put a ban on alcohol consumption, a ready supply less than 50 miles away made the island nation a key trans-shipment point for contraband.

Although the Bacardi distillery in Nassau has been closed since 2009, the Bahamas still has two breweries, and two rum distilleries. **Kalik**, brewed on the southwestern end of New Providence at Commonwealth Brewery is a nice, light ale and comes in regular, Kalik Lite, and, for the serious drinker, the stronger Kalik Gold. The beer was awarded four Monde Selection Gold Medals. Commonwealth also has a distillery, turning out **Ole Nassau** and **Ron Ricardo** rums. Brewery and distillery

tours are not available there, but you're encouraged to tour the artisanal John Watling's Distillery located on the site of the former Buena Vista hotel in Nassau. After your tour, take a seat, enjoy the breeze off the harbor and enjoy their signature Rum Dum cocktail. The newer **Sands Beer**, brewed on Grand Bahama, comes in regular and light. The line recently expanded to include stouts and lagers. Tours are available at this 20-acre brewery (☎ 242/352–4070).

## Bahamian Cocktails

**Bahama Mama.** Light rum, coconut rum, vanilla-infused rum, orange and pineapple juices.

**(A) Goombay Smash.** Light rum, coconut rum, pineapple juice, a dash of Galliano, grenadine. Created at Miss Emily's Blue Bee Bar on Green Turtle Cay, where her daughter and granddaughter still serve them daily.

**Rum Punch.** Campari, light rum, coconut rum, orange and pineapple juices.

...cy Juice. Gin, fresh coconut water, con-
...ensed milk, a sprinkle of nutmeg. Served
...ver crushed ice.

...est Beach Bars

...) **Chat 'N' Chill, the Exumas.** The restau-
...ant and 9-acre playground—an amaz-
...g white-sand beach—is the Exumas'
...arty central, particularly for the famous
...l-day Sunday pig roasts and the Friday-
...ight bonfire beach bash. Play volleyball
...n the powdery sand, slam the notorious
...oombay Smash, order what's cooking
...n the outdoor grill—fresh fish, ribs—or
...hat and chill.

...ackey's Sand Bar and Tiki Bar, South Bimini.
...oat in or take the shuttle from Bimini
...ands Resort to this party place where
...ou can get sand between your toes just
...s easily inside—where sand carpets the
...oor—as well as outside. Play a little vol-
...yball, take a dip in the pool, or snorkel
...ght off the beach between cold Kaliks.

**(C) Nippers, the Abacos.** Guana Cay's infamous party spot is a lively bar with spectacular views of the Abaco Great Barrier
Reef. The Frozen Nipper—a slushy rum-
and-fruit-juice beverage—goes down
well on a hot day. Don't miss the Sunday pig roasts, which draw everyone on
the island.

**Pete's Pub, Abaco.** This beachside tiki hut
in Little Harbour is jumping from 11 am
to sunset. Take a dip in the shallow harbor or luxuriate on the beach with a cup
of their special rum punch—the Blaster.

**Tony Macaroni's, Grand Bahama.** Follow up
Tony's famous roasted conch with a Gully
Wash (green coconut milk and gin) on
Taino Beach, arguably the island's most
spectacular. There's usually great live
music at this thatch-roof shack.

# WHEN TO GO

The Bahamas enjoys sunny days, refreshing breezes, and moderate-to-warm temperatures with little change from season to season. That said, the most pleasant time to visit is from December through May, when temperatures average 70°F–75°F. It stands to reason that hotel prices during this period are at their highest—around 30% higher than during the less popular times. The rest of the year is hot and humid and prone to tropical storms; temperatures hover around 80°F–85°F.

Whether you want to join it or avoid it, be advised that spring break takes place between the end of February and mid-April. This means a lot of vacationing college students, beach parties, sports events, and entertainment.

### Hurricane Season

Hurricane season is from June 1 through November 30, with greatest risk of a storm from August through October. Meteorology being what it is, you generally know days in advance if the area you're traveling to will be affected. Check with your hotel if a storm is on the horizon—the islands are so spread out that, just as most of the United States was unaffected when Katrina hit New Orleans, one island could be experiencing hurricane-force winds while it's nice and sunny in another.

The Bahamas has been relatively lucky when it comes to hurricanes. Nassau, the capital and central hub of the country, has not had a direct devastating hit in many decades. A glancing blow from a storm can result in some downed trees and power lines as well as localized flooding, but Bahamians have learned how to prepare for these situations and within days manage to get things pretty much back to normal. The country enforces strict building codes to guard against major structural damage from the 100-mile-an-hour winds a hurricane can bring with it. Even in the Out Islands, where more storms have come aground, the worst damage is caused by tidal flooding, which washes away quickly.

Most hotels have meticulously detailed hurricane plans that are put into action once a major storm is headed toward the country. If the storm is a major category system, extra flights are lined up to help evacuate tourists, and some hotels have hurricane policies that offer guests free stays at a later date if their vacation is interrupted by Mother Nature.

### Climate

What follows are average daily maximum and minimum temperatures for Nassau. Freeport's temperatures are nearly the same: a degree or two cooler in spring and fall, and a degree or two warmer in summer. As you head down to the more southern islands, expect temperatures to be about a degree or two warmer than the capital year-round.

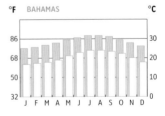

# GREAT WATER ADVENTURES

In an archipelago nation named for shallow seas that amaze even astronauts in space, don't miss having a close marine encounter. Water adventures range from a splash at the beach to shark diving. Or stay between the extremes with fishing and snorkeling.

# WHERE TO DIVE AND SNORKEL IN THE BAHAMAS

Although most water in the Bahamas is clear enough to see to the bottom from your boat, snorkeling or diving gets you that much closer to the country's true natives. Coral reefs, blue holes, drop-offs, and sea gardens abound.

Walker's Cay

Little Abaco I.

FLORIDA

Grand Bahama I.

Northwest Providence Channel

Treasure Cay

Fowl Cay Reef

Sandy Cay Reef

Great Abaco I.

Sandy Point

Paradise Point  N. Bimini

Great Stirrup Cay

Great Harbour Cay

Northeast Providence Channel

Harbour I.

S. Bimini

Berry Islands

Current Cut

Eleuthera I.

Chub Cay

Straits of Florida

Paradise I.

Nassau ★

New Providence I.

Shark Wall

Exuma Cays Land and Sea Park

**KEY**

| | |
|---|---|
| 🤿 | Best dive sites |
| 🐠 | Best snorkel sites |

Thunderball Grotto

Cat I.

Andros I.

Andros Barrier Reef/ Tongue of the Ocean

THE EXUMAS

Exuma Sound

Great Exuma I.

## BEST DIVE SITES

**Andros Barrier Reef/Tongue of the Ocean.** Go from the shallows of the world's third-largest barrier reef to the depths of the ocean.

**Fowl Cay Reef, the Abacos.** The government-protected reef is near the north coast of Man-O-War Cay. A dive operator can take you through the reef holes.

**Sandy Cay Reef, the Abacos.** Experience shallow-water diving in Pelican Cays National Park. The reef is full of life (turtles, spotted eagle rays, tarpon), thanks to its protected status.

**Shark Wall, New Providence.** Off southwest New Providence, this drop is a must for experienced divers. James Bond movies *Thunderball* and *Never Say Never Again* were filmed here.

**The Wall, Crooked Island.** The famed dive site about 50 yards off Crooked Island's coast drops from 45 feet to thousands.

Diving near New Providence Island

## BEST SNORKEL SITES

**Current Cut, Eleuthera.** Near the Current settlement in North Eleuthera there is great drift snorkel with the right tide.

**Exuma Cays Land and Sea Park.** This 176-sq-mi park was the first of its kind. Since the park is protected and its waters have essentially never been fished, you can see what the ocean looked like before humanity.

**Paradise Point, Bimini.** Off northern Bimini, this area is rich in sea life and is famous for the underwater stone path some believe marks the road to the lost city of Atlantis. Dolphins and black coral gardens are just offshore.

**Sandy Cay Reef, the Abacos.** The water surrounding this reef is just 25-feet deep, making it great for snorkeling or diving.

**Thunderball Grotto, the Exumas.** This three-story limestone-ceiling cave at the northern end of the Exumas chain was featured in the James Bond movie of the same name.

Diving near Bimini

### EXTREME DIVING ADVENTURES

Various outfitters on Grand Bahama and New Providence offer shark dives. With **Caribbean Divers** (☎ 242/373–9111 ⊕ www.bellchannelinn.com) and **UNEXSO** in Grand Bahama and **Stuart Cove's** in New Providence, you'll watch dive masters feed reef sharks which brush by you—no cage included. Dive masters control the ferocity and location of the frenzy, so the sharks' attention is on the food.

**Incredible Adventures** (☎ 800/644-7382 ⊕ www.incredible-adventures.com) in Grand Bahama offers cage diving with tiger sharks. You'll sit in the water as giant sharks come breathtakingly close, the only thing between you a few strips of metal.

Feeding sharks when humans are present make these dives controversial, especially when multiple sharks are involved and there's the possibility of a frenzy. Dive operators doing these extreme adventures are experienced and knowledgeable about shark-feeding patterns and signs of aggression, but partake in these dives at your own risk.

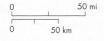

San Salvador

Rum Cay

Long I.

Crooked Island Passage

Samana Cay

The Wall
Crooked I.

Mayaguana Passage

Mayaguana I.

Acklins I.

| 0 | | 50 mi |
|---|---|---|
| 0 | | 50 km |

Little
Inagua I.

Great Inagua I.

French Angelfish

Four-Eyed Butterflyfish

Grunt

Nassau Grouper

Parrotfish

Queen Triggerfish

Sergeant Major

Snapper

Tang

Barracuda*

Lionfish*

Shark*

*dangerous fish

## WHAT YOU'LL SEE UNDER THE SEA

Reefs in the Bahamas are alive with colorful life. Vibrant hard corals—such as star, brain, staghorn, and elk—and waving purple sea fans are home to schools of myraid fish, some pictured above. Be on the lookout for lionfish; a prick from the fins of this poisonous fish is painful and could send you to the hospital. The most common sharks in the Bahamas are nurse sharks (typically non-threatening to humans) and Caribbean reef sharks. The deeper you dive, the bigger and more varied shark species get.

Generally, the further the reef is from a developed area the more abundant the marine life, but even sites around developed islands might surprise you.

# ISLAND-HOPPING

The Bahamas is a boater's paradise, with shallow protected waters and secluded, safe harbors. In small island groups, travel takes just a few hours, even minutes. The Abacos archipelago and the Exuma Cays are the best and most convenient islands to hop.

## THE ABACOS

If you're cruising from Florida, clear customs in West End, Grand Bahama; the Abaco Cays start just north.

**Grand Cay**, at the northern end of the chain, has a small community of 200 people. Most yachters find the anchorage off the community dock adequate, and the docks at Rosie's Place can take boats up to 80 feet. Double anchors are advised to handle the harbor's tidal current.

**Fox Town**, on the "mainland" of Little Abaco, is a good fuel stop, the first if you're traveling east from West End. Farther south, stock up on provisions in **Coopers Town**, Little Abaco's largest community. Just northeast is an 80-slip marina at **Spanish Cay**.

Cruising south, **Green Turtle Cay** has excellent yachting facilities. The Green Turtle Club dominates White Sound's northern end, whereas Bluff

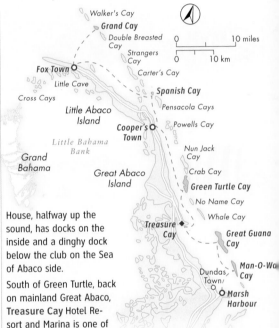

Fishing near Green Turtle Cay

House, halfway up the sound, has docks on the inside and a dinghy dock below the club on the Sea of Abaco side.

South of Green Turtle, back on mainland Great Abaco, **Treasure Cay** Hotel Resort and Marina is one of the largest marinas on the island. Here you can play golf, dine, or relax on a beautiful beach.

Straight back out in the Sea of Abaco is **Great Guana Cay** and its gorgeous 7-mi strip of pristine sand. On Sunday don't miss the famous pig roast at Nippers Bar. Just south is New England–style charmer **Man-O-War Cay**, a boatbuilding settlement with deserted beaches and 28-slip Man-O-War Marina. Fowl Cay

Park offers great snorkeling and diving just to the north.

Back on Great Abaco, **Marsh Harbour** is the capital and most populated settlement in the Abacos. Boaters consider it one of the easiest harbors to enter. It has several full-service marinas, including the 190-slip Boat Harbour Marina and the 80-slip Conch Inn Marina. This is the stop to catch up on banking and business needs. There are great restaurants and shops, too.

Exuma Cays Land and Sea Park

## THE EXUMA CAYS

To really get off the beaten path, the Exuma Cays are where it's at. This 120-mi archipelago is made up of small cays, many of which are still uninhabited or privately owned, and interspersed with sand banks and spits. Throughout is excellent diving and snorkeling. Boaters usually stock up and clear customs in Nassau, cross the yellow banks to the north of the chain, and slowly make their way south.

### BOAT TOURS

If you don't have your own boat, these outfitters will take you on island-hopping adventures.

**Captain Plug.** ☎ 242/577–0273 ⊕ www.captplug.com. $200 for a full day of island hopping in the Abacos.

**Four C's Adventures.** ☎ 242/464–1720 ⊕ www.exumawatertours.com. $1400 for a full day excursion to the Exuma Cays from Great Exuma.

**High Seas Private Excursions.** ☎ 242/363–4458 ⊕ www.highseasbahamas.com. $2500 for a full day excursion to the Exuma Cays from Nassau.

**Highbourne Cay** at the chain's northern end has a marina and food store. You can explore many of the surrounding cays by tender if you prefer to dock here. Nearby, **Allan's Cay** is home to hundreds of iguanas that readily accept food.

**Norman's Cay** has an airstrip and Norman's Cay Beach Club has a fantastic restaurant and bar. Just south is the 176-sq-mi **Exuma Cays Land and Sea Park.** It has some of the country's best snorkeling and diving. Warderick Wells Cay houses the park headquarters, which has nature trail maps and a gift shop. Just below, **Compass Cay** has a marina known for its friendly nurse sharks and a small convenience store. **Pipe Creek**, which winds between Compass and Staniel Cays, has great shelling, snorkeling, diving, and bonefishing. **Staniel Cay** is the hub of activity in these parts and a favorite destination of yachters. That's thanks to the Staniel Cay Yacht Club, the only full-service marina in the cays. It makes a good base for visiting **Big Major's Cay**, where wild pigs swim out to meet you,

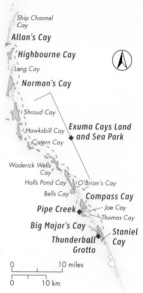

and **Thunderball Grotto**, a beautiful marine cave that snorkelers (at low tide) and experienced scuba divers can explore.

# BONEFISHING

### WHAT IS BONEFISHING?
Bonefishing is the fly-fishing sport of choice in the Bahamas. The country is full of pristine shallow flats and mangroves where stealthy "gray ghosts"— silvery white, sleek fish—school in large groups. Hooking one is a challenge, as the fish are fast, strong, and perfectly camouflaged to the sand and water.

To catch bonefish you need the right mix of knowledge, instinct, and patience. Guides are the best way to go, as their knowledge of the area and schooling patterns gives them an uncanny ability to find bonefish quickly.

### EQUIPMENT
Basics include a fly-fishing rod and reel and the right lure. Experienced anglers, guides, and fishing-supply dealers can help you gear up with the best and latest technology. Bonefishing is catch and release, so always use barbless hooks and work quickly when removing them to avoid stressing the fish. Wear comfortable, light clothing that protects much of your body from the sun, as you'll be out for hours without shade.

In many places you can just walk offshore onto the flats. Some anglers use shallow draft boats with a raised platform in the back, where they pole into extremely shallow areas.

### BEST PLACES TO BONEFISH
Bonefish hang out in shallow flats and mangrove areas. Andros, Bimini, and the Exumas have the best bonefishing; Abaco, Eleuthera, and Long Island also provide excellent adventures. If you have the time, visit the southernmost islands, like Crooked, Acklins, or Inagua, where these gray ghosts are "uneducated" to anglers.

## OTHER TYPES OF FISHING

Make sure you are familiar with fishing regulations before you begin your adventure. Visit ⊕ *www.bahamas-travel.info.*

### DEEP-SEA FISHING

Deep water is just a few miles off most islands, where anglers try for large ocean fish—tuna, wahoo, mahi mahi, shark, and marlin. Like bonefishing, the fight is what most anglers are after; however, a day on the ocean can provide a great meal. The Abacos has great deep-sea fishing, and many tournaments are held there each year.

### REEF/SHOAL FISHING

Fishing with a rod, or Bahamian "hand-lining" can be a great family fishing adventure. Anchoring near a shoal or reef, or even trolling with a lure, can be relaxing. The Out Islands are home to shoals, reefs, and wrecks that are less visited by fishing enthusiasts.

### SPEARFISHING

Most reefs are okay for free-dive spear fishing, but spear guns (guns that fire spears) are illegal in the Bahamas. Spear is the traditional Bahamian fishing method, so reefs close to more developed islands tend to have fewer fish. The Out Islands still have lesser-known spots good for spearfishing.

**WHERE TO STAY**

Bonefishing lodges are common in the Bahamas and often include top-notch guides. Accommodations are usually basic. Here are our top bonefishing lodges:

- Andros Island Bonefishing Club

- Bishop's Bonefish Resort, Grand Bahama

- Crooked Island Lodge

- Peace and Plenty Bonefish Lodge, the Exumas

- Rickmon Bonefish Lodge, the Abacos

- Small Hope Bay Lodge, Andros

(left pg) Bonefishing in Andros.
(right) A prize catch.

## SAILING

Sailing is popular in the Bahamas, and there are many regattas held here throughout the year. The Abacos, the sailing capital of the Bahamas, also host an open regatta, inviting all classes of boats and sailors to join in for a week of island hopping and racing. Large sailboats are available for charter in Marsh Harbour and Hope Town.

# NEW PROVIDENCE
# AND PARADISE
# ISLANDS

# WELCOME TO NEW PROVIDENCE AND PARADISE ISLANDS

## TOP REASONS TO GO

★ **Beach hop:**
New Providence beaches, though less secluded than those on the Out Islands, still tempt travelers with their balmy breezes and aquamarine water. Choose between the more remote beaches on the island's western end, action-packed strips on Cable Beach, or public beaches in downtown Nassau.

★ **Dine with the best of 'em:** New Providence is the country's culinary capital. Eat at a grungy local dive for one meal, then feast in a celebrity-chef restaurant for the next.

★ **Experience Atlantis:**
Explore the world's largest outdoor aquarium, splash around in the something-for-everyone water park, or dine at one of the 40+ restaurants, all while never leaving the resort property.

★ **Celebrate Junkanoo:**
This uniquely Bahamian carnival takes place the day after Christmas and New Year's Day. If you miss it, there are smaller parades in Marina Village on Paradise Island each Wednesday and Saturday at 9:30 pm.

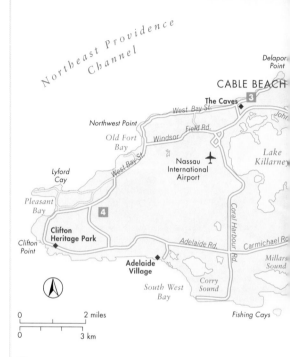

**1 Nassau.** Pink buildings dating back to the colonial era are interspersed with modern-day office complexes; horses pull their wooden carriages alongside stretch limousines; and tourists browse the local craft-centric straw market or shop for luxurious handbags at Gucci, all in this historic capital city.

**2 Paradise Island.**
P.I. (as locals call the island) is connected to downtown Nassau's east end by a pair of bridges. Atlantis, the tallest building in the Bahamas, is a beachfront resort complete with a gamut of dining options, the country's largest casino, and some of the region's fanciest shops. Most memorable, however, are the water-based activities, slides, and aquariums. Love it or despise it, it's today's face of Paradise.

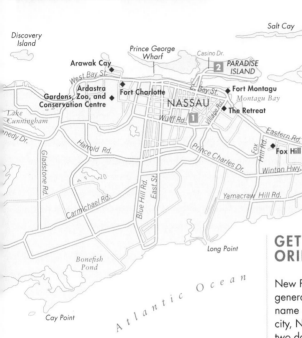

Discovery Island

Arawak Cay

West Bay St.

Ardastra Gardens, Zoo, and Conservation Centre

Fort Charlotte

Prince George Wharf

Casino Dr.

NASSAU

**2 PARADISE ISLAND**

E. Bay St.

**Fort Montagu**

Montagu Bay

**The Retreat**

Salt Cay

Sandy Cay

Rose Island

Athol Island

Wulff Rd.

**1**

Lake Cunningham

...nedy Dr.

Harrold Rd.

Prince Charles Dr.

Village Rd.

Fox Hill Rd.

Eastern Rd.

**Fox Hill**

Winton Hwy.

Eastern Point

Gladstone Rd.

Carmichael Rd.

Blue Hill Rd.

East St.

Yamacraw Hill Rd.

Bonefish Pond

Long Point

Cay Point

Atlantic Ocean

## GETTING ORIENTED

New Providence Island is generally referred to by the name of its historic capital city, Nassau. More than two dozen hotels and at least twice as many restaurants lure more than 2 million tourists to the city—and nearby Paradise Island and Cable Beach—annually. The heart of commerce and government and the bulk of the country's 300,000 people are crammed onto the 21-mile-by-7-mile island, less than 200 miles from Miami. Venturing outside the three main tourist areas will give you a better idea of true Bahamian life and a glimpse at some less-visited but worth-the-trek attractions.

**3 Cable Beach.** The crescent-shaped stretch of sand west of Nassau is in the midst of a major face-lift, transforming into a destination to rival Paradise Island. Beyond the resorts' casinos, restaurants, bars, and pretty beaches, there's not a whole lot to do here. A short walk west are a small straw market and a smattering of restaurants, cafés, and bars that cater mostly to locals.

**4 Western New Providence.** West of Cable Beach's high-rise hotels, New Providence becomes primarily residential, with small restaurants and bars along the way. West Bay Street hugs the coastline, providing spectacular ocean views. This part of the island is the least developed, so it's the perfect spot to find a secluded beach or go bird-watching.

Updated
by Jessica
Robertson

An incongruous mix of glitzy casinos and quiet shady lanes; splashy megaresorts and tiny settlements that recall a distant simpler age; land development unrivaled elsewhere in the Bahamas, and vast stretches of untrammeled territory. This is New Providence Island, a grab-bag destination. The island, home to two-thirds of all Bahamians, provides fast-paced living, nightlife that goes on until dawn, and high-end shopping strips. And when all the hustle and bustle becomes too much, it's easy to find quiet stretches of sandy white beach where the only noise is the waves rolling in.

In the course of its history, the island has weathered the comings and goings of lawless pirates, Spanish invaders, slave-holding British Loyalists who fled the United States after the Revolutionary War, Civil War–era Confederate blockade runners, and Prohibition rumrunners. Nevertheless, New Providence remains most influenced by England, which sent its first royal governor to the island in 1718. Although Bahamians won government control in 1967 and independence six years later, British influence is felt to this day.

Nassau is the nation's capital and transportation hub, as well as the banking and commercial center. The fortuitous combination of tourist-friendly enterprise, tropical weather, and island flavor with a European overlay has not gone unnoticed: each year nearly 2 million cruise-ship passengers arrive at Nassau's Prince George Wharf.

There's a definite hustle and bustle in this capital city that's not found elsewhere in the country, but that doesn't mean you have to follow suit. From shark diving and snorkeling to bicycle tours, horseback riding, tennis, and golf, active pursuits abound in New Providence. Avid water-sports fans will find a range of possibilities, including waterskiing, sailing, windsurfing, and deep-sea fishing. Or simply cruise the clear Bahamian waters for a day trip or an evening ride.

# PLANNING

## WHEN TO GO

2

With the warm Gulf Stream currents swirling and balmy trade winds blowing, New Providence is an appealing year-round destination. Temperatures usually hover in the 70s and 80s and rarely get above 90°F on a midsummer's day or below 60°F on a winter's night. June to October tend to be the hottest and wettest months, although rain is often limited to periodic afternoon showers.

The best time to visit the island is December to May, especially if you're escaping the cold. Don't mind the locals, who'll likely tell you it's too chilly to hit the beach in winter, but you may want to pack a light sweater if you plan on dining outdoors. Visitors from colder climates may find the humid summer days and nights a bit stifling. Be aware that tropical depressions, tropical storms, and hurricanes are a possibility in New Providence during the Atlantic hurricane season from early June to late November. Expect to pay between 15% and 30% less off-season at most resorts.

### TOP FESTIVALS

#### WINTER

**Bahamas International Film Festival.** In early December, the Bahamas International Film Festival in Nassau celebrates cinema in paradise, with screenings, receptions, and movie-industry panels.

**Authentically Bahamian Christmas Trade Show.** The Authentically Bahamian Christmas Trade Show on Cable Beach showcases conch-shell jewelry, straw handbags, batiks, and other island-made crafts the first weekend of December.

**Christmas Jollification.** This ongoing arts-and-crafts fair with Bahamian Christmas crafts, food, and music is held at the Retreat in Nassau.

**Junior Junkanoo Parade.** The island's schoolchildren compete for bragging rights in the Junior Junkanoo Parade in mid-December. The parade starts at 6 pm and kids in preschool through high school rush down Bay Street, putting on an exciting show.

**Junkanoo.** Once Christmas dinner is over, the focus shifts to Junkanoo. The first major parade of the season starts just after midnight in downtown Nassau. There's a second parade on New Year's Day.

#### SPRING

**International Dog Show & Obedience Trials.** In Nassau, watch dogs of all classes compete at the International Dog Show & Obedience Trials, held mid-March. Check ⊕ *www.bahamaskennelclub.org* for location.

#### SUMMER

**Goombay Summer.** Woodes Rodgers Walk is transformed during the annual Goombay Summer festival held weekends during July or August. Listen to Rake 'n' Scrape bands, watch a Junkanoo rush-out, and sample local foods.

**Fox Hill Festival.** The Nassau Fox Hill Festival in early August pays tribute to Emancipation with church services, Junkanoo parades, music, cookouts, games, and other festivities.

**FALL**

**International Cultural Weekend.** Eat and drink your way around the world at the International Cultural Weekend, hosted at the Botanic Gardens the third weekend of October.

## GETTING HERE AND AROUND

### AIR TRAVEL

Lynden Pindling International Airport (NAS) is 8 miles west of Nassau. There is no public bus service from the airport to hotels. Major car-rental companies are represented at the airport. A taxi ride for two people from the airport to downtown Nassau costs $27; to Paradise Island, $42 (this includes the $1 bridge toll); and to Cable Beach, $25. Each additional passenger is $3, and excess baggage costs $2 a bag.

### BOAT AND FERRY TRAVEL

Water taxis travel between Prince George Wharf and Paradise Island during daylight hours at half-hour intervals. The one-way cost is $3 per person, and the trip takes 12 minutes.

### BUS TRAVEL

The frequent jitneys are the cheapest choice on routes such as Cable Beach to downtown Nassau. Fare is $1.50 each way, and exact change is required. Hail one at a bus stop, hotel, or public beach. In downtown Nassau jitneys wait on Frederick Street and along the middle of Bay Street. Bus service runs throughout the day until 7 pm.

### CAR TRAVEL

Rent a car if you plan to explore the whole island. Rentals are available at the airport, downtown, on Paradise Island, and at some resorts for $40–$120 per day. Gasoline costs between $5 and $6 a gallon. Remember to drive on the left.

**Contacts Virgo Car Rental** ☎ *242/377–1275.*

### SCOOTER TRAVEL

Two people can ride a motor scooter for about $65 for a half day, $85 for a full day.

### TAXI TRAVEL

Unless you plan to jump all over the island, taxis are the most convenient way to get around. The fare is $9 plus $1 bridge toll between downtown Nassau and Paradise Island, $20 from Cable Beach to Paradise Island (plus $1 toll), and $18 from Cable Beach to Nassau. Fares are for two passengers; each additional passenger is $3. It's customary to tip taxi drivers 15%.

**Contacts Bahamas Transport** ☎ *242/323–5111.*
**Taxi Cab Union** ☎ *242/323–5818.*

# ESSENTIALS

## BANKS

Banks are open Monday through Thursday from 9:30 to 3 and Friday from 9:30 to 5. International ATMs are scattered throughout the island.

## EMERGENCIES

**Contacts Ambulance** ☎ *911, 919, 242/322-2881, 242/302-4747.*
**Police** ☎ *911, 919, 242/322-4444.*

## HOTELS

If you want to mix with locals and experience a little more of Bahamian culture, choose a hotel in downtown Nassau. Its beaches are not dazzling; if you want to be beachfront on a gorgeous white strand, stay on Cable Beach or Paradise Island's Cabbage Beach. Reasons to stay in Nassau include proximity to shopping and affordability (although the cost of taxis to and from the better beaches can add up).

The plush Cable Beach and Paradise Island resorts are big and beautiful, glittering and splashy, and have the best beaches, but they can be overwhelming. In any case, these big, top-dollar properties generally have more amenities than you could possibly make use of, a selection of dining choices, and a full roster of sports and entertainment options. Stay in Cable Beach if you don't plan to visit Nassau and Paradise Island often; you need to take a cab, and the costs add up.

## RESTAURANTS

Foodies will delight in New Providence's restaurant range, from shabby shacks serving up the kind of food you'd find in any Bahamian's kitchen, to elegant eateries where jackets are required and the food rivals that found in any major city. You'll recognize celebrity chef names like Bobby Flay, Jean-Georges Vongerichten, and Nobu Matsuhisa, all of whom have restaurants on Paradise Island.

Eating out can get expensive, particularly in resort restaurants, so a budget-friendly strategy is having brunch at one of the myriad all-you-can-eat buffets at the larger hotels on Paradise Island and Cable Beach, then a light snack to hold you over until dinnertime.

*Note: A gratuity (15%) is often added to the bill automatically. Many all-inclusive hotels offer meal plans for nonguests.*

### HOTEL AND RESTAURANT PRICES

Restaurant prices are based on the median main course price at dinner, excluding gratuity, typically 15%, which is often automatically added to the bill. Hotel prices are for two people in a standard double room in high season, excluding service and 6%–12% tax.

## VISITOR INFORMATION

The Ministry of Tourism operates tourist information booths at the airport, open daily from 8:30 am to 11:30 pm, and at the Welcome Center (Festival Place) adjacent to Prince George Wharf, open daily from 9 am to 5 pm. The Ministry of Tourism's People-to-People Program sets you up with a Bahamian family with similar interests to show you local culture firsthand.

The Royal Bahamas Police Force Band performs in front of Government House.

**Contacts Ministry of Tourism** ☎ *242/302–2000* ⊕ *www.bahamas.com.* **People-to-People Program** ☎ *242/324–9772* ⊕ *www.bahamas.com/ peopletopeople.*

## EXPLORING NEW PROVIDENCE

### NASSAU

Nassau's sheltered harbor bustles with cruise-ship activity, while a block away Bay Street's sidewalks are crowded with shoppers who duck into air-conditioned boutiques and relax on benches in the shade of mahogany and lignum vitae trees. Shops angle for tourist dollars with fine imported goods at duty-free prices, yet you'll find a handful of stores overflowing with authentic Bahamian crafts, food supplies, and other delights.

With a revitalization of downtown ongoing—the revamped British Colonial Hilton leading the way—Nassau is recapturing some of its past glamour. Nevertheless, modern influences are completely apparent: fancy restaurants, suave clubs, and trendy coffeehouses have popped up everywhere. These changes have come partly in response to the growing number of upper-crust crowds that now supplement the spring break-ers and cruise passengers who have traditionally flocked to Nassau. Of course, you can still find a wild club or a rowdy bar, but you can also sip cappuccino while viewing contemporary Bahamian art or dine by candlelight beneath prints of old Nassau, serenaded by soft, island-inspired calypso music.

A trip to Nassau wouldn't be complete without a stop at some of the island's well-preserved historic buildings. The large, pink colonial-style edifices house Parliament and some of the courts, while others, like Fort Charlotte, date back to the days when pirates ruled the town. Take a tour via horse-drawn carriage for the full effect.

### TOP ATTRACTIONS

**John Watling's Distillery.** The former Buena Vista Estate which featured in the James Bond film *Casino Royale* has been painstakingly transformed and taken back to its glory days, emerging as the new home of the John Watling's Distillery. Parts of the home date back to 1789 and the actual production of the line of John Watling's artisanal rums, gins, vodkas, and liquors are hand-made, hand bottled, and hand labelled just as they would have been in that era. Take a self-guided tour through the grounds and working estate to learn the fascinating history of the home and then walk out back to watch the rum production line from an overhead mezzanine. Sit in the Red Turtle Tavern to enjoy a cocktail and pick up a unique Bahamian souvenir in the on-site retail store. ⊠ *17 Delancy St., Nassau, New Providence Island* ☎ *242/322–2811* ⊕ *www.johnwatlings. com* ⊠ *Free* ⊙ *Daily 9–5.*

FodorsChoice **National Art Gallery of the Bahamas.** Opened in July 2003, the museum
★ houses the works of esteemed Bahamian artists such as Max Taylor, Amos Ferguson, Brent Malone, John Cox, and Antonius Roberts. The glorious Italianate-colonial mansion, built in 1860 and restored in the 1990s, has double-tiered verandahs with elegant columns. It was the residence of Sir William Doyle, the first chief justice of the Bahamas. Don't miss the museum's gift shop, where you'll find books about the Bahamas as well as Bahamian quilts, prints, ceramics, jewelry, and crafts. ⊠ *West and W. Hill Sts., across from St. Francis Xavier Cathedral, Nassau, New Providence Island* ☎ *242/328–5800* ⊕ *www.nagb. org.bs* ⊠ *$5* ⊙ *Tues.–Sat. 10–4, Sun. 12–4.*

FAMILY **Pirates of Nassau.** Take a journey through Nassau's pirate days in this interactive museum devoted to such notorious members of the city's past as Blackbeard, Mary Read, and Anne Bonney. Board a pirate ship, see dioramas of intrigue on the high seas, hear historical narration, and experience sound effects re-creating some of the gruesome highlights. It's a fun and educational (if slightly scary) family outing. Be sure to check out the offbeat souvenirs in the Pirate Shop. ⊠ *George and King Sts., Nassau, New Providence Island* ☎ *242/356–3759* ⊕ *www.pirates-of-nassau.com* ⊠ *$12* ⊙ *Mon.–Sat. 9–6, Sun. 9–12:30.*

**Pompey Square.** This open space at the western end of Bay Street overlooks the busy Nassau harbor and is the spot to catch local festivals and events, live music, and Bahamian art shows. It's also a good spot to

### PIRATES OF THE BAHAMAS

Pirates roamed the waters of the Bahamas, hiding out in the 700 islands, but they especially liked New Providence Island. Edward Teach, or Blackbeard, even named himself governor of the island. He scared enemy and crew alike by weaving hemp into his hair and beard and setting it on fire.

2

mingle with locals who gather there after work. With 24-hour security, public restrooms, an interactive water feature that delights kids of all ages, and a host of small restaurants and bars nearby, this square, which pays tribute to a slave who fought for his freedom, is the start of a strategic redevelopment of downtown Nassau. ⊠ *Bay St., Nassau, New Providence Island* ⊕ *www.downtownnassau.org.*

**WORTH NOTING**

**Balcony House.** A delightful 18th-century landmark—a pink two-story house named aptly for its overhanging balcony—this is the oldest wooden residential structure in Nassau and its furnishings and design recapture the elegance of a bygone era. A mahogany staircase, believed to have been salvaged from a ship during the 19th century, is an interior highlight. A guided tour through this fascinating building is an hour well spent. ⊠ *Market St. and Trinity Pl., Nassau, New Providence Island* ☎ *242/302–2621* ☒ *Donations accepted* ⊙ *Mon.–Wed. and Fri. 9:30–4:30, Thurs. 9:30–1.*

**Christ Church Cathedral.** It's worth the short walk off the main thoroughfare to see the stained-glass windows of this cathedral, which was built in 1837, when Nassau officially became a city. The white pillars of the church's spacious, airy interior support ceilings beamed with dark wood handcrafted by ship builders. The crucifixion depicted in the east window's center panel is flanked by depictions of the Empty Tomb and the Ascension. Be sure to spend a few minutes in the small, flower-filled Garden of Remembrance, where stone plaques adorn the walls. Sunday mass is held at 7:30, 9, 11:15 am, and 6 pm. Drop by the cathedral Christmas Eve and New Year's Eve to see the glorious church at night, and hear the music and choir. Call ahead to find out the time of the service. ⊠ *George and King Sts., Nassau, New Providence Island* ☎ *242/322–4186* ⊕ *www.christchurchcathedral.com* ⊙ *Daily 8–5.*

**Fort Fincastle.** Shaped like the bow of a ship and perched near the top of the Queen's Staircase, Fort Fincastle—named for Royal Governor Lord Dunmore (Viscount Fincastle)—was completed in 1793 to be a lookout post for marauders trying to sneak into the harbor. It served as a lighthouse in the early 19th century. A 15- to 20-minute tour costs just $1 per person and includes the nearby Queen's Staircase. ⊠ *Top of Elizabeth Ave. hill, south of Shirley St., Nassau, New Providence Island* ☎ *242/356–9085* ☒ *Free* ⊙ *Daily 8–4.*

**Government House.** The official residence of the Bahamas governor-general, the personal representative of the queen since 1801, this imposing pink-and-white building on Duke Street is an excellent example of the mingling of Bahamian-British and American Colonial architecture. Its graceful columns and broad circular drive recall the styles of Virginia or the Carolinas. But its pink color, distinctive white quoins

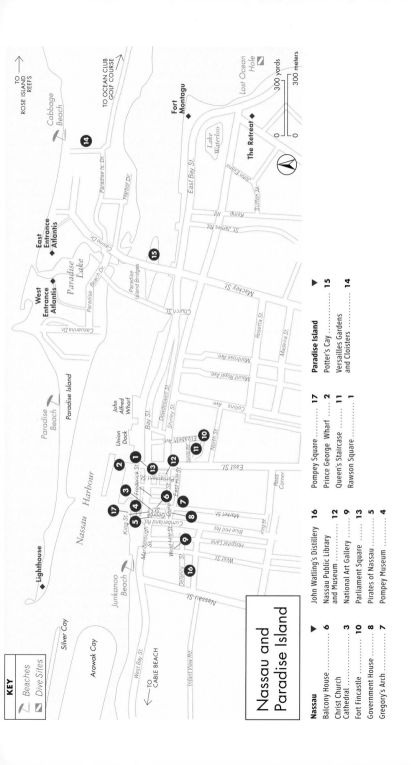

# Nassau and Paradise Island

**KEY**

◺ Beaches

◿ Dive Sites

**Nassau**

| | |
|---|---|
| Balcony House | 6 |
| Christ Church Cathedral | 3 |
| Fort Fincastle | 10 |
| Government House | 8 |
| Gregory's Arch | 7 |
| John Watling's Distillery | 16 |
| Nassau Public Library and Museum | 12 |
| National Art Gallery | 9 |
| Parliament Square | 13 |
| Pirates of Nassau | 5 |
| Pompey Museum | 4 |
| Pompey Square | 17 |
| Prince George Wharf | 2 |
| Queen's Staircase | 11 |
| Rawson Square | 1 |

**Paradise Island**

| | |
|---|---|
| Potter's Cay | 15 |
| Versailles Gardens and Cloisters | 14 |

0   300 yards
0   300 meters

(cross-laid cornerstones), and louvered wooden shutters (to keep out the tropical sun) are typically Bahamian. Here you can catch the crisply disciplined but beautifully flamboyant changing of the guard ceremony, which takes place every second Saturday of the month at 11 am. The stars of the pomp and pageantry are members of the Royal Bahamas Police Force Band, who are decked out in white tunics, red-stripe navy trousers, and spiked, white pith helmets with red bands. The drummers sport leopard skins. The governor's wife hosts a tea party open to the public from 3 to 4 pm on the last Friday of the month January–June as part of the People-to-People program. Dress is casual but elegant—no shorts, jeans, or tennis shoes. Musicians, poets, and storytellers provide entertainment. ⊠ *Duke and George Sts., Nassau, New Providence Island* ☏ *242/356–5415 ceremony schedule, 242/328–7810 tea party, 242/322–2020 Government House.*

**Gregory's Arch.** Named for John Gregory (royal governor 1849–54), this arch, at the intersection of Market and Duke streets, separates downtown from the "over-the-hill" neighborhood of **Grant's Town,** where much of Nassau's population lives. Grant's Town was laid out in the 1820s by Governor Lewis Grant as a settlement for freed slaves. Visitors once enjoyed late-night mingling with the locals in the small, dimly lighted bars; nowadays you should exhibit the same caution you would if you were visiting the commercial areas of a large city. Nevertheless, it's a vibrant section of town where you can rub shoulders with Bahamians at a funky take-out food stand or down-home restaurant.

**Nassau Public Library and Museum.** The octagonal building near Parliament Square was the Nassau Gaol (the old British spelling for jail), circa 1797. You're welcome to pop in and browse. The small prison cells are now lined with books. The museum has an interesting collection of historic prints and old colonial documents. Computers with Internet access are available for rent—$1 for 15 minutes, $4 for an hour. ⊠ *Shirley St. between Parliament St. and Bank La., Nassau, New Providence Island* ☏ *242/322–4907* ⊕ *www.bahamaslibraries.org* ▱ *Free* ☉ *Mon.–Thurs. 10–6:45, Fri. 10–4:45, Sat. 10–3:45.*

**Parliament Square.** Nassau is the seat of the national government. The Bahamian Parliament comprises two houses—a 16-member Senate (Upper House) and a 38-member House of Assembly (Lower House)—and a ministerial cabinet headed by a prime minister. If the House is in session, sit in to watch lawmakers debate. Parliament Square's pink, colonnaded government buildings were constructed in the late 1700s and early 1800s by Loyalists who came to the Bahamas from North Carolina. The square is dominated by a statue of a slim young Queen Victoria that was erected on her birthday, May 24, in 1905. In the immediate area are a handful of magistrates' courts. Behind the House of Assembly is the **Supreme Court.** Its four-times-a-year opening ceremonies (held the first weeks of January, April, July, and October) recall the wigs and mace-bearing pageantry of the Houses of Parliament in London. The Royal Bahamas Police Force Band is usually on hand for the event. ⊠ *Bay St., Nassau, New Providence Island* ☏ *242/322–2041* ▱ *Free* ☉ *Weekdays 10–4.*

The Cloisters in Versailles Gardens is possibly the most peaceful spot on the island.

**Pompey Museum.** The building, where slave auctions were held in the 1700s, is named for a rebel slave who lived on the Out Island of Exuma in 1830. The structure and historic artifacts inside were destroyed by fire in December 2011, but have been painstakingly brought back to life and new exhibits acquired and produced. Exhibits focus on the issues of slavery and emancipation and highlight the works of local artists. A knowledgeable, enthusiastic young staff is on hand to answer questions. ⊠ *Bay and George Sts., Nassau, New Providence Island* ☎ *242/356–0495* ⊕ *www.ammcbahamas.com* ☉ *Call ahead or check website.*

**Prince George Wharf.** The wharf that leads into Rawson Square is the first view that cruise passengers encounter after they tumble off their ships. Up to a dozen gigantic cruise ships call on Nassau at any one time, and passengers spill out onto downtown, giving Nassau an instant, and constantly replenished, surge of life. Even if you're not visiting via cruise ship, it's worth heading to Festival Place, a Bahamian village–style shopping emporium. Here you'll find booths for 45 Bahamian artisans; live music; Internet kiosks; vendors selling diving, fishing, and day trips; scooter rentals; and an information desk offering maps, directions, and suggestions for sightseeing. You can also arrange walking tours of historic Nassau here. ⊠ *Waterfront at Rawson Sq., Nassau, New Providence Island.*

**Queen's Staircase.** A popular early-morning exercise regimen for locals, the "66 Steps" (as Bahamians call them) are thought to have been carved out of a solid limestone cliff by slaves in the 1790s. The staircase was later named to honor Queen Victoria's reign. Pick up some souvenirs at the ad hoc straw market along the narrow road that leads to the site. ⊠ *Top of Elizabeth Ave. hill, south of Shirley St., Nassau, New Providence Island.*

**Rawson Square.** This shady square connects Bay Street to Prince George Wharf. As you enter off Bay Street, note the statue of Sir Milo Butler, the first postindependence (and first native Bahamian) governor general. Horse-drawn surreys wait for passengers along Prince George Wharf (expect to pay about $30 for a half-hour ride through Nassau's streets). Between Rawson Square and Festival Place, check out (or perhaps stop inside) the open-air **hair-braiding pavilion,** where women work their magic at prices ranging from $2 for a single strand to $100 for an elaborate do. An often-overlooked pleasure near the pavilion is Randolph W. Johnston's lovely bronze statue, *Tribute to Bahamian Women.* ⊠ *Bay St., Nassau, New Providence Island.*

> **KEEP LEFT**
>
> Driving on the left is one of the many leftovers from colonial British rule. As history goes, the Brits kept to the left so they could easily draw and use their sword on the right if an enemy approached. These days, most of the cars driven in the Bahamas are imported from the United States and are designed for right-hand driving, yet islanders still keep to the other side.

## PARADISE ISLAND

The graceful, arched Paradise Island bridges ($1 round-trip toll for cars and motorbikes; free for bicyclists and pedestrians) lead to and from the extravagant world of Paradise Island. Until 1962 the island was largely undeveloped and known as Hog Island. A&P heir Huntington Hartford changed the name when he built the island's first resort complex. In 1994 South African developer Sol Kerzner transformed the existing high-rise hotel into the first phase of Atlantis. Many years, a number of new hotels, a water park, and more than $1 billion later, Atlantis has taken over the island. From the ultraexclusive Cove hotel to the acclaimed golf course, it's easy to forget there's more to Paradise Island. It's home to multimillion-dollar homes and condominiums and a handful of independent resort properties. Despite the hustle and bustle of the megaresorts, you can still find yourself a quiet spot on Cabbage Beach, which lines the northern side of the island, or on the more secluded Paradise Beach west of Atlantis. Aptly renamed, the island *is* a paradise for beach lovers, boaters, and fun seekers.

### WORTH NOTING

**Potter's Cay.** Walk the road beneath the Paradise Island bridges to Potter's Cay to watch sloops bringing in and selling loads of fish and conch—pronounced *konk.* Along the road to the cay are dozens of stands where you can watch the conch, straight from the sea, being extracted from its glistening pink shell. If you don't have the know-how to handle the tasty conch's preparation—getting the diffident creature out of its shell requires boring a hole at the right spot to sever the muscle that keeps it entrenched—you can enjoy a conch salad on the spot, as fresh as it comes, and take notes for future attempts. Empty shells are sold as souvenirs. Many locals and hotel chefs come here to purchase the fresh catches; you can also find vegetables, herbs, and such condiments as fiery Bahamian peppers preserved in lime juice, and locally grown pineapples, papayas, and bananas. Join in on a raucous game of dominoes outside many of the stalls. Some stalls are closed on Sunday. There's also a police station and dockmaster's office, where you can book an inexpensive trip on a mail boat headed to the Out Islands. Be aware that these boats are built for cargo, not passenger comfort, and it's a rough ride even on calm seas.

> **WORD OF MOUTH**
>
> "A short walk from Atlantis will get you to the Potter's Cay (dock area) where they prepare a fresh conch salad. Pull the conch out of the shell, dice it up with veggies, and then squeeze the fresh lime over the top. It was a cheap lunch with some built in entertainment. VERY casual and 'local.'"
>
> —Michaelpl

**Versailles Gardens.** Fountains and statues of luminaries and legends (such as Napoléon and Josephine, Franklin Delano Roosevelt, David Livingstone, Hercules, and Mephistopheles) adorn Versailles Gardens, the terraced lawn at the One & Only Ocean Club, once the private hideaway of Huntington Hartford. At the top of the gardens stand the **Cloisters**, the remains of a stone monastery built by Augustinian monks in France in the 13th century. They were imported to the United States in the 1920s by newspaper baron William Randolph Hearst. (The cloister is one of four to have ever been removed from French soil.) Forty years later, Hartford bought the Cloisters and had them rebuilt on their present commanding site. At the center is a graceful, contemporary white marble statue called *Silence*, by U.S. sculptor Dick Reid. Nearly every day, tourists take or renew wedding vows under the delicately wrought gazebo overlooking Nassau Harbour. Although the garden is owned by the One & Only Ocean Club, visitors are welcome so long as they check in at the security gate. ⊠ *One & Only Ocean Club, Paradise Island Dr., Paradise Island, New Providence Island* ☏ *242/363–2501.*

## CABLE BEACH AND WESTERN NEW PROVIDENCE

From downtown Nassau, West Bay Street follows the coast west past Arawak Cay to the Cable Beach strip. If you're not driving, catch the #10 jitney for a direct ride from downtown. This main drag is lined with hotels and is being completely transformed by the Baha Mar group. A small straw market and a roadside daiquiri stall round out the area's offerings, outside of the resort and beaches.

Immediately west, the hotel strip gives way to residential neighborhoods interspersed with shops, restaurants, and cafés. Homes become more and more posh the farther west you go; Lyford Cay—the island's original gated community—is home to the original 007, Sean Connery. Hang a left at the Lyford Cay roundabout and eventually you'll come across the historic Clifton Heritage Park, the local brewery where Kalik and Heineken are brewed and bottled, a new upscale resort development whose financiers include golfers Ernie Els and Tiger Woods, and eventually the sleepy settlement of Adelaide.

The loop around the island's west and south coasts can be done in a couple of hours by car or scooter, but take some time for lunch and a swim along the way. Unless you're being taken around by a taxi or local, it's best to return to Cable Beach along the same route, as internal roads can get confusing.

## TOP ATTRACTIONS

**Arawak Cay.** Known to Nassau residents as "The Fish Fry," Arawak Cay is one of the best places to knock back a Kalik beer, chat with locals, watch or join in a fast-paced game of dominoes, or sample traditional Bahamian fare.

### SNAKES ALIVE!

The Bahamas has five types of snakes, none poisonous, but the most interesting is the Bahamian boa constrictor, threatened with extinction because Bahamians kill them on sight. The Bahamian boa is extremely unusual in that it has remnants of legs, called spurs. The male uses his spurs to tickle the female. Ask one of the trainers at Ardastra Gardens and Zoo to show you the boa, so you can see the tiny legs.

You can get small dishes such as conch fritters or full meals at one of the pastel-color waterside shacks. Order a fried snapper served up with a sweet homemade roll, or fresh conch salad (a spicy mixture of chopped conch—just watching the expert chopping is a show as good as any in town—mixed with diced onions, cucumbers, tomatoes, and hot peppers in a lime marinade). The two-story Twin Brothers and Goldie's Enterprises are two of the most popular places. Try their fried "cracked conch" and Goldie's famous Sky Juice (a sweet but potent gin, coconut-water, and sweet-milk concoction sprinkled with nutmeg). Local fairs and craft shows are often held in the adjacent field. ⊠ *W. Bay St. and Chippingham Rd., Paradise Island, New Providence Island.*

FAMILY **Ardastra Gardens, Zoo, and Conservation Centre.** Marching flamingos? These national birds give a parading performance at Ardastra daily at 10:30, 2:10, and 4:10. The brilliant pink birds are a delight—especially for children, who can walk among the flamingos after the show. The zoo, with more than 5 acres of tropical greenery and ponds, also has an aviary of rare tropical birds including the bright green Bahama parrot, native Bahamian creatures such as rock iguanas and the little (and harmless) Bahamian boa constrictors, and a global collection of small animals. ⊠ *Chippingham Rd. south of W. Bay St., Paradise Island, New Providence Island* ☎ *242/323–5806* ⊕ *www.ardastra.com* ☜ *$16 adults, $8 children* ☉ *Daily 9–5.*

FAMILY **Fort Charlotte.** Built in 1788, this imposing fort comes complete with a waterless moat, drawbridge, ramparts, and a dungeon, where children love to see the torture device where prisoners were "stretched." Young local guides bring the fort to life. (Tips are expected.) Lord Dunmore, who built it, named the massive structure in honor of George III's wife. At the time, some called it Dunmore's Folly because of the staggering expense of its construction. It cost eight times more than was originally planned. (Dunmore's superiors in London were less than ecstatic with the high costs, but he managed to survive unscathed.) Ironically, no shots were ever fired in battle from the fort. The fort and its surrounding

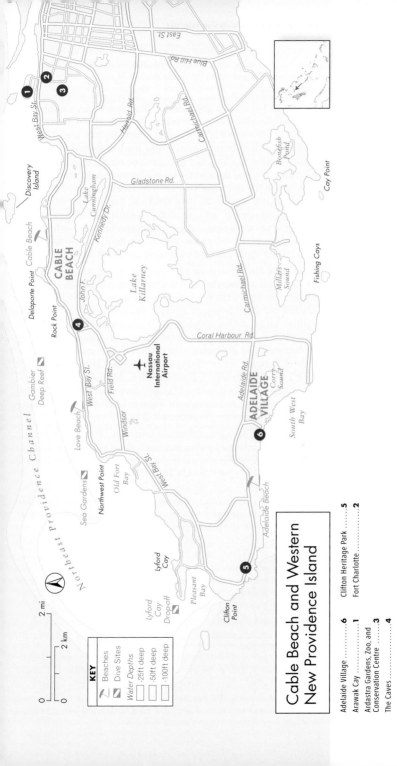

# Cable Beach and Western
# New Providence Island

**KEY**

/ Beaches

/ Dive Sites

Water Depths

- -25ft deep
- -50ft deep
- -100ft deep

0 ——— 2 mi
0 ——— 2 km

Northeast Providence Channel

Discovery Island

Cable Beach

CABLE BEACH

Delaporte Point

Rock Point

Gambier Deep Reef

Sea Gardens

Love Beach

Northwest Point

Old Fort Bay

Windsor

Lyford Cay

Lyford Cay Drop-off

Pleasant Bay

Clifton Point

Adelaide Beach

West Bay St.

Field Rd.

Nassau International Airport

Coral Harbour Rd.

Adelaide Rd.

ADELAIDE VILLAGE

Corry Sound

South West Bay

Lake Killarney

John F.

Kennedy Dr.

Lake Cunningham

Gladstone Rd.

West Bay St.

Harold Rd.

Carmichael Rd.

Carmichael Rd.

Millars Sound

Bonefish Pond

Fishing Cays

Cay Point

Blue Hill Rd.

East St.

100 acres offer a wonderful view of the cricket grounds, the beach, and the ocean beyond. ⊠ *W. Bay St. at Chippingham Rd., Paradise Island, New Providence Island* 🎫 *$5* ☉ *Tours daily 8–4.*

**WORTH NOTING**

**Adelaide Village.** The small community on New Providence's southwestern coast sits placidly, like a remnant of another era, between busy Adelaide Road and the ocean. It was first settled during the early 1830s by Africans who had been captured and loaded aboard slave ships bound for the New World. They were rescued on the high seas by the British Royal Navy and the first group of liberated slaves reached Nassau in 1832. Today, there are two sides to Adelaide—the few dozen families who grow vegetables, raise chickens, and inhabit well-worn, pastel-painted wooden houses, shaded by casuarina, mahogany, and palm trees; and the more upscale beach cottages that are mostly used as weekend getaways. The village has a primary school, some little grocery stores, and a few small restaurants serving native food.

**The Caves.** These large limestone caverns that the waves sculpted over the aeons are said to have sheltered the early Arawak Indians. An oddity perched right beside the road, they're worth a glance—although in truth, there's not much to see, as the dark interior doesn't lend itself to exploration. A daiquiri bar is situated just alongside the caves, providing a nice place for a break, and across the street is a concrete viewing platform overlooking the ocean. Just a short drive beyond the caves, on an island between traffic lanes, is **Conference Corner,** where U.S. President John F. Kennedy, Canadian Prime Minister John Diefenbaker, and British Prime Minister Harold Macmillan planted trees on the occasion of their 1962 summit in Nassau. ⊠ *W. Bay St. and Blake Rd., Paradise Island, New Providence Island.*

**Clifton Heritage Park.** It's quite a distance from just about any hotel you could stay at, but for history and nature buffs, this national park, rescued from the hands of developers, is worth the drive. Situated on a prehistoric Lucayan Village dating back to AD 1000–1500, Clifton Heritage Park allows you to walk through the ruins of slave quarters from an 18th-century plantation. There's still much work to be done to really develop this site; call ahead to arrange a tour guide for the best experience. Be sure to walk the path from the main parking lot toward the west, where you can enjoy the peace and quiet of the Sacred Space and admire the African women carved out of dead casuarinas trees by local artist Antonius Roberts. Naturalists will enjoy walking along the paths lined with native flora and fauna that lead to wooden decks overlooking mangrove swamps. ⊠ *Clifton Pier, West Bay St., Paradise Island, New Providence Island* ☎ *242/362–5121* ⊕ *www.bahamascliftonheritagepark.org* ☉ *Mon.–Fri. 9–5, weekends and holidays by appointment only.*

## EASTERN NEW PROVIDENCE

New Providence Island's eastern end is residential, although there are some interesting historic sites and fortifications here. From East Bay Street, just beyond the Paradise Island bridges, it's a 20-minute scenic drive to Eastern Point. Take Eastern Road, lined with gracious homes (and during the early summer months, the red and deep orange blooms of the Royal Poinciana tree). The following are worthy sights to see.

## TOP ATTRACTIONS

**The Retreat.** Nearly 200 species of exotic palm trees grace the 11 verdant acres appropriately known as The Retreat, which serves as the headquarters of the Bahamas National Trust. Stroll in blessed silence through the lush grounds, and be on the lookout for native birds. It's a perfect break on a steamy Nassau day. The Retreat hosts the Jollification—the unofficial start to the Christmas season—the third weekend in November. Carols, festive food and drinks, a kids' holiday craft center, and local artisans selling native and Christmas crafts make this a must-do event. ⊠ *Village Rd., Paradise Island, New Providence Island* ☎ *242/393–1317* ⊞ *$2* ⊙ *Weekdays 9–5.*

## WORTH NOTING

**Fort Montagu.** The oldest of the island's three forts, Montagu was built of local limestone in 1741 to repel Spanish invaders. The only action it saw was when it was occupied for two weeks by rebel American troops—among them a lieutenant named John Paul Jones—seeking arms and ammunition during the Revolutionary War. The small fortification is quite simple, but displays a lovely elevated view of Nassau Harbour. The second level has a number of weathered cannons. A recently renovated and restored public beach looks out upon Montagu Bay, where many international yacht regattas and Bahamian sloop races are held annually. ⊠ *East of Bay St. on Eastern Rd., Paradise Island, New Providence Island* ⊞ *Free.*

### OFFSHORE ADVENTURES

For a true beach getaway, head to one of the tiny islands just off the coast of Paradise Island. A 20-minute boat ride from Nassau, Blue Lagoon Island has a number of beaches, including one in a tranquil cove lined with hammocks suspended by palm trees. Enjoy a grilled lunch and then rent a kayak or water bike if you're feeling ambitious.

# BEACHES

New Providence is the Bahamas' most urban island, but that doesn't mean you won't find beautiful beaches. Powdery white sand, aquamarine waves, and shade-bearing palm trees are easy to come by, regardless how populated you like your beach to be. Whether you crave solitude or want to be in the middle of the action, there's a sand spot that's just right for you.

Cable Beach and the beaches near Atlantis are where you'll typically find loud music, bars serving tropical drinks, and vendors peddling everything from parasailing and Jet Ski rides to T-shirts and hair braiding. Downtown Nassau only has man-made beaches, the best being Junkanoo Beach just west of the British Colonial Hilton. But the capital city's beaches can't compare to the real thing. For a more relaxed environment, drive out of the main tourist areas. You'll likely find stretches of sand populated by locals only, or, chances are, no one at all.

The major hotels on Cable Beach have lifeguards.

## NASSAU

**Junkanoo Beach.** Right in downtown Nassau, this beach is spring-break central from late February through April. The man-made beach isn't the prettiest on the island, but it's conveniently located if you only have a few quick hours to catch a tan. Music is provided by bands, DJs, and guys with boom boxes; a few bars keep the drinks flowing. **Amenities:** food and drink; parking (no fee); toilets; water sports. **Best for:** partiers; swimming. ⊠ *Immediately west of the British Colonial Hilton, Nassau, New Providence Island.*

## PARADISE ISLAND

FAMILY
Fodor's Choice
★
**Cabbage Beach.** At this beach you'll find 3 miles of white sand lined with shady casuarina trees, sand dunes, and sun worshippers. This is the place to go to rent Jet Skis or get a bird's-eye view of Paradise Island while parasailing. Hair braiders and T-shirt vendors stroll the beach, and hotel guests crowd the areas surrounding the resorts, including Atlantis. For peace and quiet, stroll east. **Amenities:** food and drink; lifeguards; parking (fee); water sports. **Best for:** solitude; partiers; swimming; walking. ⊠ *Paradise Island, New Providence Island.*

## CABLE BEACH AND WESTERN NEW PROVIDENCE

FAMILY
**Adelaide Beach.** Time your visit to this far-flung beach on the island's southwestern shore to catch low tide, when the ocean recedes, leaving behind sandbanks and seashells. It's a perfect place to take the kids for a shallow-water dip in the sea, or for a truly private rendezvous. Popular

with locals, you'll likely have the miles-long stretch all to yourself unless it's a public holiday. **Amenities:** none. **Best for:** solitude; swimming; walking. ⊠ *Adelaide, New Providence Island.*

**Cable Beach.** Hotels dot the length of this 3-mile beach, so don't expect isolation. Music from the hotel pool decks wafts out onto the sand, Jet Skis race up and down the waves, and vendors sell everything from shell jewelry to coconut drinks right from the shell. If you get tired of lounging around, join a game of beach volleyball. Access via new hotels may be limited, but join the locals and park at Goodman's Bay park on the eastern end of the beach. **Amenities:** parking (no fee); water sports. **Best for:** partiers; sunset; swimming; walking. ⊠ *Cable Beach, New Providence Island.*

**Love Beach.** If you're looking for great snorkeling and some privacy, drive about 20 minutes west of town. White sand shimmers in the sun and the azure waves gently roll ashore. About a mile offshore are 40 acres of coral reef known as the Sea Gardens. Access is not marked, just look for a vacant lot. **Amenities:** none. **Best for:** solitude; snorkeling; sunset ⊠ *Western New Providence, New Providence Island.*

# WHERE TO EAT

*Note: A gratuity (15%) is often added to the bill. Many all-inclusive hotels offer meal plans for nonguests.*

## NASSAU

$ ╳ **Athena Café and Bar.** Gregarious owner Peter Mousis greets his guests
GREEK with a bellowing "Opa!" and he and his family serve tasty fare at moderate prices seven days a week. This Greek restaurant provides a break from the Nassau culinary routine. Sit on the second floor among Grecian statuary, or on the balcony overlooking the action below. Enjoy souvlaki, moussaka, or a hearty Greek gyro in a relaxed and friendly establishment. $ *Average main: $20* ⊠ *Bay St. at Charlotte St., Nassau, New Providence Island* ☎ *242/326–1296* ⊕ *www.athenacafebar. com* ⊗ *No dinner Sun.*

$ ╳ **Bahamian Cookin' Restaurant & Bar.** Three generations of Bahamian
BAHAMIAN women treat patrons as if they were welcoming them into their own home. And the Bahamian food whipped up in the kitchen is as close to homemade as you can get in a restaurant. This breakfast and lunch locale is bustling with local professionals during the week and has also become a popular "off the beaten path" spot for cruise ship passengers. Grandmother Mena swears their conch fritters are the "conchiest" you'll find. $ *Average main: $13* ⊠ *Trinity Place, Nassau, New Providence Island* ⊹ *Turn left off Bay St. onto Market St. toward Central Bank, then left onto Trinity Place* ☎ *242/328–0334* ⊗ *No dinner; closed Sun.*

$$$ ╳ **Café Matisse.** Low-slung settees, stucco arches, and reproductions of
ECLECTIC the eponymous artist's works set a casually refined tone at this restau-
Fodor's Choice rant owned by a husband-and-wife team—he's Bahamian, she's north-
★ ern Italian. Sit in the ground-floor garden under large white umbrellas or dine inside the century-old house for lunch or dinner. Start with beef

carpaccio, then dive into freshly made pasta with crab meat, garlic, hot pepper, cherry tomatoes, and shrimp in a spicy red-curry sauce, or such delights as pizza frutti di mar (topped with fresh local seafood). Be sure to save room for dessert and the delicious handmade cookies that come with coffee. $ *Average main: $35 ⊠ Bank La. and Bay St., behind Parliament Sq., Nassau, New Providence Island* ☏ *242/356–7012* ⊕ *www.cafe-matisse.com* ⊘ *Closed Sun., Mon., and Aug.*

> **POP THE BUBBLY**
>
> A meandering maze underneath historic Graycliff's sprawling kitchen and dining area houses more than 200,000 bottles of wine and champagne. Graycliff's wine cellar is one of the most extensive and impressive in the world. It costs $1,000 to book the elegant private cellar dining room, but tours are free.

**$$$**
CHINESE
✕ **East Villa Restaurant and Lounge.** In a converted Bahamian home, this is one of the most popular Chinese restaurants in town. The Chinese-Continental menu includes entrées such as conch with black-bean sauce, *hung shew* (walnut chicken), and steak *kew* (cubed prime fillet served with baby corn, snow peas, water chestnuts, and vegetables). The New York strip steak is nirvana. A short taxi ride from Paradise Island or downtown Nassau, this is the perfect spot if you're seeking something a little different from the typical area restaurants. Dress is casual elegance. $ *Average main: $28 ⊠ E. Bay St. near Nassau Yacht Club, Nassau, New Providence Island* ☏ *242/393–3377* ⊕ *www.eastvillabahamas.com* ⊘ *No lunch Sat.–Sun.*

**$$$$**
EUROPEAN
Fodor's Choice
★
✕ **Graycliff.** A meal at this hillside mansion begins in the elegant parlor, where, over live piano music, drinks are served and orders are taken. It's a rarefied world, where waiters wear tuxedos and Cuban cigars and cognac are served after dinner. Graycliff's signature dishes include Kobe beef, Kurobuta pork, and Nassau grouper. The wine cellar contains more than 200,000 bottles that have been handpicked by owner Enrico Garzaroli, some running into the tens of thousands of dollars. You can even buy the world's oldest bottle of wine, a German vintage 1727, for $200,000. $ *Average main: $55 ⊠ W. Hill St. at Cumberland Rd., across from Government House, Nassau, New Providence Island* ☏ *242/322–2796* ⊕ *www.graycliff.com* ⌕ *Reservations essential.*

**$**
AMERICAN
✕ **The Green Parrot.** Two locations—Green Parrot Harbourfront and Green Parrot Hurricane Hole—mean you get incomparable views of Nassau Harbour and a fresh breeze, whichever way the wind is blowing. The large Works Burger is a favorite at these casual, all-outdoor restaurants and bars. The menu includes burgers, wraps, quesadillas, and other simple but tasty dishes. The conch po'boy is a new favorite. The weekday happy hour from 5 to 9 and a DJ on Friday nights draw a lively local crowd. $ *Average main: $20 ⊠ E. Bay St., west of the bridges to Paradise Island, Nassau, New Providence Island* ☏ *242/322–9248, 242/363–3633* ⊕ *www.greenparrotbar.com.*

**$$**
BRAZILIAN
✕ **Humidor Churrascaria Restaurant.** The salad bar at this casual restaurant offers everything from simple salad fixings to scrumptious seafood salads and soups. And that is just the start. Each table setting includes a coaster that's red on one side and green on the other. Just

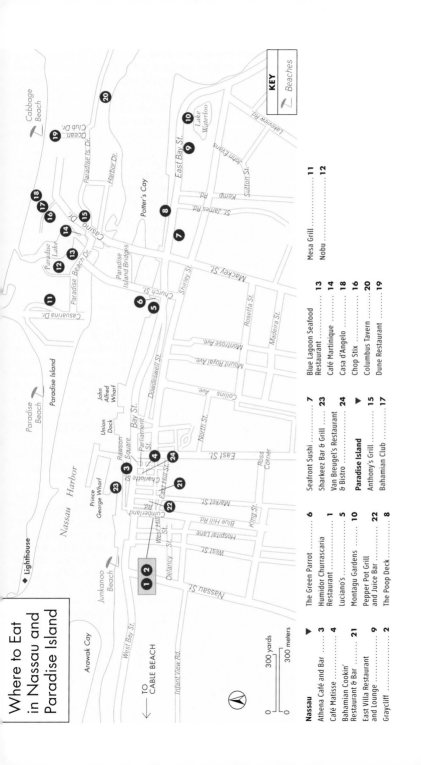

# Where to Eat in Nassau and Paradise Island

▶ Beaches

KEY

0 — 300 yards
0 — 300 meters

TO ← CABLE BEACH

**Nassau**

Athena Café and Bar ...... **3**
Café Matisse .................... **4**
Bahamian Cookin'
Restaurant & Bar ......... **21**
East Villa Restaurant
and Lounge .................... **9**
Graycliff ......................... **2**

The Green Parrot ............ **6**
Humidor Churrascaria
Restaurant ..................... **1**
Luciano's ....................... **5**
Montagu Gardens ......... **10**
Pepper Pot Grill
and Juice Bar ................ **22**
The Poop Deck ............... **8**

Seafront Sushi .............. **6**
Sharkeez Bar & Grill ..... **23**
Van Breugel's Restaurant
& Bistro ......................... **24**

**Paradise Island**          ▶

Anthony's Grill ............. **15**
Bahamian Club .............. **17**

Blue Lagoon Seafood
Restaurant .................... **13**
Café Martinique ........... **14**
Casa d'Angelo ............... **18**
Chop Stix ....................... **16**
Columbus Tavern .......... **20**
Dune Restaurant .......... **19**

Mesa Grill ..................... **11**
Nobu ............................. **12**

like a stoplight, green means go and red means stop. Waiters serve a never-ending selection of delicious skewered meats and fresh fish until you turn your coaster to red and declare uncle. When you're done, stop by the smoking lounge to see the cigar rollers in action or stroll along the garden terraces and fountains out back. [$] *Average main: $45* ✉ *W. Hill St. off Cumberland Rd., next to Graycliff Hotel, Nassau, New Providence Island* ☎ *242/328–7050* 🌐 *www.graycliff.com* 🕒 *Dinner only.*

$$$ ITALIAN 🍴 **Luciano's.** Green Roofs, the sprawling former residence of the late Sir Roland Symonette (the country's first premier), houses this harborside restaurant. The mansion's mahogany woodwork, gardens, and terraces create a romantic setting for dining on Tuscan fare, including escarole, white bean, and sausage soup; osso buco; grouper; and homemade pastas—including a delicious frutti di mar over linguine. The sweeping view of Paradise Island and the towers of Atlantis is particularly lovely at sunset. Reservations are essential for waterside tables. [$] *Average main: $38* ✉ *E. Bay St., 2 blocks west of Paradise Island bridges, Nassau, New Providence Island* ☎ *242/323–7770* 🌐 *www.lucianosnassau.com* 🕒 *Lunch weekdays; dinner daily.*

$$ SEAFOOD 🍴 **Montagu Gardens.** Angus beef and fresh native seafood—flame-grilled and seasoned with home-mixed spices—are the specialties at this romantic restaurant in an old Bahamian mansion on Lake Waterloo. The dining room opens to a walled courtyard niched with Roman-style statues and gardens that lead to a waterside balustrade. Besides seafood and steak (carnivores should try the filet mignon smothered in mushrooms), menu selections include chicken, lamb, pasta, ribs, and several Bahamian-inspired dishes such as conch fritters and cracked coconut conch. A favorite dessert is Fort Montagu Mud Pie. [$] *Average main: $25* ✉ *E. Bay St., Nassau, New Providence Island* ☎ *242/394–6347* 🌐 *www.montagugardens.com* 🕒 *Closed Sun.*

$ JAMAICAN 🍴 **Pepper Pot Grill and Juice Bar.** Jamaican transplant Keron Williams takes his role of cooking and serving up the most authentic Jamaican food in Nassau very seriously. His small, simple restaurant draws an international crowd of cruise ship workers and immigrants from the Caribbean diaspora. Awaken your taste buds with jerk pork, curry chicken, and rice and beans infused with coconut milk, then take the edge off the spiciness with a tall glass of freshly made carrot, mango, or soursop juice. Peak lunchtime gets very busy so be prepared to wait for a table. [$] *Average main: $13* ✉ *From Bay St., turn south onto Market St., then right onto King St., King St., Nassau, New Providence Island* ☎ *242/323–8177* 🕒 *No dinner.*

$$$ BAHAMIAN 🍴 **The Poop Deck.** Just east of the bridges from Paradise Island and a quick cab ride from the center of town is this favorite local haunt. There's usually a wait for a table, and it's worth waiting a little longer for one overlooking the marina and Nassau Harbour. The restaurant's popularity has resulted in a second Poop Deck on Cable Beach's west end, but for residents, this is still the place. Expect spicy dishes with names such as Mama Mary's Fish; there's also an extensive wine list. Start with Paula's Conch Fritters and then select a fresh, whole-hog snapper or lobster tail for the chef to prepare exactly how you want it.

The fish is usually served head to tail, so if you're squeamish, ask your waiter to have the head cut off before it comes out on your plate. Save room for guava duff and a calypso coffee spiked with secret ingredients. [$] *Average main: $35* ✉ *E. Bay St. at Nassau Yacht Haven Marina, east of bridges from Paradise Island, Nassau, New Providence Island* ☎ *242/393–8175* 🌐 *www.thepoopdeck.com.*

$$ SUSHI Fodor's Choice ★ 🍴 **Seafront Sushi.** One of Nassau's hot spots, this simple sushi restaurant has an extensive menu including traditional rolls, sushi, and sashimi as well as more innovative options that incorporate local delicacies like conch. The Volcano Roll topped with their special conch sauce is a favorite. There are enough non-seafood options on the menu to satisfy anyone in your group. Friday and Saturday nights are really busy and there are no reservations so be prepared to wait for a table and to be served. [$] *Average main: $20* ✉ *East Bay St., Nassau, New Providence Island* ☎ *242/394–1706* 🌐 *www.seafrontsushibahamas.com* ⏲ *Closed Sun. No lunch Sat.*

$ AMERICAN 🍴 **Sharkeez Bar & Grill.** If you arrive in Nassau aboard a cruise ship, you won't miss the sign for this second-floor, hot-spot bar and grill emblazoned atop its thatched roof. A good spot to get some basic bar food to keep you going as you tour downtown Nassau, it's also a popular spot on weekend nights for locals and tourists alike. The Sneaky Tikki, a 16-ounce fruit concoction including seven different types of rum, is a crowd-pleaser. [$] *Average main: $20* ✉ *Woodes Rogers Walk, Nassau, New Providence Island* ☎ *242/322–8144* ⏲ *No dinner Sun.–Mon.*

$$$ MODERN EUROPEAN 🍴 **Van Breugel's Restaurant & Bistro.** Dutch owner Freddy Van Breugel is enough of a character that a chance meeting with him is almost enough to make a visit to this hip spot just off Bay Street worth the effort. The Coconut Curry Conch Chowder—a delicious blend of the Bahamian staple and a Thai coconut chicken soup—is another reason. This is a popular spot for locals to grab a working lunch or catch up during Friday happy hour at the bar that runs the length of the converted Bahamian home. [$] *Average main: $33* ✉ *Charlotte St. South, Nassau, New Providence Island* ☎ *242/322–2484* 🌐 *www.vanbreugels.com* ⏲ *Closed Sun. No dinner Mon. or Tues.*

## PARADISE ISLAND

$$ AMERICAN 🍴 **Anthony's Grill.** Color is the standout feature at Anthony's: bright red, yellow, and blue tablecloths spiked with multihued squiggles; yellow-and-green walls with jaunty cloths hanging from the ceiling; booths printed with bright sea themes; and buoyant striped curtains. The lively spirit is reflected in the cheery service you'll receive at breakfast, lunch, or dinner. The extensive menu (60+ items to choose from) includes seafood pasta, grilled-to-order shrimp, grouper and salmon brochettes, steaks, burgers, ribs, and salads. [$] *Average main: $30* ✉ *Paradise Village Shopping Plaza, Paradise Island, New Providence Island* ☎ *242/363–3152* 🌐 *www.anthonysparadiseisland.com.*

$$$$ EUROPEAN 🍴 **Bahamian Club.** Reminiscent of a British country club, this handsome restaurant has walls lined with dark oak, overstuffed chairs, and leather banquettes. Meat is the house specialty—rib-eye steak, veal chop,

Jean-Georges Vongerichten designed this version of tuna tartar for Café Martinique.

herb-roasted rack of lamb, and chateaubriand for two—but grilled swordfish steak, Bahamian lobster, salmon fillet, and other fresh seafood dishes are all prepared with finesse. $ *Average main: $50* ⊠ *Atlantis, Paradise Island, New Providence Island* ☎ *242/363–3000* ⊕ *www.atlantis.com* ⌂ *Reservations essential* ☾ *No lunch.*

**$$$$**
**SEAFOOD**
✕ **Blue Lagoon Seafood Restaurant.** The interior tends toward the nautical, with hurricane lamps and brass rails, in this narrow third-floor dining room looking out to Nassau on one side and Atlantis on the other. It's a good choice for a quiet meal away from the bustle of Atlantis. Choose from simply prepared dishes such as crepes filled with seafood, stuffed grouper au gratin, lobster, or stoned crab claws. $ *Average main: $42* ⊠ *Club Land'Or, Paradise Island, New Providence Island* ☎ *242/363–2400* ⊕ *www.bluelagoonseafood.com* ⌂ *Reservations essential* ☾ *Closed Sun. No lunch.*

**$$$$**
**FRENCH**
**Fodor's**Choice
★
✕ **Café Martinique.** The original restaurant made famous in the 1965 James Bond film *Thunderball* has long been bulldozed, but with the help of renowned international chef Jean-Georges Vongerichten and New York designer Adam D. Tihany, Atlantis resurrected a classic. Nestled in the center of Marina Village on Paradise Island, Café Martinique is the height of sophistication in design, service, and cuisine. The decor includes a wrought-iron birdcage elevator and a mahogany staircase; a grand piano helps create a refined experience. The classic French gourmet menu offers simple classic dishes made spectacular thanks to the highest quality ingredients and chef Jean-George's influence. The seven-course chef's tasting menu is a special culinary treat. $ *Average main: $55* ⊠ *Marina Village, Atlantis, Paradise Island, New Providence Island* ☎ *242/363–3000* ⊕ *www.atlantis.com* ⌂ *Reservations essential.*

**$$$$** ✕**Casa D'Angelo.** At this restaurant
ITALIAN modeled after the wildly popular
Casa d'Angelo in south Florida,
chef Angelo Elia brings his famous
Tuscan-style cuisine to Paradise.
The antipasti display whets the
appetite for succulent seafood,
hearty pasta dishes, and prime cuts
of beef. The dessert pastries are
delectable. $ *Average main: $46*
*⊠ Atlantis, Paradise Island, New
Providence Island* 🕾 *242/363–
3000* ⊗ *No lunch.*

> **QUICK BITES**
>
> A quick snack or light lunch on the
> go can be picked up at most gas
> stations or bakeries on the island.
> Grab a hot patty—peppery chicken
> or beef is most popular—or a
> yellow pastry pocket filled with
> conch. One of these with a "coke
> soda"—the generic name for all
> brands of soft drink—will tide you
> over until your next real meal.

**$$$** ✕**Chop Stix.** Expect traditional Chi-
CHINESE nese favorites with a contemporary twist at this stylish restaurant. Try the
Cantonese steamed Bahamian lobster tails or grouper seared in a wok and
drizzled with a mouthwatering garlic sauce. For a late-night bite, pop in
for dim sum Friday and Saturday. The menu includes chicken spring rolls,
baked pork buns, and shrimp and lobster shu mai. $ *Average main: $33
⊠ Atlantis, Paradise Island, New Providence Island* 🕾 *242/363–3000
🖘 Reservations essential* ⊗ *Closed Mon. No lunch.*

**$$$** ✕**Columbus Tavern.** Watch the boats in Nassau Harbour through this
SEAFOOD restaurant's enormous open windows as you dine on fresh seafood deli-
cacies. This is a great spot to enjoy a traditional Bahamian breakfast of
boiled or stewed fish, though traditional American breakfast options are
also available. The tavern serves three meals a day, every day and is a
great spot to catch a romantic happy hour sunset. $ *Average main: $30
⊠ Paradise Island Dr. between Ocean Club Golf Course and Paradise
Harbor Club, Paradise Island, New Providence Island* 🕾 *242/363–5923
⊕ www.columbustavernbahamas.com.*

**$$$$** ✕**Dune Restaurant.** Feast on Jean-Georges Vongerichten's intricately
MODERN FRENCH prepared dishes while overlooking Cabbage Beach at the renowned
One & Only Ocean Club. Go for breakfast or lunch for the most reasonable prices. For breakfast, try the smoked salmon with potato pan-
cake and chive sour cream or the egg-white omelet with fresh herbs.
For dinner, share a Black Plate appetizer sampler to start and end with
the White Plate for dessert. In between, try the unique French-Asian
twists on classic entrées such as lobster, duck, beef, or mahimahi. It's
a great place to unwind amid ocean breezes. $ *Average main: $50
⊠ One & Only Ocean Club, Ocean Club Dr., Paradise Island, New
Providence Island* 🕾 *242/363–3000* ⊕ *www.oneandonlyresort.com
🖘 Reservations essential.*

**$$$$** ✕**Mesa Grill.** Bobby Flay is the latest celebrity chef to lend his name and
ECLECTIC expertise to the restaurant lineup at Atlantis. In the Cove hotel, Mesa
Grill (his first international outpost) serves the Southwestern cuisine
he is known for, but with a Bahamian twist. A fusion of local and
international herbs and spices bring extra zing to top cuts of meat and
seafood. $ *Average main: $50 ⊠ The Cove Atlantis, Paradise Island,
New Providence Island* 🕾 *242/363–3000* ⊕ *www.atlantis.com 🖘 Reservations essential* ⊗ *No lunch.*

Humidor Churrascaria Restaurant is in the Graycliff Hotel.

$$$$ SUSHI 🍴 **Nobu.** Sushi connoisseurs, celebrities, and tourists pack this Atlantis restaurant night after night. The rock shrimp and tomato ceviche and the yellowtail sashimi with jalapeño are Nobu favorites, but this restaurant also takes advantage of fresh Bahamian seafood—try the lobster shiitake salad or the cold conch shabu-shabu with Nobu sauces. The central dining room is surrounded by a Japanese pagoda, and guests seated at a long, communal sushi bar can watch chefs work. [$] *Average main: $50* ✉ *Royal Towers, Atlantis, Paradise Island, New Providence Island* ☎ *242/363–3000* 👔 *Jacket required* ⏲ *No lunch.*

## CABLE BEACH

$$$ ITALIAN 🍴 **Amici A Trattoria.** Savor delicious Italian cuisine in a casual setting overlooking the ocean. The menu features hearty pasta dishes, fresh caught seafood, and top cuts of meats. For a special treat order the Bahamian Spiny Lobster Scampi or the Short Rib Osso Bucco. [$] *Average main: $35* ✉ *Sheraton Nassau Beach Resort, Cable Beach, New Providence Island* ☎ *242/327–6000* ⏲ *No lunch.*

$$$ STEAKHOUSE 🍴 **Black Angus Grille.** This steak house offers some of the best certified Angus beef on the island. Bring your appetite if you're going to try the double porterhouse, which is carved right in front of you. It's not all about the beef, though. The skewered shrimp, ahi tuna, and seared-scallops gnocchi are delightful alternatives. Finish up with the kay lime pie made with Bahamian (instead of the traditional Floridian) citrus. [$] *Average main: $40* ✉ *Wyndham Nassau Resort, W. Bay St., Cable Beach, New Providence Island* ☎ *242/327–6200* ⏲ *Closed Sun. and Mon.; no lunch.*

**$$** ✕ **Indigo.** This eclectic restaurant doubles as an art gallery—walls are
ASIAN lined with Bahamian originals, many of them painted by the owner's
late father Brent Malone. Bahamian ingredients are transformed into
international dishes with a decidedly Asian flair. Fresh salads are a big
hit and the coconut curried conch chowder is not to be missed. The
funky inside bar is a popular local predinner hangout, and reservations
are recommended most nights and definitely on Fridays. $ *Average
main: $28* ✉ *W. Bay St. at Sandals roundabout, Cable Beach, New
Providence Island* ☎ *242/327–2524* ⊘ *Closed Sun.*

**$$** ✕ **Olive's Meze Grill.** Hip and trendy, this restaurant puts a fresh twist
MEDITERRANEAN on Mediterranean classics. The fare is simple, but locally grown greens
and fish caught in nearby waters make the meals special. It's popular
with locals for both lunch and dinner, and the small bar is hopping most
nights. Be sure to save room for desserts—the owners have taken special
pains to come up with unique sweet creations. $ *Average main: $28*
✉ *West Bay St., Cable Beach, New Providence Island* ☎ *242/327–6393.*

**$$$** ✕ **The Poop Deck at Sandyport.** A more upscale version of the other Poop
BAHAMIAN Deck, this waterside restaurant has soaring ceilings, a cool-pink-and-
aqua color scheme, and a dazzling view of the ocean. Start with grilled
shrimp and Brie before diving into the fresh catch of the day paired with
a selection from the extensive wine list. There's a smattering of choices
for the seafood-phobic. $ *Average main: $40* ✉ *W. Bay St., Cable
Beach, New Providence Island* ☎ *242/327–3325* ⊕ *www.thepoopdeck.
com* ⊘ *Closed Mon.*

**$$** ✕ **Spritz Restaurant and Bar.** This casual, open-air restaurant and bar
NORTHERN overlooks the Sandyport Canal and the pedestrians-only streets of the
ITALIAN Old Towne at Sandyport. Seating is limited, so reservations are recom-
FAMILY mended for weekend dining. The wood-fired pizzas are a local favorite, and northern Italian chef "Ciccio" brings a taste of his hometown
with a wide selection of pasta dishes. $ *Average main: $22* ✉ *Sandyport Olde Towne Marina Plaza, Cable Beach, New Providence Island*
☎ *242/327–0761* ⊕ *www.spritzrestaurant.com* ⊘ *No lunch Mon.*

**$$** ✕ **Twisted Lime.** This busy sports bar has something for everyone.
AMERICAN Indoors, the dining room and bar feature the latest games playing on
18 flat-screen TVs. Outdoors, casual canal-front dining and drinks are
available at high-tops or on plush sofas. On big game nights, it's boys'
night out, but otherwise it's become a popular option on Nassau's social
scene. The menu is quite extensive: fish tacos and nachos fiesta are good
options for starters with local flair. For a main course, try the tamarind
glazed barbecue ribs or select something from the hot dog, burger, or
flatbread menus. $ *Average main: $25* ✉ *Sandyport Marina Village,
Cable Beach, New Providence Island* ☎ *242/327–0061.*

## WESTERN NEW PROVIDENCE

**$$$** ✕ **Compass Point.** This friendly restaurant and bar has one of the best
AMERICAN sunsets on the island. Sit indoors or out on the terrace overlooking
the ocean and enjoy their simple but tasty Bahamian and island-style
American fare for breakfast, lunch, and dinner. The kitchen is open
daily until midnight, so it's a great stop for a late-night meal or snack.
The long outdoor bar stays open until the last guest leaves, and there's

live music every other Saturday. $ *Average main: $35* ✉ *W. Bay St. near Gambier Village, New Providence Island* ☎ *242/327–4500* 🌐 *www.compasspointbeachresort.com.*

$ ECLECTIC FAMILY 🍴 **Goodfellow Farms.** This unique treat is well worth the long drive to the western end of the island. The vegetable farm has a country store and small restaurant with outdoor dining under shady trees and umbrellas. Lunch is simple but delicious—cranberry-almond chicken salad wraps, flank steak, or Bahamian crawfish pasta salad served over greens picked from the farm earlier in the day. $ *Average main: $15* ✉ *W. Bay St., Mount Pleasant Village. Take left at Lyford Cay roundabout, go over the hill, entrance to farm road is signposted, New Providence Island* ☎ *242/377–5000* 🌐 *www.goodfellowfarms.com* ⏲ *No dinner.*

$$$ ECLECTIC 🍴 **Mahogany House.** A favorite with the upscale Lyford Cay crowd, Mahogany House is sophisticated simplicity at its best. Whether you're dressed to the nines or sporting flip-flops, you're bound to feel both comfortable and welcome here. Specialty ingredients like quail, foie gras, and buffalo pork belly keep things interesting, but the wood-fired pizzas (including one topped with crawfish, yellow pepper, red onion, avocado, and mozzarella) and the vast selection of cured meats and cheeses can make this a very simple yet satisfying dining experience. Save room for le grand tour: a selection of all the rich desserts to share. $ *Average main: $36* ✉ *Western Rd., Lyford Cay, New Providence Island* ☎ *242/362–6669* 🌐 *www.mahogany-house.com* ⏲ *No lunch Sat.–Sun.*

## WHERE TO STAY

### NASSAU

$$$ HOTEL 🏨 **British Colonial Hilton Nassau.** This landmark hotel is the social heart of Nassau, the setting for political meetings and the city's most important events. **Pros:** right on Bay Street; quiet but trendy beach and pool area; centrally located. **Cons:** busy with local meetings and events; man-made beach; hard to access at peak traffic times. $ *Rooms from: $329* ✉ *1 Bay St., Nassau, New Providence Island* ☎ *242/322–3301* 🌐 *www.hiltoncaribbean.com/nassau* 🛏 *288 rooms, 23 suites* 🍽 *No meals.*

$$$$ HOTEL Fodor's Choice ★ 🏨 **Graycliff.** The old-world flavor of this Georgian colonial landmark—built in the 1720s by ship captain Howard Graysmith—has made it a perennial favorite with the upscale crowd. **Pros:** one of the most luxurious accommodations on the island; lush tropical gardens; large rooms. **Cons:** centered around the busy restaurant and bar area; not easily accessible for handicapped; no beach. $ *Rooms from: $310* ✉ *W. Hill St., Nassau, New Providence Island* ☎ *242/322–2796, 800/476–0446* 🌐 *www.graycliff.com* 🛏 *7 rooms, 13 suites* 🍽 *No meals.*

$ HOTEL 🏨 **Junkanoo Beach Resort.** This simple and quiet six-floor hotel is a welcome addition to the New Providence budget-lodging market. **Pros:** walking distance from downtown; on-site restaurant open 7 am–11 pm. **Cons:** on two busy streets; popular with spring breakers; public beach is across the street. $ *Rooms from: $130* ✉ *W. Bay St. and Nassau St., Nassau, New Providence Island* ☎ *242/322–1515* 🌐 *www.junkanoobeachresort.com* 🛏 *63 rooms.*

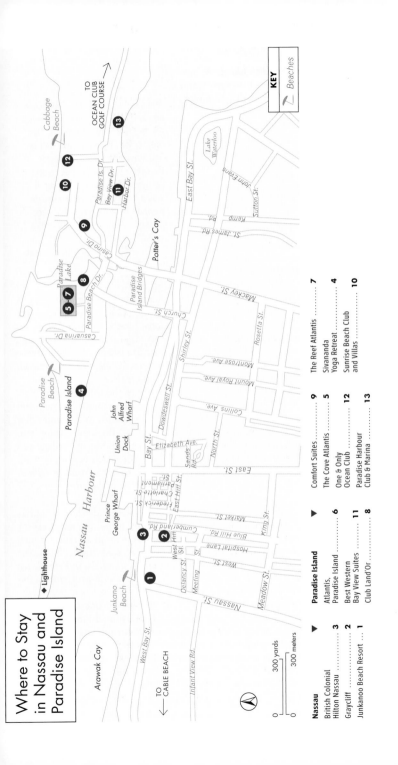

# Where to Stay in Nassau and Paradise Island

0 ⊢————⊣ 300 yards
0 ⊢————⊣ 300 meters

TO ← CABLE BEACH

← TO CABLE BEACH

Arawak Cay

Junkano Beach

Nassau Harbour

Prince George Wharf

Paradise Beach

Paradise Island

◆ Lighthouse

Paradise Beach Dr.

Casuarina Dr.

Paradise Lake

Casino Dr.

Paradise Island Bridges

Potter's Cay

Bay View Dr.
Paradise Is. Dr.
Harbour Dr.

Cabbage Beach

TO OCEAN CLUB GOLF COURSE

Lake Waterloo

East Bay St.

Kemp Rd.

John Evans

St. James Rd.

Sutton St.

Mackey St.
Church St.
Shirley St.
Montrose Ave.
Mount Royal Ave.
Collins Ave.
Rosetta St.
East Bay St.

John Alfred Wharf
Union Dock

Bay St.
Dowdeswell St.
Elizabeth Ave.
Sands Rd.
North St.
East St.

Frederick St.
Charlotte St.
Parliament St.
East Hill St.
Market St.
King St.
Cumberland Rd.
Blue Hill Rd.
Hospital Lane
West Hill St.
West St.
Meadow St.
Delancy St.
Meeting St.
Nassau St.

West Bay St.

Infant View Rd.

**Nassau** ▶

British Colonial
Hilton Nassau ........... 3
Graycliff .................... 2
Junkanoo Beach Resort ... 1

**Paradise Island** ▶

Atlantis,
Paradise Island ........ 6
Best Western
Bay View Suites ....... 11
Club Land'Or ............. 8

Comfort Suites ........... 9
The Cove Atlantis ...... 5
One & Only
Ocean Club ............. 12
Paradise Harbour
Club & Marina ......... 13

The Reef Atlantis ....... 7
Sivananda
Yoga Retreat ........... 4
Sunrise Beach Club
and Villas ............... 10

**KEY**

⌁ Beaches

## PARADISE ISLAND

**$$$$**
RESORT
FAMILY
Fodor's Choice
★

**Atlantis, Paradise Island.** A bustling fantasy world—part water park, entertainment complex, megaresort, and beach oasis—this is by far the biggest and boldest resort in the country. **Pros:** never run out of things to do; kid-friendly with some adult-only areas; incredible resort experience. **Cons:** resort is expansive and requires lots of walking; thousands of guests; food and drinks are expensive. $ *Rooms from: $670 ⊠ Casino Dr., Paradise Island, New Providence Island* ☎ *242/363–3000, 800/285–2684* ⊕ *www.atlantis.com* ⤳ *2,317 rooms and suites* ¶Ol *Multiple meal plans.*

**$$**
HOTEL

**Best Western Bay View Suites.** This 4-acre condominium resort has a lush, intimate character. **Pros:** children under 12 stay free; private "at home" vibe; free Wi-Fi in pool area. **Cons:** long walk from beach; no restaurant serving dinner on property; no organized activities on-site. $ *Rooms from: $240 ⊠ Bay View Dr., Paradise Island, New Providence Island* ☎ *242/363–2555, 800/757–1357* ⊕ *www.bwbayviewsuites.com* ⤳ *25 suites, 2 villas, 3 town houses* ¶Ol *No meals.*

**$$$**
RENTAL

**Club Land'Or.** In Atlantis's shadow just over the bridges from Nassau, this friendly time-share property has one-bedroom villas with full kitchens, bathrooms, living rooms, desks, and patios or balconies that overlook the lagoon, the gardens, or the pool. **Pros:** everything you need for an extended vacation; walking distance to Marina Village and Atlantis. **Cons:** surrounded by Atlantis resort; beach is quite a walk away. $ *Rooms from: $395 ⊠ Paradise Beach Dr., Paradise Island, New Providence Island* ☎ *242/363–2400* ⊕ *www.clublandor.com* ⤳ *72 villas* ¶Ol *Some meals.*

**$$$**
HOTEL
FAMILY

**Comfort Suites.** This all-suites, three-story pink-and-white hotel has an arrangement with Atlantis that allows you to use the megaresort's facilities. **Pros:** access to Atlantis amenities; near shops and restaurants. **Cons:** not located on a beach; in the midst of busy traffic. $ *Rooms from: $350 ⊠ Paradise Island Dr., Paradise Island, New Providence Island* ☎ *242/363–3680, 800/424–6423* ⊕ *www.comfortsuites.com* ⤳ *226 suites* ¶Ol *Breakfast.*

**$$$$**
RESORT
Fodor's Choice
★

**The Cove Atlantis.** Worlds away from its sister property Atlantis in terms of overall look, experience, and sophistication, this high-rise overlooking two stunning white sand beaches is a true grown-ups' getaway. **Pros:** adult-only pool option; incredible private beaches; amenities of Atlantis, but separated from the hustle and bustle. **Cons:** a long walk to Atlantis amenities; limited dining and bar options on-site. $ *Rooms from: $1020 ⊠ Paradise Island, New Providence Island* ☎ *242/363–3000, 800/285–2684* ⊕ *www.atlantis.com* ⤳ *663 suites* ¶Ol *Multiple meal plans.*

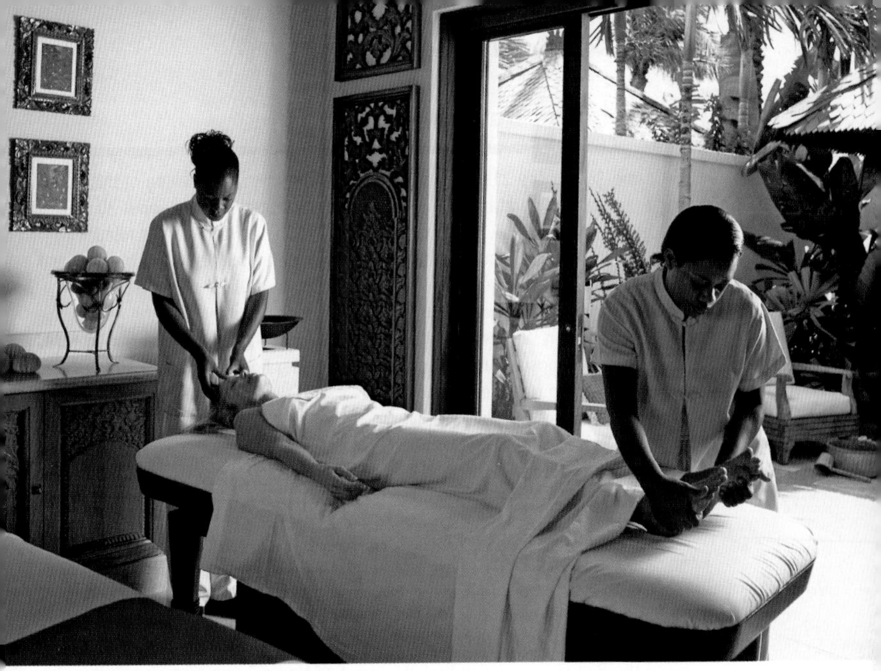

The spa at the One & Only Ocean Club offers indulgent massages.

$$$$ RESORT Fodor's Choice ★ 🏨 **One & Only Ocean Club.** Once the private hideaway of A&P heir Huntington Hartford, this exclusive resort on magnificent Cabbage Beach's quietest stretch provides the ultimate in understated—and decidedly posh—elegance. **Pros:** ultraexclusive; lovely beach; top-rated amenities. **Cons:** not within walking distance of Atlantis and its myriad restaurant and nightlife choices. [$] *Rooms from: $1945* ✉ *Ocean Club Dr., Paradise Island, New Providence Island* ☎ *242/363–2501, 800/321–3000* 🌐 *www.oneandonlyresorts.com* 🛏 *105 rooms and suites; 3 villas; 2 cottages.*

$$ RESORT 🏨 **Paradise Harbour Club & Marina.** With a marina and an enviable location, this collection of oversize, comfortable apartments is a great choice for those who want the freedom of a private residence with the facilities of a large resort. **Pros:** quiet location; cooking facilities. **Cons:** need to walk or be shuttled to and from the beach; condo built nearby towers over property. [$] *Rooms from: $240* ✉ *Paradise Island Dr., Paradise Island, New Providence Island* ☎ *242/363–2992* 🌐 *www.festiva-paradise.com* 🛏 *23 units.*

$$$$ RESORT 🏨 **The Reef Atlantis.** This 497-suite tower has exquisitely outfitted studios or one- and two-bedroom condominium-style accommodations. **Pros:** fully-equipped units; quiet; cost-effective option with Atlantis benefits. **Cons:** no restaurants or bars on property; a long walk to Atlantis amenities. [$] *Rooms from: $1025* ✉ *Paradise Island, New Providence Island* ☎ *242/363–3000, 800/285–2684* 🌐 *www.atlantis.com* 🛏 *497 condo units* 🍴 *Multiple meal plans.*

$ B&B/INN ALL-INCLUSIVE 🏨 **Sivananda Yoga Retreat.** Accessible only by boat, this resort is the antithesis of the high-rollers' Atlantis down the road. **Pros:** ideal for peace and quiet; inexpensive accommodations; free shuttle to and from Nassau. **Cons:** strict regulations; basic accommodations; no

## CLOSE UP

## Bond in the Bahamas

In *Casino Royale,* the 21st James Bond installment, Bond took on the bad guys at an embassy, which was, in reality, the lovely Buena Vista Restaurant and Hotel in Nassau, which closed shortly after filming and is now home to the John Watling's Distillery. The ruggedly handsome new Bond, Daniel Craig, also had the glamorous background of the One & Only Ocean Club resort on Paradise Island, where another Bond, Pierce Brosnan, frequently stays.

Bond and the Bahamas have a long relationship. Six Bond films have used the Bahamas as a backdrop, including *Thunderball,* filmed in 1965 with the original 007, Sean Connery. Connery loved the Bahamas so much he has chosen to live here year-round in the luxury gated community of Lyford Cay.

*Thunderball* was filmed at the Café Martinique, which, after being closed for more than a decade, reopened at Atlantis resort on Paradise Island in 2006. Scenes were also shot at the Mediterranean Renaissance–style British Colonial, built in the 1920s.

You can swim and snorkel in Thunderball Cave in the Exumas, site of the pivotal chase scene in the 1965 Sean Connery film. The ceiling of this huge, dome-shaped cave is about 30 feet above the water, which is filled with yellowtails, parrots, blue chromes, and yellow-and-black striped sergeant majors. Swimming into the cave is the easy part—the tide draws you in—but paddling back out can be strenuous, especially because if you stop moving, the tide will pull you back.

The Rock Point house, better known to 007 fans as Palmyra, the villain Emilio Largo's estate, was another Bond location, and Bay Street, where Bond and his beautiful sidekick Domino attended a Junkanoo carnival, is still the location of Junkanoo twice a year. The *Thunderball* remake, *Never Say Never Again,* was also shot in the Bahamas, using many of the same locations as the original.

Underwater shots for many of the Bond flicks were filmed in the Bahamas, including Thunderball Grotto, while Nassau's offshore reefs were the underwater locations for the 1983 film *Never Say Never Again,* the 1967 film *You Only Live Twice,* the 1977 film *The Spy Who Loved Me,* and *For Your Eyes Only,* released in 1981.

—Cheryl Blackerby

road access. [$] *Rooms from: $100* ⊠ *Paradise Island, Paradise Island, New Providence Island* ☎ *242/363–2902, 800/441–2096* ⊕ *www.sivanandabahamas.org* ⤳ *48 rooms, 36 dorm beds, 16 tent huts, 90 tent sites* ⦿| *All-inclusive.*

**$$$**  ⛿ **Sunrise Beach Club and Villas.** Lushly landscaped with crotons, coconut
**HOTEL**  palms, bougainvillea, and hibiscus, this low-rise, family-run resort on Cabbage Beach has a tropical wonderland feel. **Pros:** on one of the best beaches on the island; lively bar on property; great for families. **Cons:** no activities; lots of walking to get to rooms. [$] *Rooms from: $390* ⊠ *Casino Dr., Paradise Island, New Providence Island* ☎ *242/363–2234, 800/451–6078* ⊕ *www.sunrisebeachclub.com* ⤳ *16 rooms, 10 suites, 1 villa.*

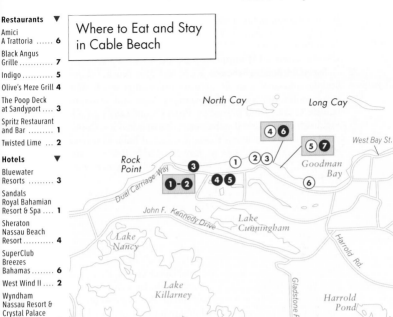

**Restaurants** ▼

Amici A Trattoria ...... 6
Black Angus Grille ............ 7
Indigo ........... 5
Olive's Meze Grill 4
The Poop Deck at Sandyport .... 3
Spritz Restaurant and Bar ......... 1
Twisted Lime ... 2

**Hotels** ▼

Bluewater Resorts ......... 3
Sandals Royal Bahamian Resort & Spa .... 1
Sheraton Nassau Beach Resort ........... 4
SuperClub Breezes Bahamas ........ 6
West Wind II .... 2
Wyndham Nassau Resort & Crystal Palace Casino .......... 5

Where to Eat and Stay in Cable Beach

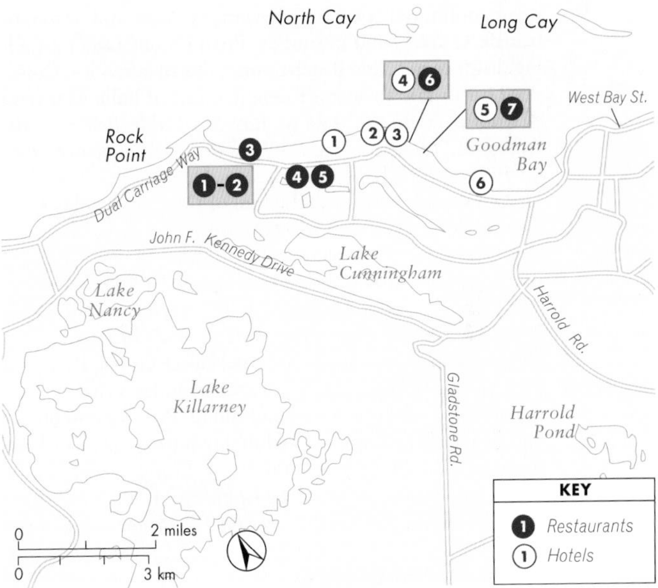


## CABLE BEACH

$$$ RESORT 🏨 **Bluewater Resorts.** These simply decorated time-share and short-term rental accommodations are perfect for young families or groups of friends traveling together. **Pros:** spring breakers not allowed; great for families; tennis courts. **Cons:** no major activities; need car to go into town; housekeeping costs extra. [$] *Rooms from: $399* ✉ *W. Bay St., Cable Beach, New Providence Island* ☎ *242/327–7568* 🌐 *www.bluewaterresortnassau.com* 🛏 *35 units* 🍴 *No meals.*

$$$$ ALL-INCLUSIVE 🏨 **Sandals Royal Bahamian Resort & Spa.** Cable Beach's most expensive spot has elegantly furnished rooms with views of the ocean, pool, or grounds replete with pillars and faux-Roman statuary as well as personal butler service for the ultimate indulgence. **Pros:** no children; lovely setting; private offshore cay. **Cons:** no children; need car or taxi to go into town; convention center popular for local functions. [$] *Rooms from: $750* ✉ *W. Bay St., Cable Beach, New Providence Island* ☎ *242/327–6400, 800/726–3257* 🌐 *www.sandals.com* 🛏 *404 rooms* 🍴 *All-inclusive.*

$$$$ HOTEL 🏨 **Sheraton Nassau Beach Resort.** Situated on 7 acres of prime beachfront property, the Sheraton has a modern, grown-up feel. **Pros:** excellent ocean views and beach access; newly renovated; many activities, including beach volleyball and live music on the weekends. **Cons:** will

be undergoing major renovations as part of the Baha Mar complex; walls somewhat thin. [$] *Rooms from: $429* ✉ *W. Bay St., Cable Beach, New Providence Island* ☎ *242/327–6000* 🌐 *www.sheratonnassau.com* 🛏 *694 rooms* 🍴 *Multiple meal plans.*

$$ ALL-INCLUSIVE 🏨 **SuperClub Breezes Bahamas.** Right on Cable Beach, this property offers couples and singles an all-inclusive rate that covers lodging, entertainment, unlimited food and beverages, land and watersports, airport transfers, taxes, and gratuities. **Pros:** no one under 14 allowed; walking distance to Cable Beach casino; lots of activities. **Cons:** no children; need car or taxi to access town; in midst of Baha Mar renovation area. [$] *Rooms from: $320* ✉ *W. Bay St., Cable Beach, New Providence Island* ☎ *242/327–5356, 800/467–8737* 🌐 *www.breezesbahamas.com* 🛏 *400 rooms* 🍴 *All-inclusive.*

$$ RESORT 🏨 **West Wind II.** Privacy is the lure of these cozy villas on Cable Beach's west end, 6 miles from downtown. **Pros:** great for families; condos sleep six; right on Cable Beach. **Cons:** no major activities; need car or taxi to go downtown; housekeeping additional. [$] *Rooms from: $300* ✉ *W. Bay St., Cable Beach, New Providence Island* ☎ *242/327–7211, 242/327–7019* 🌐 *www.westwind2.com* 🛏 *54 villas.*

$$ RESORT 🏨 **Wyndham Nassau Resort & Crystal Palace Casino.** Part of the Baha Mar project, this resort's large pool area includes a twisting waterslide, and the attached casino goes all night long. **Pros:** casino on-site; great pool and beach area. **Cons:** sprawling layout means lots of walking; in the midst of Baha Mar renovation site. [$] *Rooms from: $229* ✉ *W. Bay St., Cable Beach, New Providence Island* ☎ *242/327–6200, 800/222–7466* 🌐 *www.wyndhamnassauresort.com* 🛏 *559 rooms and suites.*

## WESTERN NEW PROVIDENCE

$$ B&B/INN 🏨 **A Stone's Throw Away.** Featuring seaside comfort in fashionable surroundings, this "gourmet bed-and-breakfast" is a luxurious hideaway. **Pros:** serene; secluded public-beach access; friendly staff. **Cons:** in flight path; long distance from anything else; hotel access up a steep staircase cut out of the limestone hill. [$] *Rooms from: $250* ✉ *Tropical Garden Rd. and W. Bay St., Gambier, New Providence Island* ☎ *242/327–7030* 🌐 *www.astonesthrowaway.com* 🛏 *8 rooms, 2 suites.*

$$$ RESORT 🏨 **Compass Point.** This whimsical-looking hotel made up of brightly colored one- and two-story cottages offers a relaxing alternative to many of the area's major resorts. **Pros:** best view on the island; access to incredible private beach. **Cons:** in flight path; not ideal for children; expensive taxi ride to town. [$] *Rooms from: $325* ✉ *W. Bay St., Gambier, New Providence Island* ☎ *242/327–4500* 🌐 *www.compasspointbeachresort.com* 🛏 *18 cottages* 🍴 *Breakfast.*

$ B&B/INN 🏨 **Orange Hill Beach Inn.** If you prefer down-home coziness over slick glamour, then this inn—on the site of a former orange plantation perched on a hilltop overlooking the ocean—is the place to stay. **Pros:** across the road from a nice beach; small; family-style service. **Cons:** long distance from town; not much by way of activities; basic accommodations. [$] *Rooms from: $160* ✉ *W. Bay St., New Providence Island* ☎ *242/327–5184* 🌐 *www.orangehill.com* 🛏 *30 rooms, 2 cottages.*

## Changes at Cable Beach

Cable Beach, a string of resorts on a white-sand beach west of Nassau, is getting a makeover so massive that it's expected to rival Las Vegas when everything is completed in December, 2014. A mammoth $3.5-billion resort called Baha Mar will include four hotels—a Grand Hyatt, Rosewood, Mondrian, and a 1,000-room luxury casino-hotel to be called the Baha Mar Casino & Hotel. The 2,200-room beachside complex is the single largest investment in the history of the Bahamas.

Cable Beach's two current resorts located next door to Baha Mar—the Sheraton Nassau Beach Resort and the Wyndham Nassau Resort & Crystal Palace Casino—are open and operating as part of Cable Beach Resorts during the building of Baha Mar. The company has already spent more than $130 million renovating these two hotels and casino. Updates at the Wyndham include flat-screen TVs and refrigerators in all guest rooms, and two bars are being added to the casino. The Sheraton Nassau Beach Resort was completely overhauled in 2007 and now presents a sophisticated lobby and contemporary room furnishings. Together, the current

resorts offer 1,100 guest rooms and suites (most with ocean views), nine restaurants and lounges, almost a mile of gorgeous white-sand beach, and a variety of water-sport activities.

When finished, Baha Mar's attractions will include a 100,000-square-foot casino, a 30,000-square-foot ESPA destination spa, 200,000 square feet of combined meeting space, a 2,000-seat performing arts center, and a shopping-and-entertainment complex—all connected by a series of canals and wide pedestrian paths—as well as an 18-hole Jack Nicklaus Signature golf course.

Michael Hong, known for his work on the $1.6-billion Bellagio Resort and Wynn Resort in Las Vegas, is leading the design team for Baha Mar, which will sprawl across 1,000 acres. The reconstruction of the landscape and the development of the hotels will be extensive, but the Baha Mar Group says it will all be done in a way that does not disturb the guest experience in current hotels.

For more information on Baha Mar, visit ⊕ *www.bahamar.com* or ⊕ *www.crystalpalacevacations.com*, or call ☎ *800/222–7466.*

# NIGHTLIFE

## NASSAU

### NIGHTCLUBS

**Bambü.** Pop into this open-air club overlooking Nassau Harbour and you may find the DJ playing the latest Top 40 dance tune. Wait a few moments and Europe's sexiest house beats will change the vibe entirely. Popular with hip young locals and cruise passengers and staff. ⊠ *Upstairs Prince George Plaza, Bay St., Nassau, Nassau, New Providence Island* ⌑ *$20* ⊙ *Tues., Fri., and Sat. 9 pm–5 am.*

**Club Waterloo.** Claiming to be Nassau's largest indoor-outdoor nightclub, this club has five bars and nonstop dancing Monday through Saturday, and live bands on the weekend. Try the spring-break-special Green Lizard, a tropical mixture of rums and punches. ⊠ *E. Bay St., Nassau, Nassau, New Providence Island* ☎ *242/393–7324* ⊕ *www. clubwaterloo.com* ☉ *Tues.–Sat. 8 pm–4 am* ☉ *Closed Sun. and Mon.*

## PARADISE ISLAND

### CASINOS

**Atlantis Casino.** At 50,000 square feet (100,000 if you include the dining and drinking areas), this is the largest casino in the Bahamas. Featuring a spectacularly open and airy design, the casino is ringed with restaurants and offers more than 1,100 slot machines, baccarat, blackjack, roulette, craps tables, and such local specialties as Caribbean stud poker. There's also a high-limit table area, and most of the eateries have additional games. ⊠ *Atlantis, Paradise Island, Paradise Island, New Providence Island* ☎ *242/363–3000* ⊕ *www.atlantis.com* ☉ *Main casino 24 hrs daily, tables open 10 am–4 am daily.*

### NIGHTCLUBS

**Aura.** This is the country's hottest nightclub, located upstairs at the Atlantis Casino. It's the place to see and be seen, though many of the celebrities who frequent the club opt for the ultraexclusive private lounge. Dancing goes on all night and the handsome bartenders dazzle the crowd with their mixing techniques. Music varies, depending on the crowd. ⊠ *Atlantis, Paradise Island, Paradise Island, New Providence Island* ☎ *242/363–3000* ⊕ *www.atlantis.com* ⊑ *$20–$100; free for Atlantis guests Tues.–Thurs.* ☉ *Tues.–Sat. 9:30 pm–4 am.*

**Oasis Lounge.** There's live piano or vocal music here every night except Sunday from 7:30 to midnight. Go early to get a good seat and take advantage of one of the best drink deals on Paradise Island—buy one, get one free and complimentary hors d'oeuvres 5–7 pm. ⊠ *Club Land'Or, Paradise Island, Paradise Island, New Providence Island* ☎ *242/363–2400* ⊕ *www.clublandor.com* ☉ *Daily 4 pm–midnight.*

## CABLE BEACH

### CASINOS

**Crystal Palace Casino.** Four hundred slot machines, craps, baccarat, blackjack, roulette, Big Six, and face-up 21 are among the games in this 35,000-square-foot space. There's a Sportsbook facility equipped with big-screen TVs that air live sporting events. Both VIPs and low-limit bettors have their own areas. Casino gaming lessons are available for beginners. ⊠ *Wyndham Nassau Resort & Crystal Palace Casino, W. Bay St., Cable Beach, Cable Beach, New Providence Island* ☎ *242/327–6200* ⊕ *www.wyndhamnassauresort.com* ☉ *24 hrs.*

The cottages at Compass Point are known for their whimsical colors.

# THE ARTS

## THEATER

**Dundas Centre for the Performing Arts.** Plays, concerts, ballets, and musicals by local and out-of-town artists are staged here throughout the year. The box office is open from 10 am to 4 pm. ⊠ *Mackey St., Nassau, New Providence Island* ☎ *242/393–3728.*

# SHOPPING AND SPAS

Most of Nassau's shops are on Bay Street between Rawson Square and the British Colonial Hotel, and on the side streets leading off Bay Street. Some stores are popping up on the main shopping thorough-fare's eastern end and just west of the Cable Beach strip. Bargains abound between Bay Street and the waterfront. Upscale stores can also be found in Marina Village and the Crystal Court at Atlantis and in the arcade joining the Sheraton Nassau Beach and the Wyndham on Cable Beach.

You'll find duty-free prices—generally 25%–50% less than U.S. prices—on imported items such as crystal, linens, watches, cameras, jewelry, leather goods, and perfumes.

## NASSAU

### BAKED GOODS

**Bahamas Rum Cake Factory.** At the Bahamas Rum Cake Factory, delicious Bahamian rum-soaked cakes are made and packaged in tins right on the premises (peek into the bakery) and make a great souvenir. Just make sure you take one home for yourself! ⊠ *E. Bay St., Nassau, New Providence Island* ☎ *242/328–3750.*

**Model Bakery.** Be sure to try the cinnamon twists or the gingerbread sticks at this great local bakery in the east end. ⊠ *Dowdeswell St., Nassau, New Providence Island* ☎ *242/322–2595.*

**Mortimer's Candies.** Mortimer's Candies whips up batches of uniquely Bahamian sweet treats daily. Pop in for a sno-cone on a hot day or buy some bags of bennie cake, coconut-cream candy, or their signature Paradise Sweets in a swirl of the Bahamian flag colors. ⊠ *East St. Hill, Nassau, New Providence Island* ☎ *242/322–5230* ⊕ *www.mortimercandies.com.*

### CIGARS

Be aware that some merchants on Bay Street and elsewhere in the islands are selling counterfeit Cuban cigars—sometimes unwittingly. If the price seems too good to be true, chances are it is. Check the wrappers and feel to ensure that there's a consistent fill before you make your purchase.

**Graycliff.** Graycliff carries one of Nassau's finest selections of hand-rolled cigars, featuring leaves from throughout Central and South America. Graycliff's operation is so popular that it has expanded the hotel to include an entire cigar factory, which is open to the public for tours and purchases. A dozen Cuban men and women roll the cigars; they live on the premises and work here through a special arrangement with the Cuban government. True cigar buffs will seek out Graycliff's owner, Enrico Garzaroli. ⊠ *W. Hill St., and departure lounge at Lynden Pindling International Airport, Nassau, New Providence Island* ☎ *242/302–9150* ⊕ *www.graycliff.com.*

### FASHION

**Brass and Leather.** Here you can find leather goods for men and women, including bags, shoes, and belts. ⊠ *Charlotte St. off Bay St., Nassau, New Providence Island* ☎ *242/322–3806.*

**Cole's of Nassau.** This is a top choice for designer fashions, sportswear, bathing suits, shoes, and accessories. ⊠ *Parliament St., Nassau, New Providence Island* ☎ *242/322–8393.*

**La Casita.** This cute boutique offers high-end straw bags and purses, as well as costume jewelry. ⊠ *Bay St. near the Straw Market, Nassau, Nassau, New Providence Island* ☎ *242/328–5988* ⊙ *Closed Sun.*

**Tempo Paris.** Tempo Paris offers men's clothing by major designers, including Ralph Lauren, Polo, and Lacoste. ⊠ *Bay St., Nassau, New Providence Island* ☎ *242/323–6112.*

*Continued on page 88*

# JUNKANOO IN THE BAHAMAS

by Jessica Robertson

It's after midnight, and the only noise in downtown Nassau is a steady buzz of anticipation. Suddenly the streets erupt in a kaleidoscope of sights and sounds—Junkanoo groups are parading down Bay Street. Vibrant costumes sparkle in the light of the street lamps, and the revelers bang on goatskin drums and clang cowbells, hammering out a steady celebratory beat. It's Junkanoo time!

Junkanoo is an important part of the Bahamas' Christmas season. Parades begin after midnight and last until midday on Boxing Day (December 26), and there are more on New Year's Day. What appears to be a random, wild expression of joy is actually a well-choreographed event. Large groups (often as many as 500 to 1,000 people) compete for prize money and bragging rights. Teams choose a different theme each year and keep it a closely guarded secret until they hit Bay Street. They spend most of the year preparing for the big day at their "shacks," which are tucked away in neighborhoods across the island. They practice dance steps and music, and they design intricate costumes. During the parade, judges award prizes for best music, best costumes, and best overall presentation.

Junkanoo costume, Grand Bahama

## JUNKANOO HISTORY

## MUSIC'S ROLE

Junkanoo holds an important place in the history and culture of the Bahamas, but the origin of the word *junkanoo* remains a mystery. Many believe it comes from John Canoe, an African tribal chief who was brought to the West Indies as a slave and then fought for the right to celebrate with his people. Others believe the word stems from the French *gens inconnus*, which means "the unknown people"—significant because Junkanoo revelers wear costumes that mask their identities.

The origin of the festival itself is more certain. Though its roots can be traced back to West Africa, it began in the Bahamas during the 16TH or 17TH century when Bahamian slaves were given a few days off around Christmas to celebrate with their families. They left the plantations and had elaborate costume parties at which they danced and played homemade musical instruments. They wore large, often scary-looking masks, which gave them the freedom of anonymity, so they could let loose without inhibition.

Over the years, Junkanoo has evolved. Costumes once decorated with shredded newspaper are now elaborate, vibrant creations incorporating imported crepe paper, glitter, gemstones, and feathers.

There's something mesmerizing about the simple yet powerful beat of the goatskin drum. Couple that steady pounding with the "kalik-kalik" clanging of thousands of cowbells and a hundreds-strong brass band, and Junkanoo music becomes downright infectious.

Music is the foundation of Junkanoo. It provides a rhythm for both the costumed revelers and crowds of spectators who jump up and down on rickety bleacher seats. The heavy percussion sound is created by metal cowbells, whistles, and oil barrel drums with fiery sternos inside to keep the animal skin coverings pliant. In the late 1970s, Junkanoo music evolved with the addition of brass instruments, adding melodies from Christmas carols, sacred religious hymns, and contemporary hits.

If you're in Nassau anytime from September through the actual festival, stand out on your hotel balcony and listen carefully. Somewhere, someone is bound to be beating out a rhythm as groups practice for the big parade.

# DRESS TO IMPRESS

Each year, talented artists and builders transform chicken wire, cardboard, Styrofoam, and crepe paper into magnificent costumes that are worn, pushed, or carried along the Junkanoo parade route. Dancers and musicians tend to wear elaborate head dresses or off-the-shoulder pieces and cardboard skirts

completely covered in finely fringed, brightly colored crepe paper—applied a single strip at a time until every inch is covered. Gemstones, referred to as "tricks" in the Junkanoo world, are painstakingly glued onto costumes to add sparkle. In recent years, feathers have been incorporated, giving the cardboard covered creations an added level of movement and flair.

In order to wow the crowd, and more importantly, win the competition, every member of the group must be in full costume when they hit Bay Street. Even their shoes are completely decorated. Massive banner pieces so big they graze the power lines and take up the entire width of the street are carried along the route by men who take turns. Every element, from the smallest costume to the lead banner, as well as the entire color scheme, is meticulously planned out months in advance.

## EXPERIENCE JUNKANOO

### SECURE YOUR SEATS

■ Junkanoo bleacher seat tickets ($10–$50) can be hard to come by as the parade date approaches. Contact your hotel concierge ahead of time to arrange for tickets or visit ⊕ www.tajiz.com, the official online retailer.

■ Rawson Square bleachers are the best seats. This is where groups perform the longest and put on their best show.

■ If you don't mind standing, make your way to Shirley Street or the eastern end of Bay Street, where the route is lined with barricades. Judges are positioned all along the way so you'll see a good performance no matter where you end up.

■ Junkanoo groups make two laps around the parade route. Each lap can take a few hours to complete, and there are many groups in the lineup, so most spectators stay only for the first round. Head to Bay Street just before dawn, and you'll be sure to score a vacant seat.

### BEHIND THE SCENES

■ During the parade, head east along Bay Street and turn onto Elizabeth Avenue to the rest area. Groups take a break in the parking lot here before they start round two. Costume builders frantically repair any pieces damaged during the first rush (Bahamian slang for parading), revelers refuel at barbeque stands, goatskin drums are placed next to a giant bonfire to keep them supple,

and in the midst of all the noise and hubbub, you'll find any number of people taking a nap to ensure they make it through a long and physically demanding night.

■ If star-stalking is your thing, scour the crowds in the VIP section in Parliament Square or look across the street on the balcony of the Scotiabank building. This is where celebrities usually watch the parades. Some who've been spotted include Michael Jordan, Rick Fox, and former New York City mayor Rudy Giuliani.

■ When the parade ends, wander along the route and surrounding streets to score a one-of-a-kind souvenir. Despite the many hours Junkanoo participants spend slaving over their costumes, by the time they're done rushing the last thing they want to do is carry it home. Finders keepers.

■ If you're in Nassau in early December, watch the Junior Junkanoo parade. School groups compete for prizes in various age categories. The littlest ones are usually offbeat and egged on by teachers and parents, but are oh-so-cute in their costumes. The high school groups put on a show just as impressive as the groups in the senior parade.

### JUNKANOO TRIVIA

■ Kalik beer, brewed in the Bahamas, gets its name from the sound of clanking cowbells.

■ An average costume requires 3,000 to 5,000 strips of fringed crepe paper to completely cover its cardboard frame.

■ Junkanoo widows are women whose husbands spend every waking moment working on their costumes or practicing music routines the weeks before the parade.

■ During the height of sponge farming in the Bahamas, a major industry in the early 1900s, many Junkanoo participants used natural sponge to create their costumes.

Junkanoo parade in Nassau

### JUNKANOO ON OTHER ISLANDS

Nassau's Junkanoo parade is by far the biggest and most elaborate, but most other islands hold their own celebrations on New Year's Day. Nassau's parades are strictly a spectator sport unless you are officially in a group, but Out Island parades are more relaxed and allow visitors to join the rush.

### JUNKANOO YEAR-ROUND

Not satisfied with limiting Junkanoo to Christmastime, the Bahamas Ministry of Tourism hosts an annual **Junkanoo Summer Festival**. Smaller scale parades are held on alternating weekends in June and July on most major islands, including Nassau. In addition to the traditional Junkanoo rush, these festivals offer arts and crafts demonstrations, conch cracking, crab catching, coconut-husking competitions, concerts featuring top Bahamian artists, and of course, lots of good Bahamian food. ☎ 242/302–2000 ✉ tourism@bahamas.com.

Marina Village on Paradise Island hosts **Junkanoo rushouts** on Wednesday (9 pm) and Saturday (9:30 pm). There are no big stand-alone pieces, but dancers and musicians wear color-coordinated costumes and headpieces. The parade is much less formal, so feel free to jump in and dance along.

The **Educulture Museum and Workshop** in Nassau gives a behind-the-scenes look at Junkanoo. Some of each year's best costumes are on display, as well as costumes from years gone by when newspaper and sponges were used as decoration. The diehard Junkanoo staff will help you make your own Junkanoo creations. Be sure to arrange your visit ahead of time. ☎ 242/328–3786 ✉ info@educulturebahamas.com.

## GIFT SHOPS

**Bahama Handprints.** Bahama Handprints fabrics emphasize local artists' sophisticated tropical prints in an array of colors. Also look for leather handbags, a wide range of women's clothing, housewares, and bolts of fabric. Ask for a free tour of the factory in back. ⊠ *Island Traders Bldg. Annex, off Mackey St., Nassau, New Providence Island* ☎ *242/394–4111* ⊕ *www.bahamahandprints.com* ⊗ *Closed Sun.*

**Linen Shop.** This shop sells fine embroidered Irish linens and lace and has a delightful Christmas corner. ⊠ *Bay St., Nassau, New Providence Island* ☎ *242/322–4266.*

**My Ocean.** Here you can find candles, soaps, salt scrubs, and lotions in island- and ocean-inspired scents and colors, all locally made. A second location is found at Festival Place. ⊠ *Prince George Plaza, Nassau, New Providence Island* ☎ *242/328–6167* ⊕ *www.myocean-bahamas. com* ⊗ *Closed Sun.*

**The Craft Cottage.** This small shop situated in a traditional wooden structure is a great place to grab locally made souvenirs and gifts including soaps and oils, handpainted glassware, straw bags, and textiles. The artists and artisans are often on-site. ⊠ *20 Village Rd., Nassau, Nassau, New Providence Island* ☎ *242/446–7373* ⊕ *www. craftcottagebahamas.com.*

## JEWELRY, WATCHES, AND CLOCKS

**Coin of the Realm.** Coin of the Realm has Bahamian coins, stamps, native conch pearls, tanzanite, and semiprecious stone jewelry. ⊠ *Charlotte St. off Bay St., Nassau, New Providence Island* ☎ *242/322–4862, 242/322–4497.*

**Colombian Emeralds International.** Colombian Emeralds International is the local branch of this well-known jeweler; its stores carry a variety of fine jewelry in addition to its signature gem. ⊠ *Bay St. near Rawson Sq., Nassau, New Providence Island* ☎ *242/326–1661.*

**John Bull.** Established in 1929 and magnificently decorated in its Bay Street incarnation behind a Georgian-style facade, John Bull fills its complex with wares from Tiffany & Co., Cartier, Mikimoto, Nina Ricci, and Yves Saint Laurent. The company has 12 locations throughout Nassau. ⊠ *284 Bay St., Nassau, New Providence Island* ☎ *242/302–2800.*

## MARKETS AND ARCADES

**International Bazaar.** This collection of shops under a huge, spreading bougainvillea, sells linens, jewelry, souvenirs, and offbeat items. There's usually a small band playing all sort of music along this funky shopping row on Bay Street at Charlotte Street in Nassau.

**Prince George Plaza.** Prince George Plaza, which leads from Bay Street to Woodes Rogers Walk near the dock, just east of the International Bazaar, has about two dozen shops with varied wares.

**Straw Market.** More than 10 years after the "world famous strawmarket" burned to the ground, vendors finally have a new permanent structure from which to sell their wares. Situated on the original site on Bay Street is a towering colonial-style marketplace housing hundreds of straw vendors selling straw bags, T-shirts, and other native souvenirs. The Straw Market is one place in the Bahamas where bartering is accepted, so it's best to wander around and price similar items at different stalls before sealing a deal.

### PERFUMES AND COSMETICS

**The Cosmetic Boutique.** This shop has beauty experts on hand to demonstrate the latest cosmetics offerings, including M.A.C., Clinique, Bobbi Brown, and La Mer. ⊠ *Bay St. near Charlotte St., Nassau, Nassau, New Providence Island* ☎ *242/323–2731.*

**Perfume Bar.** This shop carries the best-selling French fragrance Boucheron and the Clarins line of skin-care products, as well as scents by Givenchy, Fendi, and other well-known designers. ⊠ *Bay St., Nassau, New Providence Island* ☎ *242/325–1258.*

**The Perfume Shop & The Beauty Spot.** This is a landmark perfumery that has the broadest selection of imported perfumes and fragrances in the Bahamas. Experienced makeup artists are on hand to help pick out the perfect foundation or blush from a wide array of lines including Lancôme, Clinique, and Chanel. ⊠ *Bay and Frederick Sts., Nassau, New Providence Island* ☎ *242/322–2375.*

### SPAS

**Baha Retreat.** This spa, situated in an old wooden two-story Bahamian home, is popular with locals and offers a full range of spa and salon services seven days a week. Reservation are suggested, but walk-ins are welcome. They specialize in body sugaring and threading for hair removal, but massages are also good. Book a Couples Spa Day for a complete pampering treat: aromatherapy body polish, aromatherapy massage, spa manicure and pedicure, and gourmet lunch with a glass of wine each. ⊠ *East Bay St., Nassau, Nassau, New Providence Island* ☎ *242/323–6711* ⊕ *www.baharetreat.com* ✂ *Hair salon. Services: aromatheraphy, facials, hair removal, massage, nails.*

**Windermere Day Spa at Harbour Bay.** This spa has a variety of ultramodern spa treatments—such as hydrotherapy and salt glows—as well as top-quality facials, massages, manicures, and pedicures. ⊠ *E. Bay St., New Providence Island* ☎ *242/393–8788* ✂ *Hair salon. Services: aromatheraphy, facials, nassage, nails, waxing.*

## PARADISE ISLAND

### ARTS AND CRAFTS

**Bahamacraft Centre.** Bahamacraft Centre offers some top-level Bahamian crafts, including a selection of authentic straw work. Dozens of vendors sell everything from baskets to shell collages inside this vibrantly colored building. You can catch a shuttle bus from Atlantis to the center. ⊠ *Paradise Island Dr., Paradise Island, New Providence Island.*

**Doongalik Art Gallery.** This gallery showcases the artwork of more than 70 local artists. On Saturday mornings a bustling farmers' market takes place here. ⊠ *Marina Village, 18 Village Rd., Nassau, New Providence Island* ☎ *242/394–1886* ⊕ *www.doongalik.com.*

### CIGARS

**Havana Humidor.** Havana Humidor has the largest selection of authentic Cuban cigars in the Bahamas. Watch cigars being made or browse through the cigar and pipe accessories. ⊠ *Crystal Court at Atlantis, Paradise Island, New Providence Island* ☎ *242/363–5809.*

### FASHION

**Bahama Sol.** Stop here to pick up brightly designed batik cotton Androsia fabric by the yard ($16.95) or sewn into sarongs, dresses, blouses, and men's shirts. ⊠ *Paradise Island Shopping Center, Paradise Island, New Providence Island* ☎ *242/363–0605* ⊕ *www.bahama-sol.com.*

### SPAS

Fodor's Choice
★

**Mandara Spa.** Located at Atlantis but open to the public, the Indonesian-inspired Mandara Spa has treatments utilizing traditions from around the world. Plan to spend more time than your treatment or service requires to enjoy the unisex relaxation lounge, hot and cold plunge pools, and the sauna and steam room. Use of the 15,000-square-foot fitness center is complimentary for a day when you spend more than $99 on spa or salon services. The full-service salon offers hair and nail treatments as well as tooth whitening, hair extensions, and waxing. Men can get the works at the barber shop. ⊠ *Atlantis, Casino Dr., New Providence Island* ☎ *242/363–3000* ⊕ *www.mandaraspa.com* ☞ *Hair salon, hot tub, sauna, steam room. Gym with: cardiovascular machines, free weights, weight training equipment. Classes and programs: aerobics, aquaerobics, fitness analysis, nutritional analysis, nutritional counseling, personal training, Pilates, strength training, weight training, yoga.*

# SPORTS AND THE OUTDOORS

## BOATING

From Chub Cay—one of the Berry Islands 35 miles north of New Providence—to Nassau, the sailing route goes across the mile-deep Tongue of the Ocean. The Paradise Island Lighthouse welcomes yachters to Nassau Harbour, which is open at both ends. The harbor can handle the world's largest cruise liners; sometimes as many as eight tie up at one time. Two looming bridges bisect the harbor connecting Paradise Island to Nassau. Sailboats with masts taller than the high-water clearance of 72 feet must enter the harbor from the east end to reach marinas east of the bridges. A number of outfitters rent Jet Skis in front of Atlantis on Cabbage Beach.

**Atlantis.** The marina at Atlantis has 63 megayacht slips. ☎ *242/363–3000.*

**Brown's Boat Basin.** On the Nassau side, Brown's Boat Basin offers a place to tie up your boat, as well as on-site engine repairs. ☎ *242/393–3331.*

**Hurricane Hole Marina.** Ninety-slip Hurricane Hole Marina is on the Paradise Island side of the harbor. ☎ *242/363–3600* ⊕ *www.hurricaneholemarina.com.*

Paradise Island's One & Only Ocean Club has a scenic golf course.

**Lyford Cay.** At the western end of New Providence, Lyford Cay, a posh development for the rich and famous, has an excellent marina, but there is limited availability for the humble masses. ☎ *242/362–4271.*

**Nassau Yacht Haven.** On the Nassau side of the harbor, Nassau Yacht Haven is a 150-berth marina—the largest in the Bahamas—that also arranges fishing charters. ☎ *242/393–8173* ⊕ *www.nassauyachthaven.com.*

**Premier Watersports.** If your children would enjoy sitting in a row on a rubber banana and bouncing along behind a motorboat, ride the big banana at Premier Watersports, at the beach at the Riu and Atlantis. ☎ *242/324–1475, 242/427–0939 cellular.*

**Sail Nassau.** To participate in an America's Cup racing challenge, contact Sail Nassau at Paradise Island Ferry Terminal. They also offer sunset sail cruises. ☎ *242/363–1552* ⊕ *www.sailnassau.com.*

## FISHING

The waters here are generally smooth and alive with many species of game fish, which is one of the reasons why the Bahamas has more than 20 fishing tournaments open to visitors every year. A favorite spot just west of Nassau is the Tongue of the Ocean, so called because it looks like that part of the body when viewed from the air. The channel stretches for 100 miles. For boat rental, parties of two to six will pay $600 or so for a half day, $1,600 for a full day.

**Born Free Charters.** This charter company has three boats and guarantees a catch on full-day charters—if you don't get a fish, you don't pay. ☎ *242/393–4144* ⊕ *www.bornfreefishing.com.*

**Charter Boat Association.** The Charter Boat Association has 15 boats available for fishing charters. ☎ 242/393–3739.

**Chubasco Charters.** This charter company has three boats for deepsea and light tackle sportfishing. Half- and full-day charters are available. ☎ 242/324–3474 ⊕ www.chubascocharters.com.

**Nassau Yacht Haven.** Nassau Yacht Haven runs fishing charters out of its 150-slip marina. ☎ 242/393–8173 ⊕ www.nassauyachthaven.com.

## GOLF

**One & Only Ocean Club Golf Course.** Designed by Tom Weiskopf, One & Only Ocean Club Golf Course (6,805 yards, par 72) is a championship course surrounded by the ocean on three sides, which means that winds can get stiff. Call to check on current availability and up-to-date prices (those not staying at Atlantis or the One & Only Ocean Club can play at management's discretion, and at a higher rate). ⊠ *Paradise Island Dr. next to airport, Paradise Island, New Providence Island* ☎ *242/363–3925, 800/321–3000 in U.S.* ⚑ *18 holes: $270; $180 after 1 pm. Club rentals: $70* ☉ *Daily 6 am–sundown.*

## HORSEBACK RIDING

**Happy Trails Stables.** Happy Trails Stables gives guided 90-minute trail rides, including basic riding instruction, through remote wooded areas and beaches on New Providence's southwestern coast. Two morning group rides are offered, but private rides can be arranged at any time. Courtesy round-trip bus transportation from hotels is provided (about an hour each way). Tours are limited to eight people. There's a 200-pound weight limit, and children must be at least 12 years old. Reservations are required. ⊠ *Coral Harbour, Western New Providence, New Providence Island* ☎ *242/362–1820* ⊕ *www.bahamahorse.com* ⚑ *$150 per person* ☉ *Mon.–Sat. by appointment.*

## PARASAILING

**Premier Watersports.** Premier Watersports gives you the chance to be lifted into the skies for five to eight minutes—at $70 a pop. Ask for Captain Tim or his crew on Cabbage Beach in front of the large hotels. You must be at least eight years old. ☎ *242/324–1475, 242/427–0939 cellular.*

## SCUBA DIVING AND SNORKELING

### SITES

**Lost Ocean Hole.** The elusive (and thus exclusive) Lost Ocean Hole (east of Nassau, 40–195 feet) is aptly named because it's difficult to find. The rim of the 80-foot opening in 40 feet of water is studded with coral heads and teeming with small fish—grunts, margate, and jacks—as well as larger pompano, amberjack, and sometimes nurse sharks. Divers will find a thermocline at 80 feet, a large cave at 100 feet, and a sand ledge at 185 feet that slopes down to 195 feet.

**Rose Island Reefs.** The series of shallow reefs along the 14 miles of Rose Island is known as Rose Island Reefs (Nassau, 5–35 feet). The coral is varied, although the reefs are showing the effects of the heavy traffic. Still, plenty of tropical fish live here, and the wreck of the steel-hulled ship *Mahoney* is just outside the harbor.

**Gambier Deep Reef.** Off Gambier Village about 15 minutes west of Cable Beach, Gambier Deep Reef goes to a depth of 80 feet.

**Sea Gardens.** This site is off Love Beach on the northwestern shore beyond Gambier.

**Lyford Cay Drop-Off.** Lyford Cay Drop-Off (west of Nassau, 40–200-plus feet) is a cliff that plummets from a 40-foot plateau almost straight into the inky blue mile-deep Tongue of the Ocean. The wall has endless varieties of sponges, black coral, and wire coral. Along the wall, grunts, grouper, hogfish, snapper, and rockfish abound. Off the wall are pelagic game fish such as tuna, bonito, wahoo, and kingfish.

> ## CRICKET IN NASSAU
>
> If you happen to be in Nassau on a Saturday or Sunday afternoon, drop by Haynes Oval cricket field and watch the Bahamas Cricket Club members play the country's national sport. You don't have to follow what the men in white are doing, just enjoy the game from the balcony of the Cricket Club Pub over a dinner of bangers and mash, kidney pie, and a Murphy's or Guinness. The field is wedged between Fort Charlotte and a beach—all the ingredients for a great afternoon.

### OPERATORS

All dive shops listed below are Professional Association of Diving Instructors (PADI) facilities. Expect to pay about $65–$99 for a two-tank dive or beginner's course. Shark dives run $100–$125, and certification costs $450 and up.

**Bahama Divers Ltd.** The largest and most experienced dive operation in the country offers twice-a-day dive safaris as well as half-day snorkeling trips. PADI certification courses are available for $550 a person, and there's a full line of scuba equipment. Destinations are drop-off sites, wrecks, coral reefs and gardens, and an ocean blue hole. For Paradise Island guests, Bahama Divers has opened a small dive operation (which also carries snorkel equipment for rent) in the Paradise Island Harbour Resort. ☎ 242/393–1466, 800/398–3483, 954/607–7731 ⊕ *www.bahamadivers.com*.

**Stuart Cove's Dive South Ocean.** This shop, on the island's south shore, is considered by aficionados to be the island's leading dive shop. Although they're pros at teaching beginners (scuba instruction and guided snorkel tours are available), experienced thrill-seekers flock to Stuart Cove's for the famous shark dives. Also popular are his Out Island "Wilderness Safaris" and "Wall Flying Adventures," in which you ride an underwater scooter across the ocean wall. Check out the collection of celebrity photos. The shop runs dive trips to the south-shore reefs twice a day, weather permitting. The mini-sub adventure, which requires no experience, is $124; snorkeling expeditions cost $70 for adults and $45 for kids 12 and under. The shark dives are $155 for a three-hour dive. ☎ 242/362–4171, 800/879–9832 ⊕ *www.stuartcove.com*.

## TOURS

### CRUISES

**Barefoot Sailing Cruises.** The company offers regularly scheduled half-day snorkeling trips, full-day sailing tours of New Providence, and sunset Champagne trips, not to mention private charters. ☏ *242/393–0820* ⊕ *www.barefootsailingcruises.com.*

**Flying Cloud.** This catamaran in Paradise Island offers half-day sailing and snorkeling tours, full-day cruises on some Sundays, as well as sunset sails. Private charters can also be arranged. ☏ *242/394–5067* ⊕ *www. flyingcloud.com.*

### OUT ISLANDS TRIPS

**Bahamas Fast Ferries.** This isn't just a transportation company. Bahamas Fast Ferries also offers day-trips from Nassau to Harbour Island, including lunch and pick-ups at major hotels. ✉ *Potter's Cay, New Providence Island* ☏ *242/323–2166* ⊕ *www.bahamasferries.com.*

**High Seas Private Excursions.** The company offers half- or full-day powerboat excursions to such destinations as Harbour Island or the Exuma Cays, as well as private yacht charters. ☏ *242/363–4458* ⊕ *www. highseasbahamas.com.*

**Island World Adventures.** The company, which operates two 45-foot speed boats, offers regularly scheduled full-day or private-charter tours to the northern Exumas from Paradise Island. ☏ *242/363–3333* ⊕ *www. islandworldadventures.com.*

**Powerboat Adventures.** The company offers speed-filled daytrips to the Exuma Cays on two custom-made powerboats. Overnights on the company's private island, Ship Channel Cay, can also be arranged. ☏ *242/363–2265* ⊕ *www.powerboatadventures.com.*

### SPECIAL-INTEREST TOURS

**Bahamas Outdoors Ecoventures.** This outfitter offers birding and nature tours as well as biking and kayaking adventures in New Providence Island. Charters can be arranged to Andros or even Eleuthera. ☏ *242/ 362–1574* ⊕ *www.bahamasoutdoors.com.*

**Dolphin Encounters.** On Blue Lagoon Island, the company offers dolphin and sea lion interactions. Ferry transportation is offered from the Paradise Island Ferry Terminal. For an additional fee, the company offers pick-ups from Nassau. ☏ *242/363–1003* ⊕ *www. dolphinencounters.com.*

FAMILY **Graycliff Chocolate Factory.** Go behind the scenes at this boutique chocolate factory and make your own sweet souvenirs. The tour lasts about an hour and a half and after watching master chocolatiers in action and learning the history of chocolate production around the world, enter the chocolate classroom where you get to design your own creations, including a signature Graycliff chocolate bar. There is also a kids' classroom for younger chocolate lovers. ✉ *West Hill St., Nassau, New Providence Island* ☏ *242/302–9150* ⊕ *www.graycliff.com* ▥ *$49.95* ⊙ *Mon.–Sat. 11:15–2:15.*

**Seaworld Explorer.** These trips include both a short habor cruise as well as a trip on the company's semi-submersible, which allows you to view the underwater world without going into a full-fledged submarine. ☎ *242/356–2548* ⊕ *www.seaworldtours.com.*

**WALKING TOURS**

Fodor'sChoice ★ **Tru Bahamian Food Tours.** If you have three hours in Nassau, this is a great way to spend it. The eco-friendly walking tour combines the food, history, and culture of The Bahamas in a way that's sure to leave you satisfied. The seven tasting stops include some popular hot spots as well as some off-the-beaten-path gems. ⊠ *Meet outside Christ Church Cathedral, George St. and King St.* ☎ *800/656–0713, 242/601–1725* ⊕ *www.trubahamianfoodtours.com* ☒ *$75* ☾ *Mon.–Sat. 11–2.*

# GRAND BAHAMA
# ISLAND

# WELCOME TO GRAND BAHAMA ISLAND

## TOP REASONS TO GO

★ **Take endless strolls on your own private beach.** Sprawling, reef-protected shoreline and cays offer more than 50 miles of secluded white sand beaches along the southern shore.

★ **Go down under.** Between the shipwrecks, caves, coral reefs, and abundant marine life are some of the country's most varied and vivid snorkeling and diving.

★ **Get your green on.** Take part in various eco-tours to see rare birds and native curly tail lizards along stretches of undis-turbed wilderness, from the "bush" to bat caves.

★ **Party at the fish fry or a beach bonfire.** Head to Smith's Point to feast and party with locals, or dance around the bonfire at Taino by the Sea with all-you-can-eat authentic Bahamian cuisine and Bahama Mama cocktails.

★ **Swim with the dolphins or feed the sharks.** Several professional dive shops stand ready to introduce you to some of the ocean's most interesting characters.

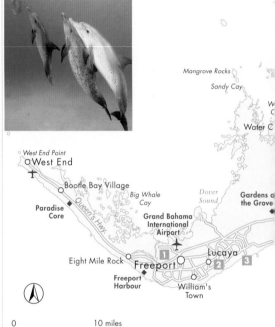

**1 Freeport.** The work-ing end of Grand Bahama, Freeport is convenient to the airport and harbor for visitors in transit. Rand Nature Centre and The Bahamian Brewery make the area worth a visit, although downtown looks a bit forlorn as developers await economic recovery.

**2 Port Lucaya.** Freeport's beachfront counterpart is more tourism-oriented, dominated by the Grand Lucayan Resort and Port

Lucaya Marketplace (the island's best shopping). It also claims the island's only casino and the finest concentration of restaurants and bars.

**3 Greater Lucaya.** The beach can get crowded at Port Lucaya, but Taino Beach and Coral Beach are nearby for those who prefer more space and solitude, as well as a hand-ful of additional hotels and restaurants.

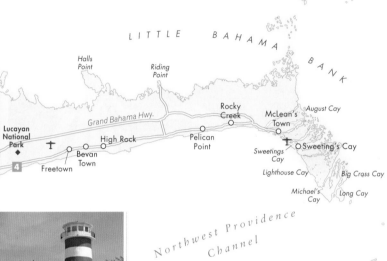

LITTLE BAHAMA BANK

Halls Point

Riding Point

Rocky Creek

McLean's Town

August Cay

Grand Bahama Hwy.

Pelican Point

Lucayan National Park

High Rock

Bevan Town

Freetown

Sweetings Cay

Sweeting's Cay

Lighthouse Cay

Big Cross Cay

Michael's Cay

Long Cay

Northwest Providence Channel

**4 Greater Grand Bahama.**
The bulk of the island lies on either side of the neighboring metropolitan duo of Freeport and Lucaya. Escaping town means discovering treasures such as Paradise Cove and Lucayan National Park, in addition to remote beaches, time-stilled fishing villages, and wooded land the locals refer to as the "bush."

## GETTING ORIENTED

Only 52 miles off Palm Beach, Florida, 96-mile-long Grand Bahama is one of the chain's northernmost islands. Freeport and Lucaya, which more or less melt into one another, are its main cities, comprising the second-largest metropolitan area in the Bahamas. Lucaya sees the most action, as Freeport struggles to regain ground lost in the hurricanes and

financial setbacks of the last decade. The town of West End is a quiet, colorful fishing village that gathers small crowds on Sunday evenings at local beach shacks. Its upscale Old Bahama Bay Resort, marina, and residential development are the extent of tourism on this end of the island. East of Freeport-Lucaya small fishing settlements, secluded beaches, and undeveloped forest stretch for 60 miles.

# LUCAYAN NATIONAL PARK

In this extraordinary 40-acre seaside land preserve, trails and elevated walkways wind through a natural forest of wild tamarind and gumbo-limbo trees, past an observation platform, a mangrove swamp, sheltered pools, and one of the largest explored underwater cave systems in the world (more than 6 miles long).

You can enter the caves at two access points; one is closed in June and July, the bat-nursing season. Twenty miles east of Lucaya, the park contains examples of the island's five ecosystems: beach, hardwood forest, mangroves, rocky coppice, and pine forest. Across the road from the caves, two trails form a loop. Creek Trail's boardwalk showcases impressive interpretive signage, and crosses a mangrove-clotted tidal creek to Gold Rock Beach, a narrow, lightly visited strand of white sand edged by some of the island's highest dunes and jewel-tone sea.

Visitors will find subtle treasures no matter what time of year they explore.

Summer can be overbearingly hot for walking, plus one of the caves closes June and July for bat season. However, that's also when certain orchids and other plants flower. Migrating birds and cooler temperatures make October–April optimal, especially mornings and low tide, when birds are most plentiful. Gold Rock Beach is best viewed when the tide is out.

### BEST WAYS TO EXPLORE

**By Kayak.** A kayak launch, near a beach where parts of the *Pirates of the Caribbean* movies were filmed, lies just east of the park entrance on the south side. From here paddlers can work their way

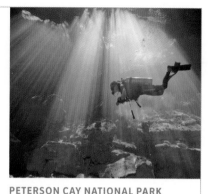

through mangrove forest to the park and its beach. Kayaking to Peterson Cay National Park, an offshore island and coral reef, is the easiest way to get there to snorkel and picnic.

**Underwater.** Snorkeling around Gold Rock Beach and its eponymous offshore Gold Rock is good. Certified cave divers can explore the intricate underwater network with Underwater Explorers Society (UNEXSO).

**On Foot.** Trails come in two parts. On the north side of the highway at the parking lot, one trail takes you into Ben's Cave and the Burial Mound Cave, where ancient Lucayan remains and artifacts have been discovered. A tricky spiral staircase descends into the dark depths of the former, and an easier wooden staircase to the latter. At both, observation platforms accommodate visitors who want to peer into the caves' clear depths. Across the highway, two flat, easy trails form a loop to the beach. Creek Trail (0.2 mile) is the easiest because its boardwalk is newer. Birds are more abundant here in the tidal creek with its low forest of mangroves at your feet. Mangrove Swamp Trail (0.3 mile) tends to be wet at high tide, and its boardwalk more difficult to negotiate (especially for small feet). Take one to the beach and the other to return to see the full range of environment here.

### PETERSON CAY NATIONAL PARK
Only accessible by boat or a long swim, Peterson Cay National Park, one of the Bahamas' smallest national parks, takes up 1½ acres 1 mile offshore from Barbary Beach. Its gorgeous, usually deserted beach and lively marine life make it worth the effort of snorkeling the reef or enjoying a quiet picnic. However, vegetation on the cay is salt-stunted and scrubby, so shade is scarce. All wildlife is protected in the park, including a quarter mile of surrounding marine environment. Local ecotour operators lead kayak and snorkel excursions.

### FUN FACT
A species of crustacean labeled *Speleonectes lucayensis* was discovered here and exists exclusively in the caverns of Lucayan National Park, where its population is protected. The rare, cave-dwelling Remipedia has no eyes or pigmentation.

Updated by
Jamie Werner

Natural beauty conspires with resort vitality to make Grand Bahama Island one of the Bahamas' most well-rounded, diverse destinations. In its two main towns, Freeport and Lucaya, visitors can find much of what the more bustling Nassau has to offer: resort hotels, a variety of restaurants, golfing, duty-free shopping, and gambling. But unlike New Providence, the touristy spots take up only a small portion of an island that, on the whole, consists of uninhabited stretches of sand and forest.

Prior to the development of Freeport, West End (the capital of Grand Bahama Island) was the epicenter of the Bahamas' logging industry and a playground for the wealthy in the 1920s. The fate of Grand Bahama changed in the 1950s when American financier Wallace Groves envisioned Grand Bahama's grandiose future as a tax-free shipping port. The Bahamian government signed an agreement that set in motion the development of a planned city, an airport, roads, waterways, and utilities as well as the port. From that agreement, the city of Freeport—and later, Lucaya—evolved. The past decade's hurricanes and economic downfall have demolished Freeport's resort glamour, and the tourism center has shifted to Lucaya, now home to the island's largest resorts.

Not much else on the island has changed since the early days, however. Outside of the Freeport-Lucaya commercial-and-resort area, fishing settlements remain, albeit now with electricity and good roads. The East End is Grand Bahama's "back-to-nature" side, where Caribbean yellow pine–and-palmetto forest stretches for 60 miles, interrupted by the occasional small settlement. Little seaside villages with white churches and concrete-block houses painted in bright pastels fill in the landscape between Freeport and West End. Many of these settlements are more than 100 years old.

# PLANNING

## WHEN TO GO

As one of the northernmost Bahama Islands, Grand Bahama experiences temperatures dipping into the 60s with highs in the mid-70s in January and February, so you may need a jacket and wet suit. On the upside, the migrant bird population swells and diversifies during that time of year. The other timing considerations are seasonal crowds and the subsequent increase in room rates. High tourist season runs from Christmas to Easter, peaking during spring break (late February to mid-April), when the weather is the most agreeable, but October through mid-December is also a good time to visit for weather.

Summers can get oppressively hot (into the mid and high 90s) and muggy, however; unless you're planning on doing a lot of snorkeling, diving, and other water sports, you may want to schedule your trip for cooler months. Afternoon thunderstorms and occasional tropical storms and hurricanes also make summer less attractive weather-wise. The island averages around 20 days of rain per month from June to September, but it usually falls briefly in the afternoon. The good news is that hotel rates plummet and diving and fishing conditions are great.

### TOP FESTIVALS

#### WINTER

**Festival Noel,** an annual holiday fest featuring music, crafts, wine tastings, and food at the Rand Nature Centre, takes place in early December.

**Bacardi Rum Billfish Tournament.** The weeklong Bacardi Rum Billfish Tournament is held in conjunction with the Bahamas Wahoo Championship. Both rotate around Grand Bahama and the Out Islands December through March.

#### SPRING

**Coconut Festival.** Experience coconut in more ways than you can count! The Coconut Festival in Pelican Point includes live music, coconut food sampling, coconut bowling, and other contests and activities held annually on Easter Monday.

#### SUMMER

**Grand Bahama Sailing Regatta.** Sailing sloops from throughout the country meet in June for the Grand Bahama Sailing Regatta, the exciting "Championship of the Seas." Onshore festivities take place at Taino Beach and include Junkanoo parades, dancing, music, and food.

#### FALL

**McLean's Town Conch Cracking Festival.** McLean's Town's annual homecoming event on the east end includes conch-cracking competitions, games, music, and various conch dishes for sample. This festival has taken place every October for more than 30 years.

**Conchman Triathlon.** The annual Conchman Triathlon at Taino Beach in November is a swimming-running-bicycling competition for amateurs that raises funds for local charities. ⊕ *www.conchman.com.*

## GETTING HERE AND AROUND

### AIR TRAVEL

**Grand Bahama International Airport (FPO)** is about 6 minutes from downtown Freeport and about 10 minutes from Port Lucaya. No bus service is available between the airport and hotels. Metered taxis meet all incoming flights. Rides cost about $17 for two to Freeport, $22 to Lucaya. The price drops to $4 per person with larger groups.

### BOAT AND FERRY TRAVEL

Balearia Bahamas Express sails from Fort Lauderdale's Port Everglades (Terminal 1) and provides fast-ferry service, making a day-trip possible, while Celebrations Cruise Line sails from Riviera Beach and is more like a small cruise ship, though hotel packages can include transportation to Grand Bahamas. Taxis meet all cruise ships. Passengers (two) are charged $16 for trips to Freeport and $24 to Lucaya. The price drops to $4–$5 per person with larger groups.

### BUS TRAVEL

Buses (usually minivans) are an inexpensive way to travel the 4 miles between downtown Freeport and Port Lucaya Marketplace daily until 8 pm. The fare is $1. Buses from Freeport to the West End cost $5 each way; to the East End, $15. Exact change is required.

### CAR TRAVEL

If you plan to drive around the island, it's cheaper and easier to rent a car than to hire a taxi. You can rent vehicles from the major agencies at the airport. Cars start at $75 for one day.

**Car Rental Contacts Cartwright's Rent-A-Car** ☎ *242/351–3002.* **Island Jeep and Car Rentals** ☎ *242/373–4001, 242/727–2207* ⊕ *www.islandjeepcarrental.com.* **KSR Car Rental** ☎ *242/351–5737, 954/703–5819* ✉ *ksr@ksrrentacar.biz* ⊕ *www.ksrrentacar.com.*

### TAXI TRAVEL

Taxi fares are fixed (but generally you're charged a flat fee for routine trips) at $3 for the first ¼ mile and 40¢ for each additional ¼ mile. Additional passengers over two are $3 each. There's a taxi waiting area outside the Grand Lucayan Resort or you can call the Grand Bahama Taxi Union for pickup.

**Contacts Grand Bahama Taxi Union** ☎ *242/352–7101.*

## ESSENTIALS

### BANKS

Banks are generally open Monday–Thursday 9:30–3 and Friday 9:30–4:30.

### EMERGENCIES

**Contacts Ambulance** ☎ *242/352–2689.* **Bahamas Air Sea Rescue** ☎ *242/727–4888, 242/359–4888* ⊕ *www.basragrandbahama.com.* **Fire Department** ☎ *911, 242/352–8888.* **Police** ☎ *911, 242/352–8280, 242/373–4112* ⊕ *www.royalbahamaspolice.org.* **Rand Memorial Hospital** ✉ *E. Atlantic Dr., Freeport, Grand Bahama Island* ☎ *242/352–2689, 242/350–6700* ⊕ *gbhs.phabahamas.org/.*

## HOTELS

Grand Bahama accommodations remain some of the Bahamas' most affordable, especially those away from the beach. The majority of these provide free shuttle service to the nearest stretch of sand. The island's more expensive hotels are beachfront, with the exception of

**FOLLOW THE SIGNS**

Roads in Grand Bahama Island are good, and the billboards are entertaining, if instructive: "Undertakers love overtakers" (i.e., people who pass).

Pelican Bay. These include the sprawling Grand Lucayan Resort; Viva Wyndham Fortuna Beach, an all-inclusive east of Port Lucaya; and the West End's elegant Old Bahama Bay Resort & Yacht Harbour. Small apartment complexes and time-share rentals are economical alternatives, especially if you're planning to stay for more than a few days.

Rates post-Easter through December 14 tend to be 25%–30% lower than those charged during the rest of the year.

## RESTAURANTS

The Grand Bahama dining scene stretches well beyond traditional Bahamian cuisine. The resorts and shopping centers have eateries that serve up everything from Italian to fine Continental and creative Pacific Rim specialties. For a true Bahamian dining experience, look for restaurants named after the owner or cook—such as Billy Joe's.

A native fish fry takes place every Wednesday evening at Smith's Point, east of Port Lucaya (taxi drivers know the way). Here you can sample fresh fish, sweet-potato bread, conch salad, and all the fixings cooked outdoors at the beach. It's a great opportunity to meet local residents and taste real Bahamian cuisine—and there's no better place than seaside under the pines and palms.

*Note: A gratuity (15%) is often added to the bill automatically; be sure to check your total before adding an additional tip.*

## HOTEL AND RESTAURANT PRICES

Restaurant prices are based on the median main course price at dinner, excluding gratuity, typically 15%, which is often automatically added to the bill. Hotel prices are for two people in a standard double room in high season, excluding service and 6%–12% tax.

## VISITOR INFORMATION

Contacts **Ministry of Tourism Grand Bahama Office** ☎ *242/352–8044, 800/224–2627* ⊕ *www.grandbahama.bahamas.com.*

# EXPLORING

## FREEPORT

Freeport, once an attractive, planned city of modern shopping centers, resorts, and other convenient tourist facilities, took a bad hit from the 2004 and 2005 hurricanes and subsequent economy downturn; its main resort and casino have not reopened. An Irish firm purchased the former Royal Oasis Resort & Casino but no plans have been made to rebuild or renovate. The International Bazaar next door is currently a ghost town with only a few crafts vendors and shops. Despite all this, Freeport's native restaurants, Rand Nature Centre, Bahamian Brewery, and beaches make it worth the visit. It's close to Lucaya (a 15-minute drive), and the airport and harbor are just a few minutes from downtown.

**Bahamas National Trust Rand Nature Centre.** On 100 acres just minutes from downtown Freeport, a half mile of self-guided botanical trails shows off 130 types of native plants, including many orchid species. The center is the island's birding hot spot, where you might spy a red-tailed hawk or a Cuban emerald hummingbird. Visit the caged one-eyed Bahama parrot the center has adopted, and a Bahama boa, a species that inhabits most Bahamian islands, but not Grand Bahama. On Tuesday and Thursday free (with admission) guided tours depart at 10:30 am. The visitor center hosts changing local art exhibits. ⊠ *E. Settlers Way, Freeport, Grand Bahama Island* ☎ *242/352–5438* ⊕ *www.bnt.bs* ☎ *$5* ⊗ *Weekdays 9–4, Sat. 9–1; guided nature walk by advance resv.*

**The Bahamian Brewery.** One hundred percent Bahamian owned, this 20-acre brewery opened in 2007, bringing to the Bahamian islands five new beers including Sands, High Rock Lager, Bush Crack, and Strong Back Stout. The brewery even makes a signature red ale served exclusively at the Atlantis Resort on Paradise Island. The brewery does everything on-site including bottling and labeling, and offers 15- to 20-minute tours that take you along each step in the brewing process. The tour ends in the tasting room where you can belly up to the bar or cocktail tables to sample each beer. Tours are $5 and walk-ins are accepted. Beer and liquor can be purchased in the retail store; Bahamian Brewery souvenirs are available in the gift shop. ⊠ *Just off Queen's Hwy., east of the turn to West End, Freeport, Grand Bahama Island* ☎ *242/352–4070* ⊕ *www.bahamianbrewery.com.*

**Perfume Factory.** Behind the now nearly defunct International Bazaar, the quiet and elegant Perfume Factory occupies a replica 19th-century Bahamian mansion—the kind built by Loyalists who settled in the Bahamas after the American Revolution. The interior resembles a tasteful drawing room. This is the home of Fragrance of the Bahamas, a company that produces perfumes, colognes, and lotions using the scents of jasmine, cinnamon, gardenia, spice, and ginger. Take a free 10-minute tour of the mixology laboratory and bottling area and get a free sample. For $30 an ounce, you can blend your own perfume using any of the 35 scents ($15 for 1½ ounces of blend-it-yourself body lotion). Sniff

## GREAT ITINERARIES

### IF YOU HAVE 3 DAYS

Begin in the morning with a shopping binge at **Port Lucaya Marketplace**. Stop at **UNEXSO** next door to make reservations for tomorrow's swim with dolphins or scuba dive excursion. Have lunch at Dive In Marina Restaurant before heading to Lucaya Beach across the street for an afternoon of sunning and water sports. Hit the restaurants and bars at the marketplace for the evening's entertainment. On Day 2, after your morning UNEXSO experience, head to Banana Bay on **Fortune Beach** to have lunch and unwind. Catch a fish fry or beach bonfire for your evening's entertainment. On Day 3, go on an ecotour and kayak through mangroves or snorkel over a blue hole. Catch an evening dinner cruise with **Bahama Mama Cruises**.

### IF YOU HAVE 5 DAYS

Spend the morning of Day 4 exploring the caves, trails, and beach at

**Lucayan National Park**. Stop at Garden of the Groves for lunch and a tour. Have dinner outside on the floating dock at Flying Fish then test your luck at the casino. The next day, rent a car for an excursion to **West End** for snorkeling at Paradise Cove and an eyeful of local culture. Stop at Pier One restaurant for dinner and shark feedings.

### IF YOU HAVE 7 DAYS

A week allows you to explore in greater depth the island's environmental treasures. On Day 6, visit the West End's Old Bahama Bay Resort and go on a fishing excursion or bonefish with a guide in the many Eastern end flats. Eat dinner in Lucaya at Red Beard's Pup or Bell Channel's Upstairs restaurant on the canal. Spend your last morning on a semisubmarine or Waverunner tour through the canals. In the afternoon, relax on Taino Beach.

mixtures until they hit the right combination, then bottle, name, and take home the personalized potion. ⊠ *Behind International Bazaar, W. Sunrise Hwy. and Mall Dr., on access road, Freeport, Grand Bahama Island* ☎ *242/352–9391, 800/628–9033* ⊕ *www.perfumefactory.com* 🖃 *Free* ⊗ *Weekdays 9:30–5, Sat. 11–3.*

## LUCAYA

On Grand Bahama's southern coast, Lucaya was developed after western neighbor Freeport as another resort center, this one on the beach and harbor. Colorful Port Lucaya Marketplace grew up along the safe harbor, known for its duty-free shops, bars, restaurants, straw market, and outdoor bandstand. This is also the home of UNEXSO, the island's famous diving and dolphin-encounter attraction. Across the street from the port, Grand Lucaya Resort is the island's biggest beach resort, complete with restaurants of various flavors, a golf course, spa, fitness center, and tennis courts. The neighboring resort, formerly Reef Village, has been purchased by Blue Diamond Hotels & Resorts and, at press time, was under renovation.

## PORT LUCAYA

FAMILY  **The Dolphin Experience.** Encounter Atlantic bottlenose dolphins in Sanctuary Bay at one of the world's first and largest dolphin facilities, about 2 miles east of Port Lucaya. A ferry takes you from Port Lucaya to the bay to observe and photograph the animals. If you don't mind getting wet, you can sit on a partially submerged dock or stand waist deep in the water and one of these friendly creatures will swim up to you. You can also engage in one of two swim-with-the-dolphins programs, but participants must be 55 inches or taller. The Dolphin Experience began in 1987, when it trained five dolphins to interact with people. Later, the animals learned to head out to sea and swim with scuba divers on the open reef. A two-hour dive program is available. You can buy tickets for the Dolphin Experience at UNEXSO in Port Lucaya, but be sure to make reservations as early as possible. ⊠ *Port Lucaya, next to Pelican Bay Hotel, Lucaya, Grand Bahama Island* ☎ *242/373–1244, 800/992–3483* ⊕ *www.unexso.com* 🖅 *Close Encounter $85, Swim with the Dolphins $179, Open-Ocean Swim $219* ⊙ *Daily 8–6.*

> ### DID YOU KNOW?
>
> The term "Lucayan" is derived from the Arawak Indian word Lukka-Cairi, or "Island People." The early tribespeople gave the Bahama Islands its first name, the Lucayas.

**Port Lucaya Marketplace.** Lucaya's capacious and lively shopping complex is on the waterfront across the street from the Grand Lucayan Resort and Treasure Bay Casino. The shopping center, whose walkways are lined with hibiscus, bougainvillea, and croton, has about 100 well-kept establishments, among them waterfront restaurants and bars, watersports operators, and shops that sell clothes, crystal and china, jewelry, perfumes, and local arts and crafts. The marketplace's centerpiece is **Count Basie Square,** where live entertainment featuring Bahamian bands appeals to joyful nighttime crowds every Thursday through Monday. Lively outdoor watering holes line the square, which is also *the* place to celebrate the holidays: a tree-lighting ceremony takes place in the festively decorated spot at the beginning of December and fireworks highlight New Year's Eve, the Fourth of July, and Bahamian Independence Day, July 10th. ⊠ *Sea Horse Rd., Lucaya, Grand Bahama Island* ☎ *242/373–8446, 242/373–2387* ⊙ *Daily 10–6. Restaurants and bars remain open at night.*

Fodor's Choice  **Underwater Explorers Society (UNEXSO).** One of the world's most respected
★  diving facilities, UNEXSO welcomes more than 50,000 individuals each year and trains hundreds of them in scuba diving. Facilities include a 17-foot-deep training pool with windows that look out on the harbor, changing rooms and showers, docks, equipment rental, an outdoor bar and grill, and an air-tank filling station. Daily dive excursions range from one-day discovery courses and dives to specialty shark, dolphin, and cave diving. ⊠ *Port Lucaya, next to Pelican Bay Hotel, Lucaya, Grand Bahama Island* ☎ *242/373–1244, 800/992–3483* ⊕ *www.unexso.com* 🖅 *One-tank reef dives $59, Discover Scuba course $109, night dives $79, dolphin dives $219, shark dives $109, equipment included* ⊙ *Daily 8–6.*

# Freeport–Lucaya

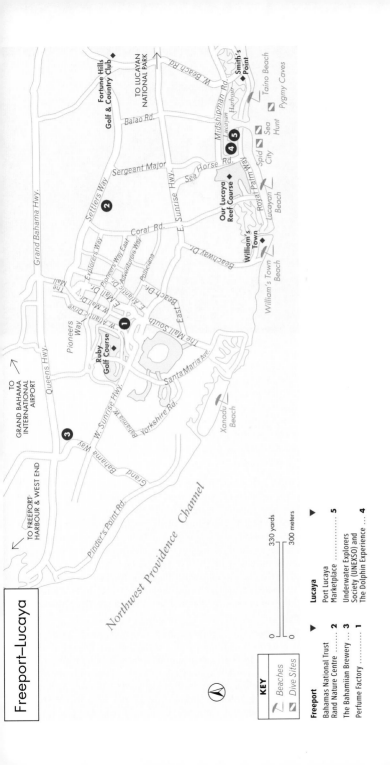

Northwest Providence Channel

TO
GRAND BAHAMA
INTERNATIONAL
AIRPORT

TO
FREEPORT HARBOUR & WEST END

Grand Bahama Hwy.

Queens Hwy.

Pinder's Point Rd.

Grand Bahama Way

W. Sunrise Hwy.

Bahama W. Sunrise Hwy.

Yorkshire Rd.

Santa Maria Ave.

Xanadu Beach

Pioneers Way

Explorer's Way

Pioneers Way East

Adventurers Way

The Mall

E. Mall Dr.

E. Mall Dr.

The Mall South

East Beach Dr.

E. Atlantic Dr.

Poinciana

Ruby Golf Course

Coral Rd.

E. Sunrise Hwy.

Settlers Way

Sergeant Major

Balao Rd.

Fortune Hills
Golf & Country Club

TO LUCAYAN
NATIONAL PARK

W. Beach Rd.

Midshipman Rd.

Sea Horse Rd.

Sunrise Hwy.

Beachway Dr.

William's
Town

William's Town Beach

Our Lucaya
Reef Course

Royal Palm Way

Lucayan Beach

Spid
City

Sea
Hunt

Taino Beach

Lucayan Harbour

Pygmy Caves

Smith's
Point

KEY
🝖 Beaches
◪ Dive Sites

| 0 | | 330 yards |
| 0 | | 300 meters |

**Freeport**

Bahamas National Trust
Rand Nature Centre ........ **2**

The Bahamian Brewery ... **3**

Perfume Factory ............. **1**

**Lucaya** ▶

Port Lucaya
Marketplace ............... **5**

Underwater Explorers
Society (UNEXSO) and
The Dolphin Experience ... **4**

More than 300 bird species call the Bahamas home, including this Bananaquit.

### GREATER LUCAYA

The lion's share of attractions, restaurants, and resorts in Lucaya are located around Port Lucaya and in particularly in the Port Lucaya Marketplace. But if you go a bit farther than you can travel easily on foot, there are also a handful of interesting establishments, including places to eat and stay that are away from the crush of tourists.

## GREATER GRAND BAHAMA

Farther out on either side of the Freeport–Lucaya development, the island reverts to natural pine forest, fishing settlements, and quiet secluded beaches. Heading west from Freeport, travelers pass the harbor area, a cluster of shacks selling fresh conch and seafood at Fishing Hole, a series of small villages, and Deadman's Reef at Paradise Cove before reaching the historic fishing town of West End and its upscale resort at the island's very tip. East of Lucaya lie long stretches of forest interrupted by the occasional small village, the Lucayan National Park, a myriad of bonefishing flats along the eastern end up to McClean's Town, and the outer Grand Bahama Cays: Sweetings, Deep Water, and Lightbourne.

**Garden of the Groves.** This vibrant 12-acre garden, featuring a trademark chapel and waterfalls, is filled with native Bahamian flora, butterflies, birds, and turtles. Interpretative signage identifies plant and animal species. First opened in 1973, the park was renovated and reopened in 2008; additions include a labyrinth modeled after the one at France's Chartres Cathedral, colorful shops and galleries with local arts and crafts, a playground, and a multideck outdoor café. Explore on your own or take a guided tour at 10 am (Monday–Saturday). Enjoy the garden under twinkling lights on Friday nights only, with dinner specials and live music. ⊠ *Midshipman Rd. and Magellan Dr., Grand Bahama Island* ☎ *242/374–7778* ⊕ *www.thegardenofthegroves.com* 💲 *$15* ⊙ *Daily 9–5; guided tours Mon.–Sat. at 10.*

**High Rock.** About 45 miles east of Lucaya and 8 miles from Lucayan National Park, it's worth the extra drive to visit an authentic, old-time island settlement affected only lightly by tourism. Its beach spreads a lovely white blanket of plump sand, with two beach clubs for food and drink. Take a walk along the beach and its parallel road (rock outcroppings interrupt the sand in places) past the cemetery to the faux lighthouse that makes a nice photographic punctuation. Although the welcome sign identifies the village as "Home of Hospitality," it holds just two small lodges. ⊠ *Eastern Grand Bahama, Grand Bahama Island.*

**Lucayan National Park.** In this extraordinary 40-acre seaside land preserve, trails and elevated walkways wind through a natural forest of wild tamarind and gumbo-limbo trees, past an observation platform, a mangrove swamp, sheltered pools, and one of the largest explored underwater cave systems in the world (more than 6 miles long). You can enter the caves at two access points; one is closed in June and July, the bat-nursing season. Twenty-six miles east of Lucaya, the park contains examples of the island's five ecosystems: beach, hardwood forest, mangroves, rocky coppice, and pine forest. Across the road from the caves, two trails form a loop. Creek Trail's boardwalk showcases impressive interpretive signage and crosses a mangrove-clotted tidal creek to Gold Rock Beach, a great place for a swim or picnic at low tide, and edged by some of the island's highest dunes and jewel-tone sea. At high tide the beach all but disappears. ⊠ *Grand Bahama Hwy., Grand Bahama Island* ☎ *242/353–4149, 242/352–5438* ⊕ *www.bnt.bs* 💲 *$5* ⊙ *Daily 9–4.*

**West End.** Once a rowdy, good-time resort area, West End still attracts party folk on Sunday evenings for friendly, casual street gatherings. Today's reputation, however, rests more firmly on its charter fishing. Day visitors stop at the bayfront conch shacks for conch salad straight from the shell (try Shebo's or Ian on the Bay) or at other tiny eateries along the way like The Chicken Nest. Overnighters stay at Old Bahama Bay Resort & Yacht Harbour, a gated resort. Non-guests are welcome at the hotel's beach side Tiki Bar for breakfast and lunch, or at the newly opened Dockside Grill for dinner. With the opening of award-winning Stuart Cove's newest scuba diving operation at Old Bahama Bay, visitors to West End can now embark on rare diving and snorkelling destinations not easily acccessed before. ⊠ *Western Grand Bahama, Grand Bahama Island.*

**Owl's Hole.** Named for the mama owl who nests here every year, this vertical fresh water cave is a popular local swimming hole. It's rimmed by a 25-foot cliff if you're up for taking a plunge. The less adventuresome can climb down a ladder into the cool but refreshing water. Take snorkel gear down with you to experience the beauty at its full potential, and if you're a certified cavern diver you can join local scuba diving excursions to explore even deeper. If your timing is right, you will see a nest full of fuzzy owlets (April–May) tucked under the ledge as you descend the ladder. The drive here feels a bit like a ride on a Bahamian bush roller coaster but it's worth it—finding the hole is half the adventure. ☒ *Off Grand Bahama Hwy., Before Lucayan National Park, Grand Bahama Island* ✛ *From Grand Bahama Hwy., turn right on last dirt road before the "dangerous curve" sign*

*(before Lucayan National Park). Drive 1.6 miles to tiny parking area on left. You've gone too far if you reach beach.*

# BEACHES

Fluffy white sand carpets in-your-dream beaches, where water sparkles like sapphires, lapis, tanzanite, emeralds, aquamarines . . . you get the picture. Grand Bahama Island has more than its share of beautiful beaches fringing the south coast of its 96-mile length. Some are bustling with watersports activity, while others lie so far off the beaten path it takes a four-wheel-drive vehicle and local knowledge to find them.

## FREEPORT

**William's Town Beach.** When the tide is high, this slice of relatively hidden beach (from East Sunrise Highway, take Coral Road south, then turn right onto Bahama Reef Boulevard) can get a little narrow, but there's a wide area at its east end, where a pig roast–jerk pit stand called Michele's Jerk Out does business. Across the road, a number of beach shacks have names such as On Da Rocks, Gone Le-Git, and Toad's on the Bay. Island Seas Resort, next to the pig roast stand, has its own modern interpretation of the local beach shack, called CoCoNuts Grog & Grub. **Amenities:** food and drink; parking (no fee); water sports. **Best for:** solitude; swimming; walking. ☒ *Freeport, Grand Bahama Island.*

**Xanadu Beach.** The old Xanadu Resort of Howard Hughes fame has been abandoned and is all but crumbling, but there is local talk that the day will come when it will be renovated. There are no longer amenities or flocks of tourists on this beach. However, the mile-long stretch of sand is still serene and worth a walk at sunset. **Amenities:** parking (no fee). **Best for:** solitude; sunrise; sunset; walking. ☒ *Freeport, Grand Bahama Island.*

## LUCAYA

### PORT LUCAYA

**Lucayan Beach.** Somewhat monopolized by the broad spread of the Grand Lucayan, nonguests of the resort can pay $15 (kids $7) for a day pass, which in addition to the beach, includes use of the hotel's pools. You must bring your own towel, and cruise-ship excursions can

# Grand Bahama Island

## Key

Beaches
Dive Sites

Water Depths
-25ft deep
-50ft deep
-100ft deep

LITTLE BAHAMA BANK

Hawksbill Cays
Upper Cay
Fox Town
LITTLE ABACO ISLAND
Sponge Cay
Little Cave Cay
Cross Cays

Big Cross Cay
Sweeting's Cay
August Cay
McLean's Town
Sweetings Cay
Lighthouse Cay
Michael's Long Cay

Rocky Creek

Great Sale Cay

Pelican Point

Riding Point

LITTLE BAHAMA BANK

Halls Point

High Rock

Grand Bahama Hwy.

Bevan Town
Freetown
Gold Rock Beach

Noss Mangrove
Sandy Harbour
Little Water Cay
Water Cay
Water Cay

Lucayan National Park

Owl's Hole

Ben's Blue Hole

Mangrove Rocks
Sandy Cay

GRAND BAHAMA ISLAND

Gardens of the Groves
Smith's Point

Fortune Beach

Theo's Wreck

Dover Sound

Mangrove Cay

Lucaya

Taino Beach
Shark Junction
Midshipman Rd.

Grand Bahama International Airport

William's Town

Sea Horse Rd.

Freeport see detail map

The Bahamian Brewery

Lucayan Beach

Big Whale Cay

Boatle Bay Village

Xanadu Beach

Freeport Harbour

West End Point
West End
Paradise Cove
Deadman's Reef
Queen's Hwy.

Northwest Providence Channel

10 mi
10 km

add to the resort's crowds. Farther west, near the famous Billy Joe's beach shack, there is no admission fee for the beach. The white sand is interrupted by rocky protrusions at places, so it's not great for strolling. Instead, spend the day people-watching, feeding jack fish, or doing multiple water sports including snorkel trips out to Rainbow Reef, parasailing, or WaveRunner tours through the canals. **Amenities:** food and drink; lifeguards; water sports. **Best for:** partiers; snorkeling; sunrise; swimming. ⊠ *Lucaya, Grand Bahama Island* 🖾 *$15.*

### GREATER LUCAYA

**Fortune Beach.** The clean white sand of Fortune Beach lies between two canal channels, and in the middle sits the Wyndham Viva Fortuna all-inclusive resort, where visitors can purchase day passes to use water sports equipment. Just steps either way from the resort, however, the beach becomes quiet and secluded and offers an endless expanse both ways for exceptional strolling, easy off-shore snorkeling and great swimming. The western end backs the Margarita Villa Sand Bar and the private homes along Spanish Main Drive, what locals refer to as "Millionaire Row." The Eastern end is home to Banana Bay, where at low tide a shallow lagoon forms alongside a long sand bar, allowing you to walk yards out to sea. **Amenities:** food and drink, parking near east end only (no fee). **Best for:** solitude, walking, windsurfing, snorkeling, swimming, sunrise. ⊠ *Fortune Bay Dr., Greater Lucaya, Lucaya, Grand Bahama Island.*

FAMILY **Taino Beach.** Arguably one of the more marvelous beaches on the island, Taino is just far enough removed from Port Lucaya to thin the crowds some, although cruise-ship passengers often make their way here on group excursions. Junkanoo Beach Club has a small food menu (compared to its long menu of 34 drinks) and water-sports operators are on hand. With lapping water that puts gemstones to shame, this fluffy-sand beach begs for exploration. A short walk down the long, gently coved beach takes you to Tony Macaroni's Conch Experience, where music plays and an all-welcome volleyball game is usually in session. A few steps farther and you arrive at Outriggers Beach Club, home to the always popular Fish Fry held every Wednesday night. Plenty of green space edges the beach, and there's a newly updated playground for families. **Amenities:** food and drink; parking (no fee); water sports. **Best for:** partiers; sunset; swimming; walking. ⊠ *W. Beach Rd., near Smith's Point, Greater Lucaya, Lucaya, Grand Bahama Island.*

## GREATER GRAND BAHAMA

**Gold Rock Beach.** Located just off the Grand Bahama Highway 26 miles outside of town, Gold Rock beach is touted by the Ministry of Tourism as Grand Bahama's "welcome mat." This secluded beach is accessible via a lovely 10-minute walk through the Lucayan National Park, and is both wide and spectacular, spanning for yards into the sea when the tide is low. The turquoise water is exceptionally clear, calm, and shallow, making it a perfect play place for families with young children. Occasional cruise ship tours visit for a couple of hours around midday, but there is enough space that you will never feel crowded. Note, however,

**CLOSE UP**

# Ecotourism on Grand Bahama

Beyond the 6-mile strip that comprises Grand Bahama Island's metropolis lie another 90 miles of unadulterated wilderness. The balance of the island is given to natural and uncrowded beaches, old-island settlements, and untamed "bush," as locals call the wilds.

The emphasis on the island's natural attributes begins below the water line with a variety of scuba diving adventures and UNEXSO's **Dolphin Experience.** UNEXSO's preoccupation with extreme diving led to the exploration of the island's unique cave system and the 1977 opening of **Lucayan National Park,** a portal to the underground labyrinth accessible to the public. One of the caves holds a cemetery of the island's aboriginals, the Lucayans. The park also gives intrepid visitors a taste of the beauty and seclusion of out-of-town beaches.

Kayaking, biking, snorkeling, boating, jeeping, and cultural safaris provide ways for visitors to take in Grand Bahama Island's most precious treasures.

**Grand Bahama Nature Tours,** a top-notch operation, follows backwater kayaking trails to Lucayan National Park and other off-the-beaten-path destinations. Knowledgeable native guides give lessons on island ecology en route.

Right in downtown Freeport, the **Bahamas National Trust Rand Nature Centre** was one of the precursors to ecotourism on Grand Bahama Island. It still provides an oasis for rare birds and resident snakes. On the island's other extreme, close to West End, **Paradise Cove** leads you below the waves to teeming healthy reefs and sand beds. Here you can rent snorkeling equipment or kayaks to experience the island's best swim-to reef—Deadman's Reef.

Ecotourism promises to be a fixture on Grand Bahama Island, attracting a different brand of island vacationer, one more adventurous and ready to experience the less-touted and richer offerings of Grand Bahama's great outback. For more information, contact the **Ecotourism Association of Grand Bahama** (☎ 242/352–8044, 800/448–3386 in the U.S.).

that the white sandy beach is almost nonexistent when the tide is high and shade is sparse, so time your visit appropriately. **Amenities:** none. **Best for:** solitude; swimming, walking. ⊠ *Grand Bahama Hwy., Lucaya, Grand Bahama Island.*

**Paradise Cove Beach.** A 15-minute drive from Freeport, this beach's spectacular swim-to reef is its best asset, with marine life that includes various rays, sea turtles, and barracudas. Paradise Cove is a small native-owned resort that will bus you out if you call ahead. The beach is short but wide with scrubby vegetation and swaying palm trees.

> **FLYING TEETH**
>
> Known in some parts as no-see-ums, the practically invisible sand fleas called "flying teeth" in the Bahamas are a force to be reckoned with, especially at the West End and in the summer months. At and after sunset they come out in force on still nights, and their bites can result in itchy red welts. Dress in long sleeves and pants or apply a repellent. Avon's Skin-So-Soft lotion or baby oil are the generally accepted deterrents.

Snorkel equipment and kayaks are available to rent, and refreshments flow at the Red Bar. There is a $3/person fee just to hang at the beach. **Amenities:** food and drink; parking (no fee); showers; toilets; water sports. **Best for:** snorkeling. ⊠ *Warren J. Levarity Hwy., Between Eight Mile Rock and West End, West End, Grand Bahama Island* ⊕ *www. deadmansreef.com* ☎ *$3* ☉ *Daily 9:30–5:30.*

# WHERE TO EAT

## FREEPORT

$    ✕ **Geneva's Place.** Geneva's sets the standard for home-cooked Bahamian
BAHAMIAN    food. Cook and owner Geneva Munroe will prepare your grouper or pork chops broiled, steamed, or fried; your conch cracked (fried light and flaky), or, for breakfast, stewed. Locals come for the chicken souse. Everything is served with a choice of comfort side dishes such as peas 'n' rice or baked macaroni and cheese. The simple dining room oozes cheerfulness in shades of yellow. If you want an authentic Bahamian meal, this is the place. $ *Average main: $18* ⊠ *E. Mall Dr. and Kipling La., across from Wendy's, Freeport, Grand Bahama Island* ☎ *242/352–5085* ☉ *Daily 7 am–9 pm.*

$    ✕ **Livity Vegetarian Juice Bar & Take-Out.** Offering the healthiest food on
VEGETARIAN    the island, this little shop (located in a shabby strip mall) doesn't look like much, but the quality of the food says differently. Livity blends up fresh fruit and vegetable juices and smoothies with names like Flu Shot, Pressure Reliever, and Incredible Hulk, with the idea that you should "Eat Smarter." Lunch includes daily specials such as chickpea stew, sautéed green beans, and mushrooms served on quinoa or wild rice, in addition to barbecued tofu and Rasta pasta. Fruit and vegetable salads, veggie fritters, soups, veggie burgers, and salmon burgers are staples on the menu. $ *Average main: $8* ⊠ *West Atlantic Dr., in Rolle's Furniture Plaza, Freeport, Grand Bahama Island* ☎ *242/352–1855* ▭ *No credit cards* ☉ *Closed Sun. No dinner.*

# LUCAYA

Most of the dining in Lucaya is in or around the Port Lucaya Marina or Port Lucaya Marketplace, which means that all the restaurants are within walking distance of each other and of the hotels in the immediate vicinity.

## PORT LUCAYA

$

BAHAMIAN

✕ **Billy Joe's on the Beach.** Eating fresh conch salad and drinking a cold beer, island music in the background and your toes in the sand: it doesn't get any better or more Bahamian. Billy Joe has been a fixture on Lucaya beach for almost 40 years, selling his freshly made-on-the-spot (watch it being prepared!) conch salad, cracked conch, roast conch, and grilled conch (minced and cooked with tomatoes, onions, and bell peppers in an aluminum packet on the barbecue). Fried lobster and ribs are also favorites, and there's even a special menu for kids. $ *Average main: $12* ⊠ *Lucaya Beach, behind the police station, Lucaya, Grand Bahama Island* ☎ *242/373–1333* ⊟ *No credit cards* ☉ *No dinner.*

$$

ASIAN

✕ **China Beach.** For fine Pacific Rim dining with a view of the ocean, have dinner here, where the menu covers the various culinary regions of China plus Thailand and Japan, with a nod to the Bahamas. Feast on sushi rolls, Japanese dumplings, stir-fried conch, Szechuan prawns, and other Asian specialties. $ *Average main: $26* ⊠ *Grand Lucayan Resort, Lucaya, Grand Bahama Island* ☎ *242/373–1333* ⊕ *www.grandlucayan. com* ☉ *Tues., Wed., Thurs., Sat. 6 pm–10 pm* ☉ *No lunch. Closed Fri., Sun., and Mon.*

$$$

STEAKHOUSE

✕ **Churchill's and Grand Bar.** Unwind in the handsome wood piano bar before enjoying a four-course dinner in the dining room, surrounded by white wainscoting and French windows. The atrium ceiling over the circular room illuminates Bahamian life with mural scenes and heavy chandeliers, and the character evokes the plantation era. The menu is Mediterranean inspired, with house specialties such as lobster and wild mushroom risotto and veal marsala, but also includes create-your-own pasta dishes, steaks, and seafoods. $ *Average main: $30* ⊠ *Grand Lucayan Resort, Lucaya, Grand Bahama Island* ☎ *242/373–1333* ⊕ *www.grandlucayan.com* ⫞ *Reservations essential* ☉ *Closed Tues. and Wed. No lunch.*

$

CARIBBEAN

FAMILY

✕ **Dive-In Marina Bar & Restaurant.** This relaxing poolside bar and grill at UNEXSO is great for lunch and weekend brunch, with delicious and creative items such as hot *antojitos* (Mexican small plates), banana bread French toast, veggie wraps, and the heaping spinach and bacon salad. Kids can splash in the pool (which has underwater windows to the marina, so bring goggles!) while adults sip Bloody Marys and tropical drinks. $ *Average main: $15* ⊠ *UNEXSO, next to Pelican Bay Hotel, Lucaya, Grand Bahama Island* ☎ *242/373–1244* ☉ *Daily 8–8.*

$$$ SEAFOOD Fodor's Choice ★ 🍴 **Flying Fish Modern Seafood.** You'll find an eclectic collection of seafood and Bahamian favorites, made with local ingredients and done with a gourmet and artistic twist, at Flying Fish, which opened in February 2012. The owners are local couple Tim and Rebecca Tibbits—Tim being the genius behind the food, Rebecca the genius behind the wine. Ask Rebecca for a pairing, and she will find something to both delight and surprise you (sake or tequila may be her choice). The restaurant is on the canal front and has an ambience that is both romantic and contemporary. But don't let all the gourmet talk fool you; it's the pub grub that attracts regulars. Sit outside on the patio or on the floating dock and choose from the bar menu that includes Chef Tim's own homemade bacon served on the BLT paired with shoestring fries. Fresh oysters are featured every Wednesday night, and Bloody Marys rock the weekend brunch. Weekly culinary classes also wow diners. [$] *Average main: $38* ✉ *Next to Pelican Bay Hotel, Lucaya, Grand Bahama Island* ☎ *242/373–4363* 🌐 *www.flyingfishbahamas.com* ✍ *Reservations essential* ☞ *Docking facilities for boaters.*

**DID YOU KNOW?**

Sands Beer made its first appearance with the opening of The Bahamian Brewery in 2008 and is now a favorite local brew, available throughout The Bahamas.

$$$ EUROPEAN 🍴 **Luciano's.** Linens, soft candlelight, and a twinkling view of the harbor add to the glamour and romance of this second-story Port Lucaya restaurant. Interior renovations and new management have given this long-standing establishment new life, but the original menu still speaks French with English subtitles, including such specialties as *coquilles St. Jacques florentine* (scallops on spinach with hollandaise), *filet au poivre vert* (tenderloin fillet with green peppercorn sauce), scampi flambé, Dover sole, stuffed quail, and chateaubriand for two. Regulars rave about the Caesar salads and the French onion soup. Dinner is served in the formal dining room or on the verandah overlooking the marina, and service can be slow, so plan to make a night of it or be frustrated. [$] *Average main: $38* ✉ *Port Lucaya Marketplace, Lucaya, Grand Bahama Island* ☎ *242/373–9100* 🌐 *www.lucianosofportlucaya.com* ✍ *Reservations essential* ⏲ *No lunch.*

$ BAHAMIAN 🍴 **Outriggers Native Restaurant.** For Bahamian food fixed by Bahamians, head to the generational property of an old island family at Taino Beach. This open-aired beach shack restaurant serves up cracked conch (pounded and fried), lobster tail, fried grouper, and barbecue chicken down-home style. On Wednesday nights the quiet little settlement comes to life when Outriggers throws its famous weekly fish fry, where you'll wait in line for the fried fish (with the head and tail still on)—make sure you try it with the lemon pepper sauce. Come early for the food, stay late for the party. Occasional beach bonfires add to the fun. [$] *Average main: $16* ✉ *Smith's Point, Lucaya, Grand Bahama Island* ☎ *242/373–4811* 🌐 *www.outriggersbeachclub.com* 💳 *No credit cards* ⏲ *Closed Sun. No lunch.*

$$ — ECLECTIC — ✕ **Sabor Restaurant and Bar.** The setting makes this restaurant the perfect place for an evening cocktail whether you sit overlooking the Port Lucaya Marina or nestled among the twinking lights and palm trees around the pool deck. The lunch and dinner menu is a fun fusion of Bahamian and American favorites with tropical twists, such as O.M.G. Jalapeño Shrimps, Kalik Cracked Conch, fresh Hog Snapper, seared tuna, and burgers to boot. Be warned that service can be slow, so it's a good thing the view is superb! Happy hour is nightly from 5 to 7. $ *Average main: $17* ⊠ *Pelican Bay Hotel at Port Lucaya, Lucaya, Grand Bahama Island* ☎ *242/373–5588* ⊕ *www.sabor-bahamas.com.*

> **CONCHING OUT**
>
> Conch harvesting is illegal in the United States and closely regulated in other tropical locations to guard against overfishing. Currently, conch harvesting is limited to six per vessel in the Bahamas, but populations, while still plentiful, are slowly becoming depleted.

$ — BAHAMIAN — ✕ **Tony Macaroni's Conch Experience.** For a taste of the local beach scene, follow the music to this weathered, thatch-roof shack at Taino Beach and get your fill of roast conch, the specialty of the "house." Operated by local personality Anthony "Macaroni" Hanna, the popular eatery also sells conch salad, roast lobster and shrimp, and Gully Wash cocktails (green coconut water, sweetened condensed milk, and gin) for noshing en plein air on a stilted deck overlooking pristine sands and sea. $ *Average main: $11* ⊠ *Taino Beach, Lucaya, Grand Bahama Island* ☎ *242/533–6766* ⊕ *www.TonyMacBahamas.com* ▭ *No credit cards.*

$ — GREEK — ✕ **Zorba's Greek Cuisine.** Besides Greek favorites, this longtime Port Lucaya tenant serves popular Bahamian dishes, too. Join the port's yacht-in clientele, shoppers, and locals alike, for breakfast, lunch, or dinner on the white-and-blue-trimmed sidewalk porch. Specialties include gyros, moussaka, Greek salad, pizza, conch fritters, fried snapper, and roasted leg of lamb. Dishes are reasonably priced and the service is consistently friendly and efficient. $ *Average main: $14* ⊠ *Port Lucaya Marketplace, Lucaya, Grand Bahama Island* ☎ *242/373–6137* ⊕ *www.zorbasbahamas.com* ⌕ *Reservations not accepted* ☽ *Daily 7 am–11 pm.*

## GREATER LUCAYA

$ — CARIBBEAN — FAMILY — Fodor's Choice — ★ — ✕ **Banana Bay Restaurant.** Directly on Fortune Beach, Banana Bay is a great place for lunch or daytime cocktails, whether you sit on the restaurant's shaded deck or on a lounger in the sand. As the tide rolls out the beach grows, creating a wonderful shallow lagoon and sand bar, perfect for wading and for frolicking kids. In addition to daily fresh fish specials, the kitchen serves up homemade warm banana bread loaves along with salads, sandwiches, wraps, and seafood appetizers like conch fritters and crab cakes. On windy days, you will have a front row seat to kite surfers in action. A few times a week, cruise ships drop off tourists en masse, so you can expect service to get a little slow . . . which will give you more time to enjoy your piña colada. $ *Average main: $12* ⊠ *Fortune Bay Dr., on Fortune Beach, Grand Bahama Island* ☎ *242/373–2960* ☽ *Daily 10–5* ☽ *No dinner.*

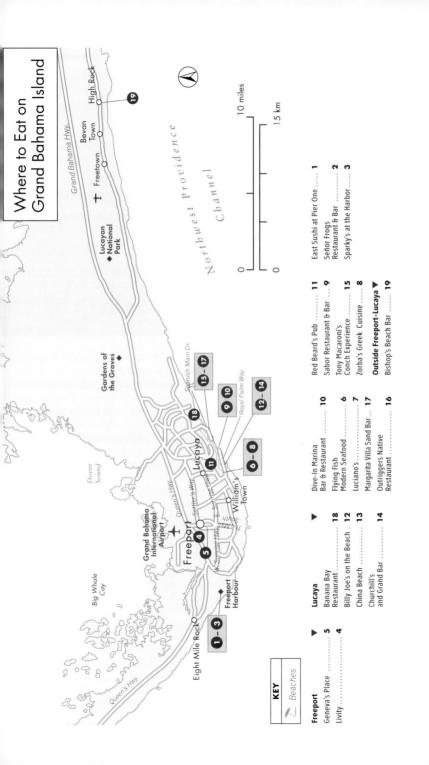

# Where to Eat on Grand Bahama Island

Northwest Providence Channel

0 — 10 miles
0 — 15 km

**KEY**
Beaches

**Freeport**
Geneva's Place ............. 5
Livity ......................... 4

**Lucaya**
Banana Bay
Restaurant ................. 18
Billy Joe's on the Beach .. 12
China Beach ................ 13
Churchill's
and Grand Bar ............ 14

Dive-In Marina
Bar & Restaurant ......... 10
Flying Fish
Modern Seafood ........... 6
Luciano's ..................... 7
Margarita Villa Sand Bar .. 17
Outriggers Native
Restaurant ................. 16

Red Beard's Pub ............ 11
Sabor Restaurant & Bar ... 9
Tony Macaroni's
Conch Experience ......... 15
Zorba's Greek Cuisine ..... 8

**Outside Freeport–Lucaya** ▶
Bishop's Beach Bar ........ 19

East Sushi at Pier One ...... 1
Señor Frogs
Restaurant & Bar .......... 2
Sparky's at the Harbor ..... 3

This sailboat is in front of Grand Lucayan Beach Resort.

$$ AMERICAN 🍴 **Margarita Villa Sand Bar.** There is no flooring in this cozy little beach bar, just sand, along with a few bartop tables and some stools along the bar. You'll feel like an old friend talking to the bartender. Party photos adorn the walls along with velvet paintings of Elvis. It's the place to be for Sunday football games (especially Miami Dolphin fans), and they also offer up free Wi-Fi, live music, and outdoor seating right on the beach. Favorites on the menu include fish and chips, conch burgers and fries, Greek salads, and Philly cheese steaks among other Bahamian and American favorites. [$] *Average main: $12* ✉ *Fortune Beach, off Spanish Main Rd., Lucaya, Grand Bahama Island* ☎ *242/373–4525* 🌐 *www.sandbarbahamas.net* 🕒 *Closes at 8 pm.*

$$ BURGER 🍴 **Red Beard's Pub.** This popular sports bar and restaurant sits across the canal from Port Lucaya Marina, serving a medley of consistently good American favorites including burgers and fries, buffalo wings, soups, salads, and homemade mozzarella sticks. The owner looks just like the pirate painted on the outside wall, and he is a perfect complement to the pirate memorabilia that adorns the interior walls (look for *Pirates of the Caribbean* movie photos that include many locals used as extras in the film). Nightly specials may include fresh fish and seafood, homemade Indian curry, or even English bangers and mash. Bring them your fresh catch (cleaned) and they will prepare it for you. Locals and expats come here, too, and join in the fun for trivia nights, karaoke, and weekly live music. [$] *Average main: $15* ✉ *2 Kings Rd., next to Bell Channel Inn, Lucaya, Grand Bahama Island* ☎ *242/374–2010* 🌐 *www.redbeardspub.com* 🕒 *Mon.–Sat. 4 pm–2 am* 🕒 *No lunch. Closed Sun. during July and Aug.* ☞ *Full dock facilities for boaters and free Wi-Fi.*

## GREATER GRAND BAHAMA

$$ BAHAMIAN 🍴 **Bishop's Beach Bar.** A longtime favorite of locals and visitors who venture out to Lucayan National Park (about 6 miles away) and into the East End's settlements, Bishop's serves all the fried Bahamian favorites with a view of the sea. The beach bar doesn't sell food, so you'll have to make the short walk across the parking lot to order in the restaurant and they will bring it out to you. Conch fritters, cracked conch, fish fingers, burgers, and crab salad are a few of the menu choices, but the food isn't what makes this place special. Bishop himself mans this kickback beach bar along with his dog, and plays great music that adds to the ambience. Come for a cold drink and stay for the beach. [$] *Average main: $15* ✉ *High Rock, Grand Bahama Island* ☎ *242/353–5485* 🌐 *www.bishopsresort.net.*

$$ SUSHI Fodor's Choice ★ 🍴 **East Sushi at Pier One.** Pier One has one of the most unique settings of any restaurant in Grand Bahama. Built on stilts above the ocean near the Harbour, it offers one-of-a-kind views of magnificent sunsets, larger than life cruise ships departing, and sharks swimming for chum. Pier One has two levels and two menus, the best one being East's. Their menu is both creative and extensive including Japanese favorites such as miso soup, seaweed salads, tempura, and a variety of rolls—try the Bahama Mama with tempura conch, avocado, mango, and chili-lime mayo for a tropical twist. Diners can eat inside either upstairs or downstairs, but the large tables on the balcony offer the best views of the shark feedings, done every hour on the hour starting at 7 pm. For those who prefer their fish cooked or Continental fare, the other menu includes grilled fish, vegetable pasta, steaks, and chicken. [$] *Average main: $25* ✉ *Freeport Harbour, Freeport, Grand Bahama Island* ☎ *242/352–6674* 🌐 *www.pieroneandeast.com* 🕒 *No lunch Sun.*

$ MEXICAN 🍴 **Señor Frog's Restaurant Bar & Souvenir Shop.** Opened in October 2012, this party place fills with cruise ship passengers when docked for the day, and sends them back to the boat happy, fed, and full of rum drinks. The location at the Freeport Harbour is open-aired and full of life, complete with a dance stage, large flat-screen TVs, a wraparound bar, and seating for more than 100 people. The music is loud, the crowd is lively, and the Mexican menu has fun Bahamian and tropical twists. Watch out for waiters who run around blowing whistles and pouring tequila down your throat, and if your party endurance is ready for a challenge, try your luck at a musical chairs game that includes two shots with every circle! [$] *Average main: $17* ✉ *Freeport Harbour, Freeport, Grand Bahama Island* ☎ *242/351–3764* 🌐 *www.senorfrogs.com* 🕒 *Closed Sun. No lunch Sat.*

$ AMERICAN 🍴 **Sparky's Harbour.** Opened in 2012, Sparky's Harbour is a sister location to Sparky's Bar at Port Lucaya Marketplace. This laid-back waterside location has fun island decor and friendly bartenders, and gets lively when the cruise ships dock. The menu boasts items such as burgers, wraps, and grilled fish sandwiches, in addition to fresh salads and popular appetizers like conch fritters and hot wings. Check weekend schedules for live music. [$] *Average main: $10* ✉ *Freeport Harbour, Terminal 4, Freeport, Grand Bahama Island* ☎ *242/352–4233.*

# WHERE TO STAY

### TIME-SHARES

Grand Bahama has a selection of time-shares in addition to regular hotels and resorts. For more information about time-share houses, apartments, and condominiums, contact the Ministry of Tourism Grand Bahama Office (☎ 800/224–2627⊕ www.grandbahama.bahamas.com).

**Freeport Resort & Club.** This property offers one- and two-bedroom suites, with 4 different layouts, in a garden setting with a pool. ⊠ *Near International Bazaar, Rum Cay Dr., Freeport, Grand Bahama Island* ☎ *242/352–5371, 877/699–9474* ⊕ *www.freeportresort.com.*

**Mayfield Beach and Tennis Club.** These 10 town houses share a pool, small beach, and tennis court. ⊠ *Port-of-Call Dr., near Xanadu Beach, Freeport, Grand Bahama Island* ☎ *242/352–9776.*

**Ocean Reef Yacht Club & Resort.** This property has 60 one- to three-bedroom apartments about 2 miles from Port Lucaya. The resort has a marina, tennis courts, pools, dive shop, and an on-site restaurant, Grouper Bar & Grill, that serves breakfast, lunch, and dinner. ⊠ *Bahama Reef Blvd., Freeport, Grand Bahama Island* ☎ *242/373–4661, 954/727–5770* ⊕ *www.oryc.com.*

## FREEPORT

**$$** 🛏 **Island Seas Resort.** This time-share property accommodates nonmembers looking for fun on the beach away from urban traffic. **Pros:** on-site restaurant; fun pool and bar area; great beach. **Cons:** fitness center is below par; other resort guests use property; property is worn and room decor is outdated. $ *Rooms from: $219* ⊠ *123 Silver Point Dr., William's Town, Freeport, Grand Bahama Island* ☎ *242/373–1271, 800/801–6884* ⊕ *www.islandseas.com* ⤵ *189 rooms* ⦿ *No meals.*

RESORT
FAMILY

## LUCAYA

### PORT LUCAYA

**$** 🛏 **Bell Channel Inn.** Right on the water and a short walk from Port Lucaya Market Place, this charming family-run (through three generations) inn with simple spacious rooms has quick and easy access to the island's best down-under sites, making it perfect for scuba-oriented and budget travelers. **Pros:** friendly, long-time staff; clean, affordable rooms; on the water. **Cons:** no beach; 10-minute walk from shopping and restaurant scene; rooms are dated but well maintained. $ *Rooms from: $85* ⊠ *Kings Rd., just off of Midshipman, Lucaya, Grand Bahama Island* ☎ *242/373–1053, 242/373–1057* ⊕ *www.bellchannelinn.com* ⤵ *32 rooms* ⦿ *No meals.*

HOTEL

**$** 🛏 **Grand Lucayan Beach & Golf Resort.** Lucaya's biggest resort (with three pools, golf, tennis, and nonmotorized water sports) boasts art deco elegance with Bahamian charm on more than 5 acres of soft-sand beach. **Pros:** across the street from Port Lucaya; great beach front activities; babysitting services. **Cons:** no shade on the beach; all-inclusive meals are average and repetitve; golf course is not championship quality.

RESORT
FAMILY

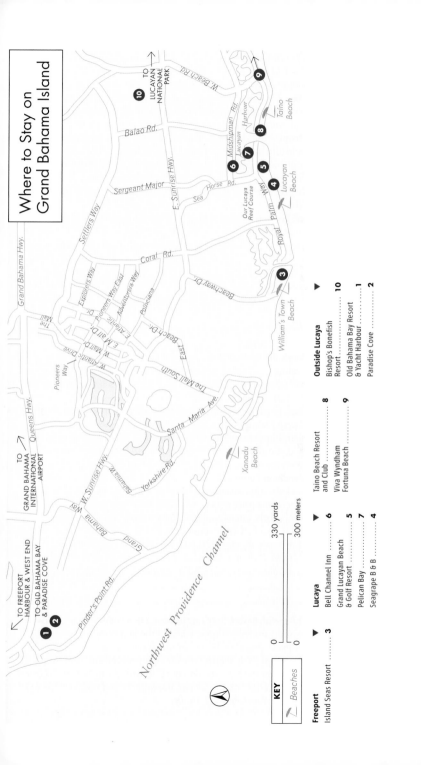

# Where to Stay on Grand Bahama Island

**KEY**

↗ Beaches

| 0 | | 330 yards |
| 0 | | 300 meters |

**Freeport**

▶ Island Seas Resort .......... 3

**Lucaya**

▶ Bell Channel Inn ............ 6
Grand Lucayan Beach
& Golf Resort ............... 5
Pelican Bay ................. 7
Seagrape B & B ............. 4

Taino Beach Resort
and Club ................... 8
Viva Wyndham
Fortuna Beach .............. 9

**Outside Lucaya**

▶ Bishop's Bonefish
Resort ..................... 10
Old Bahama Bay Resort
& Yacht Harbour ............ 1
Paradise Cove .............. 2

$ *Rooms from: $151* ⊠ *Sea Horse Rd., Lucaya, Grand Bahama Island* ☎ *242/373–1333, 866/870–7148 in U.S.* ⊕ *www.grandlucayan.com* 🛏 *540 rooms, 26 suites* ⊮ *All meals.*

$$  ⬚ **Pelican Bay.** Close to the beach, with rooms overlooking Port Lucaya
HOTEL  Marina or waterfront along the canal, Pelican Bay has a funky modern
Fodor's Choice  appeal, and suites overflow with character and decorative elements
★  collected from around the world. **Pros:** stylish and comfortable; water views; beautiful landscaping. **Cons:** no beach; fee for Wi-Fi; poolside/ marina front rooms can be noisy. $ *Rooms from: $175* ⊠ *Port Lucaya Marina, Sea Horse Rd., Lucaya, Grand Bahama Island* ☎ *242/373– 9550, 866/296–7963* ⊕ *www.pelicanbayhotel.com* 🛏 *89 rooms, 93 suites* ⊮ *Breakfast.*

$$  ⬚ **Seagrape Bed & Breakfast.** This quiet B&B offers tourists something
B&B/INN  more intimate, away from the hustle and bustle of Port Lucaya, yet mere steps from the beach and a short walk from everything else. **Pros:** free airport pickup; central location to beach and amenities; insider tips to seeing the "less traveled" sights on the island. **Cons:** only two rooms; fee for return trip to airport. $ *Rooms from: $95* ⊠ *Sea Spray Lane, Lucaya, Grand Bahama Island* ☎ *954/234–2387, 242/373–1769* ⊕ *www.seagrapehouse.com* 🛏 *2 rooms* ▭ *No credit cards* ⊮ *Breakfast.*

### GREATER LUCAYA

$$  ⬚ **Taino Beach Resort and Club.** One- and two-bedroom contemporary
RESORT  self-functioning suites, each with garden views, surrounding a large pool with a lazy river and waterslide, make this resort a haven for families. **Pros:** easy walk to Smith's Point for Fish Fry; on-site restaurant and swim-up bar; newly renovated room decor. **Cons:** no beachfront rooms; sister property Flamingo Bay Hotel with standard hotel rooms is worn and dated and not recommended. $ *Rooms from: $150* ⊠ *Jolly Roger Dr., Lucaya, Grand Bahama Island* ⊕ *www.tainobeach.com* 🛏 *156 rooms* ⊮ *No meals.*

$$  ⬚ **Viva Wyndham Fortuna Beach.** Popular with couples, families, and
ALL-INCLUSIVE  spring breakers, this secluded resort provides a casual, all-inclusive
FAMILY  getaway where one price covers meals, drinks, tips, nonmotorized water sports, and nightly entertainment. **Pros:** family-friendly; dining variety; secluded beach. **Cons:** sequestered feel; rooms are small; resort bustles. $ *Rooms from: $220* ⊠ *Churchill Dr. and Doubloon Rd., Lucaya, Grand Bahama Island* ☎ *242/373–4000, 800/996–3426 in U.S.* ⊕ *www.vivaresorts.com* 🛏 *276 rooms* ⊮ *All-inclusive.*

## GREATER GRAND BAHAMA

$  ⬚ **Bishop's Bonefish Resort.** Stay on the beach in a small settlement east of
RESORT  town, in simple, no frills rooms, without the hefty price tags and bustle of Lucaya. **Pros:** gorgeous beach; in touch with local community; near Lucayan National Park. **Cons:** far from other restaurants and shopping; spartan accommodations are dated. $ *Rooms from: $100* ⊠ *Grand Bahama Hwy., High Rock, Grand Bahama Island* ☎ *242/353–4515* ⊕ *www.bishopsresort.net* 🛏 *7 rooms.*

$$ RESORT FAMILY Fodor's Choice ★ **Old Bahama Bay Resort & Yacht Harbour.** Fishing enthusiasts, yachters, divers, and families can relax in relative seclusion at this West End, Guy Harvey Expedition Resort, comprised of beachfront and poolside suites decorated with island charm. **Pros:** top-shelf marina; close to local color; out island feel. **Cons:** limited dining choices; far from main airport, shopping and other restaurants; need a car to explore the rest of the island. [$] *Rooms from: $245* ✉ *West End, Grand Bahama Island* ☎ *242/350–6500, 888/800–8959* 🌐 *www.oldbahamabay.com* 🛏 *67 rooms, 6 suites* 🍴 *No meals.*

$ RENTAL **Paradise Cove.** Devoted snorkelers and peace-lovers will like this offbeat location (owned and operated by a local family), offering two two-bedroom stilted cottages overlooking the beach. **Pros:** on the beach; superb snorkeling; quiet in the off-hours. **Cons:** far from restaurant options, nightlife, and shopping; sometimes swarmed with bused-in visitors during the day; fee to rent snorkeling gear and kayaks. [$] *Rooms from: $175* ✉ *Warren J Levarity Hwy., 8 miles east of West End turnoff, West End, Grand Bahama Island* ☎ *242/349–2677* 🌐 *www.deadmansreef.com* 🛏 *2 cottages* 🍴 *No meals.*

## NIGHTLIFE

For evening and late-night entertainment, Port Lucaya is filled with restaurants and bars, and there's live entertainment in the middle square Thursday through Sunday. Other options include bonfire beach parties at Taino by the Sea, the Wednesday night fish fry at Smith's point, or taking a sunset cruise through the canals.

## LUCAYA

### BARS

**Bahama Mama Cruises.** The Bahama Mama hosts some of the most unique nightlife in Grand Bahama. In addition to the popular sunset "booze cruises" during the month of March for spring breakers, the Bahama Mama offers a surf-and-turf dinner with a colorful "native" show (a local term used to indicate entertainment with a traditional cultural flair); it's $83 for adults, $50 for children (ages 2–12), and both wine and Bahama Mama Rum Punch are unlimited all night. The Sunset Cruise and Show is $49 and for adults only. Reservations are essential. Both cruises are offered Wednesday and Friday. ✉ *Port Lucaya Market Place, Lucaya, Grand Bahama Island* ☎ *242/373–7863* 🌐 *www.superiorwatersports.com.*

**Club Neptune's Lounge and Nightclub.** Adorned with Tiffany lamps, couch seating, and a swanky bar, all circling the dance floor, this place is THE place to get your groove on at night. Hostesses and waitresses are decked out in bustier tops and add plenty of character, even though the place is not "R" rated. You can find respite from the rocking DJ tunes upstairs in the small lounge on your way to the restrooms. Karaoke is Wednesday, Ladies Night is Thursday, and happy hour is nightly from 7 to 9. ✉ *Port Lucaya Marketplace, Lucaya, Grand Bahama Island* ☎ *242/374–1221* 🌐 *www.neptunesportlucaya.com* ⏲ *Tues.–Sat. 7 pm–2 am* ⏲ *Closed Sun. and Mon.*

**Coral Reef Bar & Restaurant.** At the popular and long-standing time-share property Coral Beach Hotel, this spacious bar bustles with visitors and locals, too. Bartenders serve up tropical drinks and cold beer to a lively crowd with music in the background. Situated poolside and beach-front to Coral Beach, this spot is fun for lunch and a daytime drink, too. ⊠ *On the beach at Coral Rd., Royal Palm Way, Freeport, Grand Bahama Island* ☎ *242/373–2468* ⊕ *www.coralbeachonline.com.*

FAMILY **Count Basie Square.** The stage at Count Basie Square at the center of the Port Lucaya Marketplace becomes lively after dark, with live or piped-in island music and other performances (made all the more festive by surrounding popular watering holes: the Corner Bar, Sparky's, and Rum Runners). Entertainment includes stage dancers, limbo, and line dances for the crowd. ⊠ *Port Lucaya Marketplace, Sea Horse Rd., Grand Bahama Island* ☎ *242/373–8446* ⊕ *www. portlucayamarketplace.com.*

**Rum Runners.** This busy outdoor bar in Count Basie Square special-izes in keeping young barhoppers supplied with tropical frozen drinks and punches, piña coladas served in coconuts, cold beers, burgers, and conch fritters. ⊠ *Port Lucaya Marketplace, Lucaya, Grand Bahama Island* ☎ *242/373–7233.*

**Taino by the Sea Restaurant and Beach Bonfire.** This restaurant hosts one of the islands most popular tourist events—an authentic island party around a beach bonfire. The night includes a Bahamian dinner buf-fet with local specialties like coconut johnnycakes, conch and baked chicken with peas 'n' rice, all you can drink Bahama Mamas, Kamaka-zes, and fruit punch, games and activities, and a bonfire in the sand—all this in addition to the beautiful sunset on Taino Beach. Bonfires start at 6 pm every Tuesday, Thursday, and Sunday and every other Friday. Kids are welcome! Get tickets at the restaurant upon arrival, or ahead of time at your hotel. ⊠ *Taino Beach Resort, Jolly Roger Dr., Lucaya, Grand Bahama Island* ☎ *242/373–4677.*

## CASINOS

**Treasure Bay Casino.** This 17,000-square-foot, bright, tropically deco-rated adult playland has more than 320 slot machines and 33 game tables consisting of minibaccarat, Caribbean stud and three-card poker, craps, blackjack, and roulette. The casino is open from 9 am until 2 am Sunday through Thursday and 9 am to 4 am Saturday and Sunday (or at the manager's discretion); slot machines are open 24 hours on weekends. Bathing suits, bare feet, and children are not permitted. At press time, the casino was undergoing a change in man-agement and possible re-branding under a new name. ⊠ *Across the street from Port Lucaya Marketplace, Lucaya, Grand Bahama Island* ☎ *242/350–2000, 866/273–3860.*

These hand-woven souvenirs can be purchased at Port Lucaya Marketplace.

# THE ARTS

## THEATER

**Freeport Players' Guild.** A nonprofit repertory company, Freeport Players' Guild, produces American comedies, musicals, and dramas in the 300-seat Regency Theatre during its September–June season. ⊠ *West Sunrise Hwy., West of Ruby Swiss Restaurant, Freeport, Grand Bahama Island* ☎ *242/352–5533* ⊕ *www.regencytheatregbi.com.*

**Grand Bahama Performing Arts Society.** Started in 2008, the GBPAS is a charitable organization run entirely by volunteers. With a focus on music, they produce various performing arts events at venues all over the island, drawing from international and Bahamian talent. ⊠ *Freeport, Grand Bahama Island* ✍ *Email gbperform@gmail.com for event info.*

## SHOPPING AND SPAS

In the stores, shops, and boutiques in Port Lucaya Marketplace you can find duty-free goods costing up to 40% less than what you might pay back home. At the numerous perfume shops, fragrances are often sold at a sweet-smelling 25% below U.S. prices. Be sure to limit your haggling to the straw markets.

Shops in Lucaya are open Monday–Saturday from 9 or 10 to 6. Stores may stay open later in Port Lucaya. Straw markets, grocery stores, some boutiques, and drugstores are open on Sunday.

# FREEPORT

## ART

**The Glassblower Shop.** The Glassblower Shop features the work of Sidney Pratt, who demonstrates his craft in the shop's front window. ⊠ *Arcade at the International Bazaar, Freeport, Grand Bahama Island* ☏ *242/352–8585.*

**Treasure Nest.** In addition to displaying original artwork by well-known local watercolorist Sheldon Saint, this shop sells reproductions of his paintings on posters, postcards, and greeting cards. Treasure Nest also carries clothing, shoes, handbags, and accessories for ladies. ⊠ *Bullard's Shammah Plaza, West Atlantic Dr., Freeport, Grand Bahama Island* ☏ *242/352–1230* ⊕ *www.sheldonsaint. com* ⊗ *Closed Sun. and Mon.*

## PERFUMES

**Perfume Factory.** Here you can find a large variety of perfumes, lotions, and colognes by Fragrance of the Bahamas, all under $21. Its biggest-selling Pink Pearl cologne actually contains conch pearls, and Sand cologne for men has a little sterilized island sand in each bottle. You can also create your own scent and brand name and register it. ⊠ *Across from the International Bazaar, W. Sunrise Hwy. and Mall Dr., Freeport, Grand Bahama Island* ☏ *242/352–9391* ⊕ *www.perfumefactory.com.*

## SPAS

**La Spa.** This small but charming luxury day spa offers top-of-the-line treatments and specialty services such as gel manicures and pedicures, advanced facials and enzyme peels, microdermabrasion, reflexology, and hot stone massages. The technicians are knowledgeable and friendly, and you can relax with provided refreshments to the sounds of trickling water and meditative music. La Spa uses and sells retail brands such as Eminence Organics, OPI, and Essie. ⊠ *La Belle, West Atlantic Dr., Freeport, Grand Bahama Island* ☏ *242/351–3565* ⊗ *Tues.–Sat. 9:30–5:30* ⊗ *Closed Sun. and Mon.* ☞ *Services: facials, eye and lip treatments, waxing, brow and lash tinting, massage, reflexology, body polishes and scrubs, microdermabrasion, nail treatments.*

# LUCAYA

## ART

**Leo's Art Gallery.** This little shop showcases the expressive Haitian-style paintings and bahamian impressionism of famed local artist Leo Brown, each piece with its own story. ⊠ *Port Lucaya Marketplace, Lucaya, Grand Bahama Island* ☏ *242/373–1758.*

## CHINA AND CRYSTAL

**Island Galleria.** Here you can find china and crystal by Waterford, Wedgwood, Aynsley, Swarovski, and Coalport, as well as Lladró figurines. ⊠ *Port Lucaya Marketplace, Lucaya, Grand Bahama Island* ☎ *242/373–5274.*

## FASHION

**Animale.** This shop is known for the wild appeal of its fine ladies' clothing and jewelry. ⊠ *Port Lucaya Marketplace, Lucaya, Grand Bahama Island* ☎ *242/374–2066.*

**Bandolera.** Bandolera sells European-style women's fashions, bags, and jewelry for the young and flirty. ⊠ *Port Lucaya Marketplace, Lucaya, Grand Bahama Island* ☎ *242/373–7691.*

## JEWELRY AND WATCHES

**Colombian Emeralds.** Colombian Emeralds purveys a line of Colombia's famed gems plus other jewelry and crystal. ⊠ *Port Lucaya Marketplace, Lucaya, Grand Bahama Island* ☎ *242/373–8400* ⊕ *www. colombianemeralds.com.*

**Freeport Jewellers.** This jeweler caters to locals and visitors with watches, heavy gold and silver chains, larimar, and unique sea charms like conch shell jewelry. It also sells cigars, crystal, and Swiss brand watches. ⊠ *Port Lucaya Marketplace, Lucaya, Grand Bahama Island* ☎ *242/373–2776.*

## LEATHER GOODS

**Unusual Center.** Unusual Center carries eel-skin leather, peacock-feather goods, high-end bags, luggage, and jewelry. ⊠ *Port Lucaya Marketplace, Lucaya, Grand Bahama Island* ☎ *242/373–7333.*

## MARKETS AND ARCADES

**Port Lucaya Arts & Crafts Market.** This independent collection of small shops on the east side of the Port Lucaya Marketplace is comprised of individual Bahamian artisans, each selling unique arts and homemade handicrafts, many customized on request. Items for sale include seashell ornaments, candles, soaps, straw goods, dolls, and more. Don't miss seeing Mrs. Goldsmith's fun and fanciful paper hats, made from recycled cardboard. Stop by Ms. Ferguson's fruit stand for fresh coconut water. ⊠ *Port Lucaya Marketplace, Lucaya, Grand Bahama Island.*

**Port Lucaya Marketplace.** This marketplace has more than 100 boutiques and restaurants in 12 pastel-color buildings in a harborside locale, plus an extensive straw market and arts-and-crafts vendors. Live music and entertainment brings the center bandstand to life at night on the weekends. ⊠ *Sea Horse Rd., Lucaya, Grand Bahama Island* ☎ *242/373–8446* ☉ *Daily 9–6.*

**Port Lucaya Straw Markets.** Come to this collection of wooden stalls at the Port Lucaya complex's east and west ends to bargain for straw goods, T-shirts, and souvenirs. ⊠ *Sea Horse Rd., Lucaya, Grand Bahama Island.*

## MISCELLANEOUS

**Photo Specialist.** Photo Specialist carries photo and video equipment, memory cards, rechargeable batteries, cell phone chargers, and any other electronic accessory you may have forgotten to bring with you. ⊠ *Port Lucaya Marketplace, Lucaya, Grand Bahama Island* ☎ *242/373–7858.*

FAMILY **Sun & Sea Outfitters at UNEXSO.** This retail shop at UNEXSO offers the biggest shopping selection in Lucaya, including water sports equipment, toys, jewelry and accessories, brand name apparel and swimsuits, island-style housewares, and books by local authors. ⊠ *UNEXSO, next to Pelican Bay Hotel, Lucaya, Grand Bahama Island* ☎ *242/373–1244, 800/992–3483.*

### SPAS

**Senses Spa at Grand Lucayan.** This three-level spa offers a variety of luxury services including body wraps and scrubs, facials, various massage techniques, and manicures and pedicures, in addition to a full-service salon. On the top floor you will find state-of-the-art exercise equipment, including free weights and elliptical machines, a Spinning studio, and daily exercise classes for every interest. The fee is $25 for nonguests per day, which includes use of the locker room, lap pool, hot tubs, and sauna facilities. All spa services are by appointment, and Pevonia products are available for purchase. ⊠ *Grand Lucayan Beach & Golf Resort, Lighthouse Point, Lucaya, Grand Bahama Island* ☎ *242/350–5281* ⊕ *www.grandlucayan. com* ☞ *Hair salon, hot tub, sauna. Gym with: cardiovascular machines, free weights. Services: Swedish, hot stone, and couples massages, hydrobaths, sugar scrubs, body wraps and masques, manicures and pedicures. Classes: aerobics, Spinning, yoga, Pilates, Abs, step, jump rope, lap pool.*

# SPORTS AND THE OUTDOORS

## BIKING

By virtue of its flat terrain, broad avenues, and long straight stretches of highway, Grand Bahama is perfect for bicycling. There's a designated biking lane on Midshipman Road.

When biking, wear sunblock, carry a bottle of water, and keep left when riding on the road. Inexpensive bicycle rentals (about $20 a day plus deposit) are available from some resorts, and the Viva Wyndham Fortuna Beach allows guests free use of bicycles. In addition to its other ecotouring options, Grand Bahama Nature Tours offers 10-mile biking excursions that include a visit to a native settlement and Garden of the Groves for $79 per person.

## BOATING AND FISHING

### CHARTERS

Private boat charters for up to four people cost $100 per person and up for a half day. Bahamian law limits the catching of game fish to six each of dolphinfish, kingfish, tuna, and wahoo per vessel.

**Bonefish Folley & Sons.** Committed to giving you the best fishing experience possible, Bonefish Folley & Sons will take you deep-sea fishing or through the flats for bonefish and Permit. The late "Bonefish Folley" is a legend in these parts and delighted in taking people on bonefish tours for more than 60 years. He passed away in 2012 at the age of 91, but his two sons, Tommy and Carl, are continuing on in his footsteps. ⊠ *West End, Grand Bahama Island* ☎ *242/646–9504.*

### DID YOU KNOW?

Most dive operations in the Bahamas offer certification programs. If you are simply looking to try scuba on your vacation, opt for a resort course that provides enough instruction to get you into the water with equipment. If you find scuba is your new favorite adventure, get a full open-water certification. Initial certification in the Bahamas costs about $600. To save valuable vacation and bottom time, you can often begin your instruction at home or online.

**H2O Bonefishing.** Clients of this professional saltwater fly-fishing outfitter book well ahead of their arrival on island. H2O's fleet of flats boats and professional guides are available as part of a prearranged multiday package that typically includes three to six days of fishing. They cater exclusively to their anglers both on and off the water for the length of their stay, including waterfront lodging at one of Grand Bahama's finest hotels. Fly-fish year-round for trophy-size bonefish and permit as well as seasonal tarpon, or fish offshore for yellowfin tuna and mahimahi spring through summer. Light tackle and conventional fishing are also available. ✉ *Lucaya, Grand Bahama Island* ☎ *242/359–4958, 954/364–7590* ⊕ *www.h2obonefishing.com.*

**Reef Tours Ltd.** This company offers deep-sea fishing for four to six people on custom boats. Equipment and bait are provided free. All vessels are licensed, inspected, and insured. Trips run from 8:30 to 12:15 and from 1 to 4:45, weather permitting ($130 per angler, $60 per spectator). Full-day trips are also available, as are paddleboard and kayak rentals, bottom-fishing excursions, glass-bottom boat tours, snorkeling trips, sailing–snorkeling cruises, and guided Segway tours. Reservations are essential. ✉ *Port Lucaya Marketplace, Grand Bahama Island* ☎ *242/373–5880, 242/373–5891* ⊕ *www. bahamasvacationguide.com/reeftours.*

## MARINAS

**Old Bahama Bay Resort & Yacht Harbour.** The marina at Old Bahama Bay Resort has 72 slips to accommodate yachts up to 120 feet long and is only 55 nautical miles from Palm Beach, FL. Facilities include a customs and immigration office, fuel, showers, laundry, and electric, cable, and water hookups. The Dockside Bar and Grill serves dinner. ✉ *Old Bahama Bay Resort, West End, Grand Bahama Island* ☎ *242/350–6500, 954/763–6382* ⊕ *www.oldbahamabay.com.*

**Port Lucaya Marina.** Here you can find a broad range of water sports operators, free Wi-Fi, and a pump-out station; the marina has 106 slips for vessels no longer than 190 feet. Customs and immigrations officials are on-site full-time. ✉ *Port Lucaya Marketplace, Lucaya, Grand Bahama Island* ☎ *242/373–9090* ⊙ *Daily 8–6.*

## DAY CRUISES

**Reef Tours Ltd.** Family owned and operated since 1969, this company offers everything from guided Segway tours to wine and cheese evening sails aboard a catamaran. Options include fishing, snorkeling, paddleboarding, and glass bottom boat adventures. ☎ *242/373–5880, 242/373–5891, 242/373–5892* ⊕ *www.bahamasvacationguide.com/reeftours.*

FAMILY **Seaworld Explorer Semi-Submarine.** The Seaworld Explorer remains above sea level while you view the incredible marine life along Treasure Reef. Observe from your own window in the air-conditioned underwater observatory, 5 feet below the water's surface. Tours are 1½ hours, departing 3 times a day from Port Lucaya Marina. Adult tickets cost $49, Children 2–12 years are $29. Bus pick-up from all hotels is included. ✉ *Port Lucaya Marketplace, Lucaya, Grand Bahama Island* ☎ *242/373–7863* ⊕ *www.superiorwatersports.com.*

**Smiling Pat's Adventures.** Pat personally hosts all of her tours, which include historical tours through the West End and the beaches along eastern Grand Bahama, boat tours to Sandy Cay (aka Gilligan's Island) and the Abacos, and she'll even take you to the famous Wednesday night Fish Fry. She didn't get the name Smiling Pat for nothing! Her goal with each tour is to show tourists why "It's better in The Bahamas." ⊠ *Grand Bahama Island* ☎ *242/533–2946* ⊕ *www.smilingpat.com.*

**Superior Watersports.** In addition to their popular Bahama Mama cruises, Superior Watersports offers snorkeling trips and island tours. ⊠ *Port Lucaya Martketplace, Lucaya, Grand Bahama Island* ☎ *242/373–7863* ⊕ *www.superiorwatersports.com.*

## GOLF

**Fortune Hills Golf & Country Club.** Set in 17 acres of some of the highest ground in Freeport, Fortune Hills Golf & Country Club is a 3,453-yard, 9-hole, par-36 course—a Dick Wilson and Joe Lee design—with a restaurant, bar, and pro shop. This is the least expensive of the three golf courses open on Grand Bahama. The staff is friendly but both the course and the equipment are poorly maintained. ⊠ *E. Sunrise Hwy., Lucaya, Grand Bahama Island* ☎ *242/373–2222, 242/373–4500* ⊙ *Restaurant closed Mon.*

**Grand Lucayan Reef Course.** The Grand Lucayan Reef Course is a par-72, 6,930-yard links-style course. Designed by Robert Trent Jones Jr., it features lots of water (on 13 of the holes), wide fairways flanked by strategically placed bunkers, and a tricky dogleg left on the 18th. Although it is the most expensive and nicest of the three golf courses on the island, budget constraints have left it comparable to an average municipal course in the states. ⊠ *Grand Lucayan Beach & Golf Resort, Lucaya, Grand Bahama Island* ☎ *242/373–2002, 800/870–7148* ⊕ *www.grandlucayan.com* 🖃 *Resort guests $120, nonguests $130* ⊙ *Daily 10–6.*

**Ruby Golf Course.** This course reopened in 2008 with renovated landscaping but basically the same 18-hole, par-72 Jim Fazio design. It features a lot of sand traps and challenges on holes 7, 9, 10, and 18—especially playing from the blue tees. Hole 10 requires a tee shot onto a dogleg right fairway around a pond. Popular with locals, there is also a small restaurant-bar and pro shop. ⊠ *West Sunrise Hwy. and Wentworth Ave., Freeport, Grand Bahama Island* ☎ *242/352–1851* ⊕ *www.rubygolfcoursebahamas.com* ⊙ *Daily 7:30–5.*

## HORSEBACK RIDING

**Pinetree Stables.** Horseback rides are offered on eco-trails and the beach twice a day. All two-hour rides are accompanied by a guide—no previous riding experience is necessary, but riders must be at least eight years old. Plan to bring a waterproof camera because you will get wet! Reservations are essential and drinks are available for purchase. Pinetree Stables offers free shuttles from hotels and the harbour. ⊠ *Freeport, Grand Bahama Island* ☎ *242/373–3600, 305/433–4809* ⊕ *www.pinetree-stables.com.*

Pinetree Stables can take you horseback riding on the beach.

# KAYAKING

FAMILY **Calabash Eco Adventures.** This tour company (run by an island native) offers a variety of eco-excursions to areas all over Grand Bahama for sport, history, and education. Options include kayaking, snorkeling, birding, bicycling, and cavern diving into some of the island's famous inland blue holes. ☎ *242/727–1974* ⊕ *www.calabashecoadventures.com.*

Fodor'sChoice **Grand Bahama Nature Tours.** One of the most well-known eco-tour opera-
★ tors on the island for more than 20 years, Grand Bahama Nature tours is continually updating and adding to their wide variety of excursions, run mostly by Grand Bahama natives who are both entertaining and full of educational information. Popular adventures include snorkeling around Peterson Cay, kayaking through the mangroves at Lucayan National Park, Jeep safaris, off-road ATV tours, and birding through the Garden of the Groves. All tour prices include air-conditioned pick-ups and any necessary equipment. A zipline is in the works. ✉ *Grand Bahama Island* ☎ *242/373–2485, 866/440–4542* ⊕ *www. grandbahamanaturetours.com.*

# PARASAILING

**Paradise Watersports.** This company has parasailing towboats and offers flights for $70. ✉ *Island Seas Resort & Viva Wyndham Fortuna, Freeport, Grand Bahama Island* ☎ *242/373–4001, 954/237–6660 US* ⊕ *www.the-bahamas-watersports.com/paradisewatersports.*

## SCUBA DIVING

An extensive reef system runs along Little Bahama Bank's edge; sea gardens, caves, and colorful reefs rim the bank all the way from the West End to Freeport–Lucaya and beyond. The variety of dive sites suits everyone from the novice to the advanced diver, and ranges from 10 to 100-plus feet deep. Many dive operators offer a "discover" or "resort" course where first-timers can try out open-water scuba diving with a short pool course and an instructor at their side.

### SITES

**Ben's Cave and Blue Hole.** A horseshoe-shaped ledge overlooks this blue hole in 40 to 60 feet of water. Certified cavern divers can further explore the depths of the cave with guided groups from UNEXSO or Calabash Adventure Tours. Otherwise, interested visitors can view it above ground when visiting the Lucayan National Park. ⊠ *Lucayan National Park, Grand Bahama Hwy., Lucaya, Grand Bahama Island.*

**Pygmy Caves.** For moderately experienced divers, Pygmy Caves provides a formation of overgrown ledges that cut into the reef.

**Sea Hunt.** This shallow dive is named for the *Sea Hunt* television show, portions of which were filmed here.

**Shark Junction.** One of Grand Bahama Island's signature dive sites, made famous by the UNEXSO dive operation, Shark Junction is a 45-foot dive where 4- to 6-foot reef sharks hang out, along with moray eels, stingrays, nurse sharks, and grouper. UNEXSO provides orientation and a shark feeding with its dives here.

**Spid City.** Spid City has an aircraft wreck, dramatic coral formations, blue parrot fish, and an occasional shark. You'll dive about 40 to 60 feet down.

**Theo's Wreck.** For divers with some experience, Theo's Wreck, a 228-foot cement hauler, was sunk in 1982 in 100 feet of water and was the site for the 1993 Imax film *Flight of the Aquanaut.*

### OPERATORS

**Caribbean Divers.** This family-owned-and-operated dive shop offers personalized and uncrowded trips to coral reefs, wrecks, tunnels, and caverns, as well as shark dives. They also rent equipment and offer NAUI, PADI, and SSI instruction. A resort course allows you to use equipment in a pool and then in a closely supervised open dive. The professionally trained dive staff has more than 30 years of experience and the boat resides right on the channel leading out to the sea, so rides to most major sites are about 5–10 minutes. Lodging packages with Bell Channel Inn are available, in addition to snorkeling trips and private charters. ⊠ *Bell Channel Inn, King Rd., Lucaya, Grand Bahama Island* ☎ *242/373–9111, 242/373–9112* ⊕ *www.bellchannelinn.com* ☉ *Daily 8–5.*

**Stuart Cove.** The Bahamas' famed Stuart Cove opened their newest diving operation at Old Bahama Bay Resort in fall, 2012. They are best known for their two-tank, all-day shark-dive excursions to Tiger Beach, only one hour away by boat from the marina (they will equip you with all necessary equipment). In addition to diving with sharks, this shop also offers reef dives, wreck dives, night dives, and snorkeling trips to see wild dolphins. Boxed lunches are available from Old Bahama Bay's Tiki Hut café. ⊠ *Old Bahama Bay Resort, West End, Grand Bahama Island* ☎ *800/879–9832, 954/ 524–5755, 242/350–6500* ⊕ *www. stuartcove.com.*

Fodor'sChoice **UNEXSO** (*Underwater Explorers*
★ *Society*). This world-renowned scuba-diving facility with its own 17-foot dive pool, provides rental equipment, guides, and boats. A wide variety of dives is available for beginners and experienced divers, starting at $109 for a Discover

> **HERE'S WHERE**
>
> The last time locals spotted pirates on Grand Bahama Island was in 2005 when Johnny Depp and his crew were filming the second and third movies in the *Pirates of the Caribbean* series. They used a special device in Gold Rock Creek at one of the world's largest open-water filming tanks to give the illusion that the pirate ship was pitching and yawing. You can view the set near Gold Rock Beach.

Scuba Reef Diving resort course. Both the facility and its dive masters have been featured in international and American magazines for their work with sharks and cave exploration. UNEXSO and its sister company, the Dolphin Experience, are known for their work with Atlantic bottlenose dolphins. ⊠ *Next to Pelican Bay Hotel, Lucaya, Grand Bahama Island* ☎ *242/373–1244, 800/992–3483* ⊕ *www.unexso.com.*

**Viva Wyndham Fortuna Dive Shop.** Offering daily dives to various reefs and wrecks on a large boat seating 21 divers, this professional PADI-licensed shop also offers certifications for all levels (all equipment is included). With five instructors on staff, this shop also offers snorkeling trips and private boat tours. ⊠ *Viva Wyndham Fortuna Resort, Churchill and Doubloon Rd., Lucaya, Grand Bahama Island* ☎ *877/999–3223, 242/373–4000* ⊕ *www.wyndham.com.*

## SNORKELING

FAMILY **Paradise Cove.** Here you can snorkel right offshore at Deadman's Reef,
Fodor'sChoice a two-system reef with water ranging from extremely shallow to 35
★ feet deep. It's considered the island's best spot for snorkeling off the beach—you're likely to see lots of angelfish, barracudas, rays, and the occasional sea turtle. There is an access fee of $3 per person; snorkel equipment rentals are available for $15 a day. For those not wanting to swim to the reef, glass bottom kayaks are also available. Make a day of it at the beautiful beach and Red Bar, which offers burgers and fries, as well as Bahamian classics such as conch fritters and cracked conch. ⊠ *Deadman's Reef, 8 miles east of West End turnoff, Grand Bahama Island* ☎ *242/349–2677* ⊕ *www.deadmansreef.com.*

**Paradise Watersports.** This company offers a 90-minute reef snorkeling cruise for $40. They also provide Waverunner tours, glassbottom boat rides, fishing, and parasailing. ⊠ *Island Seas Resort & Viva Wyndham Fortuna, Freeport, Grand Bahama Island* ☎ *242/373–4001, 954/237–6660* ⊕ *www.the-bahamas-watersports.com/paradisewatersports.*

FAMILY **Pat & Diane Tours.** This company offers two snorkel trip options aboard a fun-boat catamaran with a 30-foot rock-climbing wall and slide into the water. One tour goes to the vibrant 1-mile-long Rainbow Reef; the other is a longer tour to a private beach and includes lunch. Free pickup and return to all hotels is included. ⊠ *Port Lucaya Marketplace, Port Lucayan Marina, Lucaya, Grand Bahama Island* ☏ *242/373–8681, 888/439–3959, 954/323–1975* ⊕ *www.snorkelingbahamas.com.*

## TENNIS

**Grand Lucayan Beach & Golf Resort.** The resort boasts four lighted courts: grass, rebound, French red clay, and deco-turf. Wimbledon-white tennis attire is required on the grass court. Racquet rental and stringing, lessons, and clinics are available. ⊠ *Grand Lucayan, Lucaya, Grand Bahama Island* ☏ *242/373–1333, 855/582–2926* ⊕ *www.grandlucayan. com* ☞ *$20–$40 per hr* ⊙ *Daily 9–5.*

## TOURS

**H.Forbes Charter & Tours.** This full-service tour operator can arrange a variety of tours for you, including van tours of the island or other experiences like sunset cruises or trips in Seaworld Explorer, including transportation from your resort. ⊠ *Grand Bahama Island* ☏ *242/352–9311, 301/637–6002* ⊕ *www.forbescharter.com.*

## WATER SPORTS

**Ocean Motion Watersports.** This is the largest water-sports operator on Grand Bahama and now operates all watersports at the Grand Lucayan resort. Located next to Billy Joe's, they offer everything from a water trampoline and banana boat rides to guided Waverunner tours through the canals and to Peterson Cay. For $70, you can parasail high above the beach and the water—kids and adults alike. In addition, Ocean Motion offers kayaks, Hobie Cat sailboats, waterskiing, and windsurfing instruction. If you'd rather keep it simple, rent snorkel equipment for the day ($40) and regular ferries will take you to Rainbow Reef and back so you get plenty of beach time, too. ⊠ *Lucayan Beach, Lucaya, Grand Bahama Island* ☏ *242/373–2139, 242/373–9603* ⊕ *www. oceanmotionbahamas.com* ⊙ *Daily 9–6.*

4

# THE ABACOS

# WELCOME TO THE ABACOS

## TOP REASONS TO GO

★ **Bonefish the Marls:** One of the most spectacular bonefishing flats anywhere, the Marls is an endless maze of lush mangrove creeks, hidden bays, and sandy cays. Hire a professional guide to show you the best spots.

★ **Cay-hop:** Rent a boat and spend a day (or more) skipping among 150 cays. Settle onto your own private strip of beach and enjoy.

★ **Beach bash:** When the Gully Roosters play on Green Turtle Cay, the island rocks. Stop in at Miss Emily's Blue Bee Bar first for a mind-altering rum, pineapple juice, and apricot brandy Goombay Smash; it's where the popular drink was born. On Great Guana Cay, Nippers' Sunday pig roast is the best beach party of the year—and it happens every week.

★ **Swim with the fishies:** With clear shallow waters and a series of colorful coral reefs extending for miles, the Abacos provide both the novice and the experienced underwater explorer plenty of visual stimulation.

## GETTING ORIENTED

The Abacos, 200 miles east of Palm Beach, Florida, are the northernmost chain of cays in the Bahamas. Covering 120 miles, this mini-archipelago offers both historic settlements and uninhabited islands. Great Abaco is the main island, the chain's largest and its most populated. Here you'll find rugged stretches of white limestone bluffs, miles of kelp-strewn beaches devoid of footprints, landlocked lakes, pine forests where wild horses and boar roam, and the Bahamas' third-largest community: the thriving commercial center of Marsh Harbour. Up north on Little Abaco, a smaller cay connected by bridge, tourism is less prominent and locals live as they have for the last hundred years. Running parallel 5 miles off the east coast of these islands are the Abaco Cays, including Green Turtle, Great Guana, Man-O-War, and Elbow, all of which offer full services for boaters and just the right sprinkling of small resorts and enchanting settlements. The majority of the other 146 cays are uninhabited.

**1 Great Abaco Island.** The Abacos' commercial center still boasts fishing and farming communities, blue holes, caves, wild parrots, and pine forests. Marsh Harbour, the island's main hub, has great restaurants and bustling nightlife. Treasure Cay has a large marina, the only public golf course, and one of the best beaches in the world. Other communities are quiet and tucked away, each with its own personality that makes them worthy day trips.

**2 Elbow Cay.** Home of the famous candy cane–striped Hope Town Lighthouse, this cay balances a historic getaway with modern conveniences. Hope Town, the main settlement, is known for neat clapboard cottages painted in pastel hues.

**3 Man-O-War Cay.** Proud of its stance as a dry island (no liquor sold), this community holds fast to its history. It's famous for its boatbuilding, which can still be seen here daily on the waterfront, where men work by hand.

**4 Great Guana Cay.** A real getaway island, here you'll find modern luxuries or empty beaches. Guana also has Nippers, a restaurant–bar with the best party scene in Abaco.

4

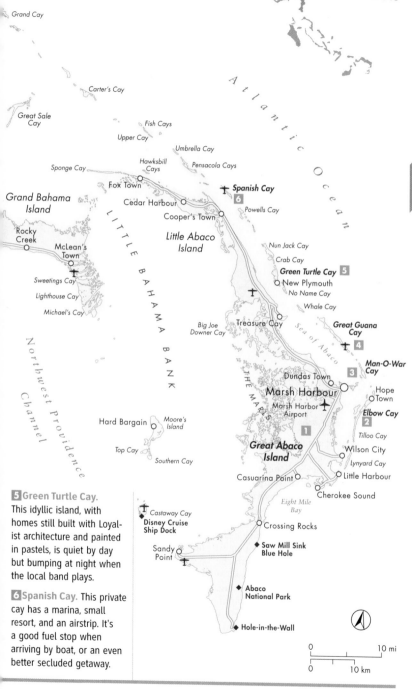

Grand Cay

*Atlantic Ocean*

Carter's Cay

Great Sale Cay

Fish Cays

Upper Cay

Umbrella Cay

Sponge Cay

Hawksbill Cays

Pensacola Cays

Fox Town

Grand Bahama Island

Cedar Harbour

Cooper's Town

Little Abaco Island

Powells Cay

✝ *Spanish Cay*
6

Rocky Creek

McLean's Town

Sweetings Cay

Lighthouse Cay

Michael's Cay

*LITTLE BAHAMA BANK*

Nun Jack Cay

Crab Cay

*Green Turtle Cay* 5

New Plymouth

No Name Cay

Whale Cay

*Northwest Providence Channel*

Big Joe Downer Cay

Treasure Cay

*Sea of Abaco*

*Great Guana Cay*
4

*Man-O-War Cay*
3

Hard Bargain

Moore's Island

Top Cay

Southern Cay

*THE MARLS*

Dundas Town

**Marsh Harbour**

Marsh Harbor Airport

1

*Great Abaco Island*

Hope Town

*Elbow Cay*
2

Tilloo Cay

Wilson City

Lynyard Cay

Casuarina Point

Little Harbour

Cherokee Sound

*Eight Mile Bay*

✝ Castaway Cay
◆ **Disney Cruise Ship Dock**

Crossing Rocks

Sandy Point

◆ **Saw Mill Sink Blue Hole**

◆ **Abaco National Park**

◆ **Hole-in-the-Wall**

0      10 mi

0      10 km

5 **Green Turtle Cay.**
This idyllic island, with homes still built with Loyalist architecture and painted in pastels, is quiet by day but bumping at night when the local band plays.

6 **Spanish Cay.** This private cay has a marina, small resort, and an airstrip. It's a good fuel stop when arriving by boat, or an even better secluded getaway.

# ABACO NATIONAL PARK

The Abaco National Park was established in 1994 as a sanctuary for the endangered Abaco parrot, of which there are fewer than 3,000. Many other birds call the park home, including the Bahama yellowthroat and pine warbler.

A 15-mile dirt track passes through the 20,500 protected acres, ending at the Hole-in-the-Wall lighthouse, a starkly beautiful and desolate location overlooking the ocean. The drive from the paved highway all the way to the lighthouse takes about 1½ hours, and can only be done in a 4X4 vehicle. The lighthouse is not technically open to visitors, but people still do climb the rickety stairs to the top where views of the island and the sea are mesmerizing. ⊠ *South end of Great Abaco Island, before you make the final turn on the main road leading to Sandy Point* ☎ *242/367–3067.*

**BEST TIME TO GO**

Berries ripen in fall and spring, and the parrots become active. The best time to spot the birds is early morning, when they move out of the forest to feed. Temperatures then are also ideal, in the 70s and 80s. The annual bird counts in North and South Abaco held at the beginning of each year are a good opportunity to work with other bird-watchers to gather information on the parrots, which is sent to the Audobon Society.

## BEST WAYS TO EXPLORE

**By Car on Your Own.** Take the 15-mile, 1½-hour drive along a dirt trail out to the lighthouse. This is the only part of the park you can drive. This lighthouse has spectacular views of the coast. Take a packed lunch and have a picnic on a ledge overlooking the ocean.

**By Guided Tour.** For the best experience, arrange a guided tour with the tourist office. A knowledgeable guide will walk or drive you through the park, pointing out plant and animal species. If you're an early riser, join a bird-watching tour to find the endangered Abaco parrot, as well as other avian beauties that reside here. Walking the park alone is not recommended, as poisonous wood saplings are a problem if you don't know how to identify them.

*Note: Friends of the Environment (☎ 242/367–2721) is a local education organization that offers more information on the park and the parrots.*

## FUN FACT

The park's pine forest is prone to summer lightning fires, but the Abaco pine is extremely resistant and actually depends on the fires to remove dense underbrush that would otherwise smother it. The Abaco parrots nest in holes in the limestone floor to escape the flames. Unfortunately, this makes them vulnerable to feral cats and raccoons that threaten their population.

## FOWL CAY NATIONAL RESERVE

This quarter-mile reef located on the ocean side of Fowl Cay is a great snorkeling and dive spot. It's well known among divers for its tunnels and wide variety of fish. On the opposite side of Fowl Cay is a small sand spit, which makes a great spot to reconvene for a sun-soaked picnic.

## PELICAN CAYS LAND AND SEA PARK

This 2,000-acre land and marine park is protected and maintained by the Bahamas National Trust. The park's preserved reef is only 25 feet under water, making it an easy snorkel excursion. It's also a great dive site, as the variety of life here is astounding. Nearby is an incredibly soft beach, great for a post-swim picnic.

4

*(above) Abaco Parrot (lower left) Hole-in-the-Wall Lighthouse*

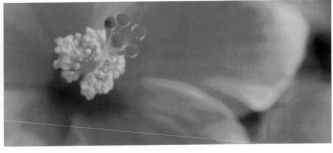

Updated
by Jessica
Robertson

The attitude of the Abacos might best be expressed by the sign posted in the window of Vernon's Grocery in Hope Town: "If you're looking for Wal-Mart—it's 200 miles to the right." In other words, the residents of this chain of more than 100 islands know that there's another world out there, but don't necessarily care to abandon theirs, which is a little more traditional, slow-paced, and out of the way than most alternatives.

Here you'll feel content in an uncrowded environment, yet still have access to whatever level of accommodations and services you desire. Ecotourism is popular, and aficionados have revitalized exploration of Abacos' Caribbean pine forests, which are home to wild boar, wild horses, the rare Abaco parrot, and myriad other bird and plant life. Hiking and biking through these forests and along abandoned beaches at the forest's edges are popular activities. Sea kayaking in pristine protected areas also provides a rewarding sense of adventure, and more conventional activities such as golf, tennis, and beach volleyball are available, too. But if you don't feel like doing anything at all, that's also a highly rated activity.

Of course, this is the Bahamas, so you shouldn't neglect activities happening in one of its most magnificent assets—the water. Snorkeling and diving have long been staple activities for visitors. Abaconians are proud of their marine environment and have worked with the government to protect some of the more vibrant reefs. The islands' calm, naturally protected waters, long admired for their beauty, have also helped the area become the Bahamas' sailing capital. Man-O-War Cay remains the Bahamas' boatbuilding center; its residents turn out traditionally crafted wood dinghies as well as high-tech fiberglass craft. The Abacos play host annually to internationally famous regattas and to a half dozen game-fish tournaments.

From island-long stretches to strips as short as your boat, with powder-white to warm-cream sand, the roar of the surf or the silence of a slow rising tide, the Abacos have a beach suited to everyone's liking. And most likely, you'll find a secluded spot to call your own.

Oceanside beaches are long expanses of white powder that change their form throughout the year depending on the surge brought in by weather. Beaches sheltered from strong winds, on the lee sides of islands, are small, narrow, and stable. Trees are taller on the lee sides of the islands and provide shaded areas for picnics. On the outer cays beaches make popular surf spots and snorkel sites, with the barrier reef running along the shore. Most Abaco beaches are secluded, but if you're looking for a beach party, head to Great Guana Cay for the Sunday pig roast.

4

# PLANNING

## WHEN TO GO

June, July, and early August are the best months for sailing, boating, and swimming, precisely why the most popular regatta and fishing tournaments are held during this time. Afternoon thunderstorms are common but usually clear quickly. Temperatures often reach the 90s.

December through May is a pleasant time to visit, with temperatures in the 70s and 80s, though sometimes dropping into the 50s at night when cold fronts blow through. Fishing, particularly deep-sea fishing, is good during this time of year.

In September and October, typically the peak of hurricane season, visitors drop to a trickle and many hotels and restaurants shut down for two weeks to two months. If you're willing to take a chance on getting hit by a storm, this can still be a great time to explore, with discounts of as much as 50% at the hotels that remain open.

### TOP FESTIVALS

#### WINTER

**Junkanoo.** Many Abaco communities have their own Junkanoo celebrations; Hope Town has a New Year's Eve children's rushout for locals and visitors to join in. Parades in the Abacos are much smaller and more intimate than in Nassau, and far less competitive.

#### SPRING

**Heritage Day.** Hope Town's annual Heritage Day in March celebrates the Loyalist settlement's history with traditional songs, speeches and exhibits on historical topics, and a boat parade.

**Island Roots Festival.** The Island Roots Festival celebrates Bahamian traditions with an outdoor party on tiny Green Turtle Cay the first weekend in May.

#### SUMMER

**Jankanoo Summer Festival.** Junkanoo Summer Festival—traditional summertime parties with dance troupes and musical groups—take place throughout summer in Marsh Harbour.

**Regatta Time.** Regatta Time in Abaco, the first week of July, stretches over several islands, with races and plenty of onshore parties.

**Treasure Cay Billfish Championship.** There are big cash prizes that increase with the number of registered boats at the Treasure Cay Billfish Championship in June. The final day includes a Lionfish Tournament designed to help save the Bahamas indigenous marine life from this relatively new predator.

## GETTING HERE AND AROUND

### AIR TRAVEL

Most flights land at the international airports in **Marsh Harbour (MHH)** or **Treasure Cay (TCB)**. Taxis wait at the main airports, and the fare to most resorts is between $15 and $30 for the first two passengers and $3 for each additional person. Cab fare between Marsh Harbour and Treasure Cay or the ferry dock is $85.

Contacts **Marsh Harbour Airport** ☎ 242/367–5500. **Treasure Cay Airport** ☎ 242/367–3067.

### BOAT AND FERRY TRAVEL

The *Legacy* mail boat leaves Potter's Cay, Nassau on Tuesday for Marsh Harbour and Green Turtle Cay, returning to Nassau on Thursday. Each one-way journey takes about 10 hours and costs $60 per person. The *Sealink* leaves Nassau on Friday and Sunday mornings for Sandy Point, at the southern tip of Great Abaco, and returns to Nassau on Fridays and Sundays. For details, call the **Dockmaster's Office.**

A good system of public ferries allows you to reach even the most remote cays. (⇨ *See Getting Here and Around within the island sections.*)

If you don't want to be bound by the somewhat limited ferry schedule, rent a small boat. The best selections are at Marsh Harbour, Treasure Cay, Hope Town, and Green Turtle Cay.

Contacts **Dockmaster's Office** ☎ 242/393–1064.

### CAR TRAVEL

On Great Abaco, renting a car is the best option if you plan on exploring outside Marsh Harbour or Treasure Cay. Rentals start at $70 a day, and gasoline costs about $6 per gallon. Cars are not necessary on most of the smaller cays in the Abacos; in fact, rental cars aren't even available in most locations.

Contacts **A & P Rentals** ⊠ *Marsh Harbour* ☎ *242/367–2655.* **Police** ☎ *911, 242/352–8280, 242/373–4112* ⊕ *www.royalbahamaspolice.org.* **Bargain Car Rentals** ⊠ *Marsh Harbour, Great Abaco Island* ☎ *242/367–0500.* **Rental Wheels of Abaco** ⊠ *Marsh Harbour* ☎ *242/367–4643* ⊕ *www.rentalwheels.com.*

### GOLF CART TRAVEL

Golf carts are the vehicle of choice on the majority of the smaller cays, including Elbow Cay, Green Turtle Cay, Great Guana Cay, and Man-O-War Cay. Rates are $40 to $50 per day, or $245 per week. Reservations are essential from April to July.

# GREAT ITINERARIES

### IF YOU HAVE 3 DAYS

Make your base in **Marsh Harbour**, the largest settlement in the Abacos, and where you'll most likely fly in. Spend the first day exploring the city or a nearby beach, then have a leisurely dinner at one of the local restaurants overlooking the busy harbor. If you arrive on a weekend you can probably find a bar with live island music. On Day 2, get up early and take the 20-minute ferry to **Hope Town**, the **Elbow Cay** settlement often considered the most lovely in the Abacos. Here you can rent a boat and take a snorkel trip out to the reefs, take a historical walk, kayak, stroll the beach, or rent a golf cart and explore outside the main settlement. Day 3 brings a choice: for another dose of Loyalist history, take the ferry again, this time to **Man-O-War Cay**, the boatbuilding capital of the region; or stay put and book a diving or fishing trip out of one of the Marsh Harbour marinas.

### IF YOU HAVE 5 DAYS

On Day 4, drive to **Treasure Cay** and hit the links, where the 18-hole course is considered one of the finest in the Bahamas and Caribbean. Afterward, catch the ferry to **Green Turtle Cay**, your base for the next two days. Stroll through **New Plymouth,** wandering through the sculpture garden and the **Albert Lowe Museum**. After lunch, spend the afternoon at a beach, then dress up for an elegant dinner at one of the two fine resorts on **White Sound**. On your last day, rent a small boat and visit some of the uninhabited nearby cays, where the snorkeling and deserted white-sand beaches are sublime.

### IF YOU HAVE 7 DAYS

On Day 6, head back to Marsh Harbour and take a ferry to **Great Guana Cay**, which has some of the most gorgeous beaches in the Abacos and one of the best party-scene restaurants, **Nippers**. On your last day, back in Marsh Harbour, rent a car and explore the southern reaches of **Great Abaco Island**, perhaps searching for the endangered Bahama parrot at the **Bahamas National Trust Sanctuary**, or checking out the bronze sculptures at **Pete Johnston's Foundry** in **Little Harbour**.

If all that sounds like too much work, consider experiencing life like a local: bring some books, sunblock, and a few swimsuits; rent a cottage, a dinghy, and a golf cart, perhaps on **Elbow Cay** or **Great Guana Cay**; and learn to practice the fine art of relaxation.

Contacts **Blue Marlin Rentals** ✉ *Treasure Cay* ☎ *242/365–8687*. **D & P Rentals** ✉ *Green Turtle Cay* ☎ *242/365–4655*. **Hope Town Cart Rentals** ✉ *Hope Town* ☎ *242/366–0064* ⊕ *www.hopetowncartrentals.com*. **Island Cart Rentals** ✉ *Hope Town* ☎ *242/366–0448* ⊕ *www.islandcartrentals.com*. **KoolKart Rentals** ✉ *Green Turtle Cay, Great Abaco Island* ☎ *242/356–4176* ⊕ *www.koolkartrentals.com*. **Man-O-War Marina** ✉ *Man-O-War Cay* ☎ *242/365–6008*. **T&N Cart Rentals** ✉ *Hope Town* ☎ *242/366–0069*.

**Island Roadrunner** ✉ *Green Turtle Cay* ☎ *242/365–4160*.

**Seaside Carts** ✉ *Green Turtle Cay* ☎ *242/365–4147*.

### TAXI TRAVEL

Taxi service is available on Great Abaco in Marsh Harbour and Treasure Cay. Hotels will arrange for taxis to take you on short trips and to the airport. Fares are generally $1.50 per mile. A 15% tip is customary.

## ESSENTIALS

### BANKS

Banks are generally open Monday–Thursday 9:30–3 and Friday until 4:30. They are sometimes closed on Wednesday. ATMs are available in Marsh Harbour at all banks.

### EMERGENCIES

Contacts **Green Turtle Cay Government Clinic** ☎ *242/365–4028.* **Hope Town Government Clinic** ☎ *242/366–0108.* **Marsh Harbour Government Clinic** ☎ *242/367–2510.* **Police or Fire Emergencies** ☎ *919.*

### HOTELS

Intimate hotels, cottage-style resorts, and rental homes are the rule in the Abacos. There are a few full-scale resorts in Marsh Harbour, Treasure Cay, Green Turtle Cay, and Hope Town—with multiple restaurants, bars, pools, and activities—but most accommodations are more homey. What you might give up in modern amenities you'll gain in privacy and beauty. Many hotels have water views, and with a cottage or private house you may even get your own stretch of beach. Air-conditioning is a standard feature, and more places are adding luxuries like satellite TV and wireless Internet. Small and remote doesn't equate with inexpensive, however; it's difficult to find lodging for less than $100 a night, and not uncommon to pay more than $300 a night for beachside accommodations with all the conveniences. Still, the Abacos remains affordable when compared to other islands.

### RESTAURANTS

Fish, conch, land crabs, and rock lobster—called crawfish by the locals—have long been the bedrock of local cuisine. Although a few menus, mostly in upscale resorts, feature dishes with international influences, most restaurants in the Abacos still serve simple Bahamian fare, with a few nods to American tastes. There are some fancier restaurants in Marsh Harbour, Treasure Cay, and Hope Town, but most restaurants are relaxed about attire and reasonably priced. Some offer live music, and shape the nightlife scene on weekends.

### HOTEL AND RESTAURANT PRICES

Restaurant prices are based on the median main course price at dinner, excluding gratuity, typically 15%, which is often automatically added to the bill. Hotel prices are for two people in a standard double room in high season, excluding service and 6%–12% tax.

### SHIPPING

**GPS Bahamas.** Renting a beach house for a week or longer? Maybe you can't take everything with you, but GPS Bahamas has air-freight service for everything from perishable foods to electronics and computers. It beats the mail boat. It also provides catalog shopping and delivery, so if you're tired of the CDs and DVDs you have, just order some new ones. ☎ *242/367–0400, 954/689–6761* ⊕ *www.gpsbahamas.com.*

**VISITOR INFORMATION**

Contacts **Abaco Tourist Office & Information Center** ⊠ *Harbor Place Bldg., Queen Elizabeth Dr., Great Abaco Island* ☎ *242/367–3067* ⊕ *www.bahamas.com.*

# GREAT ABACO ISLAND

If arriving by air, your trip will most likely begin on Great Abaco, the main island. It's bordered on its eastern side by a chain of cays that extend from the north to about midway down the island, and on the western side by a fishing flat called the Marls, a shallow-water area of mangrove creeks and islands. Great Abaco was once logged for its pine trees, and traveling by car allows you to access many old logging trails that will lead you to secluded beaches along the coast. The island is home to wild horses, cows, and boars, and the endangered Abaco parrots, who make their homes in the pine forests.

**Marsh Harbour** is the main hub of activity on the island, and where most visitors stay. Heading north on the S.C. Bootle Highway will take you to **Treasure Cay** peninsula, a resort development. There's another, smaller, airport here. Farther north are **Cooper's Town** and the small communities of **Little Abaco**, which don't provide much for visitors besides nearly total seclusion. South of Marsh Harbour off the Ernest Dean Highway are artists' retreat **Little Harbour** and **Cherokee Sound** and **Sandy Point**, both small fishing communities.

## GETTING HERE AND AROUND

To travel around Great Abaco you'll need a vehicle. Renting a car is the most convenient and economical option. If you plan on staying in one town or only making short, one-time, or one-way trips you can hire a taxi. Taxis will take you all over the island, but the farther you travel from Marsh Harbour, the more extreme rates get, sometimes in excess of a hundred dollars. The closest settlement worth a visit out of Marsh Harbour is Little Harbour, about 30 minutes away.

Golf carts are used locally in Treasure Cay and Cherokee Sound. From Marsh Harbour you can boat to Little Harbour and Cherokee Sound to the south and Treasure Cay in the north.

# MARSH HARBOUR

Most visitors to the Abacos make their first stop in Marsh Harbour, the Bahamas' third-largest city and the Abacos' commercial center. Besides having the Abacos' largest international airport, it offers what boaters consider to be one of the easiest harbors to enter. It has several full-service marinas, including the 190-slip Boat Harbour Marina and the 80-slip Conch Inn Marina.

Marsh Harbour has a more diverse variety of restaurants, shops, and grocery items than other communities. Stock up on groceries and supplies on the way to other settlements or islands. The downtown

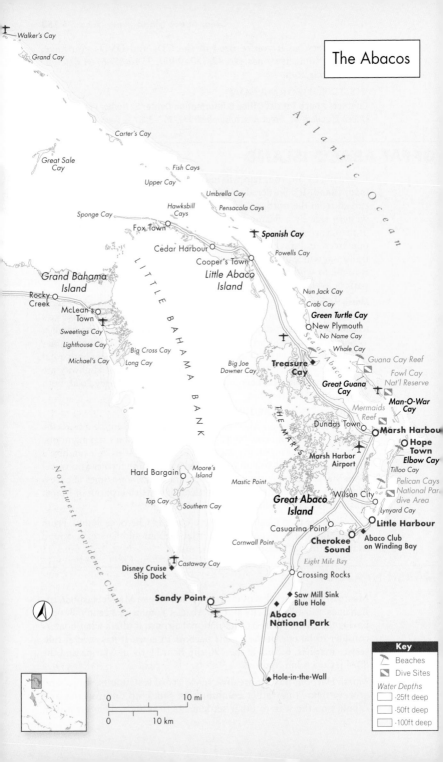

# The Abacos

Walker's Cay

Grand Cay

Carter's Cay

Great Sale Cay

Fish Cays

Upper Cay

Umbrella Cay

Hawksbill Cays

Pensacola Cays

Sponge Cay

Fox Town

Cedar Harbour

*Spanish Cay*

Cooper's Town

Powells Cay

*Little Abaco Island*

*Grand Bahama Island*

Rocky Creek

McLean's Town

Sweetings Cay

Lighthouse Cay

Michael's Cay

Big Cross Cay

Long Cay

*LITTLE BAHAMA BANK*

Nun Jack Cay

Crab Cay

*Green Turtle Cay*

New Plymouth

No Name Cay

Whale Cay

*Sea of Abaco*

Guana Cay Reef

Big Joe Downer Cay

**Treasure Cay**

*Great Guana Cay*

*Fowl Cay Nat'l Reserve*

**Man-O-War Cay**

*Mermaids Reef*

Dundas Town

**Marsh Harbour**

**Hope Town**

*Elbow Cay*

Marsh Harbor Airport

Tilloo Cay

Hard Bargain

Moore's Island

*Mastic Point*

Wilson City

*Pelican Cays National Park dive area*

*Great Abaco Island*

Top Cay

Southern Cay

Lynyard Cay

Casuarina Point

**Little Harbour**

Cornwall Point

**Cherokee Sound**

Abaco Club on Winding Bay

*Eight Mile Bay*

Disney Cruise Ship Dock

Castaway Cay

Crossing Rocks

**Sandy Point**

Saw Mill Sink Blue Hole

**Abaco National Park**

Hole-in-the-Wall

*Atlantic Ocean*

*THE MARLS*

*Northwest Providence Channel*

| Key | |
|---|---|
| | Beaches |
| | Dive Sites |
| *Water Depths* | |
| | -25ft deep |
| | -50ft deep |
| | -100ft deep |

| 0 | 10 mi |
|---|---|
| 0 | 10 km |

area has several supermarkets, as well as a few department and hardware stores. If you need cash, this is the place to get it; banks here are open every day and have ATMs, neither of which you will find on the smaller, more remote settlements or cays.

## WHERE TO EAT

$$$

BAHAMIAN

Fodor'sChoice

★

✕ **Angler's Restaurant.** Dine on roasted rack of lamb with garlic mashed potatoes or a broiled lobster tail while overlooking gleaming rows of yachts moored in the Boat Harbour Marina at the Abaco Beach Resort. White tablecloths with fresh orchid arrangements and sea-blue napkins folded like seashells create an experience a step up from typical island dining. It's not uncommon to see guests dressed in sports coats and cocktail dresses fresh off a stunning megayacht alongside other guests in shorts and T-shirts with kids in tow. Everyone can enjoy fresh grilled catch of the day—don't pass up the grilled wahoo—seafood pastas, Bahamian chicken, or charbroiled steaks. For dessert try the calorie-drenched guava duff. $ *Average main: $33* ⊠ *Abaco Beach Resort, off Bay St., Marsh Harbour, Great Abaco Island* ☎ *242/367–2158, 800/468–4799* ⊕ *www.abacoresort.com.*

$$

BAHAMIAN

✕ **Curly Tails Restaurant and Bar.** Enjoy kick-back harborside dining for lunch and dinner at the Conch Inn Hotel and Marina. Savor your meal outside on the open-air deck. At lunch, salads, burgers, cracked conch, and grouper fillets go great with a cold Kalik. Try dinner in the air-conditioned dining room. Chicken stuffed with local johnnycake or blackened grouper, snapper, mahimahi, or tuna are traditional favorites. If you're into sunsets, don't miss the daily happy hour. Sample a frozen Tail Curler or a Curlytini to go with your conch fritters. There's also live music every Thursday and Saturday night. $ *Average main: $29* ⊠ *Conch Inn Hotel and Marina, Bay St., Marsh Harbour, Great Abaco Island* ☎ *242/367–4444* ⊕ *www.abacocurlytails. com* ☉ *Closed Tues.*

$

BAHAMIAN

✕ **Jamie's Place.** There's nothing fancy about this clean, bright, diner-style eatery, but the welcome is warm, the Bahamanian dishes are well executed, and the prices are right, with most meals clocking in under $15. Choose fried chicken, cracked conch, or fresh-caught dolphin (also called mahimahi), with a side of mashed or roasted potatoes, peas 'n' rice, macaroni and cheese, or coleslaw. Jamie's is also an ice-cream parlor, with a dozen flavors. Locals love this place, and it has stayed one of Great Abaco Island's best-kept secrets. $ *Average main: $14* ⊠ *Queen Elizabeth Dr. Marsh Harbour, Great Abaco Island* ☎ *242/367–2880.*

$$

BAHAMIAN

✕ **Jib Room.** Expect casual lunches of hot wings, conch burgers, fish nuggets, and steak wraps in this harbor-view restaurant and bar, located inside the Marsh Harbour Marina. Dinner is served twice a week, and these "barbecue nights" are especially popular; on Wednesday it's baby

Mangoes waterfront restaurant sits directly on Marsh Harbour.

back ribs, fish, chicken, potato salad, slaw, and baked beans. On Saturday it's grilled steak, featuring New York strip, with fish and chicken as options along with baked potatoes and salad. If you're dying for a steak after a steady fish diet, these are the best in the Abacos. ✉ *Pelican Shores* ☎ *242/367–2700* 🌐 *www.jibroom.com* ✍ *Reservations essential* 🕒 *Closed Sun.–Tues. No dinner Thurs. and Fri.*

$ BAHAMIAN 🍴 **Junovia's Diner.** A steady stream of locals flow in and out of this unassuming diner to either dine in or grab breakfast or lunch on the run. Chicken souse is usually on the menu board. Oftentimes it's also a good place to grab boil' or stew' fish served up with a chunk of fresh-baked johnnycake and a bowl of steaming yellow grits—this is the way locals do breakfast. Not ready for fish for breakfast? Their western omelet is stuffed and delicious. [$] *Average main: $14* ✉ *Don Mackay Blvd., Marsh Harbour, Great Abaco Island* ☎ *242/367–1271* 🕒 *Mon.–Sat., 7 am–8 pm.*

$$ SEAFOOD 🍴 **Mangoes.** An open-air deck makes Mangoes a great place for waterside dining. Enjoy a traditional Bahamian breakfast; feast on cracked conch and zesty salads at lunch; and at dinner, try house specialties like smudder grouper, fried and seasoned with tomato, thyme, and pepper sauce; grilled rack of lamb; or the catch of the day grilled, fried, or blackened. If it's wahoo, order it grilled with lots of extra lime. The restaurant is housed in a complex that contains a boutique selling resort wear and fine jewelry from around the world, and a 29-slip marina—which means you can sail in from the offshore cays, tie up in front, enjoy a meal, and do some shopping. They also offer free Wi-Fi so you can check your email while grabbing a bite to eat. [$] *Average main: $26* ✉ *Bay St., Marsh Harbour, Great Abaco Island* ☎ *242/367–2366* 🌐 *www.mangoesmarina.com* 🕒 *Closed Wed.*

$ BAHAMIAN 🍴 **Show-Boo's Conch Salad Stand.** "Just be nice" implores the hand-lettered sign on this ramshackle stand between the Harbour View and Conch Inn marinas. Follow the instructions, and you'll be rewarded with what the proprietor claims to be "the world's best conch salad," often diced and mixed while you watch. Hours are erratic, especially during the September–November off-season. To find out if Show-Boo showed up for business, just swing by around lunchtime and see if there's a line forming in front of his stand. [$] *Average main: $10* ✉ *Bay St., between Conch Inn and Harbour View, Marsh Harbour, Great Abaco Island* 💳 *No credit cards* 🕒 *No dinner.*

**WORD OF MOUTH**

"If you are looking for simple, laid back, peaceful, and casual, then the Abacos are a good place to start. Before my first trip there, a friend and travel agent told me that "getting dressed for dinner in the Abacos meant putting on earrings" and I think that is still true—shorts, flip-flops, bathing suit, and you are ready to go."
—ishkribbl

$$ BAHAMIAN 🍴 **Snappas Grill and Chill.** Savvy boat people and in-the-know locals hang out here in the Harbour View Marina. The polished-wood bar is the center of gravity around which the dining room sprawls outward toward the open-air waterside deck. Killer appetizers include grilled shrimp, chicken kebabs, and sizzling onion rings. For lunch the grilled-fish Caesar salad and the Snappa Filly are hard to beat. Fresh grilled catch of the day and grilled conch are crossover items that always hit the spot. When the sun goes down—the sunsets are dazzling—order a New York steak or grilled lobster with a garden salad. Want more? Party on with live music Wednesday and Saturday nights. Happy hour lasts from 5 to 7:30 daily except Wednesdays when it goes on until 11 pm. [$] *Average main: $25* ✉ *Harbour View Marina, Bay St., Marsh Harbour, Great Abaco Island* ☎ *242/367–2278* 🌐 *www.snappasbar.com.*

$$$ BAHAMIAN Fodor's Choice ★ 🍴 **Wally's.** This two-story, pink colonial villa sits across Bay Street from the marina, fronted by green lawns, hibiscus, and white-railed verandahs. This is the Abacos' most popular restaurant—*the* place to go for good food, potent rum cocktails, and serious people-watching. Lunch is a scene, especially if you sit outside, where you'll find a mix of locals, tourists, and boat people munching on Greek or Caesar salads, spicy grouper, and mahimahi burgers. Inside there's a stylish bar, a boutique, and three dining rooms, all adorned with Haitian-style paintings. Dinner is served every night except Wednesdays and Sundays and the menu includes creamy curried shrimp, mahimahi Provençal, or a filet mignon smothered in a mushroom sauce. Save room for the irresistible key lime pie or Bahamian bread pudding with coconut and raisin, drenched in a brandy sauce. [$] *Average main: $33* ✉ *E. Bay St., Marsh Harbour, Great Abaco Island* ☎ *242/367–2074* ✍ *Reservations essential* 🕒 *Closed Sun. and Sept.–Oct. No dinner Wed.*

4

## Where to Eat and Stay in Marsh Harbour

*Sea of Abaco*

Mermaid Reef

Ferry Dock for Guana Cay

TO FERRY DOCK FOR HOPE TOWN & MAN-O-WAR

TO MARSH HARBOUR AIRPORT, SANDY POINT

*Abaco*

| KEY | |
|---|---|
| **1** | Restaurants |
| (1) | Hotels |

0 — 220 yards
0 — 200 meters

**Restaurants** ▼

Angler's Restaurant ........ **9**
Curly Tails
Restaurant & Bar .......... **7**
Jamie's Place ............... **8**
Jib Room .................... **1**
Junovia's Diner ............. **2**

Mangoes ................... **5**
Show-Boo's
Conch Salad Stand ........ **6**
Snappas Grill & Chill ...... **3**
Wally's ..................... **4**

**Hotels** ▼

Abaco Beach
Resort & Boat Harbour ..... **2**
Conch Inn
Resort & Marina ........... **3**
Lofty Fig Villas ............. **4**
Pelican Beach Villas ........ **1**

### WHERE TO STAY

$$$$ RESORT FAMILY Fodor's Choice ★ 🏨 **Abaco Beach Resort and Boat Harbour.** One of the liveliest party spots on the island, this place rocks during the half-dozen fishing tournaments it hosts every year in spring and early summer. **Pros:** ideal location for all water-related activities; easy access to town shops and restaurants; one of the best marinas in the Abacos. **Cons:** can be crowded and noisy during fishing tournaments. [$] *Rooms from: $366* ✉ *East of Conch Sound Marina, Marsh Harbour, Great Abaco Island* ☎ *242/367–2158, 800/468–4799* 🌐 *www.abacoresort.com* 🛏 *82 rooms* 🍴 *Multiple meal plans.*

$ HOTEL 🏨 **Conch Inn Resort & Marina.** This low-key, one-level marina hotel is a good choice for budget or business travelers, but make reservations well in advance. **Pros:** smack dab in the middle of everything in Marsh Harbour—marina, shops, and restaurants; easy to arrange boat rentals and diving; good value for comfortable rooms. **Cons:** far from beaches; small pool area. [$] *Rooms from: $160* ✉ *E. Bay St., Marsh Harbour, Great Abaco Island* ☎ *242/367–4000* 🌐 *www.conchinn.com* 🛏 *10 rooms.*

$ HOTEL 🏨 **Lofty Fig Villas.** The hotel owners envelop guests with exceptional hospitality, as does the superfriendly staff. **Pros:** location, location, location; good pool area for hanging out; excellent value with warm and friendly service. **Cons:** room furnishings are dated; no place to tie up a rental boat. [$] *Rooms from: $150* ✉ *Across from Mangoes Restaurant and Conch Inn Resort, Marsh Harbour, Great Abaco Island* ☎ *242/367–2681* 🌐 *www.loftyfig.com* 🛏 *6 villas.*

$$$ RENTAL 🏨 **Pelican Beach Villas.** On a quiet private peninsula opposite the main settlement of Marsh Harbour sit seven waterfront clapboard cottages cheerily painted in pale pink, yellow, blue, and green. **Pros:** tranquil beach location; near some of the best snorkeling in the Abacos; many repeat guests. **Cons:** no restaurant; need to rent a car or boat; on the expensive side for less than full-service accommodations. [$] *Rooms from: $275* ✉ *Northwest of Marsh Harbour Marina, Marsh Harbour, Great Abaco Island* ☎ *877/367–3600* 🌐 *www.pelicanbeachvillas.com* 🛏 *7 cottages.*

### NIGHTLIFE

**Curly Tails.** Stop by for live music Thursday and Saturday nights. ✉ *Conch Inn Resort & Marina, E. Bay St., Marsh Harbour, Great Abaco Island* ☎ *242/367–4444* 🌐 *www.abacocurlytails.com* 🕒 *Closed Tues.*

**Snappa's Grill and Chill.** Thursday through Saturday nights feature live music. ✉ *Harbour View Marina, Bay St., Marsh Harbour, Great Abaco Island* ☎ *242/367–2278* 🌐 *www.snappasbar.com.*

### SHOPPING

**Abaco Neem.** More than 30 different products are made using locally grown Neem trees at this shop and production plant. Salves, soaps, and lotions are organic and in many cases claim to offer medicinal benefits against skin conditions, arthritis, and even hypertension. Abaco Neem also produces an entire range of pet products. Call or email in advance to arrange a tour of the production facility and nearby farm. Tours take about 1½ hours and are free, although a $10 per person donation is welcomed. ✉ *Don Mackay Blvd., Marsh Harbour, Great Abaco Island* ☎ *242/367–4117* 🌐 *www.abaconeem.com* 🕒 *Mon.–Sat. 9–5.*

**Abaco Treasures.** At Marsh Harbour's traffic light, look for the turquoise awnings of Abaco Treasures, purveyors of fine china, crystal, perfumes, Bahamian books, and gifts. ☎ *242/367–3460.*

**Iggy Biggy.** This store, inside a bright peach-and-turquoise building, is your best bet for hats, sandals, tropical jewelry, sportswear, and souvenirs. If you are looking for gifts to take back home, you should be able to find something cool here. ⊠ *E. Bay St., Marsh Harbour, Great Abaco Island* ☎ *242/367–3596.*

**Java in Abaco.** Sip an iced latte or a strong mug of Hope Town Roasted joe while admiring the ceramics, paintings, carved wooden boats, and other locally produced creations at Java in Abaco. ⊠ *East Bay St., Royal Harbour Village, Great Abaco Island* ☎ *242/367–5523.*

**John Bull.** On the water across from the entrance to the Abaco Beach Resort, John Bull sells Rolex and other brand-name watches, fine jewelry by designers such as David Yurman and Yvel, and makeup and perfume from Chanel, Christian Dior, Clinique, and Lancôme. Fine leather goods, silk ties and scarves, and cool sunglasses are also on hand. ⊠ *E. Bay St., Marsh Harbour, Great Abaco Island* ☎ *242/367–2473* ⊕ *www.johnbull.com.*

**Sand Dollar Shoppe.** This shop sells resort wear and jewelry. Look for the locally made Abaco gold necklaces and earrings. ⊠ *East Bay St., Marsh Harbour, Great Abaco Island* ☎ *242/367–4405.*

## SPORTS AND THE OUTDOORS

### BICYCLING

**Rental Wheels of Abaco.** You can rent bicycles for $15 a day or $55 a week here. It's located on the main strip between Conch Inn Marina and the turnoff to Boat Harbour Marina. ⊠ *E. Bay St., Marsh Harbour, Great Abaco Island* ☎ *242/367–4643* ⊕ *www.rentalwheels.com.*

### BOATING

**Boat Harbour Marina.** The marina has 190 fully protected slips and a slew of amenities, including accommodations at the Abaco Beach Resort. ☎ *242/367–2158* ⊕ *www.abacobeachresort.com.*

**Conch Inn Marina.** This is one of the busiest marinas and has 80 slips, with accommodations available at the Conch Inn. ☎ *242/367–4000* ⊕ *www.conchinn.com.*

**Harbour View Marina.** The first marina on the west end of Bay Street, across from Wally's Restaurant, has extra-wide slips and 100-foot piers to accommodate boats with unlimited beam size, a private pool, wireless Internet, and Snappas Restaurant. ☎ *242/367–3910* ⊕ *www.harbourviewmarina.com.*

**Mangoes Marina.** This marina has 29 slips and a full range of amenities, including onshore showers, a pool, and a popular restaurant of the same name. ⊠ *Bay Street, Marsh Harbour, Great Abaco Island* ☎ *242/367–4255.*

The Abacos are the sailing capital of the Bahamas.

**Marsh Harbour Marina.** Marsh Harbour Marina has 68 slips and is the only full-service marina on the left side of the harbor, near Pelican Shores. It is a 10-minute drive from most shops and restaurants. ☎ *242/367–2700* ⊕ *www.jibroom.com.*

## BOAT RENTALS

**Bluewave Boat Rentals** ✉ *Marsh Harbour, Great Abaco Island* ☎ *242/ 367–3910.*

**The Moorings** ☎ *242/367–4000* ⊕ *www.moorings.com.*

**Rainbow Rentals** ☎ *242/367–4602* ⊕ *www.rainbowrentals.com.*

**Rich's Rentals** ☎ *242/367–2742.*

**Sea Horse Boat Rentals** ☎ *242/366–0023* ⊕ *www.seahorseboatrentals.com.*

## FISHING

You can find bonefish on the flats, yellowtail and grouper on the reefs, or marlin and tuna in the deeps of the Abacos.

**Justin Sands.** Premier fly-fishing guide Justin Sands works out of a state-of-the-art Hell's Bay flats skiff that will put you on tailing bones in the skinniest water. Justin was the Abacos bonefish champ for two years running, and he will guide you in the Marls or around Snake Cay, Little Harbour, and Cherokee Sound. Advance reservations are a must. ☎ *242/367–3526* ⊕ *www.bahamasvacationguide.com/justfish.html.*

**Pinder's Bone Fishing.** Buddy Pinder has 20 years' experience in the local waters, and professional Pinder's Bone Fishing provides year-round excursions in the Marls, a maze of mangroves and flats on the western side of Abaco. Advance reservations are essential. ☎ *242/366–2163.*

### SCUBA DIVING AND SNORKELING

There's excellent diving throughout the Abacos. Many sites are clustered around Marsh Harbour, including the reef behind **Guana Cay**, which is filled with little cavelike catacombs, and **Fowl Cay National Reserve**, which contains wide tunnels and a variety of fish. **Pelican Cays National Park** is a popular dive area south of Marsh Harbour. This shallow, 25-foot dive is filled with sea life; turtles are often sighted, as are spotted eagle rays and tarpon. The park is a 2,000-acre land and marine park protected and maintained by the Bahamas National Trust. Hook up your own boat to one of the moorings, or check with the local dive shops to see when trips to the park are scheduled. All of these sights can be easily snorkeled. Snorkelers will also want to visit **Mermaid Beach**, just off Pelican Shores Road in Marsh Harbour, where live reefs and green moray eels make for some of the Abacos' best snorkeling.

> **PLAY THE TIDES**
>
> If you're going bonefishing, tide pooling, or snorkeling, you'll want up-to-date tide information for the best results. A low incoming tide is usually best for bonefishing, though the last of the falling is good, too. Low tides are best for beachcombing and tide pools, although higher tides can give better coverage to your favorite reef. Ask at your hotel or a local dive shop for current tide information.

**Dive Abaco.** Located at the Conch Inn, Dive Abaco offers scuba and snorkeling trips on custom dive boats. Sites explored include reefs, tunnels, caverns, and wreck dives. ☎ 800/247–5338, 242/367–2787 ⊕ www.diveabaco.com.

**Rainbow Rentals.** This outfit rents catamarans and snorkeling gear. ☎ 242/367–4602.

**Sea Horse Boat Rentals.** Snorkeling gear is available from Sea Horse Boat Rentals. ☎ 242/367–2513.

### TENNIS

**Abaco Beach Resort.** The two lighted courts here are open to visitors. A tennis pro is on hand for clinics and private lessons for adults and children, and there are round-robin tournaments for guests. ☎ 242/367–2158.

### WINDSURFING

**Abaco Beach Resort.** Small sailboats and sea kayaks are available free of charge to hotel and marina guests at the Abaco Beach Resort. ☎ 242/367–2158 ⊕ www.abacoresort.com.

### TOURS

**Abaco Eco Kayak Tours and Rentals.** Get up close and personal with Abaco's amazing ecosystem while on a kayak tour with this environmentally sensitive operator. If you want to go it alone, rent a kayak for half a day or up to a week. ✉ Hope Town, Great Abaco Island ☎ 242/475–9616 ⊕ www.abacoeco.com.

**Brendal's Dive Center.** Whether you're looking for a close encounter with a shark, a dolphin, or a turtle, this dive operator has a tour designed just for you, plus they offer SCUBA courses, island-hopping adventures, and sunset cruises. ✉ Green Turtle Cay, Great Abaco Island ☎ 242/365–4411 ⊕ www.brendal.com.

**Froggies Out Island Adventures.** Take a day trip to one of the Bahamas' protected national parks, or on a Sunday, catch a ride to the infamous Nipper's pig roast on neighboring Guana Cay. This operator offers a variety of snorkeling and SCUBA combination tours and also certifies divers. ☎ *242/366–0431* 🌐 *www.froggiesabaco.com.*

## TREASURE CAY

Twenty miles north of Marsh Harbour is Treasure Cay, technically not an island but a large peninsula connected to Great Abaco by a narrow spit of land. This was once the site of the first Loyalist settlement in Abaco, called Carlton.



While Treasure Cay is a large-scale real-estate development project, it's also a wonderful small community where expatriate residents share the laid-back, sun-and-sea vibe with longtime locals. The development's centerpiece is the Treasure Cay Hotel Resort and Marina, with its Dick Wilson–designed golf course and a 150-slip marina that has boat rentals, a dive shop, pool, restaurant, and lively bar. Treasure Cay's commercial center consists of two rows of shops near the resort as well as a post office, self-service laundries, restaurant, a couple of well-stocked grocery stores, and BaTelCo, the Bahamian telephone company. You'll also find car-, scooter-, and bicycle-rental offices here.

### EXPLORING

**Carleton Settlement Ruins.** Tucked away toward the northwestern end of the Treasure Cay development are the ruins of the very first settlement in Abaco, founded by the Loyalists that left the Carolinas during the American Revolutionary War. The sight is not well marked, but ask a local for directions.

### BEACHES

FAMILY
Fodor's Choice ★

**Treasure Cay Beach.** This beach is world famous for its expanse of truly powderlike sand and turquoise water. On the beach's southern end is a bar and grill with a couple of shade-bearing huts. The rest of the beach is clear from development, since the land is privately owned, and almost clear of footprints. With a top-notch marina across the road and lunch a short stroll away, you have luxury; a walk farther down the beach gives you a quiet escape. **Amenities:** food and drink; parking (no fee); restrooms; water sports. **Best for:** sunrise; sunset; swimming; walking. ✉ *Treasure Cay, Great Abaco Island.*

### WHERE TO EAT

$ BAKERY

🍴 **Café La Florence.** Stop off at this bakery-café in the Treasure Cay resort's main shopping strip for just-made muffins and the best cinnamon rolls in the universe. Or go for a light lunch of lobster quiche, conch chowder, or a spicy, Jamaican-style meat patty. Anglers can order picnic lunches to go. You can also arrange for the chef to cater private dinners of lobster, steak, and the like in your rented condo. [$] *Average main: $9* ✉ *Treasure Cay, Great Abaco Island* ☎ *242/577–7358* 💳 *No credit cards.*

$ BAHAMIAN

🍴 **Coco Beach Bar.** Enjoy the stunning scenery of one of the world's top rated beaches while enjoying lunch or a cocktail at this casual, laid-back spot. Sit at the bar or on the open deck, or for the best views, enjoy your

Treasure Cay Beach is one of the most beautiful beaches on Great Abaco Island.

meal under one of the thatched shades right on the beach. A Bahamian dinner is served Tuesday nights during the high season. $ *Average main: $15* ⊠ *Treasure Cay, Great Abaco Island* ☎ *242/365–8470* ⊕ *www. treasurecay.com* ☉ *Daily 11–5* ☉ *Lunch only.*

**$$$**
BAHAMIAN

╳ **Spinnaker Restaurant and Lounge.** Ceramic-tiled floors, rattan furniture, and floral-print tablecloths accent this large resort restaurant—250 guests fit in the air-conditioned main dining area and the adjacent screened-in outdoor patio—and bar at the Treasure Cay Marina. Locals and tourists mix in an often-rowdy scene, though things quiet down in the off-season. Eggs and bacon and other American standards are whipped up for breakfast. Dinner boasts an international flair with grilled steaks and lamb chops, along with seafood pasta, grilled mahimahi, broiled lobster, and a salad bar. Even with reservations you often have to wait, but you can relax in the lounge and enjoy an array of cocktails and frozen rum drinks. $ *Average main: $32* ⊠ *Treasure Cay Marina, Treasure Cay, Great Abaco Island* ☎ *242/365–8801* ⊕ *www. treasurecay.com* ☉ *Daily 7:30–10:30 am and 6–9:30 pm* ☉ *No lunch.*

**$$**
BAHAMIAN

╳ **Touch of Class.** Ten minutes north of Treasure Cay, this locals' favorite, no-frills restaurant serves traditional Bahamian dishes such as grilled freshly caught grouper and minced local lobster stewed with tomatoes, onions, and spices. Reasonably priced appetizers, such as conch chowder and conch fritters, and a full bar make this a nice option for a night out. Free shuttle service is available from the parking lot in front of the Treasure Cay Marina. $ *Average main: $28* ⊠ *Queen's Hwy. at Treasure Cay Rd., Treasure Cay, Great Abaco Island* ☎ *242/365–8195* ☉ *No lunch.*

## WHERE TO STAY

$$$$ RESORT **Bahama Beach Club.** Ideal for families and small groups, these two- to four-bedroom condos are right off the famous Treasure Cay beach. **Pros:** luxury accommodations on one of the most sublime beaches in the world; large pool area with Jacuzzi; walking distance to the marina, restaurants, and shops. **Cons:** check-in can be slow. [$] *Rooms from: $450* ✉ *Treasure Cay, Great Abaco Island* ☎ *800/284–0382, 242/365–8500* 🌐 *www.bahamabeachclub.com* 🛏 *88 condos.*

$ HOTEL FAMILY Fodor's Choice ★ **Treasure Cay Hotel Resort & Marina.** Treasure Cay is best known for its 18-hole golf course, which *Golf Digest* frequently rates as the Bahamas' best, and its first-class 150-slip marina. **Pros:** most convenient location in Treasure Cay; good on-site restaurants and bar; Dick Wilson championship golf course. **Cons:** if you forget to make a dinner reservation in the main season you could be out of luck at the restaurant; pool area can get crowded with boat people and happy-hour patrons at the Tipsy Seagull Bar. [$] *Rooms from: $130* ✉ *Treasure Cay Marina, Treasure Cay, Great Abaco Island* ☎ *242/365–8801, 800/327–1584* 🌐 *www.treasurecay.com* 🛏 *32 suites, 32 town houses* 🍴 *Multiple meal plans.*

## NIGHTLIFE

**Tipsy Seagull.** This outside bar and grill is a fun happy-hour spot. There's usually live music on the weekend and Thursday night's Pizza Night is a big hit with locals and visitors alike. ✉ *Treasure Cay Marina, Treasure Cay, Great Abaco Island* ☎ *242/365–8814* 🌐 *www.treasurecay.com.*

## SHOPPING

**Abaco Ceramics.** Near Treasure Cay Resort is Abaco Ceramics, which offers its signature white-clay pottery with a variety of designs. The Royal fish pattern remains a favorite. ☎ *242/365–8489* 🌐 *www.abacoceramics.com* 🕓 *Closed weekends.*

## SPORTS AND THE OUTDOORS

### BICYCLING

**Wendell's Bicycle Rentals.** Rent mountain bikes by the half day, day, or week. ☎ *242/365–8687.*

### BOATING

Treasure Cay marina has 150 slips and can accommodate large yachts. It's a great base for jaunting to outer uninhabited cays for day fishing or diving trips, or to Green Turtle Cay.

Contacts **J.I.C. Boat Rentals** ☎ *242/365–8582* 🌐 *www.jicboatrentals.com.*

### FISHING

**Justin Sands.** Reservations are a must to fish with Justin Sands, the Abacos' two-time bonefish champ. ☎ *242/367–3526* 🌐 *www.bahamasvacationguide.com/justfish.html.*

**O'Donald Macintosh.** Top professional bonefish guide O'Donald Macintosh meets clients each day at the Treasure Cay Marina for full or half days of guided bonefishing in the northern Marls or outside Coopers Town. In more than 20 years of guiding, O'D has built up a large loyal base of repeat clients, so you'll need to book him well in advance—especially in the prime months of April, May, and June. ☎ *242/365–0126.*

**Treasure Cay Hotel Resort & Marina.** Arrange for local deep-sea fishing or bonefishing guides through Treasure Cay Hotel Resort & Marina. ☎ *242/365–8250* ⊕ *www.treasurecay.com/fishing.*

### GOLF

**Treasure Cay Hotel Resort & Marina.** A half mile from the Treasure Cay Hotel Resort & Marina is the property's par-72, Dick Wilson–designed course, with carts available. There's no need to reserve tee times, and the course is usually delightfully uncrowded—ideal for a leisurely round. A driving range, putting green, and small pro shop are also on-site. ☎ *800/327–1584, 242/365–8045* ⊕ *www.treasurecay.com/golf.*

### SCUBA DIVING AND SNORKELING

**No Name Cay**, **Whale Cay**, and the **Fowl Cay Preserve** are popular marine-life sites. The 1865 wreck of the steamship freighter *San Jacinto* also affords scenic diving and a chance to feed the resident green moray eel.

**Treasure Divers.** In the Treasure Cay Marina, Treasure Divers rents SCUBA and snorkeling equipment and takes divers and snorkelers out to a variety of sites. ☎ *242/365–8571* ⊕ *www.treasure-divers.com.*

### TENNIS

**Treasure Cay Hotel Resort & Marina.** The tennis courts here are six of the best courts in the Abacos, four of which are lighted for night play. Annual or monthly membership is required unless you are staying at the Treasure Cay Hotel Resort & Marina. ☎ *242/357–6779* ⊕ *www. treasurecaytennis.org* ⬛ *$25 per hour* ⊙ *Daily 7 am–8 pm.*

### WINDSURFING

**Treasure Cay Hotel Resort & Marina.** Windsurfers and a complete line of nonmotorized watercraft are available for rent at the Treasure Cay Hotel Resort & Marina. ☎ *242/365–8250.*

## SOUTH OF MARSH HARBOUR

Thirty minutes south of Marsh Harbour, the small, eclectic artists' colony of **Little Harbour** was settled by the Johnston family more than 50 years ago. Randolph Johnston moved his family here to escape the consumerist, hectic lifestyle he felt in the United States and to pursue a simple life where he and his wife could focus on their art. The family is well known for their bronze sculptures, some commissioned nationally.

Just to the south of Little Harbour is the seaside settlement of **Cherokee Sound**, home to fewer than 100 families. Most of the residents make their living catching crawfish or working in the growing tourism industry; many lead offshore fishing and bonefishing expeditions. The deserted Atlantic beaches and serene salt marshes in this area are breathtaking, and though development at Winding Bay and Little Harbour are progressing, the slow-paced, tranquil feel of daily life here hasn't changed. **Sandy Point**, a "takin' it easy, mon" fishing village with miles of beckoning beaches and a couple of bonefishing lodges, is slightly more than 50 miles southwest of Marsh Harbour, about a 40-minute drive from Cherokee.

## EXPLORING

**Abaco Club on Winding Bay.** Twenty-five minutes south of Marsh Harbour this glamorous private golf and sporting club is set on 534 acres of stunning oceanfront property. The clubhouse, restaurant, and pool, which sit on 65-foot-high white limestone bluffs, offer guests and members a mesmerizing view of the purple-blue Atlantic Ocean, and the bay has more than 2 miles of sugar-sand beaches. Amenities and activities at the club include an 18-hole tropical links golf course, a luxurious European-style spa and fitness center, scuba diving, snorkeling, tennis, bonefishing, and offshore fishing. This is a private club whose members have bought property; nonmembers can stay in the hotel-style cabanas and cottages and use all facilities one time while evaluating membership and real-estate options. ✉ *Cherokee Sound turnoff, Great Abaco Island* ☎ *242/367–0077, 800/593–8613* ⊕ *www.myabacoclub.com.*

**Abaco National Park.** The Abaco National Park was established in 1994 as a sanctuary for the endangered Abaco parrot, of which there are less than 3,000. Many other birds call the park home, including the Bahama yellowthroat and pine warbler.

A 15-mile dirt track passes through the 20,500 protected acres, ending at the Hole-in-the-Wall lighthouse, a starkly beautiful and desolate location overlooking the ocean. The drive from the paved highway all the way to the lighthouse takes about 1½ hours, and can only be done in a 4X4 vehicle. The lighthouse is not technically open to visitors, but people still do climb the rickety stairs to the top where views of the island and the sea are mesmerizing.

**Hole-in-the-Wall.** Off the Great Abaco Highway at the turn in the road that takes you to Sandy Point, a rugged, single-lane dirt track leads you to this navigational lighthouse that stands on Great Abaco's southern tip. The lighthouse was constructed in 1838 against local opposition from islanders who depended on salvaging shipwrecks for their livelihood. Over the years the lighthouse has survived sabotage and hurricanes, and was automated in 1995 to continue serving maritime interests. The Bahamas Marine Mammal Research Organisation has leased the site to monitor whale movements and conduct other ocean studies. ✉ *South of Sandy Point, Great Abaco Island.*

**Johnston Studios Art Gallery and Foundry.** Sculptor Johnston and his sons and acolytes cast magnificent lifelike bronze figures using the age-old lost-wax method at the only bronze foundry in the Bahamas. You can purchase the art in the gallery. Tours are available by appointment for $50 per person. ✉ *Little Harbour, Great Abaco Island* ☎ *242/577–5487.*

**Sawmill Sink Blue Hole.** A half-hour drive south of Marsh Harbour is a crudely marked electric pole directing you to turn right onto an old logging trail. A short drive down this road takes you to an incredible blue hole. It was featured by *National Geographic* in 2010 for the fossils found deep within it. Though you cannot dive this hole, you can swim in it. ✉ *40 mins south of Marsh Harbour, Great Abaco Island.*

### BEACHES

**Pelican Cay Beach.** In a protected park, this is a great spot for snorkeling and diving on nearby Sandy Cay reef. The cay is small and between two ocean cuts, so the water drops off quickly but its location is also what nurtures the beach's pure white sand. If you get restless, ruins of an old house are hidden in overgrowth at the top of the cay, and offer fantastic views of the park. **Amenities:** none. **Best for:** snorkeling. ⊠ *8 miles north of Cherokee Sound, South Abaco, Great Abaco Island.*

**Sandy Point Beach.** If shelling and solitude are your thing, venture 50 miles southwest of Marsh Harbour to the sleepy fishing village of Sandy Point. Large shells wash up on the sandy beaches, making it great for a stroll and shelling. The best spot for picking up one of nature's souvenirs is between the picnic site and Rocky Point. Well offshore is the private island Castaway Cay, where Disney Cruise Line guests spend a day. **Amenities:** none. **Best for:** solitude; walking. ⊠ *Sandy Point, Great Abaco Island.*

### WHERE TO EAT AND STAY

$

BAHAMIAN

✕ **Pete's Pub.** Next door to Pete's Gallery is an outdoor tiki-hut restaurant and bar where you can wiggle your toes in the sand while you chow down on fresh seafood, burgers, and cold tropical drinks. Try the mango-glazed grouper, lemon-pepper mahimahi, or coconut cracked conch while you kick back and enjoy the view of the harbor. If you want to be part of the local scene, don't miss the wild-pig roasts, which happen whenever big events take place. It's a long drive, so in the slow season, it's best to call ahead to make sure they're open. $ *Average main: $20* ⊠ *Little Harbour, Great Abaco Island* ☎ *242/577–5487* ⊕ *www.petespubandgallery.com.*

$$$$

ALL-INCLUSIVE

🛏 **Rickmon Bonefish Lodge.** Well-regarded fishing guide Ricardo Burrows operates this comfortable waterside lodge at the end of the road in Sandy Point. **Pros:** perfect location for bonefishing; some of the best professional fly-fishing guides in the Abacos; comfortable for non-fishing companions. **Cons:** average restaurant; intermittent Internet. $ *Rooms from: $500* ⊠ *Sandy Point, Great Abaco Island* ☎ *800/628–1447* ⊕ *www.angleradventures.com/rickmon* ⤴ *11 rooms* ▭ *No credit cards* ⦿❙ *All-inclusive.*

### SHOPPING

**Johnston Studios Art Gallery.** The gallery displays original bronzes by the Johnstons, as well as unique gold jewelry, prints, and gifts. ⊠ *Little Harbour, Great Abaco Island* ☎ *242/577–5487* ⊕ *www. petespubandgallery.com.*

## ELBOW CAY

### EXPLORING

**Hope Town Lighthouse.** Upon arrival in Hope Town Harbour you'll first see a much-photographed Bahamas landmark, a 120-foot-tall, peppermint-stripe lighthouse built in 1838. The light's construction was delayed for several years by acts of vandalism; then-residents feared it would end their profitable wrecking practice. Today the lighthouse is one of the Bahamas' last three hand-turned, kerosene-fueled beacons. Weekdays 10–4 the lighthouse keeper will welcome you at the top for a superb view of the sea and the nearby cays. There's no road between the lighthouse and the town proper. You can use your own boat to cross the harbor or catch a ride on the ferry before it leaves to go back to Marsh Harbour, but if you take a ferry it probably won't be back for at least an hour.

**Wyannie Malone Historical Museum.** This volunteer-run museum houses Hope Town memorabilia and photographs. Exhibits highlight Lucayan and pirate artifacts found on the island. Many descendants of Mrs. Malone, who settled here with her children in 1875, still live on Elbow Cay. ⊠ *Queen's Hwy., Hope Town, Hope Town, Elbow Cay* 🕾 *242/366–0293* 🖃 *$3 adults, $1 children* 🕙 *Nov.–July, Mon.–Sat. 10–3.*

### BEACHES

**Tahiti Beach.** This small beach at the southern tip of Elbow Cay is a popular boater's stop. The soft white sand is well protected from the close ocean cut by thick vegetation, a few barrier cays, and shallow water. This shallow area is popular for shelling, and of course simply relaxing and watching the tide rise. At low tide, the true beauty of this beach is revealed when a long sand spit emerges, perfect for picnics. It's great for young children, as the water on one side of the spit is ankle deep, stays calm, and remains warm. During peak season the beach can become a bit crowded. **Amenities:** none. **Best for:** swimming; surfing. ⊠ *Elbow Cay.*

### WHERE TO EAT

**$$** ✕ **Abaco Inn Restaurant.** Set in the country-club-style main lodge splashed
BAHAMIAN with lively Bahamian colors, the restaurant serves breakfast, lunch, and
Fodor'sChoice dinner to guests and visitors in classic island style. Attentive friendly
★ service and expansive ocean views are appetite enhancers. Fresh-baked bread, fruit, and egg dishes are breakfast highlights. But where the restaurant really shines is in its servings of the freshest seafood on the island. At lunch, sample the grilled grouper or spicy cracked conch. For dinner, grilled wahoo, hog snapper, or mahimahi can be prepared to your liking. When you make your reservation, ask for a table on the enclosed patio overlooking the ocean. Ⓢ *Average main: $27* ⊠ *2 miles south of Hope Town, Hope Town, Elbow Cay* 🕾 *242/366–0133* ⊕ *www.abacoinn.com* 🖃 *Reservations essential.*

**$** ✕ **Cap'n Jack's Restaurant and Bar.** There are a handful of booths and
BAHAMIAN a small rowdy bar, but most of this casual eatery's seating is out on the pink-and-white-striped dock–patio. Locals, boat people, and land-based tourists gather here every day for value-priced eats and drinks. The menu is nothing fancy, but provides reliable grouper burgers, pork chops, fresh fish catch-of-the-day, and cracked conch. When it's in season, there's sometimes a lobster special. Cap'n Jack's serves three meals a day, offers a full bar, and has live music Friday nights and a DJ Wednesday and Saturday nights. There are nightly drink specials and a different event each night, from trivia to sushi. Ⓢ *Average main: $15* ⊠ *Hope Town, Elbow Cay* 🕾 *242/366–0247* ⊕ *www.capnjackshopetown.com* 🕙 *Closed Sun. and mid-Aug.–Sept.*

**$$$** ✕ **Firefly Bar & Grill.** Ask anyone in the Abacos where you must eat dur-
BAHAMIAN ing your stay and there's a good chance this is it. Whether you pull in by
Fodor'sChoice golf cart or tie up by boat, it's worth the trip. Owned by the developers
★ of Firefly Vodkas, this bar carries the full line along with the Mo-Tea-To,

their take on the mojito, and the Fly Swatter, a delicious mixture that's a closely guarded secret. Seafood is their specialty and the extensive menu makes choosing just one dish a challenge. Locals travel from throughout the Abaco island chain to enjoy lunch or dinner here and catch one of the best views of the Sea of Abaco. [$] *Average main: $28* ✉ *Hope Town, Elbow Cay* ☎ *242/366–0145* 🌐 *www.fireflysunsetresort.com* 🕑 *Closed Wed.*

$$$ BAHAMIAN 🍴 **Great Harbour Room.** While casual attire is fine, this restaurant overlooking the harbor feels like an upscale establishment with dimmed lighting, quiet music, and especially attentive service. Start off with a pigeon pea bisque, then try the decadent Mike's Seafood Mac & Cheese, a trio of cheeses with a center of Bahamian spiced crab mousse. The Reef & Beef pairs a 6-ounce filet mignon with your choice of lobster tail or the catch of the day. [$] *Average main: $34* ✉ *Upper Rd., Hope Town, Elbow Cay* ☎ *242/366–0095* 🌐 *www.hopetownlodge.com* 🕑 *No lunch.*

$$ BAHAMIAN 🍴 **Harbour's Edge.** Hope Town's happening hangout for locals and tourists, this bar and restaurant's deck is the best place to watch the goings-on in the busy harbor; you can tie your boat up right in front. Kick back and have an icy Kalik or the Scattered Shower or Dark & Stormy cocktail concoctions. For lunch, try the tender conch burgers, white caps, or lobster salad. For dinner, the fresh grilled seafood and pasta dishes are some of the best in the islands. Authentic Bahamian breakfasts are served on Sunday. A band plays on Thursday and Saturday nights during high season. [$] *Average main: $23* ✉ *Lower Rd., Hope Town, Elbow Cay* ☎ *242/366–0087* 🕑 *Closed Tues.*

$ BAKERY 🍴 **Hope Town Coffee House.** Overlooking Hope Town Harbour, this upscale coffeehouse, bakery, boutique, and hot-spot café features coffees roasted right in the historic settlement, the first and only roastery in the Bahamas. It's a must for java drinks, smoothies, homemade pastries and gelato, quiches, and tapas-size savories. If you're headed out in a boat for the day, grab a shake and salad or pasta to-go. [$] *Average main: $10* ✉ *Queen's Hwy., Hope Town, Elbow Cay* ☎ *242/366–0760* 🌐 *www.hopetowncoffeehouse.com* 🕑 *Closed late Aug.–early Nov.*

$ BAHAMIAN 🍴 **On the Beach Bar and Grill.** Burgers, grilled kebabs, sandwiches, conch, fish, and icy rum drinks are served up with a terrific Atlantic view at this open-air bar and grill perched high on the beach dunes across the road from the small Turtle Hill resort. It closes at sunset because all seating is open to the elements, and a gully washer of a storm can shut the place down. Go in your bathing suit and enjoy the beach and snorkeling right out front. [$] *Average main: $13* ✉ *Queens Hwy. between Hope Town and White Sound, Hope Town, Elbow Cay* ☎ *242/366–0557* 🌐 *www.turtlehill.com* ✍ *Reservations not accepted* 🕑 *Closed Mon.*

$$ BAHAMIAN 🍴 **The Reef Bar & Grill.** Pull up a chair by the pool or on the open-air deck overlooking the beach and enjoy salads, burgers, and wraps all served up with signature dressings and sauces like Pineapple Ginger Aioli, Creamy Caribbean Petal Dressing, and Guava BBQ Sauce. Breakfast is as light or hearty as you want it. Sunday brunch features a number of different takes on classic eggs Benedict along with a complimentary mimosa. [$] *Average main: $15* ✉ *Hope Town, Elbow Cay* ☎ *242/366–0095* 🌐 *www.hopetownlodge.com* 🕑 *8:30 am–7 pm daily; coffee is served from 7 am.*

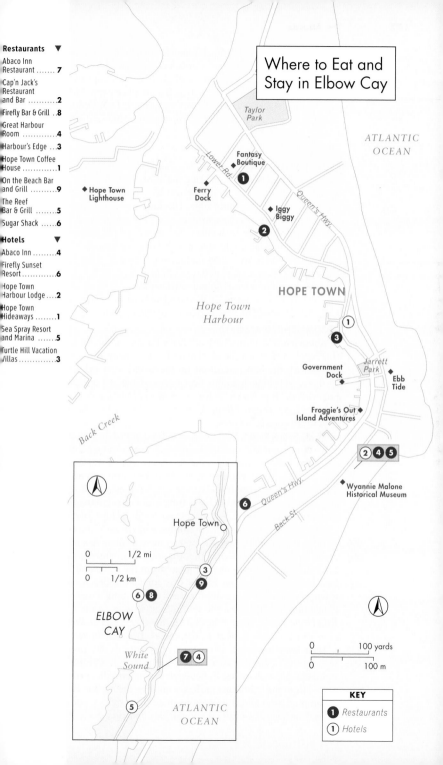

# Where to Eat and Stay in Elbow Cay

Taylor Park

ATLANTIC OCEAN

Lower Rd.

Fantasy Boutique

Hope Town Lighthouse

Ferry Dock

Iggy Biggy

Queen's Hwy.

HOPE TOWN

Hope Town Harbour

Government Dock

Jarrett Park

Ebb Tide

Froggie's Out Island Adventures

Wyannie Malone Historical Museum

Back Creek

Queen's Hwy.

Back St.

Hope Town

0    1/2 mi
0    1/2 km

ELBOW CAY

White Sound

ATLANTIC OCEAN

0    100 yards
0    100 m

**KEY**

Restaurants

Hotels

**$**
**DELI**
✕ **Sugar Shack.** This cute shack is an ice-cream parlor (14 flavors!), deli, and T-shirt shop all tied into one. Located about 1½ miles south of Hope Town, it's a worthwhile walk or ride for a cool treat or a fresh sandwich. Unique gift items such as Bahama Bee pepper jelly are available, too. $ *Average main: $7* ✉ *Centerline Rd., White Sound, Hope Town, Elbow Cay* ☎ *242/366–0788* ☉ *Mon.–Sat. 7:30 am–8 pm; Sun. 11–3* ☉ *Closed Aug.–Sept.*

## WHERE TO STAY

### PRIVATE VILLA RENTALS

**Elbow Cay Properties.** Besides being the most cost-efficient way for a family to stay a week or longer on Elbow Cay, a private house or villa is also likely to be the most comfortable. This long-standing rental agency handles a variety of properties, from cozy two-bedroom, one-bath cottages to a six-bedroom, six-bath villa better described as a mansion. Many of the rental homes are on the water, with a dock or a sandy beach right out front. The owners are set on finding you a place to match your wishes and budget. There are no Sunday check-ins, as the agency is closed, and a three-night minimum is required most weeks; a full week is required during peak holiday seasons. ✉ *Western Harborfront, Hope Town, Elbow Cay* ☎ *242/366–0569* ⊕ *www.elbowcayrentals.com.*

### RECOMMENDED RESORTS

**$$**
**B&B/INN**
🏨 **Abaco Inn.** The motto here is "Tan your toes in the Abacos," making this beachfront resort the ideal place for a getaway. **Pros:** self-contained resort with the best restaurant on the island; easy access to beaches, surfing, and fishing; hypnotic ocean views. **Cons:** 10-minute golf-cart or boat ride to Hope Town. $ *Rooms from: $210* ✉ *2 miles south of Hope Town, Hope Town, Elbow Cay* ☎ *242/366–0133* ⊕ *www.abacoinn. com* ⤳ *14 rooms, 6 villas.*

**$$$**
**HOTEL**
**Fodor's Choice**
★
🏨 **Firefly Sunset Resort.** Each of these fully equipped, beautifully appointed two-, three-, and four-bedroom cottages boasts a stunning view of the Sea of Abaco and are situated on the vast property in a way that creates privacy and a sense of true exclusivity. **Pros:** beautiful settings; large, beautifully decorated accommodations; fantastic restaurant on-site. **Cons:** golf cart or boat is a must for getting around; small man-made beach; three-day stay required. $ *Rooms from: $375* ✉ *Hope Town, Elbow Cay* ☎ *242/366–0145* ⊕ *www.fireflysunsetresort.com* ⤳ *7 houses.*

**$$$**
**HOTEL**
**Fodor's Choice**
★
🏨 **Hope Town Harbour Lodge.** You can have it all at this casually classy resort—spectacular views of the Atlantic Ocean and the beach, quality amenities, and a location steps away from the town and harbor. **Pros:** best lodging location on Elbow Cay for views, beach, and access to town; casual patio restaurant for lunch overlooking the ocean; romantic. **Cons:** Internet access can be sporadic. $ *Rooms from: $300* ✉ *Upper Rd., Hope Town, Elbow Cay* ☎ *242/366–0095* ⊕ *www.hopetownlodge. com* ⤳ *12 rooms, 6 cabanas, 6 cottages, 1 private house.*

**$$$**
**RENTAL**
🏨 **Hope Town Hideaways.** Choose one of four comfy island villas scattered on 11 acres of gardens, with access to the harbor and the beach, or go more upscale with a West Indies–style Flamingo Villa, perfectly situated across from the lighthouse at the entrance to the harbor. **Pros:** variety of accommodation and style options in all price ranges; convenient locations. **Cons:** check-in can take a while for first-time guest; do-it-yourself

vacation. $ *Rooms from: $400* ⊠ *1 Purple Porpoise Pl., Hope Town, Elbow Cay* ☎ *242/366–0224* ⊕ *www.hopetown.com* ⤴ *75 units* ☉ *No meals.*

**$$$** 🛏 **Sea Spray Resort and Marina.** Con-
RESORT sider this resort if you're planning to catch any waves, or you just want to get away from it all. **Pros:** the Atlan-
tic beach is on one side of the resort,

and the leeward-side marina on the other; self-contained relaxing retreat near the Abaco Inn; full-service marina for boaters and guests. **Cons:** res-
taurant food is just OK; 10-minute golf-cart or boat ride to Hope Town. $ *Rooms from: $325* ⊠ *South end of White Sound, Hope Town, Elbow Cay* ☎ *242/366–0065* ⊕ *www.seasprayresort.com* ⤴ *7 villas.*

**$$$** 🛏 **Turtle Hill Vacation Villas.** Bougainvillea- and hibiscus-lined walkways
RENTAL encircle the central swimming pools of this cluster of six villas, each with its own private patio. **Pros:** comfortable accommodations for fami-
lies and small groups; steps away from the beach. **Cons:** you have to golf cart out to restaurants for dinner if you don't want to cook in; extra charge for daily maid service. $ *Rooms from: $380* ⊠ *Off Queens Hwy. between Hope Town and White Sound, Hope Town, Elbow Cay* ☎ *242/366–0557* ⊕ *www.turtlehill.com* ⤴ *6 villas.*

### NIGHTLIFE

**Cap'n Jacks.** Each evening Cap'n Jacks offers a different event, including bingo and trivia, along with drink specials. After 9 pm on Wednesdays there is DJ music. This is a popular spot for young adults. ⊠ *Hope Town, Elbow Cay* ☎ *242/366–0247* ⊕ *www.capnjackshopetown.com* ⊘ *Closed Sun. and mid Aug.–Sept.*

**Harbour's Edge.** After 9 pm every Saturday, Harbour's Edge has local bands playing Bahamian and reggae music. They also play Thursday nights during peak seasons. This is a favorite spot for locals. ⊠ *Lower Rd., Hope Town, Elbow Cay* ☎ *242/366–0087* ⊘ *Closed Tues.*

**Sea Spray Resort.** Local bands perform here every Saturday night. This is a popular stop where locals and visitors can mingle and dance to classic rock-and-roll and Bahamian tunes. ⊠ *South end of White Sound, Hope Town, Elbow Cay* ☎ *242/366–0065.*

**Wine Down and Sip Sip.** Featuring a selection of 50 properly cellared wines, Wine Down and Sip Sip is a classy hangout with a high-end liquor bar, draft beer, and weekly flights and pairings. The aura is sophisticated, and complimented by a lend-and-exchange selection of books. ⊠ *Queen's Hwy., Hope Town, Hope Town, Elbow Cay* ☎ *242/366–0399.*

### SHOPPING

**Ebbtide.** This shop is on the upper-path road in a renovated Loyalist home. Come here for such Bahamian gifts as batik clothes, original driftwood carvings and prints, and nautical jewelry. Browse through the extensive Bahamian book collection. ⊠ *Hope Town, Elbow Cay* ☎ *242/366–0088.*

Tahiti Beach on Elbow Cay is a family favorite.

**Da Crazy Crab.** Here you can find a nice selection of souvenirs, beach wraps, T-shirts, arts and crafts, and Cuban cigars. ⊠ *Front Rd., Hope Town, Elbow Cay* ☎ *242/366-0537.*

**Hummingbird Cottage Art Centre.** This quaint gallery, located in a fully restored, century-old home, showcases the works of local artists and offers monthly art workshops overlooking the stunning ocean out back. ⊠ *Hope Town, Elbow Cay* ☎ *242/366-0272* ⊕ *www.hopetownart.com.*

**Iggy Biggy.** This is the only shop in Hope Town that carries the lovely Abaco ceramics handmade in Treasure Cay. It also sells home decorations, handmade dishware and glasses, wind chimes, sandals, resort wear, jewelry, and island music. ⊠ *Front Rd., Hope Town, Hope Town, Elbow Cay* ☎ *242/366-0354.*

## SPORTS AND THE OUTDOORS

### BOATING

**Hope Town Hideaways.** Hope Town Hideaways has 12 slips, mostly used for guests staying in its rental cottages and houses. Call well in advance to reserve yours. ☎ *242/366-0224.*

**Sea Spray Resort and Marina.** This full-service marina has 60 slips and boat rentals. ☎ *242/366-0065.*

### BOAT RENTALS

**Island Marine** ☎ *242/366-0282* ⊕ *www.islandmarine.com.*

**Sea Horse Boat Rentals** ☎ *242/367-5460* ⊕ *www.seahorseboatrentals.com.*

### FISHING

**Local Boy.** Deep-sea charters are available with Local Boy. ☎ *242/366-0528* ⊕ *www.hopetownfishing.com.*

**Maitland Lowe.** Book well in advance to have Maitland Lowe guide you around Snake Cay or Little Harbour. ☎ 242/366–0234 ⊕ *www. wildpigeoncharters.com.*

**Seagull Charters.** This charter company sets up guided deep-sea excursions with Captain Robert Lowe, who has more than 35 years' experience in local waters. ☎ 242/366–0266 ⊕ *www.seagullcottages.com/fishing.*

### KAYAKING

**Abaco Eco.** This company offers tours and rentals of the local area and Snake Cay. ☎ 242/475–9616, 954/889–7117 ⊕ *www.abacoeco.com.*

**Froggies Out Island Adventures.** Froggies has snorkel and dive trips, scuba and resort courses, full-day adventure tours, island excursions, and dolphin encounters. You can also rent snorkeling and diving gear to venture out on your own. Professional and friendly service has earned Froggies many repeat customers. You need to book your excursions as far in advance as possible. ☎ 242/366–0431 ⊕ *www.froggiesabaco.com.*

### PADDLE BOARDING

**Abaco Paddle Board.** Rent a paddle- or surfboard by the hour or by the day. If you're new to the sports, sign up for private lessons or the three-day surf clinic. ✉ *Hope Town, Elbow Cay* ☎ 242/475–6554, 242/366–3125 ⊕ *www.abacopaddleboard.com.*

# MAN-O-WAR CAY

Fewer than 300 people live on skinny, 2½-mile-long Man-O-War Cay, many of them descendants of early Loyalist settlers who started the tradition of handcrafting boats more than two centuries ago. These residents remain proud of their heritage and continue to build their famous fiberglass boats today. The island is secluded, and the old-fashioned, family-oriented roots show in the local policy toward liquor: it isn't sold anywhere on the island. (But most folks won't mind if you bring your own.) Three churches, a one-room schoolhouse, several boutique shops, small grocery stores, and just one restaurant round out the tiny island's offerings.

A mile north of the island you can dive to the wreck of the USS *Adirondack*, which sank after hitting a reef in 1862. It lies among a host of cannons in 20 feet of water.

### GETTING HERE AND AROUND

Man-O-War Cay is an easy 20-minute ride from Marsh Harbour by water taxi or aboard a small rented outboard runabout. The island has a 28-slip marina. No cars are allowed on the island, but you'll have no problem walking it, or you can rent a golf cart. The two main roads, Queen's Highway and Sea Road, run parallel.

### EXPLORING

**Hero's Wall.** Outside the public library is a wall adorned with plaques honoring residents who have helped to develop the community over the years. Notice that most of them share the same last name, as is often the case in small island communities. In this case, Albury and Sweeting are the most common names. ✉ *Ballfield Rd. and Queen's Hwy., Man-O-War Cay.*

**Man-O-War Heritage Museum.** Historic artifacts from the boat building industry are on display in this small museum. Built in the 1800s, the quaint white wooden building is the former "Church Corner House" commissioned by the patriarch of one of the island's best-known boat-building families. ⊠ *Queen's Hwy. and Pappy Ben Hill, Man-O-War Cay* 🖾 *Free* ⊙ *Thurs. and Sat. 11–1.*

## WHERE TO EAT

$  ✕**Dock & Dine.** The only full fare restaurant on the island sits on a covered deck overlooking the sheltered harbor. The nautical decor makes for a nice place to eat and enjoy. No liquor is served on this dry island. Food is basic Bahamian and American style with everything from salads to burgers and wraps. Try their twist on a local favorite: "chicken in da bag" is fried chicken served on a pile of fries, doused in ketchup and hot sauce, and wrapped up in foil and a paper bag to soak up the grease. $ *Average main: $18* ⊠ *Waterfront, Sea Rd., Man-O-War Cay* ☎ *242/365–6380* ⊟ *No credit cards.*

BAHAMIAN

$  ✕**Tropical Island Treats.** This small ice cream parlor has an impressive selection of flavors to choose from. If you're looking for a light bite, they also serve up basic hot dogs, nachos, and in the high season, Jamaican patties. $ *Average main: $5* ⊠ *Sea Rd., Man-O-War Cay* ☎ *242/365–6501* ⊙ *Mon.–Sat. 11:30–2:30 and 6–9.*

AMERICAN

## WHERE TO STAY

**PRIVATE VILLA RENTALS**

**Waterways Boat and Cottage Rentals.** With no hotels on the island, the only way to stay in this quaint settlement is to rent a condo or a home. Available accommodations range from a tiny dockside cottage at the entrance to the sheltered harbor to Loyalist-era houses nestled among the locals to newly constructed beachfront homes that sleep 10 comfortably and offer all the amenities of home. Most require a week's rental agreement. The company also rents boats and golf carts. ⊠ *Sea Rd. & Pappy Ben Hill, Man-O-War Cay* ☎ *242/365–6143, 242/357–6540* 🖷 *242/365–6115* ⊕ *www.waterwaysrentals.com* ⊅ *18 homes.*

## SHOPPING

**Albury's Sail Shop.** This shop is popular with boaters, who stock up on duffel bags, briefcases, hats, and purses, all made from duck, a colorful, sturdy canvas fabric traditionally used for sails. ⊠ *Lover's La. at Sea Rd., Man-O-War Cay* ☎ *242/365–6014.*

**Joe's Studio.** This store sells paintings by local artists, books, clothing, and other nautically oriented gifts, but the most interesting souvenirs are the half models of sailing dinghies. These mahogany models, which are cut in half and mounted on boards, are meant to be displayed as wall hangings. Artist Joe Albury, one of the store's owners, also crafts full, 3-D boat models. ⊠ *Sea Rd., Man-O-War Cay* ☎ *242/365–6082.*

**Sally's Seaside Boutique.** Ladies sit in the back of this small shop and sew Bahamian made Androsia fabric into original shirts, dresses, blouses, and linens for the home. You can also pick up a locally made wooden handicraft or book about the Abacos. ⊠ *Sea Rd., Man-O-War Cay* ☎ *242/365–6044.*

### SPORTS AND THE OUTDOORS

#### BOATING

**Man-O-War Marina.** This marina has 26 slips and also rents golf carts. For people coming from Marsh Harbour or other cays, the Albury Ferry dock is adjacent. ✉ *Front Rd., Man-O-War Cay* ☎ *242/365–6008*.

#### SCUBA DIVING

**DiveTime.** Learn to scuba dive in some of the most beautiful waters around. Seasoned divers can join one of the daily two-tank dives, rent equipment, or book a private charter for a maximum of six divers. Half-day snorkeling trips are also available. ✉ *Man-O-War Cay* ☎ *242/365–6235* 🌐 *www.divetimeabaco.com*.



## GREAT GUANA CAY

The essence of Great Guana Cay can be summed up by its unofficial motto, painted on a hand-lettered sign: "It's better in the Bahamas, but it's gooder in Guana." This sliver of an islet just off Great Abaco, accessible by ferry from Marsh Harbour or by private boat, is the kind of place people picture when they dream of running off to disappear on an exotic island, complete with alluring deserted beaches and grassy dunes. Only 100 full-time residents live on 7-mile-long Great Guana Cay, where you're more likely to run into a rooster than a car during your stroll around the tranquil village. Still, there are just enough luxuries here to make your stay comfortable, including a couple of small, laid-back resorts and a restaurant–bar with one of the best party scenes in the Abacos. The island also has easy access to bonefishing flats you can explore on your own.

#### GETTING HERE AND AROUND

The ferry to Great Guana Cay leaves from the Conch Inn Marina in Marsh Harbour. The ride is about 30 minutes. Golf carts are available for rent in Great Guana Cay, though most places are within walking distance.

### WHERE TO EAT AND STAY

$$ BAHAMIAN Fodor's Choice ★ 🍴 **Nippers Beach Bar & Grill.** With awesome ocean views and a snorkeling reef just 10 yards off its perfect beach, this cool bar and restaurant is a must-visit hangout. Linger over a lunch of burgers and sandwiches or a dinner of steak and lobster, then chill out in the two-tiered pool. Nurse a "Nipper Tripper"—a frozen concoction of five rums and two juices. If you down more than one or two of these, you'll be happy to take advantage of the Nippermobile, which provides free transport to and from the cay's public dock. Every Sunday, everybody who is anybody, or not, revels in the all-day party disguised as a pig roast. [$] *Average main: $30* ✉ *Great Guana Cay* ☎ *242/365–5111* 🌐 *www.nippersbar.com*.

$ BAHAMIAN 🍴 **Pirate's Cove Tiki Bar & Restaurant.** Perch on a bar stool around the tiki bar or take a seat on one of the rocking chairs on the porch and enjoy the comings and goings of Guana Cay's harbor and main road. One of the few spots to get pastries and coffee starting at 6 am, Pirate's is also a deli and ice cream parlor that turns into a popular restaurant where everything is kept simple and grilled for lunch and dinner. Locals and yachtsmen pop in for the popular Wednesday night pot-luck—bring a dish and eat for free. And if you're lucky on your fishing trip, bring it here and the chef will cook it however you want and add four sides for just $15. $ *Average main: $18* ⊠ *Great Guana Cay* ☎ *242/365–5006.*

$$$
HOTEL

🍴 **Flip Flops on the Beach.** Reserve one of the four one- or two-bedroom beachside bungalows at this casually elegant boutique resort and you can melt into the island lifestyle of sun, sand, serenity, and ocean breezes on arrival. **Pros:** beachfront location; the essence of tranquillity; quality accommodations and in-room amenities. **Cons:** remote location means there is no nightlife, shopping, or larger resort-style activities; no Internet. $ *Rooms from: $400* ⊠ *Great Guana Cay* ☎ *800/222–2646, 242/365–5137* ⊕ *www.flipflopsonthebeach.com* ⤶ *4 bungalows* ⊗ *Closed mid-Aug.–mid-Oct.* 🍴 *No meals.*

> **CELEBRATE GOOD TIMES!**
>
> All-day pig roasts are a common Sunday event, from Nippers on Great Guana Cay to Pete's Pub in Little Harbour. These events are a fun and inexpensive way to enjoy a day on the beach with lots of tasty Bahamian chow, live music, dancing, and island camaraderie. Ask at your hotel for a schedule of events.

## NIGHTLIFE

**Nippers.** Not only is this the best spot on a Sunday, but weekend nights Nippers continues to rock. ☎ *242/365–5143.*

## SHOPPING

**Gone Conchin'.** Pick up some island appropriate outfits for your vacation in this small yellow store right at the foot of the ferry dock. They also sell sea glass jewelry and other trinkets. It's the only place in Abaco that carries the full range of Bahama Handprints clothing. ⊠ *Guana Cay, Great Abaco Island* ☎ *242/365–5215* ⊗ *Daily 10–4.*

## SPORTS AND THE OUTDOORS

### BOATING

**Baker's Bay Golf & Ocean Club.** At the northwestern end of the island, Baker's Bay Golf & Ocean Club has 158 slips. ☎ *242/367–0612* ⊕ *www.discoverylandco.com.*

**Orchid Bay Yacht Club and Marina.** Orchid Bay Yacht Club and Marina has 66 deepwater slips and full services for boaters at the entrance to the main settlement bay, across from the public docks. The club office rents luxury apartments, cottages, and homes, and prime real estate is for sale. There's also a swimming pool and a restaurant that serves fresh seafood, steaks, and healthy salads on an outdoor deck overlooking the marina. ☎ *242/365–5175.*

### SCUBA DIVING

**Dive Guana.** This dive shop organizes scuba and snorkeling trips and island hopping boat tours. The shop also rents boats, kayaks, and bicycles. Renting a boat, at least for a day, is the best way to get around and enjoy other nearby cays. ☎ *242/365–5178* ⊕ *www.diveguana.com.*

# GREEN TURTLE CAY

This tiny 3-mile-by-½-mile island is steeped in Loyalist history; some residents can trace their heritage back more than 200 years. Dotted with ancestral New England–style cottage homes, the cay is surrounded by several deep bays, sounds, bonefish flats, and irresistible beaches. **New Plymouth**, first settled in 1783, is Green Turtle's main community. Many of its approximately 550 residents earn a living by diving for conch or selling lobster and fish. There are a few grocery and hardware stores, several gift shops, a post office, a bank, a handful of restaurants, and several offices.

## GETTING HERE AND AROUND

The **Green Turtle Cay Ferry** (☎ 242/365–4166) leaves the Treasure Cay airport dock at 8:30, 10:30, 11:30, 1:30, 2:30, 3:30, 4:30, and 5, and returns from Green Turtle Cay at 8, 9, 11, 12:15, 1:30, 3, and 4:30. The trip takes 10 minutes, and one-way fares are $11, same-day round-trip fare is $16. The ferry makes several stops in Green Turtle, including New Plymouth, the Green Turtle Club, and the Bluff House Beach Hotel.

Many hotels provide an occasional shuttle from the main ferry dock in Green Turtle Cay to their property, and there are a couple of taxis on the island. Most people travel via golf cart or boat. Don't worry, you won't miss having a car; even in the slowest golf cart you can get from one end of the island to the other in 20 minutes or less.

**KoolKart Rentals.** Rent your own golf cart here. ⊠ *Green Turtle Cay* ☎ *242/356–4176* ⊕ *www.koolkartrentals.com.*

## EXPLORING

**Albert Lowe Museum.** New Plymouth's most frequently visited attraction is the Bahamas' oldest historical museum, dedicated to a model-ship builder and direct descendant of the island's original European-American settlers. You can learn island history through local memorabilia from the 1700s, Lowe's model schooners, and old photographs, including one of the aftermath of the 1932 hurricane that nearly flattened New Plymouth. One of the galleries displays paintings of typical Out Island scenes by acclaimed artist Alton Lowe, Albert's son. Mrs. Ivy Roberts, the museum's director, enjoys showing visitors around and sharing stories of life in the Out Islands before the days of high-speed Internet and daily airline flights. ⊠ *Parliament St., New Plymouth, Green Turtle Cay* ☎ *242/365–4094* 🖾 *$5 adults, $3 children* ⊙ *Mon.–Sat. 9–11:45 and 1–4.*

**Captain Roland Roberts House.** Volunteers and patrons have rallied together to restore the only remaining Conch-style house left in New Plymouth and create this unique historic and environmental center. Many of the exhibits are geared towards teaching young children about the environment. If you're lucky, Richard 'Blue' Jones will be available to take you on a fascinating tour of the bush medicine garden he's planted out back. The center is run by volunteers, so opening times are often erratic. ⊠ *New Plymouth, Green Turtle Cay* 🖾 *Free, donations encouraged* ⊙ *Hours vary.*

Nippers Beach Bar & Grill is the best restaurant on Great Guana Cay.

**Memorial Sculpture Garden.** The past is present in this garden across the street from the New Plymouth Inn. (Note that it's laid out in the pattern of the British flag.) Immortalized in busts perched on pedestals are local residents who have made important contributions to the Bahamas. Plaques detail the accomplishments of British Loyalists, their descendants, and the descendants of those brought as slaves, such as Jeanne I. Thompson, a contemporary playwright and the country's second woman to practice law. This is an open garden, free to the public. ⊠ *Parliament St., New Plymouth, Green Turtle Cay.*

### WHERE TO EAT

$$$  ✕ **Captain's Table.** The colonial-style dining room serves memorable Baha-
BAHAMIAN  mian-style dinners with a Continental touch. The menu changes nightly, though there is always a choice of seafood, meat, or chicken. When it's available, don't pass up the hog snapper. The nightly fresh fish is always well prepared, and meat lovers can enjoy roasts, steaks, and chops. For dessert, don't miss the key lime pie. ⓢ *Average main: $35* ⊠ *New Plymouth Inn, Parliament St., New Plymouth, Green Turtle Cay* ☎ *242/365–4161* ⊕ *www.newplymouthinn.com* ⌕ *Reservations essential.*

$$  ✕ **Crazy Love Cafe & Grill.** The seafood at this tiny indoor restaurant is
BAHAMIAN  caught daily and the blackened snapper or grouper served on top of a fresh tomato salad is delicious. If you're all fished out, try the Prime Rib served Saturday nights. Just be sure to book in advance as seating is limited. It's also a great spot to stop in for a hearty breakfast sandwich, or at lunchtime the chicken philly sub is a big hit. ⓢ *Average main: $15* ⊠ *New Plymouth, Green Turtle Cay* ☎ *242/458–8483* ⌕ *Reservations essential.*

**$$$**

EUROPEAN

Fodor'sChoice

★

✕ **Green Turtle Club Dining.** Breakfast and lunch are served harborside on a covered, screened-in patio, while dinner takes place in the elegant dining room. At lunch, treat yourself to a lobster salad, lobster corn chowder, cheeseburger, or grilled grouper sandwich. Dinner is where the club really shines, transporting you back to the 1920s with elegant dining beneath antique chandeliers. The steaks are among the best around. The jumbo lobster and artichoke ravioli, conch trio, and stone crab claws are just some of the temptations on the extensive menu. For dessert, try the guava crème brûlée. For those who prefer a casual environment, an à la carte dinner menu is available outside on the enclosed patio. $ *Average main: $30 ⊠ Green Turtle Club, north end of White Sound, New Plymouth, Green Turtle Cay* ☎ *242/365–4271* ⊕ *Closed mid-Sept.–Oct.*

**$$**

BAHAMIAN

✕ **Harvey's Island Grill.** Sit inside and enjoy the cool air-conditioning, or grab one of the brightly painted blue and pink picnic tables on the harbor side beach across the street to enjoy your lunch or dinner. The menu is a simple mix of American and Bahamian fare. Monday's pizza night is popular as is the Friday night Fish Fry. On a hot day, grab a daiquiri or a scoop of homemade coconut or mango ice cream from the stand outside. $ *Average main: $20 ⊠ New Plymouth, Green Turtle Cay* ☎ *242/365–4389.*

**$**

AMERICAN

✕ **Jolly Roger Bar and Bistro.** This casual eatery on the water in the Bluff House Marina offers tasty meals. Sitting under an umbrella on the deck is the best way to enjoy the view of the sailboat-filled harbor, but you can also eat in the air-conditioned pub-style dining room. Menu choices range from standard Bahamian (conch fritters and burgers) to new American (roasted pork tenderloin with salsa, salads with goat cheese and roasted vegetables). Another fun option is to enjoy a rum drink from the bar while catching some rays at the pool. $ *Average main: $18 ⊠ Between Abaco Sea and White Sound, at Bluff House Beach Hotel Marina, New Plymouth, Green Turtle Cay* ☎ *242/365–4200.*

**$**

BAHAMIAN

✕ **Lizard Bar & Grill.** Dine poolside overlooking the Leeward Yacht Club marina at this casual bar and grill. The grilled lobster or fresh catch (which can be jerked, blackened, grilled, or fried) are popular menu choices as are the conch burger and conch fritters. Wash it all down with a potent Leaning Lizard. $ *Average main: $15 ⊠ Leeward Yacht Club, New Plymouth, Green Turtle Cay* ☎ *242/365–4191* ⊕ *www. leewardyachtclub.com.*

**$**

BAHAMIAN

✕ **McIntosh Restaurant and Bakery.** At this simple, diner-style restaurant, lunch means excellent renditions of local favorites, such as fried grouper and cracked conch, and sandwiches made with thick slices of slightly sweet Bahamian bread. At dinner, large portions of pork chops, lobster, fish, and shrimp are served with rib-sticking sides like baked macaroni and cheese, peas 'n' rice, and coleslaw. Save room for a piece of pound cake or coconut cream pie, baked fresh daily and displayed in the glass case up front. Breakfast is also served. $ *Average main: $12 ⊠ Parliament St., New Plymouth, Green Turtle Cay* ☎ *242/365–4625.*

4

$

BAHAMIAN

✕**Pineapples Bar & Grill.** Hang out, take a dip in the freshwater pool, and enjoy Bahamian fare with a flair. In Black Sound, at the entrance to the Other Shore Club and Marina, you'll find this simple open-air restaurant with a canopy-shaded bar and picnic tables next to the pool. Some of the best conch fritters in the islands are served from noon on. At lunch, try a fresh salad or spicy jerk chicken; for dinner, grilled daily-caught fish. The jerk-spiced grouper is sensational. Specialty drinks include a Pineapple Smash and a Yellowbird, both capable of mellowing your mood. $ *Average main: $17* ✉ *Black Sound, New Plymouth, Green Turtle Cay* ☎ *242/365–4039* ⊕ *www.othershoreclub.com* ▭ *No credit cards* ◎ *Closed Sun.*

$

BAHAMIAN

✕**The Wrecking Tree.** The wooden deck at this casual restaurant was built around the wrecking tree, a place where 19th-century wrecking vessels brought their salvage. Today it's a cool place to linger over a cold Kalik and a hearty lunch of cracked conch, fish-and-chips, or zesty conch salad. It has great pastries, too—take some back to your hotel. Dinner is served during "the season." $ *Average main: $16* ✉ *Bay St., New Plymouth, Green Turtle Cay* ☎ *242/365–4263* ▭ *No credit cards* ◎ *Closed Sun. Dinner served in the busy season only.*

## WHERE TO STAY

### PRIVATE VILLA RENTALS

**Island Property Management.** A five-bedroom, oceanfront mansion with wraparound verandah, full-time staff, and a marble fireplace could be yours. Or rent a two-bedroom cottage in the heart of New Plymouth. This agency has more than 50 cottages and houses for rent to meet different budgets and needs. It can also help arrange excursions and boat and golf-cart rentals. Most homes have water views, and some have docks for your rental boat. The offices in New Plymouth are in a blue two-story building along with Green Turtle Real Estate, just down from the ferry dock. ✉ *Various Green Turtle Cay locations, New Plymouth, Green Turtle Cay* ☎ *242/365–4047* ⊕ *www.abacoislandrentals.com.*

### RECOMMENDED RESORTS

$$

B&B/INN

🏨 **Barefoot Homes.** From its perch on a rocky bluff overlooking White Sound, this romantic hilltop hideaway provides sweeping views of the sheltered harbor or the Sea of Abaco. **Pros:** inspiring views; spacious luxury accommodations; tranquil and romantic. **Cons:** 20-minute golf-cart ride or 10-minute boat ride to New Plymouth; no reliable Internet service; no restaurant on-site. $ *Rooms from: $200* ✉ *Between Abaco Sea and White Sound, New Plymouth, Green Turtle Cay* ☎ *242/577–4092* ⊕ *www.greenturtleabacohomesforrent.com* ⤴ *4 suites, 4 villas, 5 cottages.*

$$

RESORT

🏨 **Bluff House Beach Resort & Marina.** Newly constructed, but full of old-world charm, the first stage of this property's restoration includes eight beautifully appointed suites overlooking the Sea of Abaco. **Pros:** secluded and private; new construction; beautiful decor. **Cons:** golf cart or boat required to get into New Plymouth; lots of steps up to all suites. $ *Rooms from: $225* ✉ *New Plymouth, Green Turtle Cay* ☎ *242/365–4247* ⊕ *www.bluffhouse.com* ⤴ *8 suites* ◎ *No meals.*

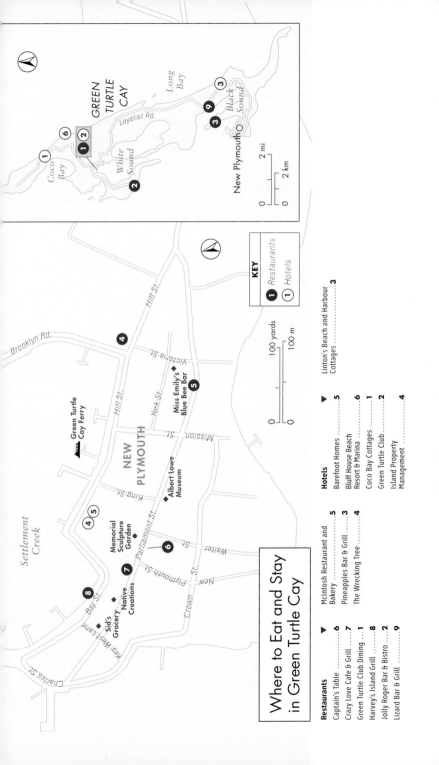

# Where to Eat and Stay in Green Turtle Cay

**Restaurants** ▶

Captain's Table .......... **6**
Crazy Love Cafe & Grill ..... **7**
Green Turtle Club Dining ... **1**
Harvey's Island Grill ....... **8**
Jolly Roger Bar & Bistro .... **2**
Lizard Bar & Grill ......... **9**

McIntosh Restaurant and
Bakery ................... **5**
Pineapples Bar & Grill ..... **3**
The Wrecking Tree .......... **4**

**Hotels** ▶

Barefoot Homes .......... **5**
Bluff House Beach
Resort & Marina .......... **6**
Coco Bay Cottages ....... **1**
Green Turtle Club ....... **2**
Island Property
Management ............ **4**

Linton's Beach and Harbour
Cottages .................. **3**

**KEY**

**1** Restaurants
**①** Hotels

NEW PLYMOUTH

Green Turtle Cay Ferry

Albert Lowe Museum

Memorial Sculpture Garden

Native Creations

Sid's Grocery

Miss Emily's Blue Bee Bar

GREEN TURTLE CAY

Coco Bay

White Sound

Long Bay

Loyalist Rd.

Black Sound

New Plymouth

Settlement Creek

Brooklyn Rd.

Hill St.

Hill St.

Victoria St.

York St.

Mission St.

King St.

Parliament St.

Walter St.

New Plymouth St.

Crown St.

Bay St.

Key West Lane

Charles St.

$$$ RENTAL **Coco Bay Cottages.** Sandwiched between one beach on the Atlantic and another calmer, sandy stretch on the bay are six spacious cottages—including two three-bedroom cottages and a four-bedroom cottage—that all have views of the water. **Pros:** spacious, well-located do-it-yourself accommodations; awesome beaches; Wi-Fi for those who can't totally get away. **Cons:** renting a boat and/or golf cart is essential; if you don't like silence, the peace and quiet will kill you. [$] *Rooms from: $350* ✉ *Coco Bay, north of Green Turtle Club, New Plymouth, Green Turtle Cay* ☎ *561/202–8149, 800/752–0166* 🌐 *www.cocobaycottages.com* 🛏 *6 cottages.*

$$ RESORT **Green Turtle Club.** The longstanding colonial tradition and tone of casual refinement continues at this well-known resort. **Pros:** excellent on-site restaurants for casual or fine dining; easy access to great beaches; personalized service. **Cons:** if you're looking for Bahamian casual, this isn't it; golf cart or boat is essential to explore the island [$] *Rooms from: $189* ✉ *North end of White Sound, New Plymouth, Green Turtle Cay* ☎ *242/365–4271, 866/528–0539* 🌐 *www.greenturtleclub.com* 🛏 *24 rooms, 2 suites, 8 villas* 🕒 *Closed Labor Day–Oct.*

$$ RENTAL **Linton's Beach and Harbour Cottages.** These three classic Bahamian-style cottages are ideally placed on 22 private acres between Long Bay and Black Sound. **Pros:** well-located do-it-yourself cottages; value priced for families and groups. **Cons:** gathering groceries and supplies can be an adventure; some beach cottages don't have phones or TV. [$] *Rooms from: $260* ✉ *S. Loyalist Rd., Black Sound, New Plymouth, Green Turtle Cay* ☎ *772/538–4680* 🌐 *www.lintoncottages.com* 🛏 *3 cottages* 💳 *No credit cards.*

## NIGHTLIFE

**Gully Roosters.** At night, Green Turtle can be deader than dead or surprisingly lively. Bet on the latter if the local favorites, the Gully Roosters, are playing anywhere on the island. Known locally as just the Roosters, this reggae-calypso band is the most popular in the Abacos. Its mix of original tunes and covers can coax even the most reluctant reveler onto the dance floor. The band's schedule is erratic, but they play every Wednesday at 9 pm under the Buttonwood tree at the **Green Turtle Club** (☎ *242/365–4271*) during the high season.

**Miss Emily's Blue Bee Bar.** Other nighttime options include a visit to Miss Emily's Blue Bee Bar, where you might find a singing, carousing crowd knocking back the world-famous Goombay Smash. (Or not—many Goombay novices underestimate the drink's potency, and end up making it an early night.) Mrs. Emily Cooper, creator of the popular Goombay Smash drink, passed away in 1997, but her daughter Violet continues to serve up the famous rum, pineapple juice, and apricot brandy concoction. The actual recipe is top secret, and in spite of many imitators throughout the islands, you'll never taste a Goombay this good anywhere else. It's worth a special trip to try one. ☎ *242/365–4181.*

**Pineapples Bar & Grill.** On the water in front of the Other Shore Club and Marina, this bar has a hopping happy hour from 4 to 6 daily and live music every Friday at 8. ☎ *242/365–4039* 🌐 *www.pineapplesbar.com.*

**Sundowner's.** Locals hang out at Sundowner's, a waterside bar and grill where attractions include a pool table and, on weekend nights, a DJ spinning dance music on the deck under the stars. ☎ *242/365–4060.*

## SHOPPING

**Native Creations.** Colorful Abaco Ceramics, handmade in Treasure Cay, are the best bet at Native Creations. The shop also sells beaded jewelry, picture frames, candles, postcards, and books. ⊠ *Parliament St., New Plymouth, Green Turtle Cay* ☎ *242/365–4206.*

**Plymouth Rock Liquors and Café.** This shop sells Cuban cigars and more than 60 kinds of rum. ⊠ *Parliament St., New Plymouth, Green Turtle Cay* ☎ *242/365–4234.*

**Sid's Grocery.** Sid's has the most complete line of groceries on the island, plus a gift section that includes books on local Bahamian subjects—great for souvenirs or for replenishing your stock of reading material. ⊠ *Upper Rd., New Plymouth, Green Turtle Cay* ☎ *242/365–4055.*

**Vert's Model Ship Shop.** Stop here to pick up one of Vert Lowe's hand-crafted two-mast schooners or sloops. Model prices range anywhere from $100 to $1,200. If Vert's shop door is locked—and it often is—knock at the white house with bright pink shutters next door. If you're still unsuccessful, inquire at the Green Turtle Club, where Vert has worked for more than 30 years. ⊠ *Corner of Bay St. and Gully Alley, New Plymouth, Green Turtle Cay* ☎ *242/365–4170.*

## SPORTS AND THE OUTDOORS

### BOATING

It's highly recommended that you reserve your boat rental at the same time you book your hotel or cottage. If you're unable to rent a boat on Green Turtle Cay, try nearby Treasure Cay or Marsh Harbour.

**Bluff House Beach Resort & Marina.** Here you can find a marina with 40 slips and a full range of services—everything from fuel to laundry facilities. ☎ *242/365–4200* ⊕ *www.bluffhouse.com.*

**Green Turtle Club.** Green Turtle Club has 40 slips and offers cable TV and Wi-Fi, as well as a full stocked commissary. ☎ *242/365–4271* ⊕ *www.greenturtleclub.com.*

**The Other Shore Club Marina and Cottages.** Tucked into quiet and protected Black Sound, the Other Shore Club Marina and Cottages is an ideal place to keep your small cay-hopping boat if you are staying in one of Green Turtle's many rental houses and cottages. The club has its own rental cottages and can arrange fishing, diving, and snorkeling trips. ☎ *242/365–4226* ⊕ *www.othershoreclub.com.*

**Boat Rentals Donnie's Boat Rentals** ☎ *242/365–4119* ⊕ *www.donniesboatrentals.com.* **Reef Boat Rentals** ☎ *242/365–4145.*

### FISHING

**Captain Rick Sawyer.** The top recommendation on Green Turtle Cay, Captain Rick Sawyer is one of the best guides in the Abacos. Rick's company, Abaco Flyfish Connection and Charters, offers bonefishing on 17-foot Maverick flats skiffs, and reef and offshore fishing aboard his 33-foot Tiara sportfisher. Book as far in advance as you can. ☎ *242/365–4261* ⊕ *www.abacoflyfish.com.*

**Ronnie Sawyer.** Considered one of the best in the business, Ronnie Sawyer has been fishing the Abaco flats professionally for nearly a quarter century. ☎ *242/365–4070* ⊕ *www.go-abacos.com/ronnie.*

## SCUBA DIVING AND SNORKELING

**Brendal's Dive Center.** This dive center leads snorkeling and scuba trips, plus wild dolphin encounters, glass-bottom boat cruises, and more. Personable owner Brendal Stevens has been featured on the Discovery Channel and CNN, and he knows the surrounding reefs so well that he's named some of the groupers, stingrays, and moray eels that you'll have a chance to hand-feed. Trips can include a seafood lunch, grilled on the beach, and complimentary rum punch. Kayak and canoe rentals are available. ☎ *242/365–4411* ⊕ *www.brendal.com.*

**Lincoln Jones.** Rent some snorkel gear or bring your own, and call Lincoln Jones, known affectionately as "the Daniel Boone of the Bahamas," for an unforgettable snorkeling adventure. Lincoln will dive for conch and lobster (in season) or catch fish, then grill a sumptuous lunch on a deserted beach. ☎ *242/365–4223* ⊕ *www.go-abacos.com/lincoln.*

5

# ANDROS, BIMINI, AND THE BERRY ISLANDS

# WELCOME TO ANDROS, BIMINI, AND THE BERRY ISLANDS

## TOP REASONS TO GO

★ **Bonefish:** Andros has a reputation for the best bonefishing in the world, and Bimini comes in a close second. Hire a fishing guide to teach you how to fly-fish, then cruise the West Side flats of Andros Island or Bimini's North Sound Lagoon in pursuit of the elusive "gray ghost."

★ **Charter a boat:** Explore the necklace of islands that comprise Bimini and the Berries. Start in Bimini and end up in Chub Cay. It's quite possible that you may choose not to come back.

★ **Dive Andros Island:** Go with the diving experts at Small Hope Bay and drop "over the wall" or explore some of Andros's magnificent reefs.

Alice Town ○ North Bimini
South Bimini
Turtle Rocks
Holm Cay
North Cat Cay     *Bimini*
South Cat Cay      **2**

Ocean Cay

**1** **Andros.** Incredible blue holes, vibrant reefs (including the third-largest barrier reef in the world), and the Tongue of the Ocean wall make diving and snorkeling some of the main reasons adventurers travel to Andros year-round. Legendary bonefishing on its West Side flats and in its creeks and bights is the other. The island is mostly flat, lush with mangroves, rimmed with white-sand beaches, and laced with miles of creeks and lakes. Exploring is best done by boat, not car, though taxis are available.

**2** **Bimini.** In spring and summer, boaters from south Florida attack nearby Bimini looking for fish and fun. Most go to North Bimini and its big modern resort or one of its older, smaller fishing lodges. South Bimini, a short ferry ride away and

home to the islands' only airport, also boasts a major resort, but appeals more to the nature-minded visitor looking for peace and beach. Uninhabited East Bimini is a maze of mangrove islands, some with beaches and the Healing Hole springs.

**3** **The Berry Islands.** For the ultimate remote island getaway, choose a Berry, any Berry island, which range from the main hub of Great Harbour Cay to private resorts such as Chub Cay. (Royal Caribbean and Norwegian cruise lines also own two private islands in the 30-cay chain.) Plan to spend your days lolling on the secluded, low-key beaches or in pursuit of game and bonefish. Chub Cay, at the Tongue of the Ocean, attracts derring-do divers.

Great Stirrup Cay

Great Harbour Cay

Hoffman's Cay

**Berry** Comfort Cay
**Islands** Bond's Cay
3

Chub Cay  Whale Cay

Joulters Cays

Lowe Sound  Morgan's Bluff
Red Bays  Nicholl's Town
Mastic Point
San Andros  *Barrier Reef*

Staniard Creek

Fresh Creek

Andros Town

**Andros Island**
1

Cargill Creek
Behring Point  *Barrier Reef*

Big Wood Cay

Moxey Town
Lisbon Creek
Yellow Cay  Mangrove Cay  Driggs Hill
Congo Town
**South Bight**  The Bluff
Kemps Bay

*Barrier Reef*

Deep Creek

Mars Bay

Water Cays  Curley Cut Cays

*G R A N D   B A H A M A   B A N K*

0 — 20 mi
0 — 30 km

NASSAU

*New Providence I.*

*Tongue of the Ocean*

## GETTING ORIENTED

The northern islands of Andros, Bimini, and Berry lie just off the east coast of Florida. Bimini, which consists of three main islands—North, South, and East Bimini—is only 50 miles from Miami. The Berry Islands are a 30-cay chain about 100 miles east of Bimini. South of Chub Cay—Berry's southernmost island—Andros comprises the Bahamas' largest land-mass—about half of all the Bahamas' land in total. North and Central Andros occupy the largest of the three major islands, while South Andros is separated from it by North and Middle Bight. South Bight splits South Andros into two parts. On their eastern shores, magnificent remote beaches stretch along most of these northern islands. Vast mangrove estuaries and swamps characterize their western leeward coasts.

5

Updated by
Paul Rubio

Legends loom large (and small) on these northwestern Bahamas islands. On Bimini, you'll hear about the lost underwater city of Atlantis, Ernest Hemingway's visits, and the Fountain of Youth. Tiny birdlike creatures known as chickcharnies are said to inhabit the pine forests of Andros Island. On both islands, along with the Berry Islands, bone-fishing has made legends of mere men.

Despite the legends, Andros, Bimini, and the Berries remain a secret mostly known to avid divers, boaters, and fishermen. These islands stash their reputation for superlative bonefishing, diving, blue holes, and other natural phenomena away from the glitter-focused eyes of visitors to nearby Nassau, just minutes away by plane but a world apart. Bimini is probably best known for its Hemingway connection and because it's an easy boat ride from Miami, which means a brisk spring and summer trade. Yet the island has virtually no cars (and only one gas station). Andros weighs in as the largest Bahamas island, accounting for more than half of the nation's landmass. Still, much of it is uninhabitable and largely undiscovered. In fact, no resort has more than 30 rooms. The 30-some cays of the Berry Islands are less known still, in spite of gorgeous beaches and destination resorts. None of the islands have traffic lights, movie theaters, or fast-food outlets—let alone water parks, shopping centers, or golf courses.

So, with that in mind, plan your trip here as an adventurer. If you're not into diving, snorkeling, fishing, kayaking, hiking, biking, or secluded beach-vegetating, these are not the islands for you. If you are into any of the above, you will be thrilled and endlessly entertained. All three islands are spoken of synonymously with bonefishing, and commercial fishing—focused on lobster, grouper, and snapper—and recreational guide fishing drive the economies of many of these communities. Andros thrives also on its harvest of land crabs, fruit and vegetable crops, and fresh water; it exports all of these products to Nassau.

# PLANNING

## WHEN TO GO

Andros, Bimini, and the Berries have a slightly different high season than most of the other Bahamas islands. Because of their close proximity to Florida, boaters make the crossing in droves from spring break through summer, especially to Bimini. Waters tend to be calmest during these months. Andros and the Berries, because of their famed fishing and diving, experience traffic also in the winter season (mid-December through Easter), but not as much as elsewhere. Fishing and diving are good throughout the year, although cold fronts December through February can cause rough seas. Temperatures usually remain steady enough to enjoy the beaches year-round, but occasionally drop into the 60s. At many resorts rates remain steady throughout the year, except in Bimini and at fishing lodges on the other islands, where they are generally higher in spring and summer. Hurricane season technically runs from June through November; August and September (the most likely months for hurricanes) can be hot and steamy, and many resorts and restaurants are closed.

### TOP FESTIVALS

#### WINTER

**Junkanoo Celebrations** take place in Fresh Creek in Central Andros, Nicholl's Town in North Andros, Alice Town in North Bimini, Bullock's Harbour Park in Great Harbour Cay, and Berry Islands on Boxing Day (December 26) and New Year's Day with festivities that include traditional Junkanoo parades, music, dancing, and food.

#### SPRING

Though bonefishing is the name of the game on the Andros islands, in April the town of Red Bays in North Andros hosts a **Snapper Tournament**.

#### SUMMER

During the second weekend in June, three days of crab races, cook-offs, live Rake 'n' Scrape music, and national musical artists comprise the **All Andros Crab Fest** in Fresh Creek, held at Queen Park. Expect wild street parties across the Bahamas on July 10, Independence Day. **The All Andros & Berry Islands Regatta** takes place the second weekend in July, featuring A, B, and C Class Bahamian sailing sloops, local cuisine, and entertainment at Andros Regatta Village on Morgan's Bluff Beach. Don't let the name fool you; **Junkanoo in June**—traditional summertime parties with Goombay dancers and musical groups—take place throughout the entire summer on Fridays (and sometimes Saturdays) in Andros, the Berry Islands, and Bimini. On-island tourism offices can provide more details. The Berry Islands celebrate everything conch—from culinary preparations to conch dance competitions—during the **Conch Festival** held in August. South Andros also hosts a similar festival in Mars Bay in mid-October. The conch-cracking contest is always a highlight there. Bimini hosts the **Bahamas Boating Flings** (formerly the Bimini Open Angling Tournament) in June and July as well as the **Annual Bimini Native Fishing Tournament** in August.

## GETTING HERE AND AROUND

### AIR TRAVEL

Direct commercial flights from the U.S. to the Bahamas' northwestern islands are few and far between. While Bimini is still accessible via direct flight from Fort Lauderdale on Silver Airways (dba United Express), the islands of Andros and Great Harbour Cay in the Berry Islands require a flight connection in Nassau unless going by private charter. Most major U.S. carriers fly to Nassau. The onward journey requires a flight on LeAir or Western Air. As strange as it may sound, connecting from North/Central Andros to South Andros or Mangrove Cay requires flying back to Nassau. Private charters and regularly scheduled charters also serve these islands. To get between the Bahamas' northwestern islands, Captain Paul W. J. Harding (☎ 242/357–9876) operates a seaplane that offers bespoke pickup and drop-off points within Bimini, Andros, and the Berry Islands (*see ⇨ Getting Here and Around in Andros*).

### BOAT AND FERRY TRAVEL

Bimini and the Berry Islands are popular with private boaters. A weekend commercial ferry connects Miami to Bimini. Regular ferries (thrice weekly) connect North/Central Andros to Nassau. Ferries do not serve the Berry Islands or Mangrove Cay/South Andros. Those wishing to reach the various islands by old-fashioned mail boat should contact the dockmaster in Potter's Cay in Nassau. All mail boats leave from Potter's Cay, and the dockmaster has the most up to date information on which boats sail where. Note that mail boats may make several stops, and due to their infrequency you may be marooned on your chosen island for days, if not weeks, until the next mail boat arrives.

Contacts **Dockmaster's Office** ☎ *242/393–1064.*

### CAR TRAVEL

Car rentals are available on Andros and on Great Harbour Cay in the Berry Islands. Don't expect major companies; rentals are done through micro-enterprises and usually arranged directly by the hotel or lodge. Make sure to call in advance to have a rental car waiting upon arrival at an airport or ferry dock. There are no car-rental agencies on Bimini. Most of Bimini can be accessed on foot, by golf cart, or by tram.

### TAXI TRAVEL

Taxis are readily available at airports to meet incoming commercial flights. Additionally, they are stationed in Alice Town, Bimini, and Fresh Creek, Central Andros, for arrival of regularly scheduled ferries and smaller ports for the arrival of mail boats.

# ESSENTIALS

### BANKS

Andros and Bimini banks are open Monday through Thursday 9:30–3 and Friday 9:30-4. All have ATMs. There are no banks on the Berry Islands.

### EMERGENCIES

**Contacts MASA** ☎ *242/393–5048.* **REVA** ☎ *954/730–9300, 800/752–4195* ⊕ *www.flyreva.com.* **Andros Medical Clinics** ☎ *242/329–2055 Nicholl's Town/ North Andros, 242/368–2038 Fresh Creek/Central Andros, 242/369–4849 Kemp's Bay/South Andros.* **Andros Police** ☎ *242/329–2103 North Andros, 242/368– 2626 Central Andros, 242/369–0083 Mangrove Cay, 242/369–4733 South Andros.* **Great Harbour Cay Medical Clinic, Berry Islands** ☎ *242/367–8400* ⊙ *Nurse on-site Mon.–Fri. 9–2.* **Berry Islands Police** ☎ *242/367–8344.* **North Bimini Medical Clinic** ☎ *242/347–2210* ⊙ *Mon.–Fri. 9–4.* **Bimini Police** ☎ *919 fire rescue, 242/347–3144.*

### HOTELS

Andros, Bimini, and the Berry Islands have accommodations to suit most tastes, from a handful of luxury properties on private cays (pronounced "keys") and remote beaches to simple fishing lodges and funky hotels with swinging nightlife on weekends. Figure out what you want—service, amenities, activities—then do your homework. Comfortable motel-style accommodations are most common, and usually have a restaurant and bar. Some fishing lodges are not well suited to overall vacationing or for families with small children. Some lodges don't have air-conditioning, in-room telephones and TVs, or Internet. Most do have a phone for guest use on the property, and some will have a computer with Internet in the lobby area. Often you must pay your hotel bill in cash. If these issues are important to you, check with the hotel before you book. And remember, even places that say they have Internet service may not have it all the time, as connections can go on the blink without warning.

Rates typically stay constant throughout the year in Andros and the Berry Islands. In Bimini, spring and summer are high season, and rates reflect that.

### RESTAURANTS

Dining in these parts is a casual experience and rarely involves anything fancy. Restaurants, lodges, and inns serve traditional Bahamian fare—fresh seafood, grilled chicken, johnnycake, cracked (deep-fried) conch, and barbecued pork with all the fixings (potato salad, coleslaw, peas 'n' rice, and macaroni and cheese). Call ahead to make sure a restaurant is open; some require you to order your dinner ahead of time. Resort restaurants are often the most dependable source of sit-down meals and most welcome nonguests. Many of the favored food outlets are take-out places. Thatched conch stands and colorful roadside bars are a treat—and a cool way to mingle with the locals.

### HOTEL AND RESTAURANT PRICES

*Restaurant prices are based on the median main course price at dinner, excluding gratuity, typically 15%, which is often automatically added to the bill. Hotel prices are for two people in a standard double room in high season, excluding service and 6%–12% tax.*

**Visitor Information Andros Tourism Offices** ☎ 242/368–2286 *Central Andros, 242/369–1688 South Andros* ⊕ *www.bahamas.com/islands/andros.* **Berry Islands Tourism Administrator** ☎ 242/367–8291 ⊕ *www.bahamas. com/islands/berry.* **Bimini Tourism Office** ✉ *Alice Town* ☎ 242/347–3529 ⊕ *www.bahamas.com/islands/bimini.* **Bahama Out Islands Promotion Board** ☎ 954/740–8740 ⊕ *www.bahamas.com.*

# ANDROS

The Bahamas' largest island (100 miles long and 40 miles wide) and one of the least explored, Andros's landmass is carved up by myriad channels, creeks, lakes, and mangrove-covered cays. The natural **Northern, Middle**, and **South Bights** cut through the width of the island, creating boating access between both coasts. Andros is best known for its bonefishing and diving, and is also a glorious ecotourism spot with snorkeling, blue-hole exploration, sea kayaking, and nature hikes.

The Spaniards who came here in the 16th century called Andros *La Isla del Espíritu Santo*—the Island of the Holy Spirit—and it has retained its eerie mystique. The descendants of Seminole Indians and runaway slaves who left Florida in the mid-19th century settled in the North Andros settlement of **Red Bays** and remained hidden until a few decades ago. They continue to live as a tribal society, making a living by weaving straw goods. The Seminoles originated the myth of the island's legendary (and elusive) chickcharnies—red-eyed, bearded, green-feathered creatures with three fingers and three toes that hang upside down by their tails from pine trees. These mythical characters supposedly wait deep in the forests to wish good luck to the friendly passerby and vent their mischief on the hostile trespasser. The rest of Andros's roughly 8,000 residents live in a dozen settlements on the eastern shore. Farming and commercial fishing sustain the economy, and the island is the country's largest source of fresh water.

Andros's undeveloped **West Side** adjoins the Great Bahama Bank, a vast shallow-water haven for lobster, bonefish, and tarpon. Wild orchids and dense pine and mahogany forests cover the island's lush green interior. The marine life–rich **Andros Barrier Reef**—the world's third largest—is within a mile of the eastern shore and runs for 140 miles. Sheltered waters within the reef average 6 to 15 feet, but on the other side ("over the wall") they plunge to more than 6,000 feet at the **Tongue of the Ocean**.

## GETTING HERE

### AIR TRAVEL

There are four airports on Andros. The San Andros airport (SAQ) is in North Andros; the Andros Town airport (ASD) is in Central Andros; the South Andros airport (TZN) is in Congo Town; and the Mangrove Cay airport (MAY) is on Mangrove Cay. Andros Town Airport sees the

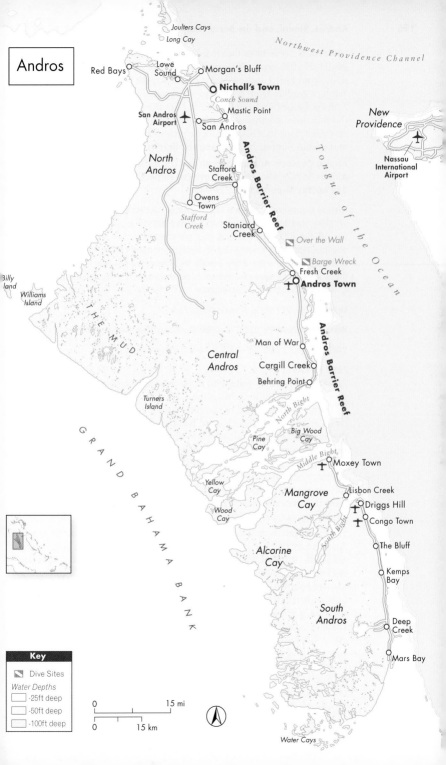

# Andros

Joulters Cays
Long Cay

Red Bays
Lowe Sound
Morgan's Bluff
**Nicholl's Town**
*Conch Sound*
Mastic Point

San Andros Airport
San Andros

*North Andros*

Stafford Creek

Owens Town

*Stafford Creek*

Staniard Creek

Andros Barrier Reef

*Over the Wall*

*Barge Wreck*
Fresh Creek
**Andros Town**

*Billy land*
*Williams Island*

THE MUD

Man of War

*Central Andros*

Cargill Creek

Behring Point

Andros Barrier Reef

Turners Island

*North Bight*

Pine Cay

Big Wood Cay

*Middle Bight*
Moxey Town

Yellow Cay

Lisbon Creek
*Mangrove Cay*
Driggs Hill
Congo Town

Wood Cay

*South Bight*

The Bluff

*Alcorine Cay*

Kemps Bay

*South Andros*

Deep Creek

Mars Bay

GRAND BAHAMA BANK

*Northwest Providence Channel*

*New Providence*

Nassau International Airport

*Tongue of the Ocean*

Water Cays

| Key | |
|---|---|
| | Dive Sites |

*Water Depths*
-25ft deep
-50ft deep
-100ft deep

0 ____ 15 mi
0 ____ 15 km

most traffic. It services flights from Nassau (LeAir) and Grand Bahama Island (SkyBahamas). Watermakers Air flies shared-charter planes twice daily from Fort Lauderdale Executive airport (EXE) to Andros Town. Western Air flies from Nassau to San Andros (North Andros) and South Andros. LeAir flies from Nassau to Mangrove Cay daily. To get between the Bahamas' northwestern islands, Captain Paul W. J. Harding operates a seaplane that offers bespoke pickup and drop-off points between and within Bimini, Andros, and the Berry Islands.

**Airport Contacts Andros Town Airport** ☎ *242/368–2724.* **Congo Town Airport** ☎ *242/369–2270.* **Mangrove Cay Airport** ☎ *242/369–0270.* **San Andros Airport** ☎ *242/329–4401.*

**Airline Contacts Capt. Paul W.J. Harding.** Paul Harding offers seamless seaplane transfers to and from Andros and Nassau. In Andros, he can drop you off directly on the beach at your preferred resort, even directly on the private island of Kamalame Cay. In addition, Harding can fly you between Andros, Bimini, and the Berry Islands. He's the only pilot who regularly offers these services between the Bahamas' northwestern islands. ☎ *242/357–9876* ⊕ *www.facebook.com/paulsseaplane.*

**LeAir** ☎ *242/377–2356* ⊕ *www.flyleair.com.*

**Watermakers Air** ☎ *954/771–0330* ⊕ *www.watermakersair.com.*

**Western Air** ☎ *242/329–4000* ⊕ *www.westernairbahamas.com.*

### FERRY TRAVEL

Andros is divided by water into three parts: Central/North Andros, Mangrove Cay, and South Andros. Only Central/North Andros can be reached by ferry. You'll first need to travel to Nassau and board your boat at Potter's Cay, the principal dock in the Bahamas capital city, located just before the bridge to Paradise Island. Commercial ferries from Bahamas Ferries run twice weekly from Potter's Cay to Fresh Creek on Central/North Andros from January to early April and three times weekly from April to December. There are no regular ferries from Potter's Cay to Mangrove Cay or South Andros; however, mail boats do travel there (*see below*). Note that once on Andros, there is no service that connects Central/North Andros to its sister landmasses, Mangrove Cay and South Andros.

For those with more time (and patience) smaller points on North/Central Andros as well as Mangrove Cay and South Andros can be reached by old-fashioned mail boat from Nassau. Riders should always consult the dockmaster in Potter's Cay in Nassau for the most up-to-date information on mail boat schedules. Note that mail boats may make several stops, and due to their infrequency you may be marooned on your chosen island for days, if not weeks, until the next mail boat arrives. From Potter's Cay Dock in Nassau, the M/V *Lisa J.* sails to Morgan's Bluff in North Andros every Wednesday, returning to Nassau the following Tuesday. The one-way trip takes five hours and costs $30. The M/V *Lady D* sails to Fresh Creek in Central Andros on Tuesday (with stops at Stafford Creek, Blanket Sound, and Behring Point) and returns to Nassau on Sunday. The trip takes five hours, and the fare is $30. The M/V *Mal Jack* sails to Kemp's Bay, Long Bay Cays, and the Bluff in South Andros on Monday at 11 pm. It returns to Nassau on Wednesday. The trip takes seven hours; the fare is $30. The M/V *Lady Gloria* departs from Nassau on Tuesday for Mangrove Cay and Cargill Creek (with two other stops) and returns on Sunday. The five-hour trip costs $30. Schedules are subject to change due to weather conditions or occasional dry-docking.

Once on Andros, it's not possible to reach Mangrove Cay or South Andros from Central/North Andros. However, it is possible to cross between Mangrove Cay and South Andros. A free government ferry makes the half-hour trip between Mangrove Cay and South Andros twice daily. It departs from Driggs Hill, South Andros at 8 am and 4 pm and from Lisbon Creek, Mangrove Cay at 8:30 am and 4:30 pm, but schedules are subject to change. Call the Commissioner's Office for information.

**Contacts Bahamas Ferries** ☎ *242/323–2166* ⊕ *www.bahamasferries.com.* **Commissioner's Office** ☎ *242/369–0331.* **Dockmaster's Office** ☎ *242/393–1064.*

### TAXI TRAVEL

Taxis meet airplanes and ferries and are available for transporting and touring around the islands. They can also be arranged ahead of time through hotels. Rates are around $1.50 a mile, though most fares are set. You should always agree on a fare before your ride begins. Cab drivers will charge $80 to $120 for a half-day tour of the island.

> ## WORD OF MOUTH
>
> "Our experiences in these islands proved that while each of the Out Islands is different from the others, they share a common denominator of welcoming and interesting islanders and visitors. It's not for everyone, but once you find yourself at home with the Out Island experience, nothing else is quite as satisfying."
> —Callaloo

# NORTH ANDROS

The northern part of Andros spreads from the settlements of **Morgan's Bluff**, **Nicholl's Town**, and **Red Bays** and ends at **Stafford Creek**. North Andros consists of long stretches of pine forests, limestone bluffs, and fields and gardens of ground crops. Seminole Indians, American slaves, and Mennonites settled this land along with the West Indian population. White-sand beaches, mostly deserted, line the island's eastern face, interrupted by creeks, inlets, and rock outcroppings. Logging supported North Andros in the '40s and '50s, and laid the foundation for its roads.

**San Andros** is home to North Andros's airport, but **Nicholl's Town** is the largest settlement here and in all of Andros. Once home to a vogue resort in the 1960s (Andros Beach Hotel), today it is mostly residential, inhabited in part by snowbirds who own the adorable Bahamian-style, brightly painted cottages that were once part of the iconic resort. Visitors driving from Central Andros should expect a bit of a wild ride as the main highway is riddled with potholes. But don't worry about traffic; you'll be lucky if you see more than a handful of cars on the highway in a single day.

## GETTING HERE AND AROUND

The San Andros airport (SAQ) has flights from Nassau via SkyBahamas and Western Air. Taxis meet incoming flights.

You can get around on foot in Nicholl's Town; car rentals are available for exploring the island's 65 miles of Queen's Highway and feeder roads in the north. They run about $70 to $85 a day. Main roads are in Central Andros are in good shape, but watch out for potholes in North Andros.

### CAR RENTALS

**A & H Car Rental** ⊠ *Fresh Creek, Andros Island* ☎ *242/329–2685.*
**Executive Car Rental** ⊠ *Nicholl's Town, Andros Island* ☎ *242/329–2636.*

## EXPLORING

**Nicholl's Town.** Nicholl's Town, at Andros's northeastern corner, is the island's largest village, with a population of about 600. This friendly community with its agriculturally based economy has stores for supplies and groceries, a few motels, a public medical clinic, a telephone station (yes, these still exist), and other shops. Adorable cottages, a throwback from the town's big resort era of the '60s, house the island's wintering population from the States and Europe. ⊠ *Nicholl's Town, Andros Island.*

**Red Bays.** Fourteen miles west of Nicholl's Town, Red Bays is the sole west coast settlement in all of Andros. The town was settled by Seminole Indians and runaway African slaves escaping Florida pre–Civil War and was cut off from the rest of Andros until a highway connected it to Nicholl's Town in the 1980s. Red Bays' residents are known for their craftsmanship, particularly basketry and wood carving. Tightly plaited baskets, some woven with scraps of colorful Androsia batik, have become a signature craft of Andros. Artisans have their wares on display in front of their homes (with fixed prices), so be on the lookout within this tiny town. Despite opening their homes to buyers, Red Bays locals don't seem very used to visitors. Expect a lot of stares and glares! ⊠ *Red Bays, Andros Island.*

**Uncle Charlie's Blue Hole.** Mystical and mesmerizing, blue holes pock Andros's marine landscape in greater concentration than anywhere else on Earth—an estimated 160-plus—and provide entry into the islands' network of coral-rock caves. Offshore, some holes drop off to 200 feet or more. Inland blue holes reach depths of 120 feet, layered with fresh, brackish, and salt water. Uncle Charlie's Blue Hole is one of Andros's most popular inland blue holes. The hole's perimeter is lined with picnic benches and a ladder leads into the mysterious (and refreshing) blue hole. The hole is 40 feet in diameter and 120 feet deep. ⊠ *300 yards off main highway in N. Andros after turnoff for Owen Town, North Andros, Andros Island.*

## BEACHES

If solitude is what you're searching for, you'll definitely find it on the beaches of North Andros. Not as manicured nor as pristine as the beaches in Central or South Andros, these beaches see visitors only during festival times and offer no facilities for visitors.

**Conch Sound.** South of Nicholl's Town, Conch Sound is a wide protected bay with strands of white sand and tranquil waters. Swimmers and bonefishers can wade on their own on the easily accessible flats. Commercial fishermen bring their catches to a little beach park where you can buy what's fresh if your timing is right (ask around to find out what time they usually come in from fishing). A small offshore blue hole beckons snorkelers a short way off the beach. Be careful if wading in the water not to fall in the blue hole! **Amenities:** none. **Best for:** solitude, snorkeling. ✉ *Nicholl's Town, Andros Island.*

**Morgan's Bluff Beach.** At the north end of North Andros near Nicholl's Town, this crescent beach is normally quiet except around regatta time. The beach of Morgan's Bluff is named after the 17th-century pirate Henry Morgan, who allegedly dropped off some of his stolen loot in the area. It is the site of Regatta Village, a colorful collection of stands and stalls that open in July when the All Andros–Berry Islands Regatta takes place. In months other than July, the beach appears to be in a state of disrepair as the broken-down stands and leftover debris remain on the beach until the following year's events. It is adjacent to Government Dock and a safe harbor, so it sees some boater traffic. **Amenities:** none. **Best for:** solitude. ✉ *Nicholl's Town, Andros Island.*

## WHERE TO STAY

$ B&B/INN 🏨 **Love at First Sight.** At the mouth of Stafford Creek, self-sufficient anglers and do-it-yourself vacationers can sit on the sundeck, sip a cold Kalik (local beer), and contemplate the vast bonefish flats of Central Andros (or take a wilderness hike through the pine forests to a remote landlocked lake). **Pros:** on-site restaurant and bar; swinging benches. **Cons:** rental car necessary; rooms extremely basic; not on beach. [$] *Rooms from: $110* ✉ *On the main highway at the mouth of Stafford Creek, Central Andros, Andros Island* ☎ *242/368–6082* 🌐 *www.loveatfirstsights.com* 🛏 *10 rooms.*

$ B&B/INN 🏨 **Pineville Motel.** A true one-of-a-kind, this eye-popping plot of land houses 16 rooms, a petting zoo, a small disco, a movie theater, a bar, and a DIY gift-shop—all constructed primarily of recycled materials like tires, reclaimed wood, and seashells. **Pros:** unique experience; cheap rates; enthusiastic owner. **Cons:** not near beach; basic accommodations; overcrowded petting zoo. [$] *Rooms from: $70* ✉ *Nicholl's Town, Andros Island* ☎ *242/329–2788* 🌐 *www.pinevillemotelandlodge.com* 🛏 *16 rooms* 🍴 *No meals.*

## NIGHTLIFE

**Big Shop.** Near the waterfront, Big Shop is as local as it gets. It's not a shop . . . more like a crumbling house with a fun bar inside. With so few islanders on Andros, the joint is open weekends only. It tends to attract North and Central Andros's younger demographic. You might be the only tourist there. ✉ *Nicholl's Town, Andros Island* ☎ *242/329–2047* 🕒 *Closed Mon.–Thurs.*

# CENTRAL ANDROS

Those arriving in Central Andros by ferry will arrive in the tiny village of **Fresh Creek**; those arriving in Central Andros by plane will arrive in neighboring **Andros Town** (the equally petite transportation and governmental hub). Both Fresh Creek and Andros Town are found mid-island, on the east coast of greater Andros Island.

Heading north from Andros Town and Fresh Creek, Central Andros extends as far north as **Stafford Creek**, whereupon the land officially becomes North Andros (though it's debated exactly where Central ends and North begins). As you head south, pine forests and later scrubby vegetation give way to hardwood hammocks. Coved beaches scallop the eastern shoreline and the sole road, Queen's Highway, will bring you to the bonefishing villages of **Cargill Creek** and then **Behring Point**, at the end of Queen's Highway. Here along the bonefish sweet spot of Northern Bight, you'll find nice homes with flowering gardens, palm trees, and sea grapes that overlook the bight along Coakley Street.

Central Andros accounts for 60% of the island's hotel inventory, but those expecting the glitz and mega-resorts of the Bahamas' more touristy islands should look elsewhere. Many of the accommodations here are dedicated to boaters and divers. Farther south the settlements cater exclusively to bonefishermen with small lodges. Guesthouse-style, they often include all-day fishing and meals.

Central Andros's famed West Side teems with mangrove estuaries rich with marine life, including lobster and bonefish. However, this uninhabited region is accessible only by private boat.

## GETTING HERE AND AROUND

LeAir flies from Nassau into Andros Town airport (ASD). Ferries arrive at Fresh Creek (FCK). Taxis meet airplanes and ferries. The fare from the airport to Fish Creek is $15; to Cargill Creek area, some 20 miles south of the airport, about $40.

A number of car-rental operators are available (rentals start at $70 a day), but if you're staying in the Cargill Creek area, you'll probably be doing most of your traveling by boat. In Andros Town you can easily get around to the local restaurants, beaches, and blue holes by bike and on foot.

### CAR RENTALS

**Adderley's Car Rental** ⊠ *Fresh Creek, Central Andros, Andros Island* ☎ *242/357–2149.*

## EXPLORING

**Andros Lighthouse.** As you enter Fresh Creek, you'll see this historical, circa 1892 lighthouse, originally built to navigate boats into the southern entrance of Fresh Creek Channel. No longer in use, the lighthouse is an island landmark and a picturesque entrance into Fresh Creek when arriving by boat or ferry. ⊠ *Fresh Creek, Central Andros, Andros Island.*

**Androsia Batik Works Factory.** Brilliantly colored batik fabric called Androsia is designed and dyed at the Androsia Batik Works Factory, a 3-mile drive from Andros Town airport and walking distance from the dock at Fresh Creek. The Small Hope Bay Lodge family started the

Andros has the third-largest barrier reef in the world (behind those of Australia and Belize).

enterprise in 1973 to provide employment for local women. Today it has been declared the official fabric of the Bahamas. You can visit the factory and see how the material is made, plus take lessons in the art of batik ($25, which includes the piece of fabric you decorate). Batik fabric is turned into wall hangings and clothing for men and women, which are sold throughout the Bahamas and the Caribbean, and are quite popular with the locals. You can stock up at the store across from the factory. ⊠ *Fresh Creek, Andros Island* ☎ *242/327–6083* ⊕ *www. androsia.com* ⊗ *Mon.–Fri. 8:30–4, Sat. 8:30–2:30.*

**Fresh Creek.** Near the Andros Town airport in Central Andros and on the north side of a creek that shares the same name and separates it from Andros Town, is the small hamlet of Fresh Creek. A few restaurants, including Hank's Place, line the waterfront, along with several boat docks. Closer to the ferry dock is the Andros Tourism Office as well as the Andros Lighthouse. The creek itself cuts over 16 miles into the island, creating tranquil bonefishing flats and welcoming mangrove-lined bays that boaters and sea kayakers can explore.

**Staniard Creek.** Sand banks that turn gold at low tide lie off the northern tip of Staniard Creek, a small island settlement 9 miles north of Fresh Creek, accessed by a bridge off the main highway. Coconut palms and casuarinas shade the ocean-side beaches, and offshore breezes are pleasantly cooling. Kamalame Cove and its nearby private cay are at the northern end of the settlement. Three creeks snake into the mainland, forming extensive mangrove-lined back bays and flats. The surrounding areas are good for wading and bonefishing.

## BEACHES

Because they're famous for their off-the-chart fishing and diving, the islands of Andros often get shorted when talk turns to beaches. This is a great injustice, especially in the case of the ungroomed beaches defining Central Andros's east coast and the abandoned way-white sand beaches of Central Andros's outlying cays.

**Big and Little Saddleback Cay.** East of Staniard Creek lie a series of serene cays, idyllic for beach drops or consummating the ultimate Robinson Crusoe fantasies. The first is Kamalame Cay, home to the luxurious resort of the same name. Just past Kamalame, uninhabited Big and Little Saddleback Cay boast sparkling, white-sand beaches and crystal clear waters. You'll need a small, private boat to reach either (note that these cays are a regular drop point for guests of Kamalame Cay). Little Saddleback is tiny with no shade; so bring plenty of sunblock. Big Saddleback has a wider crescent beach, and plenty of shade from the pine trees. Also nearby is Rat Cay, which offers excellent snorkeling especially around the adjacent blue hole. ⊠ *Central Andros, Andros Island.*

**Small Hope Bay Beach.** Small Hope Bay Lodge is planted squarely on this coved beach where from-shore snorkeling is excellent, the sand is white, and tidal limestone pools make for fun tiny sea creature exploration at low tide. It's a good, long walking beach, and you can also sign up for a resort course or diving excursion at the resort, or simply enjoy a beachside lunch buffet. **Amenities:** food and drink; parking; showers; toilets; water sports. **Best for:** snorkeling; swimming; walking. ⊠ *Small Hope Bay Lodge, Central Andros, Andros Island.*

### WHERE TO EAT

$    ✕ **Hank's Place Restaurant and Bar.** On the north side of Fresh Creek,
BAHAMIAN   a block or so east of the bridge, this restaurant and bar is shaded by coconut palms and graced with clear views of the water. Eat inside, where plastic chairs and flowered tablecloths define the vibe, or outside on the spacious deck. Bahamian specialties—steamed, fried, or baked fish or chicken; ribs; shrimp; and pork chops—make it a favorite hangout for locals and visitors, especially for the Saturday-night parties. Fresh lobster, prepared to your liking, is available in season (August–March). Hank's signature cocktail, aptly named "Hanky Panky," is a dynamite frozen rum–and–fruit juice concoction. At press time, the restaurant was open but up for sale; call ahead. $ *Average main: $14* ⊠ *Fresh Creek, Andros Island* ☎ *242/368–2447* ⊕ *www.hanks-place.com* ⌂ *Reservations essential* ⊗ *Closed Mon.–Thurs.*

### WHERE TO STAY

$$$$   ⊡ **Andros Island Bonefishing Club** (*AIBC*). If you're a hard-core bonefisher,
B&B/INN   AIBC is the place for you—guests have access to 100 square miles of lightly fished flats, including wadable (at low tide) flats right out front. **Pros:** outdoor deck and bar idyllic for fishing stories; prime location on Cargill Creek. **Cons:** not much for nonanglers other than relaxing waterside; basic accommodations. $ *Rooms from: $450* ⊠ *Cargill Creek, Andros Island* ☎ *242/368–5167* ⊕ *www.androsbonefishing.com* ⌸ *12 rooms* ⦿❘ *All meals.*

**DID YOU KNOW?**

In the Bahamas, mail is still delivered by mail boats, as it has been for decades. Mail boats leave Nassau's Potter's Cay carrying mail, cars, produce, consumer goods, and passengers on trips to more than 30 Bahamian islands, including Andros, a four-hour cruise.

$$$$ ALL-INCLUSIVE Fodor's Choice ★ **Kamalame Cay.** This 100-acre, all-inclusive, luxurious private island retreat is one of the Atlantic's best kept secrets; a mere dozen classic-yet-stylish units dot a sprawling private cay laced with white-sand beaches and coconut palms. **Pros:** discreet pampering; delicious innovative food; many daily activities. **Cons:** Wi-Fi only in reception area; eye mask needed for sleeping past sunrise; round-trip airport transfers are costly. [$] *Rooms from: $1,165* ✉ *At the north end of Staniard Creek, Central Andros, Andros Island* ☎ *242/368–6281, 800/790–7971* 🌐 *www.kamalame.com* 🛏 *5 cottages, 5 villas* 🍴 *All-inclusive.*

$$$$ B&B/INN **Mount Pleasant Fishing Lodge.** Typical of the small bonefishing lodges that have cropped up in the southern part of Central Andros, Mount Pleasant caters to fishermen who care about nothing more than being out on the water all day. **Pros:** nice beach; from-shore fishing. **Cons:** off-the-beaten-path; far from other restaurants. [$] *Rooms from: $420* ✉ *Cargill Creek, Andros Island* ☎ *242/368–5171* 🌐 *www.mtpleasantfish.com* 🛏 *6 rooms* 🍴 *All meals.*

$$$$ ALL-INCLUSIVE FAMILY Fodor's Choice ★ **Small Hope Bay Lodge.** This casual, palm-shaded oceanfront property—over 50 years strong and the Atlantic/Caribbean's original dive resort—has a devoted following of divers, snorkelers, eco-adventurers, anglers, couples, and families; it's even been listed as one of the official "1000 Things to See Before You Die" within the famous book of the same name. **Pros:** best dive operation on Andros; a/c; free Wi-Fi in public areas; free long-distance calls to the United States and Canada. **Cons:** you'll need insect repellent; no pool. [$] *Rooms from: $570* ✉ *Small Hope Bay, Fresh Creek, Andros Island* ☎ *242/368–2014, 800/223–6961* 🌐 *www.smallhope.com* 🛏 *21 cottages* 🍴 *All-inclusive.*

## NIGHTLIFE

**Green Eyed Lady Bar.** The overwater bar at Hank's Place Restaurant and Bar is *the* place to be on Fridays and Saturdays. Sunset is more of a relaxed scene; but come late night the music gets louder, people get "happier," and the dancing begins! At press time, the restaurant and bar were open but up for sale; call ahead. ✉ *Fresh Creek, Central Andros, Andros Island* ☎ *242/368–2447* 🌐 *www.hanks-place.com.*

## SHOPPING

**Androsia Store.** Adjacent to the Androsia Batik Works Factory is the Androsia Store, where you can buy original fabrics, clothing, and stuffed toys. You'll spot locals throughout Andros (and even other islands in the Bahamas) wearing Androsia's signature colorful clothing. ✉ *Fresh Creek, Andros Island* ☎ *242/368–2080* 🌐 *www.androsia.com* 🕒 *Closed Sun.*

## SPORTS AND THE OUTDOORS
### BOATING AND FISHING

Andros fishermen claim the island is the best bonefishing location, and legends at Central Andros's south end are famed for pioneering the field of fly-fishing and island fishing lodges. The four main charter fishing regions include the hard-to-reach West Side flats, the creeks (particularly Fresh Creek), Joulters Cays north of North Andros, and the bights between Central and South Andros. Fishermen will find a wealth of knowledgeable bonefish guides in the **Cargill Creek–Behring Point** area who will take you into the Northern Bight and West Side for some of the world's best bonefishing. Full-day fishing excursions cost about $600. Bonefishing–lodging-dining packages run about $500 per person per day at the half dozen lodges in the area.

Reef and deep-sea fishing excursions are also available, but are secondary and not as spectacular as on other islands, although you can catch mahimahi, wahoo, and tuna in certain seasons.

**Andy Smith.** Based in Central Andros, Andy Smith is highly recommended for guiding anglers through Andros's bights and to the bonefish-rich West Side. Andy guides both novice and professional bonefishers. ☎ *242/368–4261.*

**Charlie Neymour.** Legend and expert guide Charlie Neymour is available for fishing expeditions, namely those involving bonefish or tarpon. ☎ *242/368–4297* ⊕ *www.bigcharlieandros.net.*

**Small Hope Bay Lodge.** Small Hope Bay Lodge has bone-, deep-sea, fly-, and reef fishing, as well as a "west side overnight"—a two-night camping and bone- and tarpon-fishing trip to the island's uninhabited western end. Rates run $290–$400 for a half day and $425–$550 for a full day (full-day trips include all gear and lunch). Book in advance. ⊠ *Small Hope Bay, Fresh Creek, Andros Island* ☎ *242/368–2014, 800/223–6961* ⊕ *www.smallhope.com.*

**Tranquility Hill Fishing Lodge.** This lodge at Behring Point is your one-stop shop for bonefishing adventure. The lodge has all of Central Andros's recommended bonefishing guides on call. Lead guides are Dwain Neymour and owner/manager, Ray Mackey. Ray is available only by special request. Other top independent guides used by Tranquility include Barry Neymour, Frankie Neymour, Deon Neymour, Dwain Neymour, and Ricardo Mackey. ⊠ *Behring Point, Central Andros, Andros Island* ☎ *242/368–4132, 860/331–8467* ⊕ *www.tranquilityhilllodge.com.*

### HIKING

**Small Hope Bay Lodge.** This lodge offers four self-guided and three guided nature and cultural tours through the beach, mangroves, and blue holes, and into Fresh Creek by bike or on foot. ⊠ *Small Hope Bay, Central Andros, Andros Island* ☎ *242/368–2014, 800/223–6961* ⊕ *www.smallhope.com.*

### SCUBA DIVING AND SNORKELING

**Andros Barrier Reef.** Divers can't get enough of the sprawling Andros Barrier Reef, the world's third largest barrier reef, located just off Fresh Creek–Andros Town. Boats from local lodges and resorts bring guests to various sections of the reef to relish in complete underwater rapture. Snorkelers can explore such reefs as the Trumpet Reef, where visibility is clear 15 feet to the sandy floor and jungles of elkhorn coral snake up to the surface. Divers can delve into the 60-foot-deep coral caves of the Black Forest, beyond which the wall slopes down to depths of 6,000 feet. Anglers can charter boats to fish offshore or over the reef, and bonefishers can wade the flats on their own in Fresh Creek. While the marine life is not as rich or as diverse as one would expect from such a vibrant, healthy reef, the assemblies of coral are simply breathtaking.

**Small Hope Bay Lodge.** Andros's main dive center is full-service, with resort dives, certification courses, one- and two-tank dives, specialty dives such as shark and night, and snorkeling. One-tank dives are $90. Rental equipment is available for Small Hope Bay Lodge excursions only. Lodging-dive packages are offered. Hot showers await after long days at sea! ⊠ *Small Hope Bay, Central Andros, Andros Island* ☏ *242/368–2014, 800/223–6961* ⊕ *www.smallhope.com.*

## MANGROVE CAY

Remote Mangrove Cay is sandwiched between two sea-green bights, separating it from Central and South Andros and creating an island of shorelines strewn with washed-up black coral, gleaming deserted beaches, and dense pine forests. **Moxey Town,** known locally as Little Harbour, rests on the northeast corner in a coconut grove. Pink piles of conch shells and mounds of porous sponges dot the small harbor of this commercial fishing and sponging community. Anglers come on a mission, in search of giant bonefish on flats called "the promised land" and "land of the giants." A five-minute boat ride takes fly-fishers to Gibson Cay to wade hard sand flats sprinkled with starfish.

### GETTING HERE AND AROUND

Mangrove Cay Airport (MAY) has daily flights from Nassau via Le Air. The cay's main road runs south from Moxey Town, past the airport, then along coconut-tree-shaded beaches to the settlement of Lisbon Creek. Car rentals are available from B&I Enterprises for exploring Mangrove Cay's 8 miles of roads. They run about $70 to $85 a day. Taxis meet airplanes and ferries and are available for transporting and touring around the islands.

A free government ferry makes the half-hour trip between Mangrove Cay and South Andros twice daily. It departs from South Andros at 9 am and 5 pm and from Mangrove Cay at 8:30 am and 4:30 pm, but schedules are subject to change. Call the Commissioner's Office for information. There's no public transportation from Central Andros to Mangrove Cay.

### CAR RENTALS

**B & I Enterprises** ⊠ *Mangrove Cay, Andros Island* ☏ *242/369–0353.*

### EXPLORING

**Victoria Point Blue Hole.** On an island known for magical blue holes (water-filled caves), the Victoria Point Blue Hole is Mangrove Cay's superlative spot for snorkeling and diving. Just ask the folks at

Tiamo Resort is the best resort in South Andros.

Seascape Inn or Mangrove Cay Inn or any local to point out which of the island's myriad blue holes is the famed Victoria Point. ✉ *Mangrove Cay, Andros Island.*

### WHERE TO EAT AND STAY

**$$**
**BAHAMIAN**
✕ **Barefoot Bar and Grill.** Every table has a nice ocean view at this warm and friendly beachfront restaurant and bar at the Seascape Inn. Owners Mickey and Joan McGowan do the baking and cooking themselves. If you are staying at another inn or plan on arriving by boat, make sure to call at least one day ahead (if not more) so they can accommodate you. Grilled chicken salad, burgers, sandwiches on kaiser rolls, and at times quesadillas are ample lunch temptations. Lunch items can also be prepared to take along as picnics on a daily outing. Chicken in white wine–lime sauce, roast pork loin, grilled steaks, and fresh fish of the day are a few dinner sensations. Even if you're full, the chocolate ganache, Grand Marnier–chocolate cloud, and homemade ice creams should not be missed. $ *Average main: $22* ✉ *Seascape Inn, Mangrove Cay, Andros Island* ☎☎ *242/369–0342* ⊕ *www.seascapeinn.com* ⌁ *Reservations essential.*

**$**
**B&B/INN**
▦ **Mangrove Cay Inn.** In a coconut grove with wild orchid and hibiscus gardens, the inn caters to hardcore escapists and anglers alike. **Pros:** on-site restaurant and bar; quiet location near the beach; friendly staff. **Cons:** lots of insects; very basic accommodation; mainly for anglers. $ *Rooms from: $140* ✉ *Mangrove Cay, Andros Island* ☎ *242/369–0069* ⊕ *www.mangrovecayinn.net* ⇗ *12 rooms, 2 cottages* ▬ *No credit cards.*

**CLOSE UP**

# Undersea Adventures in Andros

Andros probably has the largest number of dive sites in the country. With the third-longest barrier reef in the world (behind those of Australia and Belize), the island offers about 100 miles of drop-off diving into the Tongue of the Ocean.

Uncounted numbers of **blue holes** are forming in the area. In some places these constitute vast submarine networks that can extend more than 200 feet down into the coral (Fresh Creek, 40–100 feet; North Andros, 40–200-plus feet; South Bight, 40–200 feet). Blue holes are named for their inky-blue aura when viewed from above and for the light-blue filtered sunlight that is visible from many feet below. Some of the holes have vast cathedral-like interior chambers with stalactites and stalagmites, offshoot tunnels, and seemingly endless corridors. Others have distinct thermoclines (temperature changes) between layers of water and are subject to tidal flow.

The dramatic Fresh Creek site provides an insight into the complex Andros cave system. There isn't much coral growth, but there are plenty of midnight parrotfish, big southern stingrays, and some blacktip sharks. Similar blue holes are all along the barrier reef, including several at Mastic Point in the north and the ones explored and filmed off South Bight.

Undersea adventurers also have the opportunity to investigate wrecks such as the *Potomac*, a steel-hulled freighter that sank in 1952 and lies in 40 feet of water off Nicholl's Town. And off the waters of Fresh Creek, at 70 feet, lies the deteriorated 56-foot-long World War II LCM (landing craft mechanized) known

only as the **Barge Wreck,** which was sunk in 1963 to create an artificial reef. Newer and more intact, the *Marian* wreck lies in 70 feet. Both are encrusted with coral and are home to a school of groupers and a blizzard of tiny silverfish. You'll find fish-cleaning stations where miniature cleaning shrimp and yellow gobies clean grouper and rockfish by swimming into their mouths and out their gills, picking up food particles. It's an excellent subject matter for close-up photography.

The multilevel **Over the Wall** dive at Fresh Creek takes novices to depths of 65–80 feet and experienced divers to 120–185 feet. The wall is covered with black coral and all kinds of tube sponges. **Small Hope Bay Lodge** is the most respected dive resort on Andros. It's a friendly, informal place where the only thing taken seriously is diving. There's a fully equipped dive center with a wide variety of specialty dives, including customized family-dive trips with a private dive boat and dive master. If you're not certified, check out the lodge's morning resort course and be ready to explore the depths by afternoon. If you are certified, don't forget to bring your C card.

If you are leery of diving but want to view the spectacular undersea world, try a snorkeling excursion. Shallow reefs, beginning in 6 feet of water, and extending down to 60 feet or more, are ideal locations for spotting myriad brightly colored fish, sea urchins, and starfish. Don't forget your underwater camera!

Winter water temperatures average about 74°F. In summer, water temperatures average about 84°F.

$ **Seascape Inn.** One of Andros's few lodging options catering to more
B&B/INN than fisherman, Seascape Inn is a small, rustic beachfront gem; five
individual, well-maintained cottages with private decks overlook the
glass-clear ocean. **Pros:** quiet beachfront location; great snorkeling and birdwatching on-site; outstanding food;
great snorkeling and birdwatching on-site. **Cons:** no a/c; no TV; insect
repellent a must. $ *Rooms from: $159* ⊠ *Mangrove Cay, Andros Island*
📠 *242/369–0342* ⊕ *www.seascapeinn.com* ⤴ *5 cottages* †○† *Breakfast.*

### NIGHTLIFE
**Green One Conch Spot.** Get fresh conch salad, hang with locals, and
play dominoes or backgammon on the beach to a reggae-and-calypso
soundtrack. ⊠ *Mangrove Cay, Andros Island.*

# SOUTH ANDROS

5

South Andros's road stretches 25 miles from **Drigg's Hill**—a small settlement
of pastel houses, a tiny church, a grocery store, the government dock, and
the Emerald Palms Resort—to Mars Bay. Eight miles farther south, the
Bluff settlement sprawls atop a hill overlooking miles of golden beaches,
lush cays, and the Tongue of the Ocean. Here skeletons of Arawak natives
were found huddled together. A local resident attests that another skeleton
was found—this one of a 4-foot-tall, one-eyed owl, which may have given
rise to the legend of the mythical, elflike chickcharnie.

### GETTING HERE AND AROUND
The Congo Town Airport (TZN) is a mile south of Drigg's Hill and
receives daily flights from Nassau via Western Air. Taxis meet incoming flights.

A free government ferry makes the half-hour trip between Mangrove Cay
and South Andros twice daily. It departs from South Andros at 9 am and
5 pm and from Mangrove Cay at 8:30 am and 4:30 pm, but schedules
are subject to change. Call the Commissioner's Office for information.
There's no public transportation from Central Andros to Mangrove Cay.

### CAR RENTALS
**Lenglo Car Rental** ⊠ *Congo Town, Andros Island* 📞 *242/369–1702.*

### WHERE TO STAY
$$$$ **Tiamo.** One of the Atlantic's last great secrets, Tiamo is a hideaway
RESORT for jetsetters in-the-know; arrival at this low-key yet sophisticated South
**Fodor's Choice** Bight eco-resort via private launch is just the beginning. **Pros:** 1.5-to-1
★ staff-to-guest ratio; spectacular private beachfront location; great food.
**Cons:** alcohol not included in rates; insect repellent a must; difficult to
reach. $ *Rooms from: $895* ⊠ *South Bight, accessible only by boat,
Driggs Hill, Andros Island* 📞 *242/359–2330* ⊕ *www.tiamoresorts.com*
⤴ *10 cottages* ☉ *Closed Sept.* †○† *All meals.*

### SPORTS AND THE OUTDOORS
#### FISHING
**Reel Tight Charters.** This renowned charter company offers a variety of
services on South Andros and throughout the Bahamas, including deep-
sea and reef fishing, plus diving, snorkeling, and spearfishing. ⊠ *Drigg's
Hill Marina, Driggs Hill, Andros Island* 📞 *242/554–0031.*

# BIMINI

Bimini has long been known as the Bahamas' big game-fishing capital. Unlike most other Bahamian islands, Bimini's strong tourist season falls from spring through summer, when calmer seas mean the arrival of fishing and pleasure boats from South Florida. The nearest of the Bahamian islands to the U.S. mainland, Bimini consists of a handful of islands and cays just 50 miles east of Miami, across the Gulf Stream that sweeps the area's western shores. Most visitors spend their time on bustling North Bimini; South Bimini is quieter and more eco-oriented. Most of the hotels, restaurants, churches, and stores in Bimini are in capital **Alice Town** along North Bimini's King's and Queen's highways, which run parallel to each other. Everything on **North Bimini**, where most of the islands' 2,000 inhabitants reside, is so close that you do not need a car to get around. The largest resort, Bimini Bay, takes up the northern quarter of the island, with a huge upscale marina development.

Sparsely populated **South Bimini** is where Juan Ponce de León allegedly looked for the Fountain of Youth in 1513, and a site with a well and natural trail memorialize it. More engaging, however, is the island's biological field station, known as the Sharklab for its study of lemon-shark behavior, among other things. The main resort on this island, Bimini Sands, is as equally marina-oriented as Bimini Bay, but much more low-key.

Salvagers, gunrunners, rumrunners, and the legendary Ernest Hemingway peopled the history of Bimini. Hemingway wrote much of *To Have and Have Not* and *Islands in the Stream* here between fishing forays and street brawls.

## GETTING HERE AND AROUND

### AIR TRAVEL

South Bimini (BIM) has a teensy airport, but blessedly with air-conditioning. It services flights from Fort Lauderdale (Silver Airways dba United Express), Nassau (Western Air), and Grand Bahama Island (Regional Air). Charters from Fort Lauderdale are available on Island Air Charters. A short taxi ride ($3) from the airport delivers you to the ferry to North Bimini, a five-minute crossing that costs $2 each way.

**Contacts Island Air** ☎ 800/444–9904 ⊕ www.islandaircharters.com. **Regional Air** ☎ 800/598–8660 ⊕ www.goregionalair.com.

### BOAT AND FERRY TRAVEL

Baleària Bahamas Express travels between Port of Miami and Alice Town, North Bimini on Fridays, Saturdays, and Sundays on the fast ferry Maverick. Those wishing to reach Bimini by old-fashioned mail boat will need to first reach Nassau. Contact the Dockmaster in Potter's Cay in Nassau for the most up-to-date information on mail boat travel from Nassau to Bimini. All mail boats leave from Potter's Cay. For information on traveling the opposite direction (from Bimini to Nassau) call the on-island mail boat contact, Miss Sherece at ☎ *242/393–1064. At press time, Bimini Mack* was leaving Potter's Cay, Nassau, Thursday afternoons for North Bimini and Cat Cay (returning on Monday morning). The trip takes about 12 hours and costs $45 one-way. Going

Sunsets in Bimini can be otherworldly.

between North and South Bimini requires a five-minute ferry crossing, managed by the local government.

Bimini accommodates private yachts and fishing boats in droves. Boaters often travel from Florida to Bimini, mostly from West Palm Beach, Fort Lauderdale, and Miami. Crossing the Gulf Stream, however, should only be done by skippers who can plot a course using charts for that purpose. The distance is 48 nautical miles. Customs and Immigrations offices are located in Alice Town next to the straw market and at both Bimini Bay and Bimini Sands resorts.

**Contacts Baleària Bahamas Express** ☎ *866/699–6988* ⊕ *www.ferryexpress.com.* **Dockmaster's Office** ☎ *242/393–1064.*

## NORTH BIMINI

Bimini's main community, **Alice Town**, is at North Bimini's southern end. It's colorful, painted in happy Caribbean pastels, but has lately taken on a glory-gone look. In a prominent location stand the ruins of the Compleat Angler Hotel, Ernest Hemingway's famous haunt, which burned down in 2006. A short walk away is the Bimini Native Straw and Craft Market, which bustles on weekends and during fishing tournaments.

In quick succession Alice Town turns into **Bailey Town**, then **Porgy Bay**—these three towns are separated only by signs heralding the change. Toward King's Highway's north end, north of Alice Town, you'll see bars, grocery shops, clothing stores, the pink medical center, and a group of colorful fruit stalls. This part of the island, from Bailey Town to the Bimini Bay Resort, is clean, fresh, and lively.

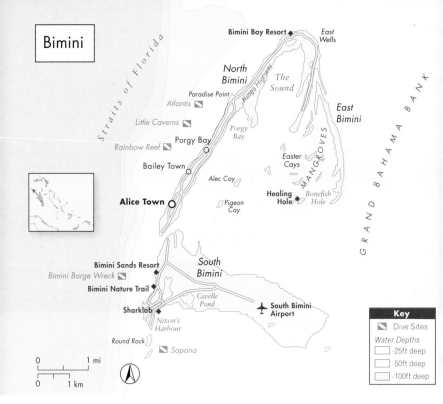

## GETTING HERE AND AROUND

If arriving by plane, catch a taxi in South Bimini at the South Bimini Airport for transportation to the ferry service between South Dock and North Dock. The entire process costs $5. Once there, walk or take one of the waiting taxis to your accommodations. Ferries cannot take you directly to your hotel or marina—to Bimini Bay Resort, for example—because government regulations protect the taxi union.

Most people get around North Bimini on gas-powered golf carts, and they are available for rent from various vendors and resorts for $70 to $100 per day, or $20 for the first hour, and $10 for each additional hour. Note that the speed limit is 25 mph, helmets are required, and that the roads follow the British system.

The Bimini Tram regularly runs the length of North Bimini to Bimini Bay for $3 per person per ride. It begins around 6:30 am and ends around 4 pm. It picks up at a number of stops along King's Highway.

**Golf Cart Rental Contacts Capt. Pat's** ⊠ *Alice Town, North Bimini* ☎ *242/347–3477.* **Uncle Tanny's Golf Cart Rentals** ⊠ *Alice Town, North Bimini* ☎ *242/347–2480.*

**Tram Contacts Bimini Tram** ☎ *242/464–5704.*

## EXPLORING

**Bailey Town.** Most of the island's residents live in Bailey Town in small, pastel-color concrete houses. Bailey Town lies on King's Highway, north of the Bimini Big Game Club and before Porgy Bay and the Bimini Bay Resort. It's also a good place to find a home-cooked meal or conch salad from shacks along the waterfront. Don't miss a bite at Joe's Conch Stand; it's a local institution. ⊠ *North Bimini, Bimini.*

**Bimini Museum.** The Bimini Museum, sheltered in the restored (1921) two-story original post office and jail—a two-minute walk from the ferry dock, across from the native straw market—showcases varied artifacts, including Adam Clayton Powell's domino set, Prohibition photos, rum kegs, old cannon balls, Martin Luther King Jr.'s immigration card from 1964, and a fishing log and rare fishing films of Ernest Hemingway. The exhibit includes film shot on the island as early as 1922. The museum is privately managed. ⊠ *King's Hwy., Alice Town, North Bimini* ☎ *242/473–1252* ⊕ *www.biminimuseum.com* ✉ *$2 donation requested* ⊙ *Daily 10–7.*

**Dolphin House.** Bimini historian and poet laureate Mr. Ashley Saunders has spent decades constructing this eclectic home and guesthouse from materials salvaged from local construction sites and the sea. Mr. Saunders offers walking tours of Alice Town, which begin with a tour of his structure—named for the 27 mosaic, sculpted, and painted dolphins throughout—then continues through Alice Town to tell the island's history. ⊠ *Alice Town between King's and Queen's Hwys., North Bimini* ☎ *242/347–3201* ✉ *Tours $20/hr* ⊙ *By appointment.*

OFF THE
BEATEN
PATH

**Healing Hole.** This is one of the few accessible spots around uninhabited East Bimini. Locals recommend a trip here for curing what ails you— gout and rheumatism are among the supposedly treatable afflictions. Ask your hotel to arrange a trip out to this natural clearing in Bimini's mangrove flats. The Dives Shop at Bimini Bay organizes three-hour kayak excursions. You can take a leap of faith into the water and, if nothing else, enjoy a refreshing dip.

**Bimini Road.** Avid divers shouldn't miss a trip to underwater Bimini Road, aka the Road to Atlantis. This curious rock formation under about 20 feet of water, 500 yards offshore at Bimini Bay, is shaped like a backward letter J, some 600 feet long at the longest end. It's the shorter 300-foot extension that piques the interest of scientists and visitors. The precision patchwork of large, curved-edge stones forms a perfect rectangle measuring about 30 feet across. A few of the stones are 16 feet square. It's purported to be the "lost city" whose discovery was predicted by Edgar Cayce (1877–1945), a psychic with an interest in prehistoric civilizations. Archaeologists estimate the formation to be between 5,000 and 10,000 years old. Carvings in the rock appear to some scientists to resemble a network of highways. ⊠ *Bimini.*

## BEACHES

In the most general terms, the beaches towards North Bimini's west coast are more for partiers in the southern reaches, especially near Alice Town, and quieter as you go north. Australian pine trees line the sensational, downy sands—what Hemingway described as "floury white" in *Islands in the Stream.*

You can kayak in North Bimini's mangrove flats.

**Radio Beach/Blister Bay.** North Bimini's west coast is one contiguous stretch of beach that runs for several miles; however, different names distinguish the various swathes of powdery white sands. From the southern start of the beach in North Bimini to north of Alice Town and roughly Bailey Town are Radio Beach and Blister Bay. Sometimes this area is also called Alice Town Beach. (Nobody really knows where Radio Beach ends and Blister Beach starts, so everyone thought the new name of Alice Town Beach was a great compromise!) This section of gem-hued waters has patches that are shaded by Australian pines and generally nice wide beaches. An iron wreck of an old salvage ship rusts at the beach's south end. Given its proximity to Alice Town the beach is usually popular with day-trippers and partiers. In fact, it's Bimini's most popular beach. During spring break, the beach is strewn with Kalik beer bottles. **Amenities:** food and drink. **Best for:** partiers; swimming. ✉ *Bimini.*

**Spook Hill Beach.** Named for its proximity to the local cemetery, Bimini Bahamas' memorial park, Spook Hill Beach tends to be quieter than Radio Beach and Blister Beach and caters mostly to families looking for quiet sands and calm waters. Shallow shores are ideal for wading and the crystal clear waters make for great snorkeling. There is a permanent snack bar here and usually a few pop-up beach bars add to the fun. The beach is heavily lined with pine trees and is not particularly wide at high tide. **Amenities:** food and drink. **Best for:** solitude; snorkeling; swimming. ✉ *North Bimini.*

## WHERE TO EAT

$ ✕ **Captain Bob's.** Across from the Sea Crest Marina, centrally located in
BAHAMIAN Alice Town, this casual joint starts serving rib-sticking American and
Bahamian breakfasts (try the conch or lobster omelet) at 6:30 am seven
days a week. This is an ideal place for anglers to start their day before
heading out to the flats or the blue water. Lunches of burgers, conch,
soups, salads, and fresh fish are served until 2 pm Monday through
Saturday and until 1 pm on Sunday. After a long day on the sea, step
in for a hearty dinner (summer only) of stuffed lobster or the popular
seafood platter. If you call ahead, fishing lunches to take out on your
boat can be prepared. $ *Average main: $16* ✉ *Queen's Hwy., Alice
Town, North Bimini* ☎ *242/347–3260* ▭ *No credit cards* ☾ *No dinner
from fall through spring.*

$$$ ✕ **Sabor.** This elegant waterfront restaurant at Bimini Bay Resort is the
BAHAMIAN most formal place you'll find on Bimini. Enjoy the view of the bay or
the display kitchen while noshing on artistic yet simple island dishes
from fresh ingredients. Start with conch fritters, ceviche, or Caesar
salad. For your entrée, try the steak frites, paella, mojo-glazed chicken,
or sesame-crusted yellowfin tuna. For dessert, order the guava duff for
a local treat when it's offered. Hours vary greatly. Call ahead to avoid
disappointment. $ *Average main: $34* ✉ *Bimini Bay Resort, North
Bimini* ☎ *242/347–2900, 866/344–8759* ⊕ *www.biminibayresort.com*
⚑ *Reservations essential.*

## WHERE TO STAY

$ ☴ **Big John's Hotel.** Seven deluxe hotel rooms—five with ocean views, two
B&B/INN with town views—are perfect for the traveler who wants to get away
from the megaresort scene, but still stay in style. **Pros:** central Alice
Town location; great value; often give 3-for-2-night deals. **Cons:** loud
noise from music downstairs; no pool; larger beach requires a walk.
$ *Rooms from: $115* ✉ *King's Hwy. across from Gateway Gallery,
Alice Town, North Bimini* ☎ *242/347–3117* ⊕ *www.biminibigjohns.
com* ⤐ *7 rooms* ▭ *No credit cards* ⦿ *No meals.*

$$ ☴ **Bimini Bay Resort and Marina.** You can choose an ocean view, a bay
RESORT view, or both at this pastel-splashed luxury resort that includes spa-
FAMILY cious suites, condominiums, and town houses with island art, seashell accents, hardwood and rattan furnishings, lavish bedrooms
and baths, and ultramodern kitchens (though some units have no
stoves). **Pros:** on-site customs and immigration; top-quality marinas
with all services; children's activity center; shuttle service around the
property. **Cons:** restaurant opening times irregular; north-end units
are long walk from town; beach can get crowded. $ *Rooms from:
$239* ✉ *King's Hwy. north of Bailey Town, North Bimini* ☎ *888/891–
2263 hotel, 877/666–2574 reservations* ⊕ *www.biminibayresort.com*
⤐ *374 units* ⦿ *No meals.*

$ ☴ **Bimini Big Game Club Resort & Marina** (*BBGC*). This low-rise lodg-
HOTEL ing fixture since 1936 reopened in 2010 after a multiyear renovation,
surfacing as the "newest" property on Bimini's dazzling coastline, and
it has frequently topped Trip Advisor's list of Bimini hotels ever since.
**Pros:** rooms and pool area renovated in 2010; excellent marina for fishing boats; excellent fishing. **Cons:** not so exciting for those not fishing;

most rooms ground level; not on the beach. $ *Rooms from: $189* ⊠ *King's Hwy., at the pink wall, Alice Town, Bimini* ☎ *242/347–3391, 800/867–4764* ⊕ *www.biggameclubbimini.com* ↝ *35 rooms, 12 cottages, 4 penthouses* ❑ *No meals.*

$    ⚐ **Sea Crest Hotel and Marina.** Tucked between the beach and the marina,
HOTEL    this three-story hotel has comfortable, simply furnished rooms with tile floors, cable TV, balconies, and one of the island's friendliest owner–management teams. **Pros:** free Wi-Fi; central location; welcoming service. **Cons:** rooms are motel style; rooms lack decor; old TVs. $ *Rooms from: $109* ⊠ *King's Hwy., Alice Town, North Bimini* ☎ *242/347–3071* ⊕ *www.seacrestbimini.com* ↝ *25 rooms, 2 suites.*

### NIGHTLIFE

**Big John's.** This self-proclaimed "Fisherman Boutique Hotel" has a newly renovated sports bar and restaurant, which happens to be one of the most popular places on-island to grab a late night cold beer. Come nightfall Thursday to Saturday, a fabulous local Bimini band offers live music combining reggae and soca. At midnight, a local DJ takes over and spins until 3 am. ⊠ *King's Hwy., across from Gateway Gallery, Alice Town, North Bimini* ☎ *239/347–3117* ⊕ *www.biminibigjohns.com.*

**End of the World Saloon** (*Sand Bar*). The back door of the small, noisy End of the World Saloon, better known by locals as "Sand Bar," is always open to the harbor. This place—with a sandy floor and visitors' graffiti, business cards, and other surprises on every surface—is a good spot to meet local folks over a beer and a lobster-and-conch pizza, while playing a game of ringtoss. The bar is near the heart of Alice Town, 100 yards from the Compleat Angler ruins, and just down the way from Big John's. ⊠ *King's Hwy., Alice Town, North Bimini* ⊘ *Closed in winter until spring break.*

### SHOPPING

**Bimini Craft Centre.** Near the Bahamas Customs Building in Alice Town, this craft center features the original straw, wood carving, and craft works of myriad islanders. Products are showcased over 17 stalls. There's also some amazing food to be had. Make sure to stop at Nathalie's Bimini Bread stand to try a loaf of decadent Bimini Bread. Think: hot challah with sugar glaze. ⊠ *Next door to Bahamas Customs Bldg., Alice Town, North Bimini* ☎ *242/347–3529.*

### SPORTS AND THE OUTDOORS

#### BOATING AND FISHING

There are numerous areas where fishermen can fish for the elusive "gray ghost." Full-day fishing excursions cost upwards of $600. Reef and deep-sea fishing excursions are also available. The best bonefish guides must be booked well in advance.

**Bonefish Ansil.** Ansil Saunders holds the world's record for the biggest bonefish ever caught. He's known around town as "Bonefish Ansil" and is one of the most sought after bonefish guides in Bimini. Ansil also has a workshop in Bailey Town where he builds boats. ☎ *242/347–2178.*

**Bonefish Ebbie.** Ebbie David is a highly recommended bonefishing guide in Bimini. ☎ *242/347–2053, 242/359–8273.*

This large bonefish was caught on Bimini's shallow flats.

**Bonefish Tommy.** Renowned bonefish guide Tommy Sewell has over 20 years experience leading bonefishing expeditions. He calls himself "the friendly guide" and prides himself on delivering excellent customer service (and big catches)! ☎ 242/347–3234.

**Capt. Jerome.** For deep-sea fishing in Bimini, Captain Jerome Stuart is your man. Stuart charges from $1,400 per day, and from $800 per half day for deep-sea fishing, with captain, mate, and gear included. Depending on the season, expect to catch snapper, grouper, Big Marlin, Bluefin Tuna, and sharks. Be aware of global declines in specific species before casting out your line. ☎ 242/347–2081 ⊕ *www.biminifishing.com*.

**Fisherman's Village Marina.** This 136-slip full-service marina, one of two marinas at Bimini Bay Resort & Marina, doubles as North Bimini's main shopping village. Adjacent to the reception area of the resort, the "village" houses Bimini Undersea dive shop; there's also a liquor and grocery store, ice-cream shop, gourmet pizza restaurant, a clothing boutique, and customs and immigration offices. ⊠ *Bimini Bay Resort & Marina, North Bimini, Bimini* ☎ 888/891–2263 ⊕ *www.biminibayresort.com/activities/fisherman's-village.aspx*.

### SCUBA DIVING AND SNORKELING

The **Bimini Barge Wreck** (a World War II landing craft) rests in 100 feet of water. **Little Caverns** is a medium-depth dive with scattered coral heads, small tunnels, and swim-throughs. **Rainbow Reef** is a shallow dive popular for fish gazing. **Moray Alley** teems with captivating moray eels and **Bull Run** is famous for its profusion of sharks. And, of course, there's **Bimini Road (aka, Road to Atlantis),** thought to be the famous "lost city." Dive packages are available through most Bimini hotels. You can also check out the best diving options through the **Bahamas Diving Association** (☎ *954/236–9292 or 800/866–DIVE* ⊕ *www.bahamasdiving.com*).

**Bimini Undersea.** Headquartered in Fisherman Village at Bimini Bay Resort, Bimini Undersea is the Dive and Watersports Center at Bimini Bay Resort & Marina. They offer myriad excursions and experiences, including scuba diving, snuba, nature boat tours, paddleboarding, fishing, and snorkeling near a delightful pod of Atlantic spotted dolphins. You can also rent or buy snorkel and diving gear. They offer two, two-tank dives a day and introductory scuba lessons. Dive packages with accommodations at Bimini Bay Resort are available, but day-trippers are also welcome to partake in Bimini Undersea's excursions. ⊠ *Bimini Bay Resort & Marina, North Bimini, Bimini* ☎ *242/347–2941, 786/462 4641 U.S. number* ⊕ *www.biminiundersea.com.*

## SOUTH BIMINI

Bigger, with better beaches and higher elevation than low-lying North Bimini, South Bimini is nonetheless the quieter of the two islands. Home to the island's only airport, it has a smattering of shops near the ferry landing where boats make regular crossings between the two islands, a short five-minute ride. Bimini Sands Resort occupies the bulk of the island with its safe-harbor marina, condos, beach club, and nature trail. It helps preserve the island's eco-focus by staying low-key and keeping much of its land undeveloped. It also helps maintain the little Fountain of Youth Park, the Sharklab, and beaches.

### GETTING AROUND

Visitors do not need a car on Bimini, and there are no car-rental agencies. A taxi from the airport to Bimini Sands Resort is $3.

### EXPLORING

**Bimini Biological Field Station Sharklab.** Showcased often on the Discovery Channel and other TV shows, the Sharklab was founded over 20 years ago by Dr. Samuel Gruber, a shark biologist at the University of Miami. Important research on the lemon and other shark species has furthered awareness and understanding of the misunderstood creatures. Visitors can tour the lab at low tide. The highlight is wading into the bay where the lab keeps several lemon sharks, rotating them on a regular basis. The tour leader gets in the pen with the sharks, captures one in a net, and speaks about its behaviors and common misconceptions people have of the lemon. Tours are offered daily but visitors must call in advance for times. ⊠ *South Bimini, South Bimini* ☎ *242/347–4538* 🎫 *Free* ⊙ *Call ahead for tour time.*

FAMILY **Bimini Nature Trail.** Developed by Bimini Sands Resort on undeveloped property, this mile-loop trail is one of the best of its kind in the Bahamas. Its slight rise in elevation means a lovely shaded walk under hardwood trees such as gumbo-limbos, poisonwood (marked with "Don't Touch" signs), and buttonwood. Check out the ruins of the historic Conch House, a great place for sunset-gazing. There is also a pirate's well exhibit devoted to the island's swashbuckling history. Excellent signage guides you through the island's fauna and flora if you prefer doing a self-guided tour. However, for the best interpretation and learning experience, book a guided tour with Bimini Sand's resident biologists Grant Johnson or Katie Grudecki. Kids always love petting the indigenous Bimini boa on the guided tour. ⊠ *South Bimini, South Bimini* 🕾 *242/347–3500* 🕮 *Free. Tours $12 adults, $6 kids* ⊗ *Daily sunrise–sunset.*

## BEACHES

South Bimini claims Bimini's prettiest beaches, with some of the best from-shore snorkeling around. Because of its convenient boat docks right near the beach, there tends to be a party crowd, but there's plenty of room to spread out.

**Bimini Sands Beach.** Patrons of Bimini Sands Resort & Marina are not the only ones who love Bimini Sands Beach. In fact, this gorgeous stretch of white-sand beach is so enticing, that vacationers on North Bimini often take the quick ferry ride over for the day. Beachgoers can set up headquarters at the Bimini Sands Beach Club, where public boat docks (including one with a customs and immigration office for those making the trip from Florida by boat), volleyball, tiki umbrellas, restaurants, and bars provide convenience and action. The beach gets particularly busy during spring break time. **Amenities:** food and drink; showers; toilets; water sports. **Best for:** partiers; sunrise; swimming; walking. ⊠ *South Bimini, Bimini.*

**Shell Beach.** Arguably Bimini's most pristine beach, Shell Beach, lies on South Bimini's undeveloped west coast, around the point from Bimini Sands Resort's beach on the island's west side. Head here for seclusion. The beach stretches out, long and natural, and calm waters typically prevail. The snorkeling is also great. As the name implies, the beach is strewn with colorful seashells. A small picnic shelter is the only concession to facilities, but Bimini Sands' restaurants and bars are a short walk away. **Amenities:** none. **Best for:** solitude; snorkeling; sunset; swimming. ⊠ *South Bimini, Bimini.*

## WHERE TO EAT

$$
SEAFOOD
Fodor'sChoice
★

✕ **Bimini Twist.** One of the top dining spots in Bimini, Bimini Twist at the Bimini Sands' Beach Club has an exceptional sushi bar and an elegant dining room. Time dinner for the sunset show if possible. If you'd rather not do sushi, start with conch, shrimp, lobster, or tomato ceviche. The chef is at the top of his game and will prepare special requests with panache. Entrées provide good variety from pasta pomodoro and conch linguine to chicken sautéed with mushroom and onions, and sirloin steak. $ *Average main: $26* ⊠ *Bimini Sands Resort, South Bimini* 🕾 *242/347–4500* ⊕ *www.biminisands.com* ⚏ *Reservations essential.*

## WHERE TO STAY

$$
RESORT
FAMILY
Fodor'sChoice
★

🛏 **Bimini Sands Resort and Marina.** Overlooking the Straits of Florida, this well-designed property rents one- to three-bedroom condominiums with direct beach access. **Pros:** two good restaurants (including a sushi bar); great nature trail on property; good tour operations; full-service marina with customs clearance. **Cons:** limited nightlife on South Bimini (party is daytime here); near marina, beach is crowded with day-trippers; sometimes shortage of lounge chairs. $ *Rooms from:* $260 ✉ *South Bimini, South Bimini* ☎ *242/347–3500, 800/737–1007* ⊕ *www.biminisands.com* ⇨ *206 condominiums.*

### NIGHTLIFE

**Mackey's Sand Bar.** With its beachfront location, sand floor, and eight flat screen TVs, Mackey's Sand Bar is South Bimini's one and only hot

**PLAN AHEAD**

Even though you're going to the laid-back islands, you need to reserve your guides, boats, cars, and golf carts in advance. And if you ask, these friendly islanders might include an airport greeting and transfer to your hotel.

spot. Folks often make the water-taxi ride from North Bimini for dinner and cocktailing. Wednesday night is the night to be here. There's a super cheap happy hour, karaoke, and live music in spring and summer. ✉ *Bimini Sands, South Bimini, Bimini* ☎ *242/347–4500* ⊕ *www.biminisands.com/bahamas/mackeys.*

### SPORTS AND THE OUTDOORS

#### BOATING AND FISHING

**Bimini Sands Marina.** This marina on South Bimini is a top-notch 60-slip marina capable of accommodating vessels up to 100 feet. Convenient customs clearance for guests is at the marina. Rent a 20- to 22-foot Twin Vee for either the half-day or full-day. Rental fishing gear (flats and blue water) is also available. The Bimini Sands Resort has a variety of eco and other boat excursions including snorkeling and a shark-feeding tour. ✉ *Bimini Sands Resort & Marina, South Bimini* ☎ *242/347–3500* ⊕ *www.biminisands.com.*

#### SCUBA DIVING AND SNORKELING

Bimini has excellent diving opportunities, particularly for watching marine life. Off the shore of South Bimini the concrete wreck of the **S.S. *Sapona*** attracts snorkelers as well as partiers.

**Bimini Sands Resort & Marina.** For guests of the hotel and day-trippers, Bimini Sands Resort & Marina has an excellent recreation program that includes snorkeling excursions to reefs, wrecks, and the Bimini Road to Atlantis. It also offers kayaking trips, boat tours, shark encounters, tours of the Bimini Nature Trail, and Kid's Club activities. ✉ *South Bimini, Bimini* ☎ *242/347–3500* ⊕ *www.biminisands.com.*

# THE BERRY ISLANDS

Remote, undiscovered, and pristine in beauty, the Berry Islands consist of more than two dozen small islands and almost a hundred tiny cays stretching in a sliver moon–like curve north of Andros and New Providence Island. Although a few of the islands are privately owned, most of them are uninhabited—except by rare birds who use the territory as their nesting grounds, or by visiting yachters dropping anchor in secluded havens. The Berry Islands start in the north at **Great Stirrup Cay,** where a lighthouse guides passing ships, and they end in the south at **Chub Cay,** only 35 miles north of Nassau.

Most of the islands' 700 residents live on **Great Harbour Cay,** which is 10 miles long and 1½ miles wide. Great Harbour, the largest of the Berry Islands, is sedate, self-contained, and oriented toward family beach and water-sport vacationing. Its main settlement, **Bullock's Harbour,** more commonly known as "the Village," has a couple of good restaurants near the marina, plus a grocery store and some small shops. The Great Harbour Cay resort and beach area, a few miles away from Bullock's Harbour, was developed in the early 1970s. More homes have been built since then, and many of the older beach villas and cottages have been remodeled.

Although the area has long been geared toward offshore fishing, in recent years family vacations and bonefishing have become more popular. Both Chub and Great Harbour cays are close to the Tongue of the Ocean, where big-game fish roam. Remote flats south of Great Harbour, from Anderson Cay to Money Cay, are excellent bonefish habitats, as are the flats around Chub Cay. Deeper water flats hold permit and tarpon.

## GETTING HERE AND AROUND

### AIR TRAVEL

In the Berry Islands the government airport in Great Harbour Cay (GHC) receives regular flights from Nassau (Le Air). There are no longer direct flights from Fort Lauderdale following the end of Gulfstream International (dba as Continental Connection and United Express) and the end of international flights by SunAir. Direct flights from Grand Bahama have also ceased since the dissolution of Flamingo Air. Private charters from south Florida and other Bahamas islands still make the trip to Great Harbour Cay. Chub Cay (CCZ) has a private airport; there are currently no regularly scheduled flights to Chub Cay. There's another private airport on Big Whale Cay.

The Great Harbour Cay airport is within walking distance of resorts, but taxis are available at the airport. You can get around the main settlement of Bullock's Harbour on foot.

Contacts **LeAir** ☎ 242/377–2356 ⊕ www.flyleair.com.

### ISLAND TRANSPORTATION

On Great Harbour Cay you can get most places on foot, but you can also rent a bike, car, or golf cart. Golf-cart rentals go for about $50 a day. Car rentals run about $60 per day.

They are the most common and convenient source of transportation off the water.

Rentals **Happy People's Rental** ✉ Great Harbour Cay ☎ 242/367–8117.

## BEACHES

The clarity of Bahamian waters is particularly evident when you reach the Berry Islands. Starfish abound, and you can often catch a glimpse of a gliding stingray or eagle ray.

**Great Harbour Cay Beach.** One of two crescent beaches that scoop the coastline of Great Harbour Cay, this beach is within walking distance of the airport and Great Harbour Village and town. The 5-mile sweep appeals to beachgoers who like the conveniences of food, drink, and hotel with their sand. The Beach Club restaurant and some houses line its length. **Amenities:** food and drink. **Best for:** sunset; swimming; walking.

**Sugar Beach.** For the best seclusion on Great Harbour Cay's 7 miles of beach, move to its second main beach 5 miles north, where rock bluffs divide the gorgeous, fine white sand into "private" beaches roughly 1 mile in length. Exploring the Sugar Beach Caves is an added attraction. The calm waters along these coved beaches make them great for snorkeling. **Amenities:** none. **Best for:** solitude; sunrise; snorkeling; swimming; walking.

### EARLY-BIRD DINNERS

Dinner is commonly served in most restaurants starting at 6 pm and can be over by 8:30. It is always best to call ahead for reservations, and to let the restaurant know you are coming for sure, as hours can be irregular, or restaurants can just decide to close if they think they aren't going to be busy. Some like to have your order ahead of time.

## WHERE TO EAT

$ BAHAMIAN 🍴 **The Beach Club.** This is the island's cool locale for breakfast and lunch, across the road from the airport, overlooking the beach and turquoise water. At breakfast, go for the eggs and ham with home grits. At lunch, have a grilled cheeseburger or whatever fresh fish is on the menu for the day. Takeout is available, including fishing lunches. Dinner is available on request, but if you eat at the open-air tables, be sure to have insect repellent, especially if the wind is down and especially at sunset. Hours and days are irregular, so talk to the locals or go by to see if it's open. [$] *Average main: $16* ✉ *Across from Great Harbour Airport, Great Harbour Cay* ☎ *242/367–8108* 💳 *No credit cards.*

$$ BAHAMIAN 🍴 **Coolie Mae Restaurant.** Expats, locals, and visitors rate Mae's food as the best on the island. Her bright sign makes the casual 60-seat restaurant in the Village, on the north side of the marina entrance, easy to find. Mae's secret is simple: she uses the best and freshest ingredients available each day to serve up wonderful home-style chow. Midday, try the conch salad, panfried grouper, or a tasty burger. Broiled lobster, steaks, pork chops, and fried conch along with peas 'n' rice and macaroni and cheese are dinner specialties. The menu changes daily, but the world famous Guava Duff is always available for dessert. Place your order in advance or call days ahead for a reservation. [$] *Average main: $21* ✉ *The Village, Great Harbour Cay* ☎ *242/367–8730* 💳 *No credit cards* 🕓 *Closed Sun.*

$$$ BAHAMIAN 🍴 **Tamboo Club.** A tradition at the Great Harbour Marina, this supper club—once a private club for the likes of Cary Grant and Brigitte Bardot—is now public and open on Saturday and other nights with reservations depending on the season. There is usually a lively crowd enjoying both local and international fare such as grilled seafood, rack of lamb, beef tenderloin, pork loin, baked duck, Cornish hen, and Bahamian specialties like smothered chicken with macaroni and cheese. The bar has satellite TV and backgammon. At press time, the restaurant was open but up for sale; call ahead. [$] *Average main: $38* ✉ *Great Harbour Marina, Great Harbour Cay* ☎ *242/367–8203* 💳 *No credit cards* 🕓 *Sometimes closed in Aug. and Sept.; call ahead.*

Kayaks line the beach at Little Stirrup Cay in the Berry Islands.

## WHERE TO STAY

$ B&B/INN 🏨 **Great Harbour Inn.** Perched at the water's edge on the marina in Great Harbour Cay, this inn has convenient access to the area's few restaurants, shops, and activities. **Pros:** good choice for a no-frills economical getaway; easy access to nearby beaches and fishing. **Cons:** no TV or Internet service; can be hot and buggy when the wind is down; not always easy to reach. [$] *Rooms from: $120* ✉ *On the waterfront at Great Harbour Marina, Great Harbour Cay* ☎ *242/367–8370* 🛏 *5 suites.*

## SPORTS AND THE OUTDOORS

### BOATING

The water's depth is seldom more than 20 feet here. Grass patches and an occasional coral head or flat coral patch dot the light-sand bottom. You might spot the odd turtle, and if you care to jump over the boat's side with a mask, you might also pick up a conch or two in the grass. Especially good snorkeling and bonefishing, and peaceful anchorages, can be found on the lee shores of the Hoffmans and Little Harbour cays. When it's open, **Flo's Conch Bar,** at the southern end of Little Harbour Cay, serves fresh conch prepared every way you can imagine.

**Great Harbour Cay Marina.** In the upper Berry Islands, the full-service Great Harbour Cay Marina has 80 slips that can handle boats up to 150 feet. Accessible through an 80-foot-wide channel from the bank side, the marina has one of the Bahamas' most pristine beaches running along its east side. The marina is also one of the best hurricane holes in the Bahamas. Fuel can be obtained at a separate dock west of the marina. ☎ *242/367–8005.*

**Happy People.** At Great Harbour Cy Marina, Happy People has boats available for exploring the island. They also rent golf carts and jeeps. ✉ *Great Harbour Cy Marina, Great Harbour Cay* ☎ *242/367–8117.*

**FISHING**

**Percy Darville.** Percy Darville knows the flats of the Berries better than anyone, and two of his brothers guide with him. Call him as far in advance as possible to book the Darville brothers as they are in hot demand. ☎ *242/464–4149, 242/367–8119.*

# ELEUTHERA AND
# HARBOUR ISLAND

# WELCOME TO ELEUTHERA AND HARBOUR ISLAND

## TOP REASONS TO GO

★ **Play in pink sand:** Glorious, soft pink sand, the ethereal shade of the first blush of dawn, draws beach connoisseurs to Harbour Island, which boasts a world-famous 3-mile stretch. Plenty of pretty pink beaches also dot Eleuthera's east and north coasts.

★ **Ogle island architecture:** Lovely 18th- and 19th-century homes with storybook gables and gingerbread verandahs are the norm on Harbour Island and Spanish Wells. Picturesque Victorian houses overlook Governor's Harbour in Eleuthera.

★ **Savor soulful sounds:** Nights here rock with the hot new Bahamian group Afro Band, the hip-hop of TaDa, the traditional sound of Jaynell Ingraham, the calypso of Dr. Sea Breeze, the soul music of Ronnie Butler, and the impromptu performances of local resident Lenny Kravitz (who built a recording studio in Gregory Town).

**1 Gregory Town and North Eleuthera.** Eleuthera's undeveloped, serene north holds some of the island's most iconic natural wonders: the Glass Window Bridge, a heart-racing span between 80-foot cliffs often buffeted by a raging Atlantic; the 17th-century Preacher's Cave; and the thrilling waves of Surfer's Beach.

**2 Hatchet Bay.** "The Country's Safest Harbour" is Hatchet Bay's claim to fame. The naturally protected harbor is a popular place to anchor sailboats and fishing vessels, and is mid-Eleuthera's only marina.

**3 Governor's Harbour.** The pretty Victorian town, with a lively harbor that's a frequent stop for mail boats, ferries, and yachts, offers upscale restaurants and down-home conch cafés, boutique inns, and inexpensive apartments.

**4 Rock Sound and South Eleuthera.** Rock Sound, the original capital of Eleuthera, is a quaint seaside settlement with 19th-century homes. Thirty miles away, yachties stop at Cape Eleuthera peninsula for a few nights of luxury in elegant town houses. Environmentalists also come here from around the world to learn about the self-sustaining Island School.

**5 Harbour Island.** Dunmore Town, the first capital of the Bahamas, may be the country's loveliest place, with its historic Loyalists' houses. White picket fences, some with cutouts of pineapples and boats, are festooned with red bougainvillea and tumbling purple morning glories. Luxurious inns, renowned restaurants, and the magnificent pink beach attract a parade of celebrities.

**6 Spanish Wells.** A quaint town of tidy clapboard white houses is on windswept St. George's Cay, a destination for those who don't want to bump elbows with other tourists. Idyllic white- and pink-sand beaches are the main attractions.

**6**

# GETTING ORIENTED

Eleuthera, at the center of the Bahamas chain, is made up of three distinctly different islands. The mainland is the largest island, a narrow, 110-mile long iguana-shaped landmass with two-lane Queen's Highway running from top to bottom. The fierce, deep-blue Atlantic is to the east, and the usually placid azure and teal shallows of the Bight of Eleuthera and Great Bahama Bank are to the west. The island is divided into North, Central, and South sections; Governor's Harbour, the government center and capital of Eleuthera, is mid-island and has the largest of three airports on the island. Eleuthera's mainland holds the majority of the island's residents, about 8,000. The rest of the 3,000 residents are split between 3-mile Harbour Island, 1 mile off Eleuthera's northeast coast, and 2-mile Spanish Wells, 1 mile off Eleuthera's northern coast. Both are reachable by 10-minute ferry rides from North Eleuthera. The island is 200 miles east of Florida and 50 miles east of Nassau.

# THE HARBOUR ISLAND LIFESTYLE

There are Out Islands and then there are "In" Islands (think fashionable St. Bart's), where the person at the next beachside table could be a film star, supermodel, or Grammy-winning musician. Harbour Island is both, an island where celebrities and billionaires gallivant freely, wearing flip-flops and driving old four-seater golf carts.

There are no high-rise condos, no luxurious spas, but plenty of fresh fish and lobster, one of the world's most magnificent beaches, elegant intimate inns, bakeries that rival any in Paris, good weather, and good cheer. When you're here you don't have to live the pampered life of the rich and famous; go fishing (regulars develop relationships with their fishing guides that last longer than some of their marriages), diving, and kayaking—or just sit back on the beach and watch how the beautiful people do it.

**CLAIMS TO FAME**

**Celebrities:** Both homeowners and visitors are detailed below.

**Photo Shoots:** 2006 swimsuit issue of *Sports Illustrated*; *Vogue* fashion spreads.

**TV Shows:** *House Hunters International* episodes on HGTV (the real-estate agent on both episodes was Robert Arthur, co-owner with his wife of Arthur's Bakery).

## HOW TO DO HARBOUR ISLAND

**Know Your Golf Cart Etiquette.** A friendly hello and wave separate the insiders from the visitors. Use hand signals to indicate turns—another thing newcomers don't do which causes some confusion on the narrow lanes. And drive on the left, for goodness sake! Americans have a habit of drifting toward the right, especially when they're looking at the scenery.

**Plan Your Sunsets.** The hallowed daily ritual of watching the sun set is best complemented by food and a libation: a glass of Italian wine and crab cakes at Acquapazza, lobster dumplings on the porch of the Landing, refreshing gazpacho on the terrace of the posh Rock House, conch fritters at Sunsets Bar and Grille, or cold Kaliks at Valentine's Marina. So many choices, so few vacation days.

**Who's Here?** Bahamians are famously unimpressed with celebrities, but ask the staff at shops and restaurants, and they usually don't mind telling you who's in town. It's nice to know what famous musician is on the island, just in case there's an impromptu bonfire sing-along.

**Pronounce it Like a Local.** Islanders have a shorthand name for their island: Briland. But say it right: BRI (rhymes with dry)-land.

**Bring Your Pooch.** To really blend in with the locals, you should take your dog—everywhere. You will look right at home with your furry best friend riding in the golf cart, frolicking on the beach, sharing a table on the terrace of a café, and going on long walks down the narrow lanes. There's no quarantine, just an import permit available at ⊕ *www.bahamas.com*, a $10 fee, and your vet's health certificate.

### WHO'S WHO OF HARBOUR ISLAND

Homeowners include **Wayne Huizenga,** former owner of the Miami Dolphins; Revlon Chairman **Ron Perelman;** media mogul **Barry Diller** and his fashion designer wife **Diane von Furstenberg;** duty-free tycoon **Robert Miller;** J. Crew CEO **Mickey Drexler;** supermodel **Elle Macpherson;** and **India Hicks,** English model and goddaughter of Prince Charles. Island Records founder **Chris Blackwell** started the influx of the ultra-wealthy when he bought Pink Sands Resort in 1992; guests have included **Martha Stewart** and the **Duchess of York. Dave Matthews, Tyra Banks, Jimmy Buffett,** and **Mick Jagger** all rent homes on Harbour Island.

Updated by
Julianne Hoell

You haven't experienced a real escape until you've vacationed in Eleuthera. Simple luxury resorts are the norm, deserted expanses of white- or pink-sand beaches are your playground, and islanders are genuinely friendly. Although the low-key, relax-and-relax-some-more island vacation isn't for everyone, Eleuthera is the place to go when you need to recharge your batteries. Seclusion, sun, and starry skies—just what the doctor ordered.

Eleuthera was founded in 1648 by a British group fleeing religious persecution; the name is taken from the Greek word for freedom. These settlers, who called themselves the Eleutheran Adventurers, gave the Bahamas its first written constitution. "Adventurers" has taken on new meaning as a clarion call to sailors, tourists, and, more recently, retirees looking for adventures of their own.

Largely undeveloped rolling green hills and untrammeled sandy coves, along with sleepy 19th-century towns, offer an authentic Bahamas experience that is quickly disappearing. Try not to notice the ubiquitous HG Christie and Sotheby's "For Sale" signs unless, of course, you're so smitten you want to stay. Rent a car—or even better, an SUV—for washboard back roads, and explore the island's secluded beaches and sandy coves fringing turquoise and aqua water that rivals anything in the Caribbean. The island is among the prettiest in the Bahamas, with gentle hills, unspoiled "bush" (backwoods), and gardens of tumbling purple lantana and sky-blue plumbago. Hotels and inns are painted in the shades of Bahamian bays and sunset, which is best watched from the comfort of inviting verandahs and seaside decks.

If you're looking for all of this and a bit more action, ferry over to Harbour Island, Eleuthera's chic neighbor. With its uninterrupted 3-mile pink-sand beach, top-notch dining, and sumptuous inns, the island has long been a favorite hideaway for jet-setters and celebrities. For splendid beaches with few, if any, tourists, head to Spanish Wells, a quiet, secluded island.

Eleuthera and Harbour Island beaches are some of the best in the world, thanks to their pristine beauty and dazzling variety. Deep-blue ocean fading to aqua shallows makes gorgeous backdrops for gourmet restaurants and the wooden decks of fishing shacks. The sand is for bonfires, celebrity-watching, Friday-night fish fries, dancing, and music, as much as it is for afternoon naps and stargazing.

Tranquil coves' sparkling white sand are as calm as a pool on the west side of Eleuthera, while the Atlantic's winter waves challenge skilled surfers on the east side, which has long stretches of pink sand. On Harbour Island, pink sand is on the ocean side and the white-sand coves face the calm channel. Home to shells that tumble in with every wave and starfish resting just offshore, the island's occasional glitz can't compete with the beaches' natural beauty.

# PLANNING

## WHEN TO GO

High season in Eleuthera runs December through April, when residents of cold-weather climates head to the Bahamas to defrost and soak up some rays. Low temperatures might dip into the 60s, and the water can be chilly. Bring a sweater and a jacket, especially if you are boating. Expect to pay higher rates for rooms, boat rentals, and airfare during this time. For the cheapest hotel rates and some of the best deals on water-sports packages, visit in summer or fall, when the ocean is generally calm and warm. But beware, hurricane season runs June through November, with most risk of storms from August to October. During this time weather can be steamy and rainy.

For those who want to catch some action, the liveliest times to visit Eleuthera are Christmas during the annual Junkanoo celebration, the Pineapple Festival and Conch Fest in June, and the North Eleuthera Sailing Regatta in October. Reserve hotel rooms early.

### TOP FESTIVALS

#### WINTER

**Junkanoo** is celebrated in Tarpum Bay on Christmas Day, and in Rock Sound and Harbour Island on December 26. Celebrations start around 7 pm.

#### SPRING

Cyclists from around the globe come in April to ride the 100-mile **Ride for Hope**, an event that benefits cancer care and research. Riders of all ages and skill levels can ride 10 miles or 100. The route starts at Governor's Harbour. ⊕ *www.rideforhopebahamas.com.*

#### SUMMER

**Conch Fest.** Deep Creek's annual Conch Fest in June has lots of conch, Rake 'n' Scrape, and arts and crafts.

**Eleuthera Pineapple Festival.** In June, Gregory Town hosts the four-day Eleuthera Pineapple Festival, with a Junkanoo parade, crafts displays, tours of pineapple farms, the annual 40-mile Cycling Race—as well as an opportunity to sample what Eleuthera natives proclaim to be the sweetest pineapple in the world.

**FALL**

**Softball Playoff Games.** Softball is the top sport in Eleuthera, and you can't beat Softball Playoff Games in September for excitement and camaraderie with locals. The winner competes in the national tournament. Games are held in Palmetto Point, Rock Sound, Governor's Harbour, and James Cistern.

**North Eleuthera/Harbour Island Sailing Regatta.** The North Eleuthera/Harbour Island Sailing Regatta in October provides five days of exciting competition of Bahamian Class A, B, and C boats. Onshore activities based on Harbour Island include live bands, Bahamian music, cultural shows, food, and drink.

## GETTING HERE AND AROUND

### AIR TRAVEL

Eleuthera has three airports: **North Eleuthera (ELH)**, mid-island **Governor's Harbour (GHB)**, and **Rock Sound (RSD)** in the south. Taxis usually wait for scheduled flights at the airports. Taxi service for two people from North Eleuthera Airport to the Cove is $20 ($60 from Governor's Harbour Airport); from Governor's Harbour to Pineapple Fields, $35; from Rock Sound airport to Cape Eleuthera, $70. Visitors going to Harbour Island and Spanish Wells should fly into North Eleuthera Airport.

**Contacts North Eleuthera Airport** ⊠ *Eleuthera Island* ☎ *242/335–1242.* **Governor's Harbour Airport** ⊠ *Governor's Harbour, Eleuthera Island* ☎ *242/332–2321.* **Rock Sound Airport** ⊠ *Rock Sound, Eleuthera Island* ☎ *242/334–2177.*

### BOAT AND FERRY TRAVEL

Mail boats leave from Nassau's Potter's Cay for the five-hour trip to Eleuthera. One-way tickets cost $35. M/V *Current Pride* sails to Current Island, Hatchet Bay, the Bluff, and James Cistern on Thursday, returning Tuesday to Nassau. M/V *Bahamas Daybreak III* leaves Nassau on Monday and Wednesday for Harbour Island, Rock Sound, and Davis Harbour, returning to Nassau Tuesday and Friday. The *Eleuthera Express* sails for Governor's Harbour, Rock Sound, Spanish Wells, and Harbour Island on Monday and Thursday, returning to Nassau on Tuesday and Sunday. Contact the **Dockmaster's Office. Bahamas Ferries,** high-speed catamarans, connect Nassau to Harbour Island, Governor's Harbour, and Spanish Wells. The trip takes two hours and costs $131 round-trip.

**Contacts Bahamas Fast Ferries** ⊠ *Eleuthera Island* ☎ *242/323–2166* ⊕ *www.bahamasferries.com.* **Dock Master's Office** ⊠ *Eleuthera Island* ☎ *242/393–1064.*

### CAR TRAVEL

Rent a car if you plan to travel around Eleuthera. North to south is about a three-hour drive. Daily rentals run about $70. Request a four-wheel drive if you plan to visit Preacher's Cave or Surfer's Beach.

## GREAT ITINERARIES

### IF YOU HAVE 3 DAYS

Fly into North Eleuthera and take the ferry to **Harbour Island**. Base yourself at a hotel near the famous 3-mile pink-sand beach or in historic Dunmore Town. Relax on the beach and have lunch at an ocean-side restaurant. Stroll through **Dunmore Town** in the afternoon, stopping at crafts stands and fashionable shops, admiring colonial houses along Bay Street, and visiting historic churches. At night, dine at one of the island's fine restaurants, such as the Landing, Rock House, Pink Sands, or Acquapazza. On Day 2, go scuba diving or snorkeling, or hire a guide and try to snag a canny bonefish. Visit the conch shacks on Bay Street for a low-key beachside dinner. On Day 3 get some last-minute color on the beach or some in-room spa pampering; stop by Vic-Hum Club or Gusty's for late-night music.

### IF YOU HAVE 5 DAYS

Head back to **Eleuthera** for the next two days. Rent a car at the North Eleuthera Airport (reserve in advance) and drive south past the **Glass Window Bridge**, where you can stand in one spot and see the brilliant-blue and often-fierce Atlantic Ocean to the east and the placid Bight of Eleuthera to the west. Continue to **Governor's Harbour**, the island's largest town, and grab lunch at Tippy's or the Beach House, upscale, laid-back beach bistros overlooking the Atlantic Ocean. Stay at one of the beach resorts and enjoy the incredible water views. Head into town if you're looking for some nightlife or dining options.

### IF YOU HAVE 7 DAYS

On your last two days, drive back to **North Eleuthera**, base yourself at the Cove, and relax on the resort's two beaches. On your final day take the ferry to **Spanish Wells**, where you can rent a golf cart and spend a half day exploring the tiny town and relaxing on a white-sand beach with no tourists. Or stay put and explore Surfer's Beach.

Contacts **Dingle Motor Service** ⊠ *Rock Sound, Eleuthera Island* ☎ *242/334–2031.* **Gardiner's Automobile Rentals** ⊠ *Governor's Harbour, Eleuthera Island* ☎ *242/332–2665.* **Stanton Cooper** ⊠ *Governor's Harbour, Eleuthera Island* ☎ *242/359–7007.*

### GOLF CART TRAVEL

You'll want a golf cart if you spend more than a couple of days on Harbour Island or Spanish Wells. Four-seater carts start at about $50 a day. Carts can be rented at most hotels and at the docks.

Contacts **Abner's Rentals** ⊠ *Spanish Wells, Eleuthera Island* ☎ *242/333–4090.* **Dunmore Rentals** ⊠ *Harbour Island* ☎ *242/333–2372.* **Johnson's Rentals** ⊠ *Harbour Island* ☎ *242/333–2376.* **Kam Kourts** ⊠ *Harbour Island* ☎ *242/333–2248.*

### TAXI TRAVEL

Taxis are almost always waiting at airports and at the North Eleuthera and Harbour Island water taxi docks. Your hotel can call a taxi for you; let them know a half hour before you need it.

Contacts **Amos at Your Service** ☎ *242/422–9130.* **Stanton Cooper** ☎ *242/359–7007.*

## ESSENTIALS

### BANKS

Banks are open Monday through Thursday from 9:30 to 3, Friday from 9:30 to 4:30. ATMs are available at most banks.

### EMERGENCIES

**Contacts Medical Clinics** ☎ *242/332–2774 Governor's Harbour, 242/333–2227 Harbour Island, 242/334–2226 Rock Sound, 242/333–4064 Spanish Wells.* **Police** ☎ *242/332–2117 Governor's Harbour, 242/333–2111 Harbour Island, 242/334–2244 Rock Sound, 242/333–4030 Spanish Wells, 919 Police.*

### HOTELS

Harbour Island, more than any other Out Island, is where the cognoscenti come to bask in ultra-luxurious inns and atmospheric small resorts. Follow the celebrities to $600-a-night cottages with views of the pink-sand beach or ultra-elegant rooms in Dunmore Town. Eleuthera offers elegant intimate resorts next to pink- and white-sand beaches happily empty of crowds. Those on tight budgets have a range of friendly, tidy, and affordable inns, a few on the beach, for around $100 a night. For urbanites who want all-out American luxury, there are modern town houses with stainless-steel appliances and granite in the kitchens, and bedrooms for the entire family. Whether you spend a lot or a little, the staff on this friendly island will know your name after a day. Many hotels are closed in September and October.

### RESTAURANTS

Don't let the outdoor dining on rustic wood tables fool you—Harbour Island and Eleuthera offer sophisticated cuisine that rivals that of any restaurants in Nassau. Although the place is usually casual and you never have to wear a tie, food is taken seriously. Of course, island specialties such as cracked conch, barbecued pork or chicken, and the succulent Bahamian lobster most locals call crawfish still abound, but you'll also find cappuccinos, steak, and lobster ravioli. Stop by Harbour Island's conch shacks on Bay Street north of Government Dock, where you can eat fresh conch salad on decks next to the water.

Most eateries are closed Sunday. Many restaurants have entertainment on regular nights so plan your dining schedule accordingly.

#### HOTEL AND RESTAURANT PRICES

*Restaurant prices are based on the median main course price at dinner, excluding gratuity, typically 15%, which is often automatically added to the bill. Hotel prices are for two people in a standard double room in high season, excluding service and 6%–12% tax.*

### VISITOR INFORMATION

**Contacts Eleuthera Tourist Office** ⊠ *Governor's Harbour, Eleuthera Island* ☎ *242/332–2142.* **Harbour Island Tourist Office** ⊠ *Dunmore Street, Harbour Island* ☎ *242/333–2621.* **Out Islands Promotion Board** ⊕ *www.myoutislands.com.*

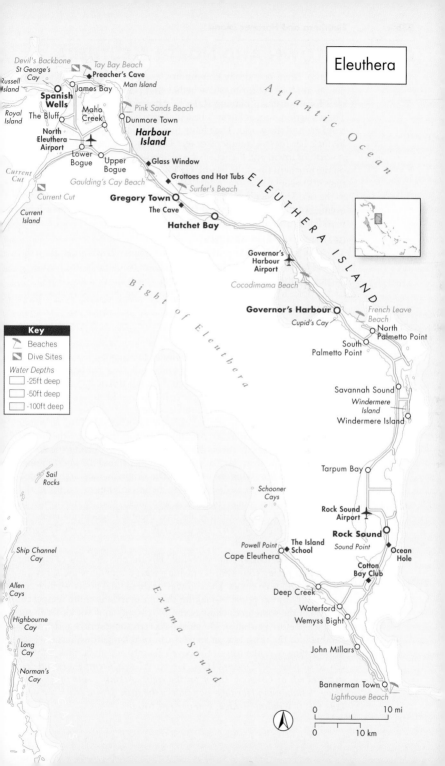

# Eleuthera

**Atlantic Ocean**

**ELEUTHERA ISLAND**

*Devil's Backbone*
*St George's Cay*
*Tay Bay Beach*
◆ **Preacher's Cave**
○ James Bay
*Man Island*

*Russell Island*
**Spanish Wells**
○ Maho Creek
*Pink Sands Beach*
○ **Dunmore Town**

*Royal Island*
The Bluff ○
North Eleuthera Airport ✈
○ Lower Bogue
○ Upper Bogue
*Harbour Island*

*Current Cut*
◆ Glass Window
◆ Grottoes and Hot Tubs
*Surfer's Beach*
◆ The Cave
**Gregory Town** ○
*Gaulding's Cay Beach*

*Current Island*
○ **Hatchet Bay**

Governor's Harbour Airport ✈
*Cocodimama Beach*

**Governor's Harbour** ○
*French Leave Beach*
*Cupid's Cay*
○ North Palmetto Point
South Palmetto Point ○

○ Savannah Sound
*Windermere Island*
○ Windermere Island

*Bight of Eleuthera*

Tarpum Bay ○

Rock Sound Airport ✈
**Rock Sound** ○
Powell Point
Cape Eleuthera ◆ The Island School
*Sound Point*
○ Ocean Hole
◆ **Cotton Bay Club**

Deep Creek ○
Waterford ○
Wemyss Bight ○

*Exuma Sound*

John Millars ○

Bannerman Town ○
*Lighthouse Beach*

**Sail Rocks**

*Schooner Cays*

**Ship Channel Cay**

**Allen Cays**

**Highbourne Cay**

**Long Cay**

**Norman's Cay**

| Key | |
|---|---|
| 🏖 | Beaches |
| ◥ | Dive Sites |

*Water Depths*
☐ -25ft deep
☐ -50ft deep
☐ -100ft deep

0 — 10 mi
0 — 10 km

# GREGORY TOWN AND NORTH ELEUTHERA

Gregory Town is a sleepy community, except on Friday nights when people are looking for music, whether that is speakers blasting reggae or a local musician playing Rake 'n' Scrape at a roadside barbecue. There's action, too, at Surfer's Beach, where winter waves bring surfers from around the world. They hang their surfboards from the ceiling at Elvina's Bar for free summer storage. The famous Glass Window Bridge is north of town, and Preacher's Cave, landing of the earliest settlers, is on the northern tip of the island. Gregory Town is home to a little more than 400 people, residing in small houses on a hillside that slides down to the sea. The town's annual Pineapple Festival begins on the Thursday evening of the Bahamian Labor Day weekend, at the beginning of June, with live music continuing into the wee hours.

## GETTING HERE AND AROUND

The North Eleuthera Airport is closer to Gregory Town hotels than the airport in Governor's Harbour. The taxi fare from the North Eleuthera Airport to the Cove Eleuthera, the area's most upscale inn, is $35 for two people. Rent a car at the airport unless you plan to stay at a resort for most of your visit.

## EXPLORING

Fodor's Choice   **Glass Window Bridge.** At a narrow point of the island a few miles north
★        of Gregory Town, a slender concrete bridge links two sea-battered bluffs that separate the island's Central and North districts. Sailors going south in the waters between New Providence and Eleuthera supposedly named this area the Glass Window because they could see through the natural limestone arch to the Atlantic on the other side. Stop to watch the northeasterly deep-azure Atlantic swirl together under the bridge with the southwesterly turquoise Bight of Eleuthera, producing a brilliant aquamarine froth. Artist Winslow Homer found the site stunning, and painted *Glass Window* in 1885. The original stone arch, created by Mother Nature, was destroyed by a combination of storms in the 1940s. Subsequent concrete bridges were destroyed by hurricanes in 1992 and 1999. Drive carefully, because there is frequent maintenance work going on. ⊠ *Queen's Hwy., north of Gregory Town, Gregory Town, Eleuthera Island.*

**Grottoes and Hot Tubs.** If you're too lulled by the ebb and flow of lapping waves and prefer your shores crashing with dramatic white sprays, a visit here will revive you. The sun warms these tidal pools—which the locals call "moon pools"—making them a markedly more temperate soak than the sometimes chilly ocean. Be careful, and ask locals about high seas before you enjoy. On most days refreshing sprays and rivulets tumble into the tubs, but on some it can turn dangerous; if the waves are crashing over the top of the cove's centerpiece mesa, pick another day to stop here. ⊠ *Queen's Hwy., Gregory Town, Eleuthera Island* ✛ *5 miles north of Gregory Town on the right (Atlantic) side of Queen's Hwy. A Bahamian Heritage sign marks the turn. If you reach the one-lane Glass Window Bridge, you've gone too far.*

**Preacher's Cave.** At the island's northern tip, this cave is where the Eleutheran Adventurers (the island's founders) took refuge and held services when their ship wrecked in 1648. Note the original stone altar inside the cave. Across from the cave is a long succession of deserted pink-sand beaches. ✉ *North Eleuthera, Eleuthera Island* ✣ *Follow Queen's Hwy. to the T intersection at the north end of the island. Turn right and follow signs to the cave.*

### PINEAPPLE EXPRESS

Pineapples remain Eleuthera's most famous product, even though the industry has been greatly reduced since the late 1800s, when the island dominated the world's pineapple market. These intensely sweet fruits are still grown on family farms, primarily in northern Eleuthera. Don't miss Gregory Town's Pineapple Festival in June.

## BEACHES

**Gaulding's Cay Beach.** Snorkelers and divers will want to spend time at this beach, 3 miles north of Gregory Town. You'll most likely have the long stretch of white sand and shallow aqua water all to yourself, and it's great for shelling. At low tide, you can walk or swim to Gaulding's Cay, a tiny rock island with a few casuarina trees. There's great snorkeling around the island; you'll see a concentration of sea anemones so spectacular it dazzled even Jacques Cousteau's biologists. **Amenities:** none. **Best for:** snorkeling; sunset. ✉ *Queen's Hwy., across from Daddy Joe's restaurant.*

**Surfer's Beach.** This is Gregory Town's claim to fame and one of the few beaches in the Bahamas known for surfing. Serious surfers have gathered here since the 1960s for decent waves from December to April. If you don't have a jeep, you can walk the ¾ mile to this Atlantic-side beach—take a right onto the paved road past the Hatchet Bay silos, just south of Gregory Town. Look for a young crowd sitting around bonfires at night. **Amenities:** none. **Best for:** surfing; walking. ✉ *Queen's Hwy., Gregory Town, Eleuthera Island.*

**Tay Bay Beach.** Steps from historical Preacher's Cave, this beach offers a long expanse of pink powdery sand. The area is remote, so you're likely to have the beach to yourself. There are plenty of palmetto trees to relax underneath for a quiet afternoon. Just offshore is Devil's Backbone, where the Eleutheran Adventurers shipwrecked and sought shelter in the cave. **Amenities:** parking. **Best for:** solitude; walking. ✉ *North Eleuthera, Eleuthera Island* ✣ *Follow the Queen's Hwy. to the T intersection at the north end of the island. Turn right and follow signs to Preacher's Cave.*

## WHERE TO EAT

$$$ EUROPEAN

🍴 **The Cove Eleuthera Restaurant.** The spacious, window-lined dining room serves three meals a day, blending classic Continental with Bahamian to produce delights such as Eleuthera pineapple with feta, braised short ribs, Bahamian grouper, and spiny lobster. It's one of the nicest restaurants on the island. Be sure to order dessert—you won't be disappointed. [$] *Average main: $33* ✉ *Queen's Hwy., Gregory Town, Eleuthera Island* ☎ *242/335–5142, 888/776–3901* 🌐 *www.thecoveeleuthera.com* ✍ *Reservations essential.*

$ | × **The Laughing Lizard Café.** This eco-minded café is perched high atop a hill just off the Queen's Highway, north of Gregory Town. The colorful restaurant uses local produce to create island-inspired wraps, panini, and salads. They also have a full bar where you can order tropical smoothies, Bahamian beer, or fresh herbal iced tea. Jamaican owner Petagay Hollinsed-Hartman is committed to a green philosophy—all to-go utensils and plates are biodegradable, and aluminum cans are crushed and sent to Nassau to support the Cans for Kids program. $ *Average main: $10* ⊠ *Queen's Hwy., Gregory Town, Eleuthera Island* ☎ *242/470–6992* ⊕ *www. laughinglizardcafe.com* ⚏ *No credit cards* ☉ *Closed Sun. and Mon.*

CAFÉ

> **GREGORY TOWN SOUND**
>
> In 2009, Grammy Award–winning musician Lenny Kravitz built a multimillion-dollar recording studio called Gregory Town Sound, and he and his band often slip into Elvina's Bar down the road for inspiration. Kravitz, who lives in Gregory Town part-time, has said, "This is the place I love being the most. Some of the nicest people I've ever met in my life are here."

## WHERE TO STAY

$$$ | 🏨 **The Cove Eleuthera.** Forty secluded acres studded with scenic beach cottages set the tone for this relaxing island escape, which underwent a sweeping renovation in 2013. **Pros:** sandy beaches; top-rated amenities; one of the most luxurious places to stay on the island. **Cons:** need a car if you want to do anything outside the property. $ *Rooms from: $395* ⊠ *Queen's Hwy., 1½ miles north of Gregory Town, Gregory Town, Eleuthera Island* ☎ *242/335–5142, 888/776–3901* ⊕ *www. thecoveeleuthera.com* ⟿ *120 rooms* ⏁ *No meals.*

RESORT
Fodor's Choice
★

## SHOPPING

Fodor's Choice
★

**Island Made Shop.** This shop, run by Pam and Greg Thompson, is a good place to shop for Bahamian arts and crafts, including Androsia batik (made on Andros Island), driftwood paintings, Abaco ceramics, and prints. Look for the old foam buoys that have been carved and painted into fun faces. ⊠ *Queen's Hwy., Gregory Town, Eleuthera Island* ☎ *242/335–5369* ☉ *Closed on Sun.*

## SPORTS AND THE OUTDOORS

### ADVENTURE TOURS

**Bahamas Out-Island Adventures.** This tour operator gives overnight kayaking and surfing lessons. ☎ *242/335–0349* ⊕ *www.bahamasadventures.com.*

### ISLAND TOURS

**Arthur Nixon Tours** ☎ *242/332–2052, 242/359–7879.*

**Eleuthera Adventure Tours** ☎ *242/334–2356* ⊕ *www.eleutheraadventuretours.com.*

**Freedom Tours** ☎ *242/335–1700.*

### SCUBA DIVING AND SNORKELING

**Devil's Backbone.** In North Eleuthera, Devil's Backbone offers a tricky reef area with a nearly infinite number of dive sites and a large number of wrecks. Contact a local dive shop to schedule a trip. ⊠ *North Eleuthera, Eleuthera Island.*

### SURFING

**Rebecca's Beach Shop.** In Gregory Town, stop by Rebecca's Beach Shop, a general store, crafts shop, and, most important, a surf shop, where local surf guru "Ponytail Pete" rents surfboards, snorkel gear, and more. A chalkboard lists surf conditions and tidal reports. He also gives surf lessons. ⊠ *Queen's Hwy., Gregory Town, Eleuthera Island* ☎ *242/335–5436.*

# HATCHET BAY

Hatchet Bay, which has mid-Eleuthera's only marina, is a good place to find a fishing guide and friendly locals. Take note of the town's side roads, which have such colorful names as Lazy Road, Happy Hill Road, and Smile Lane. Just south of town, the Rainbow Inn and Restaurant is the hub of activity for this stretch of the island. Bay Inn Bed and Breakfast opened in late 2009, and has been busy since the first day.

"The Country's Safest Harbour" is Hatchet Bay's claim to fame. The naturally protected harbor is a popular place to anchor sailboats and fishing vessels when storms are coming. One of the most memorable days for the harbor, however, wasn't a storm but the day years ago when Jackie Kennedy Onassis came in on a friend's yacht.

The pastoral scenery outside of Hatchet Bay is some of the island's most memorable—towering, long-empty grain silos, windswept green hillsides, and wild cotton, remnants of the old cotton plantations. Don't miss James Cistern, a seaside settlement to the south.

### GETTING HERE AND AROUND

Hatchet Bay is equidistant between the Governor's Harbour and North Eleuthera airports. The taxi fare from either airport is about $50 for two people. Rent a car at the airport unless you plan to stay at a resort for most of your visit.

## EXPLORING

**The Cave.** North of Hatchet Bay lies a subterranean, bat-populated tunnel complete with stalagmites and stalactites. Pirates supposedly once used it to hide their loot. An underground path leads for more than a mile to the sea, ending in a lofty, cathedral-like cavern. Within its depths, fish swim in total darkness. The adventurous may wish to explore this area with a flashlight (follow the length of guide string along the cavern's floor), but it's best to inquire first at one of the local stores or the Rainbow Inn for a guide. ⊠ *Queen's Hwy., Hatchet Bay, Eleuthera Island* ✛ *2 miles north of Hatchet Bay, turn left at sign for "Hatchet Bay Caves."*

## WHERE TO EAT

**$$** ╳ **The Front Porch.** This little roadside restaurant features a beautiful view
ECLECTIC of the bay, particularly at sunset when the orange horizon is freckled
with the silhouettes of moored sailboats. The menu is island-inspired
European cuisine and always includes fresh seafood. In addition to serv-
ing lunch and dinner, The Front Porch also rents kayaks and windsurf-
ing gear, and can arrange captains and tour guides. $ *Average main:
$24* ⊠ *Queen's Hwy., Hatchet Bay, Eleuthera Island* ☎ *242/335–0727*
✆ *Closed Wed.*

**$$$** ╳ **The Rainbow Inn Steakhouse.** With a classy but no-fuss aura and exhi-
EUROPEAN bition windows that face gorgeous sunsets, this restaurant is well
known for its steaks, including 14-ounce New York strip, 8-ounce
filet mignon, and 20-ounce rib eye, which are flown in daily. Grouper, conch, mahimahi, and cobia are also fresh, caught daily. Guests
have 180-degree views of the ocean from the screened patio or dining room. The restaurant has live music on Monday, Wednesday,
and Saturday nights (in high season). They are open for breakfast.
$ *Average main: $35* ⊠ *Queen's Hwy., 2½ mi south of Hatchet Bay,
Hatchet Bay, Eleuthera Island* ☎ *242/335–0294* ✆ *Closed Sun. and
end of Aug.–mid-Oct.*

## WHERE TO STAY

**$** ☷ **Bay Inn Bed and Breakfast.** You can't miss the lime-green, yellow,
B&B/INN and pink clapboard buildings and lush landscaping at this bed-and-
breakfast, which opened in June 2009. **Pros:** Continental breakfast;
relaxing outdoor space; helpful staff. **Cons:** not on the beach or bay;
no water views; not close to shops. $ *Rooms from: $120* ⊠ *West off
Queen's Hwy., Hatchet Bay, Eleuthera Island* ☎ *242/335–0730* ⤴ *11
rooms* ¶⦿¶ *Breakfast.*

**$** ☷ **Rainbow Inn.** Immaculate, generously sized cottages, some octago-
RENTAL nal—all with large private porches—have sweeping views of the ocean.
Fodor's Choice **Pros:** superspacious cottages at reasonable prices; great water views;
★ friendly service. **Cons:** not on the beach; not close to a town or shops.
$ *Rooms from: $155* ⊠ *Queen's Hwy., 2½ miles south of Hatchet Bay,
Hatchet Bay, Eleuthera Island* ☎ *242/335–0294* ⊕ *www.rainbowinn.
com* ⤴ *4 cottages, 2 villas* ✆ *End of Aug.–mid-Oct.* ¶⦿¶ *Some meals.*

## NIGHTLIFE

**Dr. Sea Breeze.** The debonair Cebric Bethel, better known as Dr. Sea
Breeze, strums his acoustic guitar while singing island songs at the
Rainbow Inn in Hatchet Bay, Unique Village in Governor's Harbour,
and Daddy Joe's in Gregory Town. To be sure you don't miss him, call
beforehand to confirm his schedule.

The beach at Governor's Harbour.

## GOVERNOR'S HARBOUR

Governor's Harbour, the capital of Eleuthera and home to government offices, is the largest town on the island and one of the prettiest. Victorian-era houses were built on Buccaneer Hill, which overlooks the harbor, bordered on the south by a narrow peninsula and Cupid's Cay at the tip. To fully understand its appeal, you have to settle in for a few days and explore on foot—if you don't mind the steep climb up the narrow lanes. The town is a step into a gentler, more genteel time. Everyone says hello, and entertainment means wading into the harbor to cast a line, or taking a painting class taught by Martha's Vineyard artist Donna Allen at the 19th-century pink library on Monday mornings. You can see a current movie at the balconied Globe Princess, the only theater on the island, which also serves the best hamburgers in town. Or swim at the gorgeous beaches on either side of town, which stretch from the pink sands of the ocean to the white sands of the Bight of Eleuthera. There are three banks, a few grocery stores, and some of the island's wealthiest residents, who prefer the quiet of Eleuthera to the fashionable party scene of Harbour Island.

### GETTING HERE AND AROUND

Fly into Governor's Harbour Airport north of town, or arrive by mail boat from Nassau. You will want to rent a car at the airport, even if you plan to stay in Governor's Harbour, to best explore the beaches and restaurants. If you stay at Duck Inn or Laughing Bird Apartments, you'll be able to walk to nearby restaurants.

## EXPLORING

**Haynes Library.** The heart of the community, this 19th-century building offers art classes and Tuesday morning coffee hours for visitors and residents. The library has a wide selection of books and Internet terminals, with gorgeous views of the harbor. ⊠ *Cupid's Cay Rd., Governor's Harbour, Eleuthera Island* ☎ *242/332–2877* ⊕ *hayneslibrary.blogspot.com* ⊙ *Mon.–Thurs. 9–6, Fri. 9–5, Sat. 10–4* ⊙ *Closed Sun.*

**Leon Levy Native Plant Preserve.** Walk miles of scenic trails in this 25-acre nature preserve located on Banks Road. Funded by the Leon Levy Foundation and operated by the Bahamas National Trust, the preserve serves as an environmental education center with a focus on traditional bush medicine. Follow the boardwalk over a small waterfall and take the path to the Observation Tower to see hundreds of indigenous trees, plants, and wildlife such as mangroves, five-finger plants, and bullfinches. Group tours are available, or if you'd prefer to tour the preserve on your own, the welcome center will provide you with a map and a plant identification guide. ⊠ *Banks Rd., Governor's Harbour, Eleuthera Island* ☎ *242/332–3831* ⊕ *www.levypreserve.org* 💰 *$5* ⊙ *Daily 9–5.*

**Windermere Island.** About halfway between Governor's Harbour and Rock Sound, distinguished Windermere Island, 5 miles long with a lovely pink-sand beach, is the site of vacation homes of the rich and famous, including Mariah Carey and members of the British royal family. Don't plan on any drive-by ogling of these million-dollar homes, though; the security gate prevents sightseers from passing. ⊠ *Queen's Hwy., Windermere, Eleuthera Island.*

## BEACHES

**French Leave Beach.** This stretch of pink sand was Club Med's famed beach before the resort was destroyed by a hurricane in 1999; it will soon be home to the new French Leave Marina Village. The gorgeous Atlantic-side beach is anchored by fantastic bistros like the Beach House and Tippy's. The wide expanse, ringed by casuarina trees, is often deserted and makes a great outpost for romantics. **Amenities:** food and drink. **Best for:** solitude; swimming; walking. ⊠ *Banks Rd.*

**French Leave Beach.** This stretch of pink sand was Club Med's famed beach before the resort was destroyed by a hurricane in 1999, and will soon be home to the new French Leave Marina Village. The gorgeous Atlantic-side beach is anchored by fantastic bistros like the Beach House and Tippy's. The wide expanse, ringed by casuarina trees, is often deserted and makes a great outpost for romantics. **Amenities:** food and drink. **Best for:** solitude; swimming; walking. ⊠ *Banks Rd., Governor's Harbour, Eleuthera Island.*

FAMILY **Cocodimama Beach.** Many necklaces and shell decorations come from Cocodimama, which, along with Ten Bay Beach at South Palmetto Point, is well known for perfect small shells. The water at this secluded beach, 6 miles north of Governor's Harbour, has the aqua and sky blue shades you see on Bahamas posters, and is shallow and calm, perfect for children and sand castles. The Cocodimama Resort is next to the beach, and makes a perfect lunchtime respite for pasta and wine.

A Governor's Harbour home.

**Amenities:** food and drink; parking. **Best for:** sunset. ✉ *Cocodimama Resort, Queen's Hwy., Governor's Harbour, Eleuthera Island* 🌐 *www.cocodimama.com.*

## WHERE TO EAT

$ DELI 🍴 **Banks Road Deli.** For the perfect beach picnic, stop by Banks Road Deli to pick up freshly made sandwiches, chips, and homemade cookies. Located in the same building as Pineapple Field's Gift Store, the deli also serves pastries and coffee in the morning, which you can enjoy in their quiet outdoor seating area. The small gourmet grocery section is great for stocking up on wine and chocolate. [$] *Average main: $9* ✉ *Banks Rd., Governor's Harbour, Eleuthera Island* ☎ *242/332–2221* 🌐 *www.pineapplefields.com/index.php/dining/banks-road-deli.html* 🕒 *Closed Sun.*

$$ EUROPEAN Fodor's Choice ★ 🍴 **The Beach House Tapas Restaurant.** On a gorgeous pink-sand beach, this outdoor restaurant offers stunning views and exquisite Spanish appetizers and entrées such as shrimp with goat cheese and prosciutto, and jumbo crab–and-lobster ravioli. There is live music on Monday and Thursday nights, so be sure to arrive early to secure a table, or sit at the bar for the best view of the band. [$] *Average main: $25* ✉ *Banks Rd., Governor's Harbour, Eleuthera Island* ☎ *242/332–3387* 🕒 *Dinner served Mon. and Thurs. only* 🕒 *Closed Oct.*

$$ ECLECTIC 🍴 **The Bistro at Sky Beach Club.** In addition to oceanview seating in its outdoor dining room, the Bistro also features a swim-up bar, perfect for a leisurely lunch. Relax in the infinity-edge pool while you savor a mango daiquiri and cheeseburger, and take in the magnificent view

of the Atlantic. Dinner is decidedly more sophisticated, with options such as grouper creole, seafood linguini, or steak served with butternut squash and chèvre. While you are invited to enjoy the pool and beach without being a hotel guest, an afternoon at Sky Beach Club may have you booking your next stay there. $ *Average main: $23* ⊠ *Sky Beach Club, Queen's Hwy., Governor's Harbour, Eleuthera Island* ☎ *242/332–3422* ⊕ *www. skybeachclub.com.*

$$ ✕ **Buccaneer Club.** On the top of
BAHAMIAN     Buccaneer Hill overlooking the town and harbor, this mid-19th-century farmhouse is now a restaurant serving three meals a day, with an outdoor dining area surrounded by a garden of bougainvillea, hibiscus, and coconut palms. The beach is a leisurely five-minute stroll away, and the harbor, where you can also swim, is within shouting distance. Sample such native specialties as grouper, conch, and crawfish. $ *Average main: $21* ⊠ *Haynes Ave., Governor's Harbour, Eleuthera Island* ☎ *242/332–2000* ▭ *No credit cards* ◔ *No dinner Sun. and Wed.*

$ ✕ **Governor's Harbour Bakery.** A Governor's Harbour staple since 1989,
BAKERY     this bakery serves up delicious pastries and breads, baked fresh daily. Stop in to pick up come of the popular Danish coffee cake, or sample johnnycakes and hot patties—Bahamian favorites. The bakery also makes fresh doughnuts, éclairs, and other homemade treats. Be sure to buy extra: once you get them home, these pastries tend to disappear quickly. $ *Average main: $4* ⊠ *Gibson La., Governor's Harbour, Eleuthera Island* ☎ *242/332–2071* ▭ *No credit cards* ◔ *Closed Sun.*

$ ✕ **Mate & Jenny's Restaurant & Bar.** A few miles south of Governor's Har-
PIZZA     bour, this casual neighborhood restaurant specializes in pizza; try one topped with conch. Sandwiches and Bahamian specialties are also served. The walls are painted with tropical sunset scenes and decorated with photos and random memorabilia, and the ongoing dart games add to the joint's local color. Pizza prices range from $10 to $25, depending on the toppings. $ *Average main: $14* ⊠ *S. Palmetto Point, Governor's Harbour, Eleuthera Island* ☎ *242/332–1504* ▭ *No credit cards* ◔ *Closed Tues.*

$$ ✕ **Tippy's.** Despite its barefoot-casual environment (old window shutters
ECLECTIC     used as tabletops, sand in the floor's crevices), the menu at this open-air
Fodor'sChoice     beach bistro is a sophisticated mix of Bahamian and European cuisine,
★     with items that change daily based on the availability of fresh local products. Expect things like lobster salad, specialty pizzas, and fresh fish prepared with some sort of delectable twist. This place may look like a beach shack, but everything has been well planned—the owners even imported a French chef to satisfy discriminating palates. Try to grab a table on the outdoor deck, which has a fantastic view of the beach. Locals and visitors keep this place hopping year-round, and there's

---

**PINK SAND BEACHES**

Contrary to popular opinion, pink sand comes primarily from the crushed pink and red shells of microscopic insects called foraminifera, not coral. Foraminifer live on the underside of reefs and the sea floor. After the insects die, the waves smash the shells, which wash ashore along with sand and bits of pink coral. The intensity of the rosy hues depends on the slant of the sun.

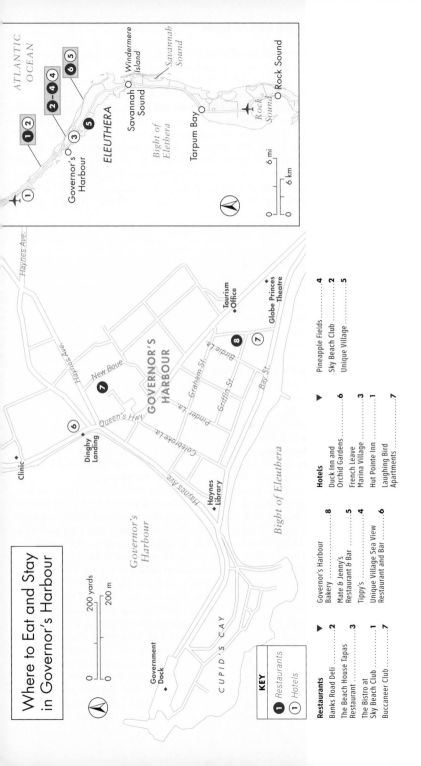

# Where to Eat and Stay in Governor's Harbour

## KEY

▶ Restaurants ①
① Hotels

**Restaurants**

| | |
|---|---|
| Banks Road Deli | **2** |
| The Beach House Tapas Restaurant | **3** |
| The Bistro at Sky Beach Club | **1** |
| Buccaneer Club | **7** |
| Governor's Harbour Bakery | **8** |
| Mate & Jenny's Restaurant & Bar | **5** |
| Tippy's | **4** |
| Unique Village Sea View Restaurant and Bar | **6** |

**Hotels**

| | |
|---|---|
| Duck Inn and Orchid Gardens | **6** |
| French Leave Marina Village | **3** |
| Hut Pointe Inn | **1** |
| Laughing Bird Apartments | **7** |
| Pineapple Fields | **4** |
| Sky Beach Club | **2** |
| Unique Village | **5** |

ATLANTIC OCEAN

ELEUTHERA

Governor's Harbour

Savannah Sound

Windermere Island

Savannah Sound

Bight of Eleuthera

Tarpum Bay

Rock Sound

Rock Sound

0   6 mi
0   6 km

Haynes Ave.

Clinic

Haynes Ave.

New Boue

Queen's Hwy.

Dinghy Landing

Colebroke La.

Pinder La.

Graham St.

Griffin St.

Birdie La.

Bay St.

Tourism Office

Globe Princes Theatre

GOVERNOR'S HARBOUR

Haynes Library

Haynes Ave.

Governor's Harbour

Bight of Eleuthera

CUPID'S CAY

Government Dock

0   200 yards
0   200 m

live music on Wednesday and Saturday nights. $ *Average main: $25* ⊠ *Banks Rd., Governor's Harbour, Eleuthera Island* ☎ *242/332–3331* ⊕ *www.pineapplefields.com/index.php/dining/tippys.html* ⚘ *Reservations essential* ⊘ *Closed Mon. and mid-Sept.–Oct.*

$$
BAHAMIAN

✕ **Unique Village Sea View Restaurant and Bar.** Bahamas home cooking is the reason to come to this octagonal restaurant, with its pagoda-style natural-wood ceiling, wraparound covered deck, and panoramic view of the beach. The restaurant–bar is a popular spot for locals and visitors, especially for the live music on Sundays. Specialties include cracked conch, the chef's snapper special with peas 'n' rice, homemade bread, and coconut tarts for dessert. $ *Average main: $27* ⊠ *North Palmetto Point, Banks Rd., Governor's Harbour, Eleuthera Island* ☎ *242/332–1830.*

## WHERE TO STAY

$
B&B/INN

**Duck Inn and Orchid Gardens.** Facing west into the sunset, overlooking beautiful Governor's Harbour, two colonial cottages and a two-story home built in the 1850s are surrounded by a tropical garden with a superb orchid collection. **Pros:** historic buildings; harbor views; lush orchid gardens. **Cons:** not on the beach; only a few restaurants and shops within walking distance. $ *Rooms from: $150* ⊠ *Corner of Pine and Queen's Hwy., Governor's Harbour, Eleuthera Island* ☎ *242/332–2608* ⊕ *www.theduckinn.com* ⤳ *2 cottages, 1 house* ⦿ *No meals.*

$$$$
RESORT

**French Leave Marina Village.** This new Governor's Harbour resort, which welcomed its first guests in August 2013, offers gorgeous waterfront bungalows, and by summer 2014 will include a bar and grill, a freshwater pool, and dozens of other luxurious amenities. **Pros:** new resort, beautiful harbor views, luxurious amenities. **Cons:** you'll need a car if you want to explore the islnad; at press time, constuction was ongoing. $ *Rooms from: $450* ⊠ *Queen's Hwy., Governor's Harbour, Eleuthera Island* ⚘ *info@frenchleaveresort.com* ⊕ *www. frenchleaveresort.com* ⤳ *37 cottages* ⦿ *No meals.*

$$
B&B/INN

**Hut Pointe Inn.** Those looking for history and luxury will find much to like about this historic building constructed in 1944 by the first premier of the Bahamas, Sir Roland Symonette. **Pros:** historic building; wonderfully landscaped grounds; upscale amenities. **Cons:** within a few feet of the Queen's Highway; not on beach; 10 minutes from town. $ *Rooms from: $281* ⊠ *Queen's Hwy., Governor's Harbour, Eleuthera Island* ☎ *760/908–6700, 242/332–3530* ⊕ *www.hutpointe.com* ⤳ *7 suites* ⦿ *No meals.*

$
B&B/INN

**Laughing Bird Apartments.** Jean Davies and her son Pierre own these four tidy apartments on an acre of land across the street from Laughing Bird Beach. **Pros:** nice view of beach through garden foliage; roomy guest rooms with full kitchens. **Cons:** needs refurbishing and redecorating. $ *Rooms from: $100* ⊠ *Gibson La., Governor's Harbour, Eleuthera Island* ☎ *242/332–2012* ⤳ *4 apartments* ⦿ *No meals.*

$$
RENTAL
FAMILY
Fodor's Choice
★

**Pineapple Fields.** Across the street from a pink-sand Atlantic beach and Tippy's oceanfront bistro, Pineapple Fields is the perfect base for a disappearing act. **Pros:** modern facilities and amenities; large units; secluded beach and Tippy's across the street. **Cons:** sterile American-style condo; will need to drive to town. $ *Rooms from: $220*

Dr. Sea Breeze performs at the Rainbow Inn.

✉ *Banks Rd., Governor's Harbour, Eleuthera Island* ☎ *242/332–2221, 877/677–9539* 🌐 *www.pineapplefields.com* 🛏 *32 condo units* 🕒 *Closed Oct.* 🍴 *No meals.*

$$$ RESORT 🏨 **Sky Beach Club.** Perched on 22 acres of oceanfront property, this modern resort rents poolside bungalows and large four-bedroom houses. **Pros:** secluded pink-sand beach; restaurant on-property; close to airport. **Cons:** need a car to get to town. [$] *Rooms from: $325* ✉ *Queen's Hwy., Governor's Harbour, Eleuthera Island* ☎ *242/332–3422* 🌐 *www.skybeachclub.com* 🛏 *3 bungalows, 4 houses.*

$ HOTEL 🏨 **Unique Village.** Just south of Governor's Harbour near North Palmetto Point on marvelous pink Poponi Beach, this resort has large, refurbished rooms with French doors opening to private balconies. **Pros:** on a gorgeous pink beach; steps to large pool and restaurant. **Cons:** must go down many wood stairs to access beach; a 10-minute drive to Governor's Harbour. [$] *Rooms from: $130* ✉ *North Palmetto Point, Banks Rd., Governor's Harbour, Eleuthera Island* ☎ *242/332–1830* 🌐 *www.uniquevillage.com* 🛏 *10 rooms, 4 villas* 🍴 *No meals.*

## NIGHTLIFE

**Dr. Sea Breeze.** Dr. Sea Breeze plays calypso at Unique Village resort in Palmetto Point; at Rainbow Inn, south of Hatchet Bay; and at Daddy Joe's, north of Gregory Town. Be sure to call ahead to make sure he's scheduled.

**Globe Princess.** The Globe Princess shows current movies, one show each night at 8:15 pm. Movies change weekly. The concession serves the best hamburgers in town. ✉ *Queen's Hwy., Governor's Harbour, Eleuthera Island* ☎ *242/332–2735* 🎟 *$5.50* 🕒 *Closed Thurs.*

**Ronnie's Hi-D-Way.** With a pool table, outdoor basketball court, and large dance floor, Ronnie's is the most popular local hangout in Governor's Harbour. The scene really takes off on Friday and Saturday nights, when the bar hosts a DJ. If you drop in for a drink on the weekend, expect to stay a while for dancing to popular reggae and hip-hop tunes. ⊠ *Cupid's Cay, Governor's Harbour, Eleuthera Island* ☎ *242/332–2307.*

## SHOPPING

**The Beach House Gift Shop.** The shop at The Beach House Tapas Restaurant is full of fabulous resortwear and island-chic gifts. You'll also find jewelry, sandals, and other great accessories. ⊠ *The Beach House Tapas Restaurant, Bay St., Governor's Harbour, Eleuthera Island* ☎ *242/332–3387.*

**The Gift Shop at Pineapple Fields.** You'll find Bahamian handcrafted art, locally made jewelry, and elegant beachwear in this gift shop, located in the same building as Pineapple Fields' office and Banks Road Deli. ⊠ *Bay St., Governor's Harbour, Eleuthera Island* ☎ *242/332–2221* ⊕ *www.pineapplefields.com* ⊙ *Closed Oct.*

## SPORTS AND THE OUTDOORS

### FISHING

**Paul Petty.** Paul is one of the best in the business for guiding anglers through the flats in Governor's Harbour. With his help, you're sure to hook a bonefish. He is also a knowledgeable reef-fishing and deep-sea-fishing guide. ⊠ *Governor's Harbour, Eleuthera Island* ☎ *242/332–2963.*

### HORSEBACK RIDING

**Oceanview Farm.** The island's only horseback riding facility offers two trail rides daily, at 9:30 am and 11 am, through mangroves and wild orchids, around a lake, and onto a pink-sand beach. The fee is $100 per person, with group rates available. Prior experience is not necessary, but riders must be 12 years of age or older. ⊠ *Banks Rd., Governor's Harbour, Eleuthera Island* ☎ *242/332–3671* ⊕ *www.oceanview242. com* ⊙ *Mon.–Sat. 9–4* ⊙ *Closed Sun.*

# ROCK SOUND AND SOUTH ELEUTHERA

One of Eleuthera's largest settlements, the village of **Rock Sound** has a small airport serving the island's southern part. Front Street, the main thoroughfare, runs along the seashore, where fishing boats are tied up. If you walk down the street, you'll eventually come to the pretty, whitewashed St. Luke's Anglican Church, a contrast to the deep blue and green houses nearby, with their colorful gardens full of poinsettia, hibiscus, and marigolds. If you pass the church on a Sunday, you'll surely hear fervent hymn singing through the open windows. Rock Sound has the island's largest supermarket shopping center, where locals stock up on groceries and supplies.

The tiny settlement of **Bannerman Town** (population 40) is 25 miles from Rock Sound at the island's southern tip, which is punctuated by an old cliff-top lighthouse. Rent an SUV if you plan to drive out to it; the rutted sand road is often barely passable. The pink-sand beach here is gorgeous, and on a clear day you can see the Bahamas' highest point, Mt. Alvernia (elevation 206 feet), on distant Cat Island. The town lies about 30 miles from the residential Cotton Bay Club, past the quiet little fishing villages of Wemyss Bight (named after Lord Gordon Wemyss, a 17th-century Scottish slave owner) and John Millars (population 15), barely touched over the years.

### GETTING HERE AND AROUND

Fly into Rock Sound Airport and rent a car. The airport is just north of town, and The Island School is a 22-mile drive south. If you fly into Governor's Harbour, plan to rent a car at the airport—Rock Sound is about 34 miles south. Taxis are available at both airports, but can be expensive.

---

> **LEARNING IN PARADISE**
>
> The Island School is a pioneering 14-week program for high-school students that's a model of sustainability—students and teachers work together to run a campus where rainwater is captured for use, solar and wind energy are harnessed, food comes from its own small farm, wastewater is filtered and reused to irrigate landscaping, and biofuel is made from cruise ships' restaurant grease to power vehicles and generators. This "mind, body, and spirit experience" aims to inspire students to be responsible, caring global citizens. Call the school and see if someone's available to give a tour. ☎ 242/334–8551.

## EXPLORING

**Ocean Hole.** A small inland saltwater lake a mile southeast of Rock Sound is connected by tunnels to the sea. Steps have been cut into the coral on the shore so visitors can climb down to the lake's edge. Bring a piece of bread or some fries and watch the fish emerge for their hors d'oeuvres, swimming their way in from the sea. A local diver estimates the hole is about 75 feet. He reports that there are a couple of cars at the bottom, too. Local children learn to swim here. ⊠ *Queen's Hwy.* ✛ *A Bahamas Heritage sign, across the street from a church, marks the path to the Ocean Hole.*

**St. Luke's Anglican Church.** This idyllic seaside church on Front Street, which runs along the shore, has a pretty belfry and a garden of poinsettia, hibiscus, and marigolds. ⊠ *Queen's Hwy., Rock Sound, Eleuthera Island.*

## BEACHES

**Lighthouse Beach.** You'll need an SUV to cross the rocky terrain to get to this beach, but the drive is well worth the breathtaking views. Lighthouse beach has it all: dramatic cliffs, a pink sand beach, plenty of shade beneath the trees—and you'll likely have it entirely to yourself. Reefs just off the beach make it a great place to spend the day snorkeling. Be aware that there can be a strong current. **Amenities:** none. **Best for:** snorkeling; walking; solitude. ⊠ *Southern tip of Eleuthera, Bannerman Town, Eleuthera Island.*

## WHERE TO EAT

**$$** ✕ **Pascal's.** Located on a small beach with a breathtaking sunset view,
CARIBBEAN Pascal's serves both traditional Bahamian fare and French-Caribbean
fusion cuisine. The conch fritters are some of the best in the area, and
the quesadillas are popular for lunch. Dinner options vary, but often
include island-inspired pizzas, fresh fish, and seafood curry. Be sure to
try the signature Parrot Punch cocktail. The restaurant is large and can
accommodate big groups for weddings or other functions. $ *Average
main: $25 ⊠ Queen's Hwy., Rock Sound, Eleuthera Island* ☎ *242/334–
2778* ▭ *No credit cards* ✆ *Closed Sun.*

**$** ✕ **Sammy's Place.** This spotless stop is owned by Sammy Culmer and
BAHAMIAN managed by his friendly daughter Margarita. It serves conch fritters,
fried chicken, lobster and fish, and peas 'n' rice. When it's available
in season, don't miss the guava duff dessert, sweet bread with swirls
of creamy guava. It's open for breakfast, too. $ *Average main: $19
⊠ Albury La., Rock Sound, Eleuthera Island* ☎ *242/334–2121* ▭ *No
credit cards.*

## WHERE TO STAY

**$** 🏠 **Northside Cottages.** These quaint cottages are nestled into a hillside
RENTAL with an extraordinary view of the Atlantic. **Pros:** beachfront; restaurant
on-property; friendly staff. **Cons:** steep walk down to the beach; the
area is remote. $ *Rooms from: $120 ⊠ Northshore Dr., Rock Sound,
Eleuthera Island* ✥ *Turn off Queen's Hwy. in Rock Sound onto Fish St.
Turn left at T intersection onto Northshore Dr., then right at the end
of the pavement* ☎ *242/334–2573* ⊕ *www.northsideinneleuthera.com*
↪ *3 cottages* ▭ *No credit cards* ⦿ *No meals.*

# HARBOUR ISLAND

Harbour Island has often been called the Nantucket of the Caribbean
and the prettiest of the Out Islands because of its powdery pink-sand
beaches (3 miles' worth!) and its pastel-color clapboard houses with
dormer windows, set among white picket fences, narrow lanes, cute
shops, and tropical flowers.

The frequent parade of the fashionable and famous, and the chic small
inns that accommodate them, have earned the island another name:
the St. Bart's of the Bahamas. But residents have long called it Briland,
their faster way of pronouncing "Harbour Island." These inhabitants
include families who go back generations to the island's early settle-
ment, as well as a growing number of celebrities, supermodels, and
tycoons who feel that Briland is the perfect haven to bask in small-
town charm against a stunning oceanscape. Some of the Bahamas'
most handsome small hotels, each strikingly distinct, are tucked within
the island's 2 square miles. At several, perched on a bluff above the
shore, you can fall asleep with the windows open and listen to the
waves lapping the beach. Take a walking tour of the narrow streets
of **Dunmore Town,** named after the 18th-century royal governor of the
Bahamas, Lord Dunmore, who built a summer home here and laid

A stroll through Dunmore Town on Harbour Island is a must for any visitor.

out the town, which served as the first capital of the Bahamas. It's the only town on Harbour Island, and you can take in all its attractions during a 20-minute stroll.

**GETTING HERE AND AROUND**

Access Harbour Island via a 10-minute ferry ride from the North Eleuthera dock. Fares are $5 per person in a boat of two or more, plus an extra dollar to be dropped off at the private Romora Bay Club docks and for nighttime rides.

The best way to get around the island is to rent a golf cart or bike, or hire a taxi, since climbing the island's hills can be strenuous in the midday heat. If you plan to stay in Dunmore Town, you'll be able to walk everywhere.

## EXPLORING

**Lone Tree.** If you stroll to the end of Bay Street and follow the curve to the western edge of the island, you'll find the Lone Tree, one of the most photographed icons of Harbour Island. This enormous piece of driftwood is said to have washed up on shore after a bad storm and anchored itself on the shallow sandbar in a picturesque upright position, providing the perfect photo op for countless tourists. ⊠ *Bay St, Harbour Island.*

**Loyalist Cottage.** The most photographed house on the island is the pretty turquoise-and-white Loyalist Cottage, one of the original settlers' homes (circa 1797) on Bay Street. You can't go inside; it's privately owned. Many other old houses are in the area, with gingerbread trim and picket fences. Amusing names include Beside the Point, Up Yonder, and The Royal Termite. ⊠ *Bay St., Harbour Island.*

**St. John's Anglican Church.** The first church built by the Eleutheran Adventurers and the Bahamas' oldest Anglican church was constructed in 1768. It still welcomes churchgoers after almost 250 years. Services are Sunday at 8 am and 7 pm. ⊠ *Dunmore St., Harbour Island.*

**Straw Crafts.** A row of straw-work stands are on Bay Street next to the water, including Pat's, Eva's, and Sarah's, where you'll find straw bags, hats, and T-shirts. Food stands sell conch salad, Kalik beer, coconut water, and fruit juices. ⊠ *Bay St., Harbour Island.*

> ### A SWINGING TIME
>
> In Eleuthera the game that brings the crowds is fast-pitch softball. The Eleuthera Twin City Destroyers were the men's champions of the 2006 Bahamas Softball Federation tournament. On most any weekend afternoon from March to November you can find the team playing at Rock Sound or Palmetto baseball parks on the island, known as the Softball Capital of the Bahamas. Eleuthera pitchers and brothers Edney and Edmond Bethel are both players for the Bahamas National Team, which has been consistently in the top 10 in the world.

## BEACHES

**Pink Sands Beach.** This is the fairest pink beach of them all: 3 miles of pale pink sand behind some of the most expensive and posh inns in the Bahamas. Its sand is of such a fine consistency that it's almost as soft as talcum powder, and the gentle slope of the shore makes small waves break hundreds of yards offshore; you have to walk out quite a distance to get past your waist. This is the place to see the rich and famous in designer resort wear or ride a horse bareback across the sand and into the sea. **Amenities:** food and drink; toilets. **Best for:** sunrise; swimming; walking; partiers. ⊠ *Harbour Island.*

## WHERE TO EAT

*Note that many Harbour Island hotels and restaurants are closed from September through mid- to late October.*

**$$$**  ✕ **Acquapazza.** Briland's only Italian restaurant offers a change of pace
ITALIAN  from the island's standard fare, and a change of scenery, too. It's located on the island's south end at the Harbour Island Marina, with a dockside terrace where you can take in the sunset while sipping one of its exclusively imported Italian wines. Chef and owner Manfredi Mancini's hearty portions of fried calamari and pasta *e fagioli* (with beans) don't disappoint, and the seafood entrées are always a good choice. ⓢ *Average main: $30* ⊠ *Harbour Island Marina, south end of island off Queens Hwy., Dunmore Town, Harbour Island* ☎ *242/333–3240* ⊕ *www.acquapazzabahamas.com* ⌂ *Reservations essential.*

**$**  ✕ **Arthur's Bakery and Cafe.** Bread and pastries are baked every morning
CAFÉ  by *White Shadow* screenwriter and local real-estate agent to the stars Robert Arthur and his Trinidadian wife Anna. The friendly café has a

quiet garden nook where you can savor your morning brew with an apple turnover, banana pancakes, or any of the daily breakfast offerings. The most popular item to take back is the jalapeño-and-cheese bread. Computers with Internet access are available for a fee. $ *Average main: $14 ⊠ Crown St. and Dunmore St., Dunmore Town, Harbour Island* ☎ *242/333–2285* ═ *No credit cards* ⊘ *Closed Sun.*

**$$** ✕ **The Beach Bar at Coral Sands.** For lunch with a view, try Coral Sands'
ECLECTIC oceanfront bar and restaurant, just steps from the pink-sand beach. Executive Chef Ken Gomes creates delicious lunch options that go perfectly with a tropical cocktail or a glass of white wine. In addition to seafood options like conch fritters, lobster rolls, and grouper sandwiches, the restaurant also serves fresh salads and gourmet pizzas. $ *Average main: $20 ⊠ Chapel St., Dunmore Town, Harbour Island* ☎ *242/333– 2350* ⊕ *www.coralsands.com* ⊘ *No dinner. Closed Sept. to mid-Oct.*

**$$** ✕ **The Blue Bar at Pink Sands.** Head to the beach for lunch outside at this
ECLECTIC lively oceanfront restaurant. Situated just above the pink-sand beach,
Fodor's Choice you'll have an unbeatable view for sipping one of the signature cocktails
★ and enjoying fish tacos, a grouper ciabatta, or any of the other island-inspired menu options. If you're in the mood for a cheeseburger, try the Blue Water Burger on a brioche roll. During the summer, the Blue Bar is also open for dinner. $ *Average main: $20 ⊠ Pink Sands Resort, Chapel St., Dunmore Town, Harbour Island* ☎ *242/333–2030* ⊕ *www. pinksandsresort.com* ⊘ *Closed Sept.*

**$$$** ✕ **The Dunmore.** Start with a signature cocktail at the handsome mahog-
CARIBBEAN any bar before enjoying dinner under the stars on the ocean-view porch at this recently renovated restaurant at The Dunmore. Chef Cindy Hutson creates island-inspired dishes that change seasonally. On Tuesday nights, the restaurant often offers a barbecue buffet with a live local band. $ *Average main: $36 ⊠ The Dunmore, Gaol La., Dunmore Town, Harbour Island* ☎ *242/333–2200* ⊕ *www.dunmorebeach.com* ⌕ *Reservations essential* ⊘ *Closed mid-Aug.–mid-Nov.*

**$** ✕ **Dunmore Deli.** Patrick Tully's exceptional deli satisfies the epicurean
DELI demands of Briland's more finicky residents and visitors, while its shaded wooden porch, filled with hanging plants and bougainvillea, makes this the perfect spot for a lazy breakfast or lunch. Treat yourself to the Briland Bread Toast, the amazingly fluffy take on French toast, or pick up one of the inventive deli sandwiches for a picnic on the beach. While here, you can also stock up on a variety of international coffees, imported cheeses, produce, and other gourmet items you won't find anywhere else on the island. $ *Average main: $12 ⊠ King St., Dunmore Town, Harbour Island* ☎ *242/333–2644* ⊘ *Closed Sun.*

**$$$$** ✕ **The Garden Terrace at Pink Sands.** Enjoy an elegant candlelit dinner in
CARIBBEAN Pink Sands' exquisitely decorated indoor dining room, or alfresco in their lush garden. Executive Chef Ed Boncich, who previously worked with Bobby Flay in New York City, emphasizes fresh seafood and his Caribbean bistro cuisine. The menu changes based on the availability of fresh ingredients, but often features gazpacho or calamari to start, followed by filet mignon or Bahamian grouper with coconut rice. $ *Average main: $40 ⊠ Pink Sands Resort, Chapel St., Dunmore Town, Harbour Island* ☎ *242/333–2030* ⊕ *www.pinksandsresort.com* ⌕ *Reservations essential* ⊘ *No lunch. Closed Sept.–Oct.*

6

**Restaurants** ▼

Acquapazza .... **10**

Arthur's Bakery & Cafe ............ **2**

The Beach Bar at Coral Sands .... **15**

The Blue Bar at Pink Sands ..... **14**

Dunmore Deli ....**4**

The Dunmore ..**12**

The Garden Terrace at Pink Sands ..**13**

The Landing .....**6**

Ma Ruby's ........**9**

Queen Conch ....**3**

The Rock House ............**7**

Runaway Hill Inn .........**11**

Sip Sip ...........**1**

Sunsets Bar & Grille ......**8**

Tropic Hut ........**5**

**Hotels** ▼

Baretta's Seashell Inn .....**1**

Coral Sands Hotel .............**3**

The Dunmore ....**4**

The Landing .....**5**

Pink Sands .......**2**

Rock House ......**6**

Romora Bay Club & Resort ..**10**

Runaway Hill Inn ...............**7**

Tingum Village Hotel .............**8**

Valentine's Resort & Marina ...........**9**

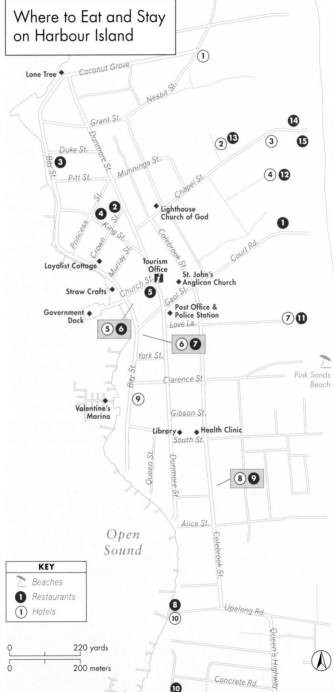

# Where to Eat and Stay on Harbour Island

ATLANTIC OCEAN

Lone Tree ◆   Coconut Grove

Nesbit St.

Grant St.

Duke St.   Dunmore St.   Munnings St.

Bay St.   Pitt St.

Chapel St.

Princess St.   King St.   Crown   Murray St.

◆ Lighthouse Church of God

Colebrook St.   Court Rd.

Loyalist Cottage ◆

Tourism Office

St. John's Anglican Church ◆

Straw Crafts ◆   Church St.

Government Dock ◆

Post Office & Police Station ◆

Love La.

York St.

Bay St.   Clarence St.

Pink Sands Beach

Valentine's Marina

Gibson St.

Library ◆   ◆ Health Clinic

South St.

Queen St.   Dunmore St.

Alice St.   Colebrook St.

*Open Sound*

## KEY

🌴 *Beaches*

① *Restaurants*

① *Hotels*

Upalong Rd.

Queen's Highway

0 ——— 220 yards

0 ——— 200 meters

Concrete Rd.

$$$$ ECLECTIC Fodor's Choice ★ 🍴 **The Landing.** You never know which actor or rock star you'll rub elbows with—Richard Gere and Dave Matthews like to dine here—at the Hemingway-esque bar, but none of it matters once you've moved on to the dining room and are under the spell of Swedish chef Vincent Vitlock, whose dishes soar with a Southeast Asian flair. Standouts include the goat-cheese ravioli with shrimp, walnut-crusted fresh fish, and banana upside-down cake. One of the Caribbean's top dining destinations, the Landing also offers an impressive wine selection. If the weather is nice, request a romantic table on the porch. [$] *Average main: $45* ✉ *The Landing, Bay St., Dunmore Town, Harbour Island* ☎ *242/333–2707* 🌐 *www.harbourislandlanding.com* ✍ *Reservations essential* ⏲ *No lunch. Closed Wed.*

## HEAVENLY MUSIC

The best live music on Harbour Island is at the Lighthouse Church of God on Chapel Street in Dunmore Town on Sunday mornings. Mick Jagger and Lenny Kravitz have dropped by to hear Pastor Samuel Higgs, drummer and bass player, and guitarist Rocky Sanders, both of whom played Europe's clubs for years before settling down on the island.

$ BAHAMIAN 🍴 **Ma Ruby's.** Although you can sample local Bahamian fare at this famous eatery, the star of the menu is the cheeseburger, purportedly the inspiration for Jimmy Buffett's "Cheeseburger in Paradise" song. Maybe it's the rustic charm of the breezy patio, or the secret seasonings on the melt-in-your-mouth patty, but this burger served between thick slices of homemade Bahamian bread is definitely otherworldly. Dinner specialties include cracked conch and fish stew. Be sure to save room for Ma's coconut tart or key lime pie. [$] *Average main: $10* ✉ *Tingum Village Hotel, Colebrooke St., Dunmore Town, Harbour Island* ☎ *242/333–2161* 💳 *No credit cards.*

$ BAHAMIAN 🍴 **Queen Conch.** Four blocks from the ferry dock on Bay Street, with a deck overlooking the water, this colorful snack stand—presided over by Lavaughn Percentie—is renowned for its freshly caught conch salad ($10), which is diced in front of you, mixed with fresh vegetables, and ready to eat right at the counter. On weekends, get there early to put in your order, as visitors from the world over place large orders to-go. [$] *Average main: $10* ✉ *Bay St., Dunmore Town, Harbour Island* ☎ *242/333–3811* 💳 *No credit cards* ⏲ *Closed Sun.*

$$$$ MODERN AMERICAN Fodor's Choice ★ 🍴 **The Rock House.** Splendid harbor views and a transporting Mediterranean-loggia vibe create the perfect backdrop for Chef Jennifer Learmonth's California Continental menu, infused with tropical accents. Imaginative dishes include curried Colorado lamb chops and Thai-style stone crab and lobster spring rolls. The Rock House also takes its drinks seriously, with an extensive list showcasing California boutique wines. Dining here is refined and serene, thanks to the flawless service, so linger over coffee and one of the decadent desserts, like red velvet cake or homemade "hokey pokey" turtle ice cream. [$] *Average main: $40* ✉ *The Rock House Hotel, Bay St., Dunmore Town, Harbour Island* ☎ *242/333–2053* 🌐 *www.rockhousebahamas.com* ✍ *Reservations essential* ⏲ *Closed Aug.–mid-Nov.*

Harbour Island is a tranquil place to spend some time.

**$$$$**
CARIBBEAN

✕ **Runaway Hill Inn.** Enjoy a moonlit dinner on Runaway Hill's beach-front verandah. The atmosphere feels like a private club with a handsome 1920s interior. Chef Luc Castiloux specializes in international fusion cuisine, combining Bahamian ingredients with global flavors. The menu always features a fresh catch of the day, and often includes Bahamian lobster and stone crabs. $ *Average main: $40* ⊠ *Cole-brooke St., Dunmore Town, Harbour Island* ☎ *242/333–2150* ⊕ *www. runawayhill.com* ⚓ *Reservations essential* � *Closed Mon.*

**$$**
BAHAMIAN
**Fodor's**Choice
★

✕ **Sip Sip.** Locals and travelers alike seek out this popular snow-cone-green house overlooking the beach for a little "sip sip" (Bahamian for gossip) and delicious inspired food. Chef and owner Julie Lightbourn uses whatever is fresh, local, and in season to create "Bahamian with a twist" dishes, so check what daily specials are on the blackboard. Conch chili is one of her signatures; consider yourself lucky if the lobster quesadillas are available, and don't miss the decadent carrot cake with ginger-caramel. Sip Sip is open for lunch only, from 11:30 to 4. $ *Average main: $25* ⊠ *Court Rd., Dunmore Town, Harbour Island* ☎ *242/333–3316* ☾ *No dinner. Closed Tues. and mid-Aug.–Nov.*

**$$**
BAHAMIAN
FAMILY

✕ **Sunsets Bar & Grille.** This waterfront pavilion at the Romora Bay Club perfectly frames sunsets over Harbour Island, so be sure to get here in time to snag a good seat for the show. Popular with locals, the restaurant serves midpriced Bahamian specialties such as conch fritters for a casual lunch or dinner. The bartender is always happy to create drinks just to suit your vibe, and be sure to greet Goldie the parrot, who has held court over the bar for more than 50 years. $ *Average main: $20*

✉ *Romora Bay Club, Dunmore St., Dunmore Town, Harbour Island* ☎ *242/333–2325* 🌐 *www.romorabay.com* ⏲ *Closed Aug.–Nov.*

$ PIZZA 🍴 **Tropic Hut.** If you're in the mood to dine at home, this centrally located restaurant is the perfect place for pizza take-out. In addition to a multitude of toppings, the menu also includes wings, wraps, burgers, and subs. It may lack the elegant ambience of most Harbour Island restaurants, but for a relatively inexpensive meal, this pizza joint is a great option. [$] *Average main: $10* ✉ *Dunmore St., Dunmore Town, Harbour Island* ☎ *242/333–3700* ⏲ *Closed Sun.*

## WHERE TO STAY

$ B&B/INN 🏨 **Baretta's Seashell Inn.** If all you need is a clean, affordable room that's close to the beach, Baretta's is the place for you. **Pros:** well-maintained rooms; close to the beach; locally owned business. **Cons:** only partial ocean views from the second floor over the tops of trees; off-the-beaten-path; limited services. [$] *Rooms from: $160* ✉ *Nesbitt St., Dunmore Town, Harbour Island* ☎ *242/333–2361* 🌐 *www.barettasseashellinn.com* 🛏 *12 rooms* 🍽 *No meals.*

$$$ RESORT FAMILY 🏨 **Coral Sands Hotel.** An elegant yet energetic flair accents this 9-acre oceanfront resort, right on the pink-sand beach. **Pros:** direct ocean access; trendy beach resort vibe; billiard room. **Cons:** rooms vary in quality and style; some rooms feel cramped; only one private cottage. [$] *Rooms from: $335* ✉ *Chapel St., Harbour Island* ☎ *242/333–2350, 800/468–2799* 🌐 *www.coralsands.com* 🛏 *39 rooms* ⏲ *Closed Sept.–mid-Oct.* 🍽 *Breakfast.*

$$$$ RESORT 🏨 **The Dunmore.** This recently renovated hotel with private cottages evokes a 1940s club in the tropics—with its mahogany bar, casual yet elegant dining room, and faded paperbacks in the clubhouse library, it's a favorite with the New England yachting set. **Pros:** on the beach with ocean-side bar service; spacious bathrooms; private terraces and lawn chairs for every cottage. **Cons:** cottages too close for real privacy; small clubhouse. [$] *Rooms from: $450* ✉ *Gaol La., Dunmore Town, Harbour Island* ☎ *242/333–2200, 877/891–3100* 🌐 *www.dunmorebeach.com* 🛏 *15 cottages* ⏲ *Closed mid-Aug.–mid-Nov.* 🍽 *No meals.*

$$ B&B/INN 🏨 **The Landing.** Spare white walls and crisp white linens evoke a timeless, understated chic at the Landing, which is acclaimed as much for its singular style as for its superb cuisine. **Pros:** chic and comfortable rooms; glorious outdoor shower; acclaimed dining. **Cons:** 10 am check-out time; limited hotel services; not on the beach. [$] *Rooms from: $225* ✉ *Bay St., Dunmore Town, Harbour Island* ☎ *242/333–2707* 🌐 *www.harbourislandlanding.com* 🛏 *12 rooms* ⏲ *Closed Oct.* 🍽 *No meals.*

$$$$ RESORT Fodor's Choice ★ 🏨 **Pink Sands.** Harbour Island's famed beachfront resort has long been praised by celebrities—Martha Stewart, Nicole Kidman, and Brooke Shields—and honeymooners alike for its 25 private cottages scattered over 26 secluded acres. **Pros:** truly private cottages; state-of-the-art media room; discreet and well-trained staff. **Cons:** some cottages quite a walk from the main house and beach (better drive your golf cart on a hot day); resort is a hike from the center of town [$] *Rooms from: $600* ✉ *Chapel St., Dunmore Town, Harbour Island* ☎ *242/333–2030* 🌐 *www.pinksandsresort.com* 🛏 *25 cottages* ⏲ *Closed Sept.* 🍽 *Breakfast.*

6

Fresh seafood can be found at the Landing in Dunmore Town.

$$$ HOTEL Fodor's Choice ★ 🏨 **Rock House.** With a drawing room straight out of a villa on the Amalfi Coast, the Rock House is Harbour Island's most luxurious boutique hotel. **Pros:** heavenly beds; stellar service; best gym on the island. **Cons:** not on the beach; lack of views from some rooms. [$] *Rooms from: $300* ✉ *Bay St., Dunmore Town, Harbour Island* ☎ *242/333–2053* 🌐 *www.rockhousebahamas.com* 🛏 *7 rooms, 3 suites* 🕓 *Closed Aug.–mid-Nov.* 🍴 *Breakfast.*

$$$ RESORT FAMILY 🏨 **Romora Bay Club & Resort.** Three pink Adirondack chairs on the dock welcome you to this colorful and casual resort situated on the bay side of the island. **Pros:** friendly staff; water views from every room; private bayside beach. **Cons:** sloping steps from dock to cottages are a hassle for luggage; main house has been converted into a resort showroom. [$] *Rooms from: $300* ✉ *South end of Dunmore St., Dunmore Town, Harbour Island* ☎ *242/333–2325* 🌐 *www.romorabay.com* 🛏 *18 rooms* 🕓 *Closed end of Aug.–Nov.* 🍴 *No meals.*

$$$$ B&B/INN 🏨 **Runaway Hill Inn.** Set on gorgeous rolling grounds, this quiet seaside inn feels far removed from the rest of the island, which is precisely the point. **Pros:** oceanfront location with direct beach access; well-stocked library; intimate character. **Cons:** limited service; not as chic a vibe as nearby resorts. [$] *Rooms from: $425* ✉ *Colebrooke St., Dunmore Town, Harbour Island* ☎ *242/333–2150, 843/278–1724* 🌐 *www.runawayhill.com* 🛏 *10 rooms, 1 cottage, 1 house* 🕓 *Closed mid-Aug.–mid-Nov.* 🍴 *No meals.*

$ B&B/INN FAMILY 🏨 **Tingum Village Hotel.** Each of the rustic cottages on this property, owned by the Percentie family, is named after a different island of the Bahamas. **Pros:** family-friendly; local flavor; Ma Ruby's restaurant. **Cons:** no-frills interior and furnishings; not on beach or harbor;

rustic grounds. $ *Rooms from: $95* ✉ *Colebrooke St., Harbour Island* 🏠 *242/333–2161* 🛏 *12 rooms, 7 suites, 2 cottages* ⊟ *No credit cards* ⊘ *No meals.*

$$ 🏨 **Valentine's Resort and Marina.** With the largest marina on Harbour
RESORT Island, equipped with 50 slips capable of accommodating yachts up to
FAMILY 160 feet, this resort is ideal if you are a self-sufficient traveler or family
that doesn't require many amenities but enjoys spacious condo-style
rooms and water-focused activities. **Pros:** modern rooms; state-of-the-
art marina; large swimming pool. **Cons:** not oceanfront; impersonal
condo-style quality; lack of hotel service. $ *Rooms from: $295* ✉ *Bay
St., Dunmore Town, Harbour Island* 🏠 *242/333–2142* ⊕ *www.
valentinesresort.com* 🛏 *41 rooms* ⊘ *No meals.*

## NIGHTLIFE

**Beyond the Reef.** The party starts at this waterfront bar at sunset and
extends well into the evening. Drink specials are available all day and
you can find great Bahamian food at any one of its neighboring vendors.
✉ *Bay St., Dunmore Town, Harbour Island* 🏠 *242/333–3478.*

**Daddy D's.** This is the place to be on the weekends and holidays in Har-
bour Island. The dance floor takes off around midnight and is a popular
spot for young locals and tourists alike. DJ and owner Devon "Daddy
D" Sawyer spins pop music, hip-hop, and reggae tunes late into the
night. ✉ *Dunmore St., Dunmore Town, Harbour Island.*

**Gusty's.** Enjoy a brew on the wraparound patio of Gusty's, on Harbour
Island's northern point. This lively hot spot has sand floors, a few tables,
and patrons shooting pool. On weekends, holidays, and in high season,
it's an extremely crowded and happening dance spot with a DJ, espe-
cially after 10 pm. ✉ *Coconut Grove Ave., Dunmore Town, Harbour
Island* 🏠 *242/333–2165.*

**Vic-Hum Club.** Vic-Hum Club, owned by "Ma" Ruby Percentie's son
Humphrey, occasionally hosts live Bahamian bands in a room deco-
rated with classic record-album covers; otherwise, you'll find locals
playing Ping-Pong and listening and dancing to loud recorded music,
from calypso to American pop and R & B. Mick Jagger and other rock
stars have dropped by. Look for the largest coconut ever grown in the
Bahamas—33 inches in diameter—on the bar's top shelf. ✉ *Barrack St.,
Dunmore Town, Harbour Island* 🏠 *242/333–2161.*

## SHOPPING

*Most small businesses on Harbour Island close for a lunch break between
1 and 3.*

### ART GALLERIES

**Princess Street Gallery.** Princess Street Gallery displays original art by
local and internationally renowned artists, as well as a diverse selec-
tion of illustrated books, home accessories, and locally made crafts.
✉ *Princess St., Dunmore Town, Harbour Island* 🏠 *242/333–2788*
⊘ *Closed Sun.*

## CLOTHING

**Blue Rooster.** This is the place to go for festive party dresses, sexy swimwear, fun accessories, and exotic gifts. ⊠ *King St., Dunmore Town, Harbour Island* ☎ *242/333–2240* ⊘ *Closed Sun.*

**Briland's Androsia.** This shop has a unique selection of clothing, beachwear, bags, and home items handmade from the colorful batik fabric created on the island of Andros. ⊠ *Coconut Grove Ave., Dunmore Town, Harbour Island* ☎ *242/333–2342* ⊘ *Closed weekends.*

**Miss Mae's.** Miss Mae's sells an exquisite and discerningly curated collection of fashion-forward clothing, accessories, and gifts from international designers and artisans. ⊠ *Dunmore St., Dunmore Town, Harbour Island* ☎ *242/333–2002* ⊘ *Closed Sun.*

**Sugar Mill.** Here you can find a glamorous selection of resort wear, accessories, and gifts from designers around the world. ⊠ *Bay St., Harbour Island* ☎ *242/333–3558* ⊘ *Closed Sun.*

**The Sand Dollar.** This boutique specializes in resortwear made from Trinidadian cloth. You'll also find jewelry, handbags, shoes, and other accessories. ⊠ *King St., Dunmore Town, Harbour Island* ☎ *242/333–3576* ⊘ *Closed Sun.*

## FOOD

**Patricia's Fruits and Vegetables.** This is where locals go for homemade candies, jams, and other Bahamian condiments. Her famous hot sauce and native thyme (sold in recycled Bacardi bottles) make memorable gifts. ⊠ *Duke St., Dunmore Town, Harbour Island* ☎ *242/333–2289.*

## GIFTS AND SOUVENIRS

**Bahamian Shells and Tings.** This shop sells island wear, souvenirs, and crafts, many handmade on Harbour Island. ⊠ *Coconut Grove Ave., Dunmore Town, Harbour Island* ☎ *242/333–2839* ⊘ *Closed Sun.*

**Dilly Dally.** Here you can find Bahamian-made jewelry, maps, T-shirts, CDs, decorations, and other fun island souvenirs. ⊠ *Dunmore St., Dunmore Town, Harbour Island* ☎ *242/333–3109* ⊘ *Closed Sun.*

**Pink Sands Gift Shop.** This shop offers a trendy selection of swimwear, accessories, casual clothing, and trinkets. ⊠ *Pink Sands Resort, Chapel St., Dunmore Town, Harbour Island* ☎ *242/333–2030.*

**The Plait Lady.** You'll find novelty gifts, locally crafted baskets, and other straw goods at this Bay Street store. ⊠ *Bay St., Dunmore Town, Harbour Island* ☎ *242/333–3799, 242/225–3900* ⊘ *Closed Sun.*

**The Shop at Sip Sip.** The Shop at Sip Sip sells its own line of T-shirts and a small but stylish selection of handmade jewelry, custom-designed totes, Bahamian straw work, and gifts found by owner Julie Lightbourn on her far-flung travels. ⊠ *Court Rd., Dunmore Town, Harbour Island* ☎ *242/333–3316* ⊘ *Closed Tues.*

## SPAS AND SPA SERVICES

**The Island Spa.** For romantic couples massages in the privacy of your own room, book Karen at The Island Spa. She makes in-room visits and offers evening beach massages, body scrubs, and aromatherapy. In addition to massages, The Island Spa can also do bridal hair and makeup, manicures, and pedicures—ideal for a destination wedding. ✉ *Harbour Island* ☎ *242/333–3326* ⊕ *www.theharbourislandspa.com* ✆ *Services: aromatherapy, massage, nail treatment, scrubs, wedding hair and makeup.*

## SPORTS AND THE OUTDOORS

### BIKING

**Michael's Cycles.** Bicycles are a popular way to explore Harbour Island; rent one—or golf carts, motorboats, Jet Skis, and kayaks—at Michael's Cycles. ✉ *Colebrooke St., Dunmore Town, Harbour Island* ☎ *242/333–2384.*

### BOATING AND FISHING

There's great bonefishing right off Dunmore Town at **Girl's Bank**. Charters cost about $350 for a half day. The Harbour Island Tourist Office can help organize bone- and bottom-fishing excursions, as can all of the major hotels.

**Stuart Cleare.** Bonefish Stuart is one of Harbour Island's best bonefishing guides. You'll want to call well in advance to arrange a trip with him. ✉ *Harbour Island* ☎ *242/333–2072, 242/464–0148.*

### SCUBA DIVING AND SNORKELING

**Ocean Fox Diving and Deep-sea Fishing Center.** Ocean Fox Diving and Deep-sea Fishing Center provides dive trips. ✉ *Harbour Island Club and Marina, Dunmore Town, Harbour Island* ☎ *242/333–2323.*

**Valentine's Dive Center.** This dive center rents and sells equipment and provides all levels of instruction, certification, and dive trips. ✉ *Valentine's Resort and Marina, Bay St., Dunmore Town, Harbour Island* ☎ *888/462–0462* ⊕ *www.valentinesdive.com.*

# SPANISH WELLS

Off Eleuthera's northern tip lies St. George's Cay, the site of **Spanish Wells**. The Spaniards used this as a safe harbor during the 17th century while they transferred their riches from the New World to the Old. Residents—the few surnames go back generations—live on the island's eastern end in clapboard houses that look as if they've been transported from a New England fishing village. Descendants of the Eleutheran Adventurers continue to sail these waters and bring back to shore fish and lobster (most of the Bahamas' langoustes are caught here), which are prepared and boxed for export in a factory at the dock. So lucrative is the trade in crawfish, the local term for Bahamian lobsters, that the 1,500 inhabitants may be the most prosperous Out Islanders.

### GETTING HERE AND AROUND

You can reach Spanish Wells by taking a five-minute ferry ride ($7) from the Gene's Bay dock in North Eleuthera. You can easily explore the area on foot, or rent a golf cart.

## WHERE TO EAT

$$ DINER 🍴 **The Generation Gap.** This casual diner is a hub of activity during lunch hours. In addition to American soda shop favorites like cheeseburgers, subs, and hot dogs, the menu also includes Bahamian fare such as fried grouper sandwiches and conch dishes. The Gap, as it's known locally, serves a great milk shake, and their crushed ice makes it the best spot to stop for a cold drink on the island. [$] *Average main: $24* ✉ *13th and Samuel Guy Sts., Spanish Wells, Eleuthera Island* ☎ *242/333–4230* 🕒 *Closed Sun.*

$ BAKERY 🍴 **Kathy's Bakery.** Located on the corner of Samuel Guy Street and 17th Street, Kathy's Bakery makes breads, pies, and cakes. You can custom order ahead of time, or choose from the daily selection. The bakery is also home to the island's best johnnycakes, a Bahamian specialty. [$] *Average main: $5* ✉ *17th and Samuel Guy Sts., Spanish Wells, Eleuthera Island* ☎ *242/333–4405* 🕒 *Closed Sun.*

## WHERE TO STAY

$ RENTAL FAMILY 🏨 **Abner's Rentals.** These two-bedroom oceanside rentals include the discounted use of a golf cart so you can explore the island and pick up groceries at one of the local shops. **Pros:** all four houses have washers and dryers. **Cons:** Spanish Wells is very quiet and remote. [$] *Rooms from: $170* ✉ *Between 12th and 13th Sts., Spanish Wells, Eleuthera Island* ☎ *242/333–4890, 954/237–6266* 🌐 *www.abnersvacationrentals.com* 🛏 *4 houses* 🍽 *No meals.*

# THE EXUMAS

7

# WELCOME TO THE EXUMAS

## TOP REASONS TO GO

★ **Party like a local:** Hot spots include the Fish Fry on weekends for conch salad and fresh fish and Chat 'N' Chill on Stocking Island for Sunday pig roasts.

★ **Island-hop:** You'll want to spend a couple of days boating through the 365 cays (one for every day of the year, as the locals say), most uninhabited, some owned by celebrities. Get ready for iguanas, swimming pigs, and giant starfish.

★ **Enjoy empty beaches:** Beautiful stretches of bleach-white sand are yours to explore, and more often than not you'll be the only person on them, even at noon on a Saturday.

★ **Explore the Land and Sea Park:** Underwater attractions in the 176-square-mile Exuma Land and Sea Park, one of the best snorkel sights in the Bahamas, include queen conchs, starfish, and thriving coral reefs. Keep a lookout for the endangered hawksbill and threatened green and loggerhead turtles.

**1 Great Exuma.** Capital George Town sees most of the action on this mainland, including the 12-day George Town Cruising Regatta and the Bahamian Music and Heritage Festival. But dazzling white beaches and fish fries offering cold Kaliks and conch salad crop up along the coasts of the entire island. Visitors come to fish—especially to stalk the clever bonefish—dive and snorkel, and stay in atmospheric inns and luxurious resorts, where you can find complete solitude or hopping beach parties.

**2 Little Exuma.** The Tropic of Cancer runs through the chain's second-largest island, which is duly noted on the steps leading to Tropic of Cancer Beach, one of the most spectacular on the island. *Pirates of the Caribbean* 2 and 3 were filmed on Sandy Cay, just offshore; stop by Santana's Grill on the beach in historic Williams Town and ask

to see their famous-people photo book while you feast on fresh-cracked lobster.

**3 The Exuma Cays.** If you're looking for a true escape—a vacation where you're more likely to see giant starfish, wild iguanas, swimming pigs, dolphins, and sharks than other people—boat over to the cays. This is also where celebrities come to buy their own spectacular islands—Johnny Depp, Faith Hill and Tim McGraw, David Copperfield, and Nicholas Cage all have 'em. The renowned Exuma Cays Land and Sea Park, toward the chain's north end, has some of the most gorgeous crystal clear water and white sand on earth.

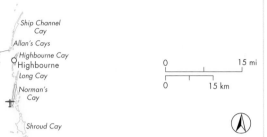

Sail Rocks

Ship Channel Cay

Allan's Cays

Highbourne Cay
Highbourne

Long Cay

Norman's Cay

Shroud Cay

Hawksbill Cay

Cistern Cay

**Exuma Cays Land and Sea Park** ③

Waderick Wells Cay

Halls Pond Cay
O'Brian's Cay

Bells Cay
Fowl Cay    Compass Cay
**Pipe Creek** ◆    Joe Cay
Sampson Cay    Thomas Cay
Big Major's Cay    Staniel Cay
Harvey's Cays

*Exuma Sound*

O Black Point

Great Guana Cay

*GRAND BAHAMA BANK*

*EXUMA CAYS*

Big Farmer's Cay

Musha Cay    Cave Cay
Rudder Cut Cay

Darby Island    Young Island

Block Cay    Normans Pond Cay
Lee Stocking Island

Brigantine Cays    Barraterre
◆ **Starfish Reserve**
O Rolleville
O Steventon
*Great Exuma Island* ①    Queen's Hwy.
Exuma Int'l Airport    O Mt. Thompson
Moss Town O    **Elizabeth Harbour**
Fish Fry    *Stocking Island*
George Town O    Elizabeth Harbour
Channel Cays    **Rolle Town Tombs**
Rolle Town    O Forbes Hill
**St. Christopher's**    ②
**The Hermitage**    *Little Exuma Island*    Williams Town

0 ___ 15 mi
0 ___ 15 km

## GETTING ORIENTED

Thirty-five miles southeast of Nassau, Allan's Cay sits at the top of the Exumas' chain of 365 islands (most uninhabited) that skip like stones for 120 miles south across the Tropic of Cancer. Flanked by the Great Bahama Bank and Exuma Sound, the islands are at the center of the Bahamas. George Town, the Exumas' capital and hub of activity, so to speak, is on Great Exuma, the mainland and largest island, near the bottom of the Exumas' chain. Little Exuma is to the south and connected to the mainland by a bridge. Together, these two islands span 50 miles.

7

# EXUMA CAYS LAND AND SEA PARK

Created by the Bahamas National Trust in 1958, the 176-square-mile Exuma Cays Land and Sea Park was the first of its kind in the world—an enormous open aquarium with pristine reefs, an abundance of marine life, and sandy cays.

The park appeals to divers, who appreciate the vast underworld of limestone, reefs, drop-offs, blue holes, caves, and a multitude of exotic marine life including one of the Bahamas' most impressive stands of rare pillar coral. Since the park's waters have essentially never been fished, you can see what the ocean looked like before humanity. For landlubbers there are hiking trails and birding sites; stop in the main office for maps. More than 200 bird species have been spotted here. At Shroud Cay, jump into the strong current that creates a natural whirlpool whipping you around a rocky outcropping to a powdery beach. On top of the hill overlooking the beach is Camp Driftwood, made famous by a hermit who dug steps to the top leaving behind pieces of driftwood. ⊠ *Between Conch Cut and Wax Cay Cut* ☎ *242/225–1791, VHF Channel 9 or 16* ⊕ *www.exumapark.info.*

### BEST TIME TO GO

In summer the water is as warm as bathwater and usually just as calm. The park has vastly fewer boats than in the busy winter season, when the channel becomes a blue highway for a parade of sailing and motor vessels. Bring insect repellent in summer and fall.

### BEST WAYS TO EXPLORE

**By Boat.** Boaters can explore the sandy cays and many islets that are little more than sandbars. The water is so clear it's hard to determine depths without a depth finder, so go slow and use your charts. Some routes are only passable at high tide. Get detailed directions before you go into the park, and be sure to stop by the park headquarters on Warderick Wells Cay for more information. Make sure you have a VHF marine radio on the boat or carry a handheld VHF radio so you can call for help or directions.

**On Foot.** The park headquarters has a map of hiking trails—most are on Warderick Wells Cay—that range from 2-mile walks to two-hour treks. Wear sturdy shoes, because trails are rocky. You'll see red, black, and white mangroves; limestone cliffs; and lots of birds—white-tail tropic birds, green herons, blue herons, black-bellied plovers, royal terns, and ospreys. Take sunscreen and water, and be aware that there's very little shade.

**By Kayak.** Visitors do sometimes take kayak trips from neighboring cays into the park and camp on the beach. The park has two kayaks that can be used free of charge by boaters moored in the park. As you paddle, look for sea turtles, which might pop up beside you.

**Underwater.** You have to go underwater to see the best part of the park—spiny lobsters walking on stilt legs on the sandy floor, sea grass waving in the currents, curious hawksbill turtles

(critically endangered), solemn-faced groupers, and the coral reefs that support an astonishing range of sea life. Bring your own equipment.

**FUN FACT**
The park has one native land mammal—the hutia, a critically endangered nocturnal rodent that looks similar to a gray squirrel.

**MAKING A DIFFERENCE**
How successful has the Exuma Cays Land and Sea Park been? About 74% of the grouper in the northern Exumas' cays come from the park. Crawfish tagged in the park have been found repopulating areas around Cat Island 70 miles away. The concentration of conch inside the park is 31 times higher than the concentration outside. This conservatively provides several million conchs outside the park for fishermen to harvest each year.

*(above) Boats anchored in the bay at Warderick Wells Cay, the park's headquarters.*

Updated by
Julianne Hoell

The Exumas are known for their gorgeous 365 cays — most uninhabited, some owned by celebrities. Get the wind and sea salt in your hair as you cruise through the pristine 120-mile chain. The water here is some of the prettiest in the world, and comes in every shade of blue and green (you'll grow tired trying to name the exact color); beaches are dazzling white. Combine that with fresh seafood and friendly locals, and you have yourself one of the best vacation destinations in the Bahamas.

Yes, the Exumas are Out Islands in the fullest sense of the word; there isn't a casino or cruise ship in sight. Those who love the remote beauty of the windswept cays keep coming back, people like Jimmy Buffett, who once docked his seaplane behind the historic Club Peace and Plenty and amused islanders by fishing from the cockpit. A vacation here revolves around uncrowded beaches, snorkeling, fishing, and enjoying a freshly caught dinner at an outdoor restaurant by the beach.

In 1783 Englishman Denys Rolle sent 150 slaves to Great Exuma to build a cotton plantation. His son Lord John Rolle later gave all of his 5,000 acres to his freed slaves, and they took the Rolle name. On Great Exuma and Little Exuma you'll still find wild cotton, testaments from plantations first established by Loyalists after the Revolutionary War. But today the Exumas are known as the Bahamas' onion capital, although many of the 7,000 residents earn a living by fishing and farming, and, more recently, tourism.

The Exumas attract outdoorsmen and adventurers, particularly fishermen after bonefish, the feisty breed that prefers the shallow sandy flats that surround these islands. And the healthiest coral reefs and fish populations in the country make for excellent diving and snorkeling. But for those simply seeking secluded beaches, starry skies, and a couple of new friends, the Exumas won't disappoint.

You can't go wrong with any of the beaches in the Exumas. They're some of the prettiest in the Bahamas—powdery bleach-white sand sharply contrasts the glittery emerald and sapphire waves. You can even stake your umbrella directly on the Tropic of Cancer. And the best part of all? You'll probably be the only one there.

The Exumas are made up of 365 cays, each and every one with pristine white beaches. Some cays are no bigger than a footprintless sandbar. But you won't stay on the sand long; Perrier-clear waters beckon, and each gentle wave brings new treasures—shells, bits of blue-and-green sea glass, and starfish. Beaches won't be hard to find on the tiny cays; on Great Exuma, look for "Beach Access" signs on the Queen's Highway.

# PLANNING

## WHEN TO GO

High season is December through April, when weather is in the 70s (although lows can dip into the 60s). Be warned that hotels will sell out for events such as the George Town Cruising Regatta and the Bahamian Music and Heritage Festival in March, and the National Family Islands Regatta in April.

Summer room rates are cheaper than the winter high season, but fall (late August through November) offers the best deals. That's because it's hurricane season (June–November), with the most chance of a storm from August to November. Weather during this time can be rainy and hot. Some inns close for September and October.

### TOP FESTIVALS
#### WINTER
**Junkanoo.** The Exumas' Junkanoo Parade on Boxing Day (Dec. 26) starts around 3 pm in George Town, ending at Regatta Park. Dancing, barbecues, and music happen before and after the parade.

**Annual New Year's Day Cruising Regatta.** The Annual New Year's Day Cruising Regatta at the Staniel Cay Yacht Club marks the finale of a five-day celebration.

**George Town Cruising Regatta.** The George Town Cruising Regatta in March is 12 days of festivities including sailing, a conch-blowing contest, dance, food and entertainment, and sports competitions.

**Bahamian Music and Heritage Festival.** March's Bahamian Music and Heritage Festival brings local and nationally known musicians to George Town, along with arts and crafts, Bahamas sloop exhibitions, storytelling, singing, poetry reading, and gospel music.

#### SPRING
**National Family Islands Regatta.** In April the National Family Islands Regatta is the Bahamas' most important yachting event. Starting the race in Elizabeth Harbour in George Town, island-made wooden sloops compete for trophies. Onshore, the town is a weeklong riot of Junkanoo parades, Goombay music, and arts-and-crafts fairs.

## GREAT ITINERARIES

### IF YOU HAVE 3 DAYS

Fly into **George Town**, relax on the beach or at the pool, and if it's a Friday night drive to the Fish Fry, a collection of outdoor fish shacks and bars just north of George Town; eat your dinner on a picnic table next to the beach. Finish the night at Club Peace and Plenty, the heart of George Town for more than 50 years. On Day 2, pick an activity: golfing at Sandals Emerald Bay; diving, snorkeling, or kayaking (make arrangements the night before at your resort); bonefishing; or drive to a beautiful secluded beach. Get gussied up (sun dresses and linen shirts) for a nice dinner in town. On Day 3, head out to **Stocking Island** for some beach volleyball and that it's-five-o'clock-somewhere cocktail. Stay for dinner and sunset. If it's Sunday, a pig roast at noon brings all the islanders over.

### IF YOU HAVE 5 DAYS

On Day 4, head to the **Exuma Cays** for some island-hopping: snorkel in Thunderball Grotto, feed swimming pigs and the rare Bahamian iguanas, or find your own secluded sand bar. Spend the night at Staniel Cay Yacht Club, and enjoy a festive dinner at the bar. On Day 5, head to the Exuma Cays Land and Sea Park, and spend the day snorkeling, hiking, and beach snoozing.

### IF YOU HAVE 7 DAYS

For the last two days, on your way back from the cays, relocate to Grand Isle or Sandals Emerald Bay for a luxurious end to your vacation. Relax on the beach, go to the spa, and enjoy that gorgeous blue water one last time. Eat at some of the finer restaurants on the island, or at beach shacks off the resort property.

### SUMMER

**Junkanoo Summer Festival.** The Junkanoo Summer Festival in June and July is held beachside at the Fish Fry in George Town, and features local and visiting bands, kids' sunfish sailing, arts and crafts, and boatbuilding displays. It takes place Saturdays at noon.

### FALL

**Bahamas Sunfish Festival.** The annual Bahamas Sunfish Festival in October at Little Farmer's Cay features exciting races to prepare young sailors for international competition.

## GETTING HERE AND AROUND

### AIR TRAVEL

The **Exuma International Airport (GGT)** (☎ 242/345–0002) is 10 miles north of George Town. Taxis wait at the airport for incoming flights; a trip to George Town costs $30 for two people; to Williams Town, $80; to February Point, $30; to Emerald Bay, $20; to Barraterre, $50. Each additional person is $3. Staniel Cay Airport accepts charter flights and private planes.

### BOAT AND FERRY TRAVEL

M/V *Grand Master* travels from Nassau to George Town on Tuesday and returns to Nassau on Thursday. The trip takes 12 hours and costs $45 each way. M/V *Captain Sea* leaves Nassau on Tuesday for Staniel

Cay, Big Farmer's Cay, Black Point, and Barraterre, returning to Nassau on Saturday. The trip is 14 hours and costs $70. Contact the **Dockmaster's Office** (☎ 242/393–1064) for information.

*Eastwind* travels from Nassau to George Town on Monday and the Sealink makes the trip on Wednesday, each arriving in Exuma the next day (on Tuesday and Thursday). The trip takes 10 hours and costs $63 one-way, $116 round-trip. Contact **Bahamas Ferries** (☎ 242/323–2166).

To reach Stocking Island from George Town, **Club Peace and Plenty Ferry** (☎ 242/336–2551) leaves the hotel at 10 am and 1 pm. It's free for guests and $12 round-trip for nonguests. **Elvis Ferguson** (☎ 242/464–1558 or VHF 16) operates a boat taxi from Government Dock to Chat 'N' Chill on the hour throughout the day. If you plan on leaving the island after 6 pm, tell the captain in advance. If you want to explore the Exuma cays, you'll appreciate the freedom of having your own boat.

### CAR TRAVEL

If you want to explore Great Exuma and Little Exuma, you'll need to rent a car. Most hotels can arrange car rentals.

Contacts **Airport Rent a Car** ✉ George Town Airport, George Town, Great Exuma Island ☎ 242/345–0090. **Exuma Transport** ✉ George Town, Great Exuma Island ☎ 242/336–2101. **Thompson's Rentals** ✉ George Town, Great Exuma Island ☎ 242/336–2442.

### TAXI TRAVEL

Taxis are plentiful on Great Exuma, and most offer island tours. A half-day tour of George Town and Little Exuma is about $150 for two people.

Contacts **Exuma Travel and Transportation Limited** ☎ 242/345–0232. **Kendal "Dr. K" Nixon** ✉ Great Exuma Island ☎ 242/422–7399. **Leslie Dames Taxi Service** ✉ Great Exuma Island ☎ 242/357–0015. **Luther Rolle Taxi Service** ✉ Great Exuma Island ☎ 242/357–0662.

## ESSENTIALS

### BANKS

Banks in George Town are open Monday–Thursday 9:30–3 and Friday until 4:30. All have ATMs.

### EMERGENCIES

Contacts **George Town Clinic** ✉ Queens Hwy., George Town, Great Exuma Island ☎ 242/336–2088. **Nurse Lydia King-Rolle Health Center** ✉ Queen's Hwy., Steventon, Great Exuma Island ☎ 242/358–0053. **Police** ☎ 911, 242/336–2666 George Town, 242/355–2042 Staniel Cay.

### HOTELS

Accommodations in the Exumas are more wide-ranging than on most Bahamian Out Islands. You can stay in simple stilt cottages, fabulous rooms with butler service, atmospheric old inns, modern condo rentals, all-inclusives, eco-lodges, or bed-and-breakfasts—temporary homes-away-from-home for every taste and price point. Most places have lots of personality and are distinctive in some marvelous way—a great hangout for fishermen, a peaceful place of tranquillity with no distractions, or action-packed resorts with head-spinning activity choices. Meal plans are available at some hotels.

The mainland of Great Exuma has had an energetic growth spurt that includes some of the country's most luxurious hotels: the new Sandals Emerald Bay, which opened in 2010; Grand Isle Resort and Spa; and February Point Resort Estate.

## RESTAURANTS

Exuma restaurants are known for terrific Bahamian home cooking—cracked conch, pan-seared snapper caught that morning, coconut fried shrimp, fried chicken served with peas 'n' rice, or macaroni baked with egg and loads of cheese. Try conch salad at the cluster of wooden shacks called the Fish Fry, just north of George Town. Pea soup and dumplings (made with pigeon peas) is a specialty here, and many local restaurants serve it as a weekly lunch special, usually on Wednesday.

Restaurants at larger resorts have upscale dining, including Continental twists on local cuisine—fresh snapper with mango salsa—as well as imported steaks, rack of lamb, and gourmet pizzas.

### HOTEL AND RESTAURANT PRICES

*Restaurant prices are based on the median main course price at dinner, excluding gratuity, typically 15%, which is often automatically added to the bill. Hotel prices are for two people in a standard double room in high season, excluding service and 6%–12% tax.*

### VISITOR INFORMATION

**Contacts Exuma Tourist Office** ⊠ *Queen's Hwy., George Town, Great Exuma Island* ☎ *242/336–2430* ⊕ *www.exuma.bahamas.com.* **Out Islands Promotion Board** ⊕ *www.myoutisland.com.*

# GREAT EXUMA

**George Town** is the capital and largest town on the mainland, a lovely seaside community with darling pink government buildings overlooking Elizabeth Harbour. The white-pillared, colonial-style Government Administration Building was modeled on Nassau's Government House and houses the commissioner's office, police headquarters, courts, and a jail. Atop a hill across from it is the whitewashed St. Andrew's Anglican Church, originally built around 1802. Behind the church is the small, saltwater Lake Victoria. It was once used for soaking sisal used for making baskets and ropes. The straw market, a half-dozen outdoor shops shaded by a huge African fig tree, is a short walk from town. You can bargain with fishermen for some of the day's catch at the Government Dock, where the mail boat comes in.

# The Exumas

Sail Rocks

Ship Channel Cay
Allan's Cays
Leaf Cay
Highbourne Cay
Highbourne
Long Cay
Norman's Cay

Windmere Island

Tarpum Bay

Schooner Cays

Rock Sound Airport

ELEUTHERA ISLAND

Powell Point

Rock Sound

Deep Creek
Greencastle
Waterford
Wemyss Bight

John Millars

Bannerman Town

Arthur's Town

Bennett's Harbour

Little San Salvador

Stevenson

CAT ISLAND

New Bight

Exuma Cays Land And Sea Park

Shroud Cay

Hawksbill Cay
Cistern Cay

Waderick Wells Cay

Halls Pond Cay
O'Brian's Cay

Bells Cay
Fowl Cay
Compass Cay
Joe Cay
Pipe Creek
Thomas Cay
Sampson Cay

Big Major's Cay
Staniel Cay
Harvey's Cays
Thunderball Grotto

Black Point

Great Guana Cay

Exuma Sound

Devil's Point

E X U M A

G R A N D   B A H A M A   B A N K

C A Y S

Little Farmer's Cay
Big Farmer's Cay
Musha Cay
Cave Cay

Darby Island
Young Island
Block Cay
Normans Pond Cay
Lee Stocking Island

Brigantine Cays
Barraterre
Starfish Reserve

Rolleville
Steventon

Great Exuma Island

Queen's Hwy.
Angel Fish Blue Hole
Jolly Hall Beach
Stocking Island Mystery Cave

Mt. Thompson
Exuma Int'l Airport
Moss Town
Fish Fry
George Town

Stocking Island
Chat'N'Chill
Elizabeth Harbour
Rolle Town Tombs
The Hermitage

Channel Cays
Rolle Town
St. Christopher's

Little Exuma Island

Williams Town

Hog Cay
Sandy Cay

Tropic of Cancer Beach

## Key

- Beaches
- Dive Sites

*Water Depths*
- -25ft deep
- -50ft deep
- -100ft deep

0        15 mi

0        15 km

Small settlements make up the rest of the island. **Rolle Town,** a typical Exuma village devoid of tourist trappings, sits atop a hill overlooking the ocean 5 miles south of George Town. Some of the buildings are 100 years old. **Rolleville** overlooks a harbor 20 miles north of George Town. Its old slave quarters have been transformed into livable cottages. The Hilltop Tavern, a seafood restaurant and bar, is guarded by an ancient cannon.

### GETTING AROUND

If you are going to sightsee on your own and plan to eat at restaurants and visit beaches outside your resort, you should rent a car, since taxis can get expensive. If you plan to stay at your resort most of your vacation, you can use taxis.

## EXPLORING

**Fish Fry.** Fish Fry is the name given to a jumble of one-room beachside structures, such as Charlie's and Honeydew, about 2 miles north of George Town. They're favored by locals for made-to-order fish and barbecue. Some shacks are open weekends only, but most are open nightly until at least 11 pm. There's live Rake 'n' Scrape Monday nights and DJs on Friday and Saturday. Eat at picnic tables by the water and watch the fishing boats come into the harbor. This is a popular after-work meeting place on Friday nights, and a sports bar attracts locals and expats for American basketball and football games. ⊠ *Queen's Hwy., George Town, Great Exuma Island.*

**Mt. Thompson.** From the top of Mt. Thompson, rising from the Three Sisters Beach, there is a pleasing view of the **Three Sisters Rocks** jutting above the water just offshore. Legend has it that the rocks were formed when three sisters, all unwittingly in love with the same English sailor, waded out into deep water upon his departure, drowned, and turned into stone. If you look carefully next to each "sister," you'll see smaller boulders—the children with which the fickle sailor left them. Mt. Thompson is about 12 miles north of George Town, past Moss Town. ⊠ *Queen's Highway, Mount Thompson, Great Exuma Island.*

**Rolle Town Tombs.** Seek out the three Rolle Town Tombs, which date back to Loyalists. The largest tomb bears this poignant inscription: "Within this tomb interred the body of Ann McKay, the wife of Alexander McKay who departed this life the 8th November 1792. Aged twenty-six years and their infant child." The tombs are off the main road; look for a sign. The settlement has brightly painted buildings, several more than 100 years old. ⊠ *Rolle Town, Great Exuma Island.*

Fodor's Choice
★

**Stocking Island.** Slightly more than a mile off George Town's shore lies Stocking Island. The 4-mile-long island has only 10 inhabitants, the upscale Hotel Higgins Landing, lots of walking trails, a gorgeous white beach rich in seashells and popular with surfers on the ocean side, and plenty of good snorkeling sites. Jacques Cousteau's team is said to have traveled some 1,700 feet into Mystery Cave, a blue-hole grotto 70 feet beneath the island. Don't miss Chat 'N' Chill, a lively open-air restaurant and bar right on the point. Volleyball games, board games under the trees, and the new Conch Bar make for fun in the sun. The restaurant picks up guests at Government Dock on the hour. Club Peace and Plenty's ferry runs over to Stocking Island twice daily at 10 am and 1 pm and charges $12 for nonguests. Near the Stocking Island pier, Peace and Plenty Beach Club provides changing rooms (with plumbing) and operates a lunch spot where Dora's hamburgers and famous conch burgers are the eats of choice. Stocking Island is the headquarters for the wildly popular George Town Cruising Regatta.

### PEACOCKS

During your walks, you might glimpse peacocks on Great Exuma. Originally, a peacock and a peahen were brought to the island as pets by a man named Shorty Johnson, but when he left to work in Nassau he abandoned the birds, which gradually proliferated into a colony. The birds used to roam the streets, but development has forced them into the bush, so they are rarer sights these days.

## BEACHES

**Chat 'N' Chill.** The restaurant and 9-acre playground—an amazing white-sand beach—is the Exumas' party central, particularly for the famous all-day Sunday pig roasts. Play volleyball in the powdery sand, order what's cooking on the outdoor grill—fresh fish, ribs—or chat and chill. There are dances on the beach from January to the end of April when 200-plus sailboats populate the harbor. The new Conch Bar on the beach serves conch fritters, conch salad, and lobster fritters. The beach is quieter on weekdays, and usually not crowded in summer and fall. **Amenities:** food and drink; toilets. **Best for:** partiers. ✉ *Stocking Island, Great Exuma Island* ☎ *242/357–0926* 🌐 *www.chatnchill.com.*

**Jolly Hall Beach.** A curve of sparkling white sand shaded by casuarina trees, this long beach is located just north of Palm Bay Beach Club. It's quiet and the shallow azure water makes it a great spot for families or romantics. When it's time for lunch, walk over to Palm Bay, Exuma Beach Resort, or Augusta Bay, three small nearby inns. Watch your bags when high tide comes in; much of the beach is swallowed by the sea. That's the signal for a cold Kalik and grouper sandwich. **Amenities:** none. **Best for:** solitude; sunrise; swimming; snorkeling. ✉ *Queen's Hwy., George Town, Great Exuma Island.*

## WHERE TO EAT

$ BAHAMIAN 🍴 **Big D's Conch Shack.** For the freshest—and according to locals, best—conch salad and the coldest beer, look for the splatter-painted seaside shack a stone's throw from Grand Isle Resort. You can't get a better water view, and the beach is great; bring a swimsuit. [$] *Average main: $10* ✉ *Queen's Hwy., Steventon, Great Exuma Island* ☎ *242/358–0059* 💳 *No credit cards* 🕒 *Closed Mon.*

$ ECLECTIC 🍴 **Blu Bistro.** With a stunning view of the Three Sisters Rocks, this charming beachfront restaurant offers dinner à la carte every night but Wednesday, and themed dinners three times a week: Mexican Mondays with margaritas, Indian Fridays, and Bahamian Sundays with barbecue and live

music. Blu Bistro also serves lunch on the beachfront terrace every day, but you'll need to call ahead. Menu options include burgers, sandwiches, and chicken tenders. $ *Average main: $16* ✉ *Exuma Palms Hotel, Queen's Hwy., Mount Thompson, Great Exuma Island* ☎ *242/358-4040* ⊕ *www.exumapalms.com* ⊙ *No dinner Wed.*

> ### THE GOLDEN TICKET
>
> Sandals restaurants aren't open to nonguests—unless you buy a $150 pass that includes all you can eat and drink from 6 pm to 2 am, a $180 pass for 10 am to 6 pm, or an all-day pass for $310.

**$$$**
ECLECTIC
✕ **Catch a Fire Bar and Grill.** Sip a tropical cocktail and enjoy the sunset at this waterfront bar and grill. Tastefully decorated with teak benches, a handsome bar, and infinity pool, Catch a Fire is a fun place to go for dinner and for dancing on Wednesday and Saturday nights when the restaurant has live entertainment. It can be busy, so call ahead for reservations. $ *Average main: $30* ✉ *George Town, Great Exuma Island* ☎ *242/357-0777* ⊙ *Closed Sun. and Mon.*

**$**
BAHAMIAN
Fodor'sChoice
★
✕ **Chat 'N' Chill.** Yacht folks, locals, and visitors alike rub shoulders at Kenneth Bowe's funky open-air beach bar on the point at Stocking Island. All of the food is grilled over an open fire; awesome conch burgers with secret spices and grilled fish with onions and potatoes attract diners from all over Great Exuma. Dances and bonfires on the beach during the winter season are famous island-wide. Sunday pig roasts, which start around noon, are legendary, but call first to make sure it's scheduled. Most guests arrive by sailboat but you can get here by water taxi (☎ *242/464-1558; or call Capt. Elvis Ferguson on VHF radio channel 16*) from the Government Dock, which leaves on the hour during the day. $ *Average main: $14* ✉ *1 Stocking Island, Great Exuma Island* ☎ *242/357-0926* ⊕ *www.chatnchill.com* ▬ *No credit cards.*

**$**
BAHAMIAN
✕ **Cheater's Restaurant and Bar.** Disregard the lack of ambience, this popular restaurant serves some of the best food on the island. Fresh fish and fried chicken dinners are the house specialties. Free transportation is available to those staying at hotels within 4 miles of the restaurant. $ *Average main: $15* ✉ *Queen's Hwy., 1½ miles south of, George Town, Great Exuma Island* ☎ *242/336-2535* ▬ *No credit cards* ⊙ *Closed Sun. and Mon.*

**$$**
EUROPEAN
✕ **Club Peace and Plenty.** The legendary hotel's restaurant has a fabulous view of the pool and harbor, along with traditional Bahamian specialties including conch fritters and grilled fish, and a 12-ounce New York strip steak. This is one of the nicer places to dine on the island, perfect for a romantic dinner or family celebration. For breakfast start your day with boiled snapper and johnnycakes or an omelet. $ *Average main: $29* ✉ *Club Peace and Plenty, Queen's Hwy., George Town, Great Exuma Island* ☎ *242/336-2551* ⊕ *www.peaceandplenty.com.*

**$**
DELI
✕ **Driftwood Café.** Located in central George Town just across from the Peace & Plenty, this café is a pleasant spot for a cup of coffee and hot breakfast sandwich in the morning. Driftwood Café also offers lunch, with specialties such as quiche, subs, and salads served with fresh lemonade or iced tea. Choose between air-conditioned seating inside or tables outside on the private terrace. $ *Average main: $10* ✉ *Queen's Hwy., George Town, Great Exuma Island* ☎ *242/336-3800* ⊙ *Closed Sun. No dinner.*

7

Sandals Emerald Bay on Great Exuma has one of the island's best beaches.

$ 🍴 **Eddie's Edgewater.** Fried chicken, lobster, T-bone steak, and cracked
BAHAMIAN conch are the delicious reasons people eat at this modest lakeside establishment. [$] *Average main: $15* ✉ *Charlotte St., George Town, Great Exuma Island* ☎ *242/336–2050.*

$$ 🍴 **Exuma Yacht Club.** The newly opened Exuma Yacht Club, located in the
ITALIAN hustle and bustle of central George Town, has a magnificent view of the
Fodor's Choice ★ harbor. Enjoy the ocean breeze from the bar on the balcony, or dine in the chic indoor seating area. The lunch menu includes burgers, salads, and a fresh catch of the day. Dinner is decidedly more sophisticated, with an Italian menu comprised of fantastic seafood and pasta dishes. [$] *Average main: $29* ✉ *Queen's Hwy., George Town, Great Exuma Island* ☎ *242/336–2578* 🌐 *www.theexumayachtclub.com.*

$$$ 🍴 **Latitudes.** Enjoy the ocean view at Exuma Beach Resort for lunch,
CARIBBEAN dinner, or over one of their famous cocktails. Highlights of the lunch menu are the ½-pound gourmet Angus beef burger, sushi-grade ahi tuna wrap, and flatbread pizzas. Dinner options include the popular mango-chutney shrimp curry and grilled Bahamian lobster. Latitudes has karaoke on Tuesday nights, live entertainment on Friday nights, and Happy Hour on Sunday. Be sure to try one of their signature cocktails: the 22.5 degrees North is named for the latitude of the Tropic of Cancer, which runs through Exuma, and the Chocolatini is the best dessert in the house. [$] *Average main: $36* ✉ *Queens Hwy., George Town, Great Exuma Island* ☎ *242/336–3100.*

$$$ 🍴 **Palappa Pool Bar and Grill at Grand Isle Resort.** This poolside restaurant
EUROPEAN serves three meals a day. The extensive menu equally features American classics and Bahamian specialties. Dinner highlights include ahi

tuna steak, shrimp pasta, prime rib eye, and baby back ribs. A fun drink list including many frozen concoctions complements the food. $ *Average main: $37* ⊠ *Queen's Hwy., Emerald Bay, Great Exuma Island* ☎ *242/358–5000* ⊕ *www.grandisleresort.com* ⌂ *Reservations essential.*

$    × **Prime Island Meats and Deli.** Stop by this deli to stock up on gourmet
DELI  meats, cheeses, and wine for your stay. Owners Ron and Susan Kemp also sell delicious chicken salad, crab salad, potato salad, and more. All are homemade and perfect for a beach picnic. The rotisserie chicken is extremely popular, as is the quality beef. $ *Average main: $8* ⊠ *Queen's Hwy., George Town, Great Exuma Island* ☎ *242/336–3627* ⊘ *Closed Sun. and Mon.*

$      × **Splash Bar & Grill at Palm Bay Beach Club.** Restaurant highlights for
BAHAMIAN  lunch are fish burgers, conch burgers, and regular burgers. Dinner specialties include grilled grouper, cracked conch, and pizza. The restaurant circles a lively bar, a popular hangout for locals as well as guests who enjoy the view of the harbor and Stocking Island. $ *Average main: $13* ⊠ *Queen's Hwy., George Town, Great Exuma Island* ☎ *242/336–2787* ⊘ *Closed Sept.*

$      × **Towne Café.** This George Town restaurant serves breakfast (especially
BAHAMIAN  popular on Saturday)—consider trying the stew' fish or chicken souse— and lunches of grilled fish or seafood sandwiches with three sides. It's open until 3 pm. Don't miss the baked goods, especially the giant cinnamon rolls. $ *Average main: $14* ⊠ *Marshall Complex, Queen's Hwy., George Town, Great Exuma Island* ☎ *242/336–2194* ▭ *No credit cards* ⊘ *Closed Sun. No dinner.*

## WHERE TO STAY

$$      ⌂ **Augusta Bay Bahamas.** The perfect balance of luxury and casual chic,
RESORT  without the megaresort feel, this 16-room resort on 300 feet of nar-
Fodor'sChoice  row beach is a mile north of George Town. **Pros:** luxurious rooms;
★     great water views; friendly service. **Cons:** beach almost disappears at high tide; need a car to drive to town and shops. $ *Rooms from: $277* ⊠ *Queen's Hwy., George Town, Great Exuma Island* ☎ *242/336–2250* ⊕ *www.augustabaybahamas.com* ⌐ *16 rooms* ⦿ *Breakfast.*

$      ⌂ **Club Peace and Plenty.** The first Exumas' hotel and granddaddy of the
HOTEL  island's omnipresent Peace and Plenty empire, this pink, two-story lodge is in the heart of the action in George Town. **Pros:** guests are in middle of the George Town action; friendly staff; ocean-view balconies in some rooms. **Cons:** no beach; have to take a water taxi to Stocking Island. $ *Rooms from: $180* ⊠ *Queen's Hwy., George Town, Great Exuma Island* ☎ *242/336–2551, 800/525–2210* ⊕ *www.peaceandplenty.com* ⌐ *32 rooms* ⦿ *No meals.*

$      ⌂ **Coral Gardens Bed and Breakfast.** Extremely popular with Brits and
B&B/INN  Europeans, the sprawling two-story B&B, owned and run by British expats Betty and Peter Oxley, is on a hilltop with an inviting verandah. **Pros:** superb hilltop view of water in the distance; peaceful location; friendly hosts. **Cons:** not on the beach; need a car to go to George Town and the beach. $ *Rooms from: $100* ⊠ *Off Queen's Hwy., 3*

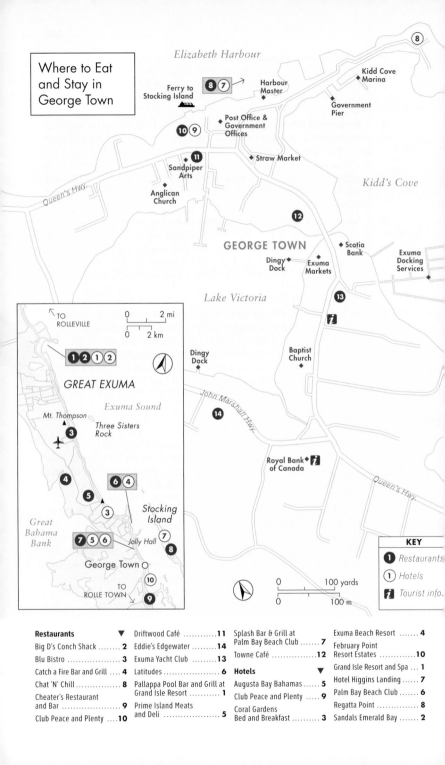

## Where to Eat and Stay in George Town

*Elizabeth Harbour*

Kidd Cove
Marina

Harbour
Master

**8 7** Ferry to
Stocking Island

Government
Pier

Post Office &
Government
Offices

**10 9**

Straw Market

**11**
Sandpiper
Arts

*Kidd's Cove*

Anglican
Church

**12**

**GEORGE TOWN**

Scotia
Bank

Dingy
Dock

Exuma
Markets

Exuma
Docking
Services

*Lake Victoria*

**13**

*i*

TO
ROLLEVILLE

0        2 mi

0     2 km

*GREAT EXUMA*

**1 2 1 2**

Dingy
Dock

Baptist
Church

*Exuma Sound*

Mt. Thompson

Three Sisters
Rock

John Marshall Hwy.

**3**

**14**

**4**

**5**

**3**

**6 4**

*Stocking
Island*

*Great
Bahama
Bank*

**7 5 6**

Jolly Hall

**7**

**8**

Royal Bank
of Canada

*i*

Queen's Hwy.

George Town

**10**

TO
ROLLE TOWN

**9**

0      100 yards

0      100 m

### KEY

**1** *Restaurants*

**(1)** *Hotels*

*i* *Tourist info.*

| Restaurants ▼ | | | |
|---|---|---|---|
| Big D's Conch Shack ........ **2** | Driftwood Café ............**11** | Splash Bar & Grill at Palm Bay Beach Club ....... **7** | Exuma Beach Resort ....... **4** |
| Blu Bistro .................. **3** | Eddie's Edgewater ........**14** | Towne Café ................**12** | February Point Resort Estates .............**10** |
| Catch a Fire Bar and Grill .... **4** | Exuma Yacht Club ........**13** | | Grand Isle Resort and Spa ... **1** |
| Chat 'N' Chill .............. **8** | Latitudes .................... **6** | **Hotels ▼** | Hotel Higgins Landing ...... **7** |
| Cheater's Restaurant and Bar ..................... **9** | Pallappa Pool Bar and Grill at Grand Isle Resort ........... **1** | Augusta Bay Bahamas...... **5** | Palm Bay Beach Club ...... **6** |
| | Prime Island Meats and Deli .................... **5** | Club Peace and Plenty ..... **9** | Regatta Point .............. **8** |
| Club Peace and Plenty ....**10** | | Coral Gardens Bed and Breakfast .......... **3** | Sandals Emerald Bay ....... **2** |

*miles north of George Town, 12 Garden Rd., George Town, Great Exuma Island* ☎ *242/336–2880* 🌐 *www.coralgardensbahamas.com* 🛏 *3 rooms, 2 apartments* ⏲ *Closed Sept.–mid-Oct.* 🍴 *Breakfast.*

$ RESORT **Exuma Beach Resort.** This newly renovated beachfront resort just outside of George Town boasts eight guest rooms and one exceptional suite. **Pros:** modern accommodations; centrally located. **Cons:** backs into main road; resort can feel cramped. [$] *Rooms from: $175* ✉ *Queen's Hwy., George Town, Great Exuma Island* ☎ *242/336–3100* 🌐 *www.exumabeachresort.com* 🛏 *9 rooms, including 1 suite* 🍴 *Breakfast.*

### TAKING PICS OF THE WATER

"My pictures will never show the incredible shades of blue in this water." You're likely to hear this on your vacation, maybe straight from your own mouth. Here are a few tips: shoot early—before 9—on a sunny day, or late in the afternoon. Make sure the sun is behind you. Use a tripod, or hold the camera still. Find a contrasting color—a bright red umbrella or a yellow fishing boat.

$$$$ RESORT Fodor's Choice ★ **February Point Resort Estates.** This gated residential community and resort is made up of 42 villas and privately owned homes—20 of the villas are available as guest accommodations. **Pros:** elegant accommodations that feel like an ultraluxurious home away from home. **Cons:** more like a gated community than a resort. [$] *Rooms from: $850* ✉ *Queen's Hwy., George Town, Great Exuma Island* ☎ *242/336–2695, 877/839–4253* 🌐 *www.februarypoint.com* 🛏 *20 villas.*

$$$ RESORT Fodor's Choice ★ **Grand Isle Resort and Spa.** This luxurious 78-villa complex boasts one of the island's few spas, an infinity pool overlooking the ocean, and a poolside patio restaurant. **Pros:** the ultimate in luxury accommodations; friendly staff; on-site spa and restaurant. **Cons:** 20-minute drive from Georgetown and not much to do near the resort. [$] *Rooms from: $300* ✉ *Off Queens Hwy., Emerald Bay, Great Exuma Island* ☎ *242/358–5000* 🌐 *www.grandisleresort.com* 🛏 *78 villas* 🍴 *No meals.*

$$$$ HOTEL **Hotel Higgins Landing.** Laid out on undeveloped Stocking Island is this eco-hotel that is 100% solar powered—though everything still works when the weather's overcast. **Pros:** the ultimate in luxury for the eco-minded; plenty of walking trails and great beaches; nonmotorized water sports. **Cons:** property is remote; have to take a water taxi to George Town. [$] *Rooms from: $445* ✉ *Stocking Island, Great Exuma Island* ☎ *242/357–0008* 🌐 *www.higginslanding.com* 🛏 *4 cottages* ⏲ *Closed Sept.–Oct.* 🍴 *Some meals.*

$$ RESORT FAMILY **Palm Bay Beach Club.** Palm Bay, one of George Town's most modern accommodations, is all about light and color. **Pros:** luxurious, roomy accommodations; friendly young staff. **Cons:** beach all but disappears at high tide. [$] *Rooms from: $250* ✉ *1 mile from George Town, Queen's Hwy., Great Exuma Island* ☎ *888/396–0606, 242/336–2787* 🌐 *www.palmbaybeachclub.com* 🛏 *43 rooms* ⏲ *Closed Sept.* 🍴 *Some meals.*

$$ HOTEL **Regatta Point.** Soft pink with hunter-green shutters, this handsome two-story guesthouse overlooks Kidd Cove from its own petite island. **Pros:** in George Town but has the feel of a private island; has beach and fantastic harbor views. **Cons:** water at the beach doesn't look

The Straw Market in George Town features handmade crafts.

clean; no restaurant. ⓢ *Rooms from: $248* ✉ *Kidd Cove, George Town, Great Exuma Island* ☎ *242/336–2206, 800/688–0309* ⊕ *www. regattapointbahamas.com* ⤵ *6 suites* ▭ *No credit cards.*

**$$$$**
**ALL-INCLUSIVE**
**Fodor'sChoice**
★

🍽 **Sandals Emerald Bay.** The former luxurious Four Seasons is now the even more luxurious Sandals Emerald Bay, an all-inclusive resort of pink and aqua buildings facing a 1-mile-long stretch of powdery white sand. **Pros:** all-inclusive; magnificent beach and swimming pools; great water sports. **Cons:** the resort is isolated. ⓢ *Rooms from: $750* ✉ *Queen's Hwy., Emerald Bay, Great Exuma Island* ☎ *242/336–6800, 800/SANDALS* ⊕ *www.sandals.com* ⤵ *245 suites* 🍴 *All-inclusive.*

## NIGHTLIFE

**Club Peace and Plenty.** In season, the Thursday-night poolside bashes at Club Peace and Plenty, fueled by live bands, keep Bahamians and vacationers on the dance floor. ✉ *Queen's Hwy., George Town, Great Exuma Island* ☎ *242/336–2551.*

**Eddie's Edgewater.** On Monday, head to Eddie's Edgewater for rousing Rake 'n' Scrape music. The front porch is a popular spot, where locals hang out all week long, especially come Friday night, when a DJ plays. ✉ *Charlotte St., George Town, Great Exuma Island* ☎ *242/336–2050.*

**Fish Fry.** There's always something going on at the Fish Fry, a cluster of shacks 2 miles north of George Town. On Monday nights there's a Rake 'n' Scrape band; a DJ is usually there on Friday and Saturday. ✉ *Queen's Highway, George Town, Great Exuma Island.*

## SHOPPING

### GIFTS AND SOUVENIRS

**Exuma Markets.** At this grocery store located in the center of George-town, yachties tie up at the skiff docks in the rear, on Lake Victoria. FedEx, emergency email, and faxes for visitors are also accepted here. ⊠ *Across from Scotia Bank, Queen's Hwy., George Town, Great Exuma Island* ☎ *242/336–2033.*

**Sandpiper Arts & Crafts.** Here you can find upscale souvenirs, from high-quality cards and books to batik clothing and art. ⊠ *Queen's Hwy., George Town, Great Exuma Island* ☎ *242/336–2084.*

**Straw Market.** The Straw Market offers a wide range of Bahamian straw bags, hats, and beachwear at a half dozen open-air shops under a huge African fig tree. Prices are negotiable. ⊠ *Queen's Hwy., George Town, Great Exuma Island.*

**Red Lane Spa.** Located on the Sandals Emerald Bay property, this elegant spa has 16 treatment rooms, a steam room, and a fitness center. Couples massages and "sun lover" relief are among the treatments offered. The spa is also open to nonguests, but you'll need to call ahead to make your appointment. ⊠ *Sandals Emerald Bay, Queen's Hwy., George Town, Great Exuma Island* ☎ *242/336–6800* ⊕ *www.sandals. com* ☞ *Steam room. Gym with: cardiovascular machines, free weights, weight-training equipment. Services: body wraps, facials, massage, scrubs, nail treatment. Classes and programs: Pilates, yoga.*

## SPORTS AND THE OUTDOORS

### BOATING

Because of its wealth of safe harbors and regatta events, the Exumas are a favorite spot for yachtsmen. Renting a boat allows you to explore the cays near George Town and beyond, and a number of area hotels allow guests to tie up rental boats at their docks. For those who want to take a water jaunt through Stocking Island's hurricane holes, sailboats are ideal.

### FISHING

In the shallow flats off Exuma's windward coast the elusive bonefish, the "ghosts of the sea," roam. Patient fishermen put featherweight, thumb-nail-size flies on the lines, calculate the tides and currents, and cast out about 50 feet in hope of catching one. For sure success, avid fishermen pay guides about $300 a day to help them outsmart the skinny gray fish that streak through crystal water. Most hotels can arrange for expert locals guides, and a list is also available from the Exuma Tourist Office. The season is year-round and highly prized among fly fishermen.

**Fish Rowe Charters.** This charter company has a 40-foot Hatteras that holds up to four fishermen. Deepwater charters run $800 for a half day, $1,200 for ¾ day, and $1,600 for a full day. ☎ *242/357–0870* ⊕ *www. fishrowecharters.com.*

**Steve Ferguson.** Stevie is an experienced guide who will help you hook feisty bonefish. ⊠ *Great Exuma Island* ⊕ *www.bonefishstevie.com.*

You'll swim among multicolored tropical fish at Staniel Cay.

### GOLF

**Sandals Emerald Bay.** Golf legend Greg Norman designed the 18-hole, par-72 championship course, featuring six oceanside holes, at Sandals Emerald Bay, the island's only golf course. There are preferred tee times for hotel guests, who pay $150, including golf cart; the fee for nonguests is the same. ⊠ *Queen's Hwy., Great Exuma Island* ☎ *242/336–6800.*

### KAYAKING

**Gully's Sea Kayaking.** Gully rents kayaks for $60/day for a single and $80/day for a double. Discounts are available for longer rentals. ⊠ *Great Exuma Island* ☎ *242/524–4213.*

### SCUBA DIVING

**Angel Fish Blue Hole.** This popular dive site, just minutes from George Town, is filled with angelfish, spotted rays, snapper, and the occasional reef shark.

**Dive Exuma.** This outfitter provides dive instruction, certification courses, and scuba trips. Two-tank dives are $135; blue-hole one-tank dives are $85. ☎ *242/357–0313, 242/336–2893* ⊕ *www.dive-exuma.com.*

**Stocking Island Mystery Cave.** This site is full of mesmerizing schools of colorful fish but is for experienced divers only.

### SNORKELING

**Minn's Water Sports.** Minn's rents snorkeling gear for $10/day. ⊠ *Queen's Hwy., George Town, Great Exuma Island* ☎ *242/336–2604* ⊕ *www.mwsboats.com.*

## TENNIS

**February Point.** Nonguests can use the two Laykold cushion–surfaced courts and adjacent fitness center at February Point for $40 a month. ✉ *February Point Resort, Queen's Hwy., George Town, Great Exuma Island* ☎ *242/336–2693, 877/839–4253.*

# LITTLE EXUMA

Scenes from two *Pirates of the Caribbean* movies were filmed on the southern end of Little Exuma—only 12 square miles—and on one of the little cays just offshore. The movies' stars, Johnny Depp and Orlando Bloom, often roamed around the island and ate at Santana's open-air beach shack, the island's best-known restaurant. But that's just one of the reasons people are drawn to this lovely island connected to Great Exuma to the north by a narrow bridge. Rolling green hills, purple morning glories spilling over fences, small settlements with only a dozen houses, and glistening white beaches make a romantic afternoon escape. Near **Williams Town** is an eerie salt lake, still and ghostly, where salt was once scooped up and shipped away. You can hike old footpaths and look for ruins of old plantation buildings built in the 1700s near the Hermitage, but you'll have to look beneath the bushes and vines to find them. Little Exuma's best beach is Tropic of Cancer Beach (also known as Pelican's Bay Beach); it is a thrill to stand on the line that marks the spot. You're officially in the tropics now.

### GETTING HERE AND AROUND

You need a car or a scooter to explore Little Exuma. It's possible to walk or ride a bike around the island, but it's hot and there's very little shade.

## EXPLORING

**Hermitage.** The Hermitage estate ruins are testaments to the cotton plantation days. The small settlement was built by the Ferguson family from the Carolinas, who settled here after the American Revolutionary War. Visitors can see the foundations of the main house and tombs that date back to the 1700s. The tombs hold George Butler (1759–1822), Henderson Ferguson (1772–1825), and Constance McDonald (1755–59). A grave is believed to be that of an unnamed slave. ✉ *Williams Town, Little Exuma.*

**St. Christopher's Anglican.** This is the island's smallest church, built in 1939 when the parish priest Father Marshall heard that a schooner loaded with timber from the Abacos had wrecked off Long Island. He visited the local Fitz-Gerald family and suggested they use the timber to build a church, which they did. Visitors can see the church and pews, all built of salvaged wood. ✉ *Queen's Hwy., Ferry, Little Exuma.*

## BEACHES

**Tropic of Cancer Beach** (*Pelican's Bay Beach*). This is the beach most visitors come to the Exumas for, although don't be surprised if you're the only one on it at noon on a Saturday. It's right on the Tropic of Cancer; a helpful

# Island of the Stars

The Bahamas have served as a source of inspiration for countless artists, writers, and directors. The country's movie legacy dates back to the era of silent films, including the now-legendary original black-and-white version of **Jules Verne**'s 20,000 Leagues Under the Sea, which was filmed here in 1907. Since the birth of color film, the draw has only increased—directors are lured by the possibility of using the islands' characteristic white sands and luminous turquoise waters as a backdrop. Among the more famous movies shot in the Bahamas are Jaws: The Revenge, the cult favorite whose killer shark has terrified viewers for more than three decades; Flipper, the family classic about a boy and a porpoise; Splash, whose main character is a mermaid who becomes human; and Cocoon, about a group of elderly friends who discover an extraterrestrial secret to immortality. Most recently, parts of the two sequels to Pirates of the Caribbean, Dead Man's Chest and At World's End, were shot on location in the Exumas. Thunderball and Never Say Never Again were both shot on location in Staniel Cay, one of the northernmost islands of the Exumas' chain.

**Ernest Hemingway** wrote about the Bahamas as well. He visited Bimini regularly in the 1930s, dubbing it the "Sportsfishing Capital of the World." His hangout was the Compleat Angler, a bar that housed a small Hemingway museum until it burned down in January 2006. Among the items the museum displayed were Hemingway's drawings for The Old Man and the Sea—rumor has it that the protagonist looks suspiciously like one of the Angler's former bartenders.

The Bahamas not only seem to spark the imaginations of artists, but have also become a playground for the rich and famous. **Lenny Kravitz** and **Patti LaBelle** own homes in Eleuthera, while the stars of Cocoon, the late **Hume Cronyn** and **Jessica Tandy,** were regular visitors to Goat Cay, a private island just offshore from George Town, Exuma. **Johnny Depp** purchased a cay in the Exumas after filming on location for Pirates of the Caribbean, and **Nicolas Cage** and **Faith Hill** and **Tim MacGraw** own private islands in the area as well. Many world-famous celebrities and athletes hide out at **Musha Cay,** an exclusive retreat in the northern part of the Exumas, where a week's stay sets you back $24,750 for the entire island. **David Copperfield** bought Musha and its five houses in 2006 for $50 million, renaming it Copperfield Cay. Although the cay won't name its guests, the all-knowing taxi drivers at the George Town airport mention **Oprah Winfrey** and **Michael Jordan** as a couple of the esteemed visitors.

line marking the spot on the steps leading down to the sand makes a great photo op. The beach is a white-sand crescent in a protected cove, where the water is usually as calm as a pond. A shady wooden cabana makes a comfortable place to admire the beach and water. *Pirates of the Caribbean* 2 and 3 were filmed on nearby Sandy Cay. Have lunch at the cast's favorite place, the open-air Santana's in Williams Town, a 10-minute drive from the beach. **Amenities:** none. **Best for:** solitude; snorkeling; swimming; walking. ⊠ *Williams Town, Little Exuma.*

## WHERE TO EAT

$ BAHAMIAN Fodor's Choice ★ 🍴 **Santana's Grill Pit.** This seaside open-air restaurant—you can't miss the orange-and-yellow building—is the hot spot in Little Exuma, and the closest restaurant to the Tropic of Cancer Beach. Dinner highlights include cracked lobster, cracked conch, shrimp, and grilled grouper, all served with peas 'n' rice or baked macaroni and cheese. Ask to see the photo book of celebrities who have eaten here; it was popular with the *Pirates of the Caribbean* cast and crew. [$] *Average main: $16* ✉ *Queen's Hwy., Williams Town, Little Exuma* ☎ *242/345–4102* 💳 *No credit cards* 🕒 *Closed Sun.*

## WHERE TO STAY

$$$$ HOTEL 🏨 **Turquoise Cay.** In the place of the old Peace and Plenty Bonefish Lodge, the island's first luxury boutique hotel opened in summer 2013. **Pros:** the resort has docks if you choose to rent a boat; peaceful; great sunset views. **Cons:** secluded; need a car to leave the property. [$] *Rooms from: $400* ✉ *Queen's Hwy., Ferry, Little Exuma* ☎ *242/345–5010* 🌐 *www.turquoisecay.com* 🛏 *8 rooms* 🍽 *No meals.*

# THE EXUMA CAYS

7

A band of cays—with names like **Rudder Cut**, **Big Farmer's**, **Great Guana**, and **Leaf**—stretches northwest from Great Exuma. It will take you a full day to boat through all 365 cays, most uninhabited, some owned by celebrities (Faith Hill and Tim McGraw on Goat Cay, Johnny Depp on Halls Pond Cay, and David Copperfield on Musha Cay). Along the way you'll find giant starfish, wild iguanas, swimming pigs, dolphins, sharks, and picture-perfect, footprintless sandbars. The Land and Sea Park, toward the northern end of the chain, is world-renowned.

### GETTING HERE AND AROUND

Most people visit the cays with their own boats; you'll need one to island-hop, although you can fly into Staniel Cay. The channels are confusing for inexperienced boaters, especially at low tide, and high tide can hide reefs and sandbars just underneath the surface. If this sounds nerve-racking, look into booking a boat tour. Once on a cay, most are small enough to walk. Golf carts are popular on Staniel Cay.

## EXPLORING

**Allan's Cay.** Allan's Cay is at the Exumas' northernmost tip and home to the rare Bahamian iguana. Bring along some grapes and a stick to put them on, and these little guys will quickly become your new best friends.

**Big Major's Cay.** Just north of Staniel Cay, Big Major's Cay is home to the famous swimming pigs. These guys aren't shy; as you pull up to the island they'll dive in and swim out to greet you. Don't forget to bring some scraps; Staniel Cay restaurant gives guests bags before they depart.

**Compass Cay.** Explore the many paths on the island, which is 1½ miles long and 1 mile wide, or sit on the dock and watch the sharks swim below—don't worry, they're harmless nurse sharks. There are four houses for rent on the island, all come with a 13-foot Boston Whaler. There's also a small convenience store stocked with snacks and beverages.

**Exuma Cays Land and Sea Park.** Created by the Bahamas National Trust in 1958, the 176-square-mile Exuma Cays Land and Sea Park was the first of its kind in the world—an enormous open aquarium with pristine reefs, an abundance of marine life, and sandy cays.

The park appeals to divers, who appreciate the vast underworld of limestone, reefs, drop-offs, blue holes, caves, and a multitude of exotic marine life including one of the Bahamas' most impressive stands of rare pillar coral. Since the park is protected and its waters have essentially never been fished, you can see what the ocean looked like before humanity. For landlubbers there are hiking trails and birding sites; stop in the main office for maps. More than 200 bird species have been spotted here. At Shroud Cay, jump into the strong current that creates a natural whirlpool whipping you around a rocky outcropping to a powdery beach. On top of the hill overlooking the beach is Camp Driftwood, made famous by a hermit who dug steps to the top leaving behind pieces of driftwood. ⊠ *Between Conch Cut and Wax Cay Cut* ☎ *242/225–1791 VHF Channel 9 or 16* ⊕ *www.exumapark.info*.

**Little Farmer's Cay.** If you're looking for a little civilization, stop off at Little Farmer's Cay, the first inhabited cay in the chain, about 40 minutes (18 miles) from Great Exuma. The island has a restaurant and a small grocery store where locals gather to play dominoes. But don't expect too big of a party; just 70 people live on the island. A walk up the hill will reward you with fantastic island views.

⇨ *For information on the Exuma Cays Land and Sea Park, see the feature at the front of the chapter.*

**Pipe Creek.** Boaters will want to explore the waterways known as Pipe Creek, a winding passage through the tiny islands between Staniel and Compass cays. There are great spots for shelling, snorkeling, diving, and bonefishing. The Sampson Cay Yacht Club at the creek's halfway point is a good place for lunch or dinner.

**Staniel Cay.** This is the hub of activity in the cays, and a favorite destination of yachters. That's thanks to the Staniel Cay Yacht Club, the only full-service marina in the cays. Shack up in one of the cotton candy–color cottages, some perched on stilts right in the water. The club's restaurant is the place to be for lunch, dinner, and nightlife. The

The famous swimming pigs of Big Major's Cay will be happy to meet you at your boat.

island has an airstrip, one hotel, and paved roads. Virtually everything is within walking distance. Oddly enough, as you stroll past brightly painted houses and sandy shores, you are as likely to see a satellite dish as a woman pulling a bucket of water from a roadside well. At one of three grocery stores, boat owners can replenish their supplies. The friendly village also has a small red-roof church, a post office, and a straw vendor. Staniel Cay is a great home base for visiting the Exuma Cays Land and Sea Park.

**Starfish Reserve.** Just off the mainland of Great Exuma, locals call the water surrounding the first few cays the Starfish Reserve, where tons of giant starfish dot the shallow ocean floor. As long as you don't keep them out of the water for too long, it's okay to pick them up.

**Thunderball Grotto.** Just across the water from the Staniel Cay Yacht Club is one of the Bahamas' most unforgettable attractions: Thunderball Grotto, a lovely marine cave that snorkelers (at low tide) and experienced scuba divers can explore. In the central cavern, shimmering shafts of sunlight pour through holes in the soaring ceiling and illuminate the glass-clear water. You'll see right away why this cave was chosen as an exotic setting for such movies as 007's *Thunderball* and *Never Say Never Again,* and the mermaid tale *Splash.*

## BEACHES

**Warderick Wells Cay.** Next to the park headquarters in Exuma Cays Land and Sea Park is a lovely white beach, but you won't be looking at the sand when you first arrive. The beach is dominated by the stunningly huge skeleton of a sperm whale that died in 1995 because it consumed plastic. The skeleton was fortified in its natural form and makes an emotion-packed statue that no artist could duplicate. Equally striking is the gorgeous blue shades of water and the glistening white sand. Check out the snorkel trail in the park when you've soaked in enough sun.

## WHERE TO EAT

$ AMERICAN 🍴 **Sampson Cay Yacht Club.** A favorite of boaters passing through the cays, this restaurant has American classics like burgers and fish sandwiches for lunch. Save room for dessert—pineapple upside-down cake, coconut cake, and chocolate cake. Lunch is served from noon to 3. [$] *Average main: $18* ✉ *Sampson Cay, Exuma Cays* ☎ *242/355–2034, 877/633–0305* 🌐 *www.sampsoncayclub.com* 🕒 *Closed Sun. No dinner.*

$$$ BAHAMIAN 🍴 **Staniel Cay Yacht Club.** Hand-painted tablecloths cover the tables in the screened-in dining room that serves Bahamian specialties such as cracked conch, fresh grouper, snapper, and grilled lobster with homemade bread. Many of the vegetables come from the restaurant's garden. Don't miss the key lime pie for dessert. A dinner bell rings when dinner is ready and diners move from the bar to the dining room. You must place your dinner order by 5 pm. Three meals are served daily. [$] *Average main: $30* ✉ *Staniel Cay, Exuma Cays* ☎ *242/355–2024* 🌐 *www.stanielcay.com.*

## WHERE TO STAY

$$$$ RENTAL 🏨 **Compass Cay.** Four spacious houses on the island, which is 1½ miles long and 1 mile wide, are so far apart and separated by lush palm and hardwood hammocks that you feel you have the island to yourself. **Pros:** remote tranquillity; boat included. **Cons:** expensive to get to. [$] *Rooms from: $650* ✉ *Compass Cay, Exuma Cays* ☎ *207/667–0618* 🌐 *www.compasscay.com* 🛏 *4 houses* 🍽 *No meals.*

$ RENTAL ALL-INCLUSIVE Fodor's Choice ★ 🏨 **Staniel Cay Yacht Club.** The club once drew such luminaries as Malcolm Forbes and Robert Mitchum. **Pros:** simple cottages that give an authentic Bahamian experience; great restaurant. **Cons:** expensive to get to if you don't have your own boat or plane. [$] *Rooms from: $165* ✉ *Staniel Cay, Exuma Cays* ☎ *242/355–2024, 954/467–6658* 🌐 *www.stanielcay.com* 🛏 *12 cottages* 🍽 *All-inclusive.*

## NIGHTLIFE

**Staniel Cay Yacht Club.** Staniel Cay Yacht Club has a relatively busy bar, hopping with yachters from all over the world. ☎ *242/355–2024.*

Staniel Cay Yacht Club is justifiably famous among fishermen.

## SPORTS AND THE OUTDOORS

### BICYCLING

Staniel Cay Yacht Club rents beach cruisers if you want to pedal around the island.

### BOATING AND FISHING

**Staniel Cay Yacht Club.** Rent a 13-foot Whaler and arrange for a fishing guide at Staniel Cay Yacht Club, a prime destination for serious bone fishers. But regular excursions can also be arranged for any resort guest. ✉ *Staniel Cay, Exuma Cays* ☎ *242/355–2024* ⊕ *www.stanielcay.com.*

### GUIDED TOURS

**BOAT TOURS**

**Charter World.** This company offers a variety of yacht charters. ☎ *954/603–7830* ⊕ *www.charterworld.com.*

**Exuma Cays Adventures.** This company offers several tour options, including a trip through the Exuma Cays, a snorkeling excursion to Long Island, and tours of Elizabeth Harbour in a glass bottom boat. ☎ *242/357–0390* ⊕ *www.exumacaysadventures.com.*

**Exuma Water Sports.** Come here for guided Jet Ski tours through the Exuma Cays, as well as a scenic boat cruise that includes snorkeling at Thunderball Grotto. ☎ *242/357–0770, 242/357–0100* ⊕ *www.exumawatersports.com.*

**Four C's Adventures.** Various private and group charters are available through Four C's Adventures, including snorkeling, fishing, and sightseeing tours. ☎ *242/464–1720* ⊕ *www.exumawatertours.com.*

## ISLAND TOURS

**Exuma Travel and Transportation Limited.** This company provides bus tours of Great Exuma and Little Exuma and can accommodate large parties. ☎ *242/345–0234.*

**Kendal "Dr. K" Nixon.** Dr. K gives tours of Great Exuma and Little Exuma by car, for up to six passengers. ☎ *242/422–7399.*

**Luther Rolle.** Luther's 4-hour guided tour of the island by car is fully customizable and can be split between days to best suit your vacation schedule. ☎ *242/357–0662.*

## SCUBA DIVING AND SNORKELING

**Exuma Cays Land and Sea Park** and **Thunderball Grotto** are excellent snorkeling and dive sites.

**Staniel Cay Divers.** Operating out of the Staniel Cay Yacht Club, the resort's dive operation has a boat and offers full dive courses as well as Snuba. There is a 38-foot custom dive boat. You can also come here to rent masks and fins for snorkeling. Dive trips can be arranged for as few as two divers, but rates are expensive ($180 for a two-tank dive, but snorkelers can ride along for $35 per person). Complete dive and stay packages can be arranged through Staniel Cay resort. ✉ *Staniel Cay Yacht Club, Staniel Cay, Exuma Cays* ☎ *242/225–9668* ⊕ *www.stanielcaydivers.com.*

**Minns Water Sports** ☎ *242/336–3483, 242/336–2604* ⊕ *www.mwsboats.com.*

# THE SOUTHERN
# OUT ISLANDS

# WELCOME TO THE SOUTHERN OUT ISLANDS

## TOP REASONS TO GO

★ **Stage a disappearing act:** Discover your inner castaway on islands way off the trampled tourist track. Pink or white sand, calm azure coves, or rolling ocean waves—you'll have your pick.

★ **Tell your own tall fishing tale:** Whether deep-sea fishing past the Wall off southern Inagua or bonefishing in the crystal clear shallows on Cat Island's east coast, your fish-capades will be ones to remember.

★ **Explore historic lighthouses:** Surrounded by treacherous shoals and reefs, the southern Out Islands have the country's most famous 19th-century lighthouses, most of which you can climb for stunning views.

★ **Set sail:** Sailing regattas are huge here at the gateway to the Caribbean. It's thrilling to watch the first boats come into view and race across the horizon in full sail, and the regatta site parties are fun and lively.

**1 Cat Island.** Stunning pink and white beaches, the highest hilltop in the country (the 206-foot Mt. Alvernia), 200-year-old deserted stone cottages, and a cuisine all its own (spicy grits and crab, anyone?) attract loyal visitors. More than a half dozen small resorts offer low-key luxury for those who want an Out Island experience with creature comforts.

**2 San Salvador.** Located on one of the largest reefs in the world, the tiny island's crystal clear waters are a scuba diver's dream. The beach at Club Med is gorgeous, with soft white sand and blinding turquoise water.

**3 Long Island.** Ringed with stunning natural beaches that reach out into the Bahamas Banks and dip easterly into the deep Atlantic, this island is off the beaten path, yet an adequate infrastructure allows visitors to travel from one end of the island to the other. It boasts a rich history, the world's deepest blue hole, and is populated by friendly, accommodating people.

**4 Crooked and Acklins islands.** These islands make great outposts for the self-sufficient adventurer. Fishing and more fishing are

the reasons to come here, except when you take the day off to dive and snorkel. The Wall, a famed dive site about 50 yards off Crooked Island's coast, drops from 45 feet to thousands.

Arthur's Town

Cat Island 1

New Bight
Mt. Alvernia
Port Howe

Exuma Sound

Conception Cay

Stella Maris

Great Exuma Island

Deadman's Cay

Ragged Island Range

## GETTING ORIENTED

The southernmost Bahamas islands are remote, exposed to the open Atlantic, and ruggedly dramatic. One hundred thirty miles southeast of Nassau, Cat Island lies to the west of diminutive San Salvador, about the size of Manhattan. Long Island, which is indeed long, stretches 80 miles across the Tropic of Cancer, due south of Cat Island. Windswept Crooked and Acklins islands, each with about 400 residents, are southeast of Long Island. And way down at the southernmost point of the country is Inagua, only 55 miles northeast of Cuba and 60 miles north of Haiti.

*San Salvador*

Cockburn
Town

2

Rum Cay
Port Nelson

*Atlantic*

**Long Island**
3
Clarence
Town

Samana
Cay

*Crooked Island Passage*

**Crooked
Island** Colonel Hill

*O c e a n*

Long Cay
4
Richmond

Guana Cay

Spring Point

Plana
Cay

*Mayaguana Passage*

Mayaguana
Island

**Acklins
Island**

**5 Inagua.** The biggest attraction here is undoubtedly the island's 70,000 flamingos. The first sighting is a thrilling shock to the senses; some birds stand as tall as 5 feet. Flocks, ranging in size from a half dozen to hundreds, live all over the island, but the highest concentration are at the salt ponds and in the park. Anglers come to fish with famed fishing guide Ezzard Cartwright, and to dive in search of the Spanish galleons that sank off the coast.

Little
Inagua Island

**Great Inagua
Island**
5

Lake
Windsor

Matthew
Town

0                    30 mi

0                    30 km

8

# INAGUA NATIONAL PARK

Nothing quite prepares you for your first glimpse of the West Indian flamingos that nest in Inagua National Park: brilliant crimson-pink, up to 5 feet tall, with black-tipped wings. A dozen flamingos suddenly fly across a pond, intermixed with fantastic pink roseate spoonbills.

It's a moving experience, and yet because of the island's remote location, only about 50 people witnessed it in 2009. In 1952, Inagua's flamingos dwindled to about 5,000. The gorgeous birds were hunted for their meat, especially the tongue, and for their feathers. The government established the 287-square-mile park in 1963, and today 70,000 flamingos nest on the island, the world's largest breeding colony of West Indian flamingos. The birds like the many salt ponds on Inagua that supply their favorite meal—brine shrimp.

You must contact the **Bahamas National Trust**'s office (☎ *242/393–1317* ⊕ *www.bnt.bs*) or **Warden Henry Nixon** (☎ *242/225–0977*) to make reservations for your visit. All visits to the park are by special arrangement. ⊠ *10 miles west of Matthew Town.*

**BEST TIME TO GO**
Flamingos are on the island year-round, but for the greatest concentration, visit during nesting season, from the end of February through June. Early morning and late afternoon are the best times to come. If you visit right after their hatching, the flocks of fuzzy, gray baby flamingos—they can't fly until they're older—are entertaining.

## BEST WAYS TO EXPLORE

**With a Guide.** Warden Henry Nixon leads all tours into the park and to Union Creek Reserve. He'll drive you by small flocks of flamingos in the salt ponds and answer questions. Nixon is difficult to reach by phone, but your best chance is in the early evening.

**By Kayak.** You can't kayak in the park's salt ponds because they're too shallow, but you can in Lake Windsor, also called Lake Rosa, a huge inland lake. Its eastern half is in the park. Because of badly washed-out dirt roads, a truck is necessary to reach the lake.

**On Foot.** The best way to see flamingos up close is by parking the car and walking, or sitting quietly for a while in a thicket of mangroves. Flamingos are skittish and easily spooked. Although the ponds and mangroves look a lot like the Florida Everglades, there are no alligators or poisonous snakes here. Make sure you have insect repellent on before you take off; the mosquitoes are brutal.

## FLAMINGO FACTS

Flamingos are the country's national bird, and they're protected from hunters by law.

Female flamingos lay one egg a year, and both parents take turns sitting on it for 28 days. Both parents also produce milk in the crop at the base of the neck for the chick, for three months. The par-

ents' feathers turn white while they feed the chick because they lose carotene.

Flamingos are monogamous and usually mate for life, but are extremely social birds that like to live in groups.

Their "knees," which seem to bend backward, are actually ankles (the knees are tucked under their feathers). What looks like the leg is actually the foot extending from the ankle.

Standing on one leg is the most comfortable position for a flamingo.

Brine shrimp, the flamingo's main source of food is what gives the mature bird its brilliant deep pink.

**8**

# RAKE 'N' SCRAPE

There's something about Rake 'n' Scrape music that makes you want to dance. The contagious, unique cadence accompanied by the "chink-chink," "kalik-kalik," "scratch-scratch" sound created by the unique instruments, made mostly from recycled objects, brings on a particularly strong urge to get up and shake it.

Most closely linked in sound, rhythm, and composition to zydeco music out of New Orleans, Rake 'n' Scrape is folk music at its best. It's unclear just where Rake 'n' Scrape originated, but most believe it has roots in Africa, made the voyage to the Bahamas with slaves, and was adapted over the years. Today's Rake 'n' Scrape was cultivated on remote Cat Island. Lacking money for and access to modern things, the resourceful locals made use of whatever supplies were available. Years later, many of these musicians could have their pick of shiny, finely tuned instruments, but they stick with what they know makes beautiful music.

**HAVE A LISTEN**

International recording artist and Cat Island native **Tony McKay**, who went by the stage name Exuma, incorporated Rake 'n' Scrape into his music. He paid homage to the style with the song "Goin' to Cat Island."

**George Symonette**'s "Don't Touch Me Tomato" gained infamy in a recent television commercial for Cable Bahamas. Symonette is associated with Goombay, a music style popular in Nassau in the 1950s. Goombay soon died out, giving way to closely related Rake 'n' Scrape.

Comprised of six Harbour Island natives, **the Brilanders** have toured with Jimmy Buffet. Their hit song "Backyard Party" is a sound-track standard at just about any Bahamian party.

## INSTRUMENTS

An authentic Rake 'n' Scrape band uses recycled objects to make music. An ordinary saw held in a musician's lap, then bent and scraped, becomes an instrument. A piece of wood, some fishing line, and a tin washtub is a good stand-in for the brass section. Plastic juice bottles are filled with pigeon peas, painted in bright colors, and turned into maracas. Add a goatskin drum, and you have all you need for a Rake 'n' Scrape ensemble, although many bands now add a concertina, guitar, or saxophone.

## MAJOR PLAYERS

Authentic Rake 'n' Scrape is a dying art. The handful of groups scattered throughout the Bahamas are comprised of older men, as younger Bahamians prefer more modern sounds. Today **Ophie and the Websites**, **The Brilanders**, **Thomas Cartwright**, and Bo Hogg are among the few groups still performing old style Rake 'n' Scrape. Other modern Bahamian musicians, such as **K.B.**, **Phil Stubbs**, and **Ronnie Butler** work the sound and rhythm into their own signature styles.

The popular 4-day **Rake 'N' Scrape Festival** each June on Cat Island hosts dozens of bands from all over the Bahamas and the Caribbean.

On Harbour Island, **Gusty's** and **Vic-Hum Club** usually work at least one night of Rake 'n' Scrape into the weekly live music schedule. **The Brilanders** often play at **Seagrapes**.

## DANCE LIKE A LOCAL

The Rake 'n' Scrape rhythm is so captivating that even the most rhythmically challenged will be hard-pressed to stand still. As the first beats are played, look around and see what the old folk do. It's not unusual to see a man stick his leg out (whether he's sitting or standing), lift his pants leg a bit, and let his footwork get fancy.

At festivals, schoolchildren usually dance the quadrille or heel-toe polka. If you ask a Bahamian to show you how to "mash de roach" or dance "the conch style," they may jump up and put on a show.

Updated by
Jamie Werner

Wild and windswept, the southern Bahamian islands are idyllic Edens for those adventurers who want to battle a tarpon, dive a "wall" that drops thousands of feet, photograph the world's largest group of West Indian flamingos, or just sprawl on a sun-splashed beach with no sign of life—except maybe for a Bahama parrot pelting seeds from a guinep tree.

The quiet, simpler way of life on the southern Out Islands is startlingly different from Nassau's fast-paced glitz and glamour, and even more secluded than the northern Out Islands. You won't find huge resorts, casinos, or fast-food restaurants here, not to mention stoplights. Instead, you'll be rewarded with a serene vacation that will make your blood pressure drop faster than a fisherman's hook and sinker.

# PLANNING

## WHEN TO GO

Few visitors make it to these southern islands, but those who do come at different times. Europeans tend to arrive in summer and stay for a month or longer. Sailors come through on their way to the Caribbean in fall and return to the Bahamas in spring on trips back to the United States. Fishermen arrive all year and divers like the calm seas in summer. Those looking for a winter warm-up visit from December to April, when temperatures are in the 70s. These months have the lowest rainfall of the year, but the ocean is chilly and rough for divers and boaters. Christmas and New Year's are usually booked, so reserve rooms months in advance.

Many inns and resorts are closed September and October for hurricane season, which technically runs from June through November. Mosquito repellent is usually needed year-round, but is imperative in summer and fall, especially after a period of rain when both mosquitoes and no-see-ums come out in full force. Note that they remain in the sand on your feet and towels even after you leave the beach, so make sure to rinse or leave your towel outside your room.

The southern islands are generally warmer than Nassau, but you may need a windbreaker in winter, particularly on a boat. If possible, time your visit for Junkanoo, sailing regattas, and special events such as the Cat Island's Rake 'N' Scrape Festival.

## TOP FESTIVALS

### WINTER

**Junkanoo.** Inagua puts on a spirited Junkanoo parade on Boxing Day, December 26, and New Year's Day. Parades start at 4:30 am; you have to make the decision to stay up all night or get up early. There's food at the Fish Fry at Kiwanis Park in the center of town, where the parades end.

### SUMMER

**Long Island Sailing Regatta.** The annual Long Island Sailing Regatta, featuring Bahamian-made boats, is a three-day event the first weekend of June. Held in Salt Pond, the regatta is the island's biggest event, attracting contestants from all over the islands. Booths featuring handmade crafts and Bahamian food and drink dot the site and local bands provide lively entertainment beginning at sundown. Salt Pond is 10 miles south of Simms.

**Cat Island Rake 'N' Scrape Festival.** The Cat Island Rake 'N' Scrape Festival in June celebrates the Bahamas' indigenous Rake 'n' Scrape music, and includes food, crafts, and entertainment.

**Cat Island Regatta.** The annual Cat Island Regatta in August has parties, live music, games, dancing, and lots of island cooking.

### FALL

**Discovery Day Festival.** San Salvador's annual Discovery Day Festival in October celebrates Christopher Columbus's discovery of the Americas (the island is his reputed landing place). The festival is held at Graham's Harbour at the small settlement of United States. There are live music, games, food, church services, and a sloop regatta sail.

## GETTING HERE AND AROUND

### AIR TRAVEL

All of the southern out island have at least one airport, and several have multiple airports. Flights are primarily on charters on local carriers, but there also a handful of flights on major carriers out of Florida (primarily Fort Lauderdale or Miami). *See individual island sections for more details.*

### BOAT AND FERRY TRAVEL

Mail boats link all of these islands to Nassau, but there are also a handful of ferries. See individual island sections for more details, but you can also check schedules by calling the dockmaster's office in Nassau.

**Contacts Mailboat Port/Dockmaster's Office in Nassau** ⊠ *New Providence Island* ☏ *242/393–1064.*

### CAR AND TAXI TRAVEL

You cant rent a car on all the islands. Taxi service is also available. Regardless, transportation tends to be expensive because of the isolation and cost of fuel.

## ESSENTIALS

### BANKS

Banks are generally open half days (9–2) Monday through Thursday and 9–5 on Fridays. There are no banks on Crooked and Acklins islands.

### EMERGENCIES

Contacts **Acklins Island Police** ☎ 242/344–3126 Salina Point, 242/344–3666 Spring Point. **Cat Island Police** ☎ 242/354–2046 Arthur's Town, 242/342–3039 New Bight. **Inagua Police** ☎ 242/339–1444. **Long Island Police** ☎ 242/337–3919 Clarence Town, 242/337–0999 Deadman's Cay, 242/338–8555 Simms, 242/338–2222 Stella Maris. **San Salvador Police** ☎ 242/331–2010.

### HOTELS

The inns in the southern Out Islands are small and intimate, and usually cater to a specific crowd such as anglers, divers, or those who just want a quiet beach experience. Club Med–Columbus Isle, an upscale resort on San Salvador, is the exception, with 236 rooms and a wide range of activities.

Most inns are on the beach, and many have one- and two-bedroom cottages with private verandahs. Most inns offer three meals a day for their guests, kayaks, and bikes, and will pick you up at the airport, arrange car rentals, fishing guides, and dive trips. Off-season rates usually begin in May, with some of the best deals available in October, November, and early December. Club Med–Columbus Isle offers early-bird booking bonuses and runs pricing promotions year-round.

### RESTAURANTS

Out Island restaurants are often family-run and focus on home-style dishes. You'll probably eat most of your meals at your hotel, since there aren't many other places. If you want to dine at a restaurant or another inn, it's crucial to call ahead. Dinner choices largely depend on what the fishermen and mail boats bring in; be prepared for few choices.

Don't expect gourmet food, but do anticipate fresh fish, lobster, conch, fresh-baked bread, and coconut tarts. Don't miss "flour cakes," another Cat Island specialty, which taste similar to large vanilla wafers (visit Alnor's Bakery and Lennora will warm them up for you). A good bet for Friday or Saturday nights is an outdoor fish fry at a colorful beach shack, such as Regatta Beach on Cat Island or Kiwanis Park on Inagua.

### HOTEL AND RESTAURANT PRICES

*Restaurant prices are based on the median main course price at dinner, excluding gratuity, typically 15%, which is often automatically added to the bill. Hotel prices are for two people in a standard double room in high season, excluding service and 6%–12% tax.*

## VISITOR INFORMATION

**Contacts The Out Islands of The Bahamas** ⊕ *www.myoutislands.com.*
**The Bahamas Ministry of Tourism** ☎ *242/302–2000* ⊕ *www.bahamas.com.*

Sportsmen are drawn to the southern islands to outsmart the swift bonefish, and fish for marlin, black and bluefin tuna, wahoo, and swordfish. Yachties roam these islands on their way to the Caribbean, and vacationers rent Hobie Cats and kayaks. Divers and snorkelers come to see healthy reefs and abundant underwater wildlife. Romantics and honeymooners head south for the glorious sunsets viewed from the verandahs of beachside cottages, and for the lovely pink beaches. Bird-watchers arrive with binoculars in hand to see the green and red Bahama parrots, the Bahama woodstar hummingbirds, Bahama pintails, tricolored and crested night herons, and, of course, flamingos.

The friendliness of residents is well known, but visitors are often taken aback by their instant inclusion in the community. You can't walk 100 feet without someone offering a welcome ride on a hot day. Ask an islander where a certain restaurant is and they will walk with you until you see it. Express any disappointment such as not seeing a flamingo up close, and the person standing behind you at the store will get on their cell phone. (There's a big flock now at the Town Pond!) The scenery is gorgeous, but this genuine rapport is what brings regulars back time and again to these tiny communities.

# CAT ISLAND

You'll be purring on Cat Island's exquisite pink-sand beaches and sparkling white-sand-ringed coves, as calm and clear as a spa pool. Largely undeveloped, Cat Island has the tallest hill in the Bahamas, a dizzying 206 feet high, with a tiny stone abbey on top, a lovely spot for meditation or a picnic. The two-lane Queen's Highway runs the 48-mile length of the island from north to south along a gorgeous sandy coastline, through adorable seaside settlements and past hundreds of abandoned stone cottages; some are 200-year-old slave houses, crumbling testaments to cotton and sisal plantation days. Trees and vines twist through spaces that used to be windows and roofs and the deep-blue ocean can be seen through missing walls. In 1938 the island had 5,000 residents and today only about 1,500. Many of the inhabitants left the cottages long ago out of necessity, to find work in Nassau and Florida, but the houses remain because they still mark family land.

Cat Island was named after a frequent visitor, the notorious pirate Arthur Catt, a contemporary of Edward "Blackbeard" Teach. Another famous islander is Sir Sidney Poitier, who grew up here before leaving to become an Academy Award–winning movie actor and director.

## GETTING HERE AND AROUND
### AIR TRAVEL
Cat Island has two airports: Arthur's Town (ATC) in the north and the Bight (TBI) mid-island. Cat Island Air flies daily to the Bight from Nassau and is the best and cheapest service to the southern part of the island. Southern Air flies from Nassau to Arthur's Town and is the best

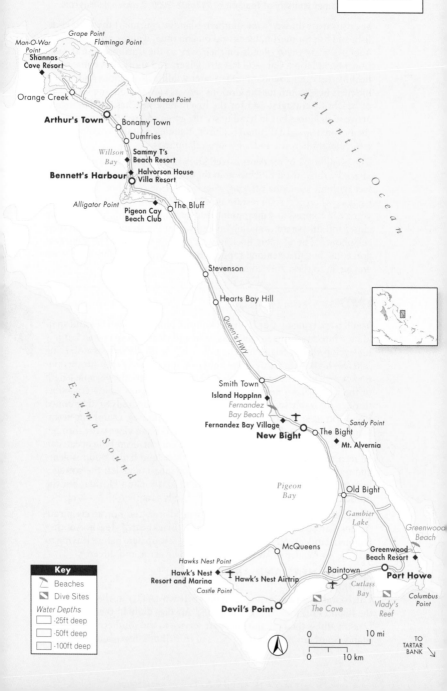

# Cat Island

Atlantic Ocean

Exuma Sound

*Man-O-War Point*
*Grape Point*
*Flamingo Point*

**Shannas Cove Resort**

Orange Creek

*Northeast Point*

**Arthur's Town**

Bonamy Town

Dumfries

*Willson Bay*

Sammy T's Beach Resort

**Bennett's Harbour**

Halvorson House Villa Resort

*Alligator Point*

Pigeon Cay Beach Club

The Bluff

Stevenson

Hearts Bay Hill

Queen's HWY

Smith Town

Island HoppInn

*Fernandez Bay Beach*

**Fernandez Bay Village**

**New Bight**

The Bight

*Sandy Point*

Mt. Alvernia

*Pigeon Bay*

Old Bight

*Gambier Lake*

*Greenwood Beach*

McQueens

Greenwood Beach Resort

*Hawks Nest Point*

**Hawk's Nest Resort and Marina**

Hawk's Nest Airtrip

Baintown

**Port Howe**

*Castle Point*

*Cutlass Bay*

*Columbus Point*

**Devil's Point**

The Cave

Vlady's Reef

## Key

- Beaches
- Dive Sites

*Water Depths*
- -25ft deep
- -50ft deep
- -100ft deep

0          10 mi

0          10 km

TO TARTAR BANK

service for the northern portion of the island. Sky Bahamas Air also flies from Nassau to both the Bight and Arthur's Town. Florida Coastal Air flies into the Bight from Fort Lauderdale. If you are going to Fernandez Bay Village, Island HoppInn, Greenwood Beach Resort, or Hawk's Nest Resort, fly into the Bight. If you are going to Pigeon Cay Halvorson House, or Shanna's Cove, fly to Arthur's Town.

**Contacts Arthur's Town Airport** ☎ *242/354–2036.*
**The Bight Airport** ☎ *242/342–2016.*

### BOAT TRAVEL

Mail boats that bring supplies to the island each week make an adventurous mode of transportation. You'll ride with groceries, large and small appliances, automobiles, and sometimes even livestock. All boats depart from Potter's Cay in Nassau. Schedules change frequently. The *East Wind* leaves Tuesday for Smith Bay and Old and New Bight, returning Thursday (10 hours; $60 one-way).

**Contacts Mailboat Port/Dockmaster's Office in Nassau** ⊠ *New Providence Island* ☎ *242/393–1064.*

### CAR TRAVEL

The New Bight Service Station and Gilbert's New Bight Market rent cars on the southern end of Cat Island and will pick you up from the Bight airport. Robon Enterprises rents cars for the north (for those flying into Arthur's Town). All inns and resorts can arrange rental cars for you upon arrival. Rates depend on the number of days you're renting, but $80 per day plus gas, is the average.

The best way to enjoy the overall Cat Island experience is to rent a car, at least for one day, and do some exploring on your own. You'll need one if you want to check out various settlements, as they're not within walking distance. The two-lane, potholed Queen's Highway runs the 48-mile length of the island from north to south. You can also tour the island with a guide from Cat Island Experience.

**Contacts Gilbert's Car Rentals and Market.** From this little convenience store, Ms. Nora Gilbert rents cars for pick up/return on the southern end of Cat Island only. She also sells cold drinks, dry goods, snacks, and toiletries—it's a good stop if you forgot to bring bug spray. ⊠ *Across from Gilbert's Inn, New Bight, Cat Island* ☎ *242/342–3011.* **New Bight Service Station.** Cars rented from New Bight Service station cost $95/day, plus gas, which is more or less the going rate on the island. These rental cars are available for pick up/return on the southern end of the island only. ⊠ *New Bight, Cat Island* ☎ *242/342–3014.*

**Robon Enterprises Car Rental.** Situated on the north end of Cat Island, this is the place to rent a car if you fly into Arthur's Town. ⊠ *Arthur's Town, Cat Island* ☎ *242/354–6120, 242/359–9725.*

### TAXI TRAVEL

Taxis wait for incoming flights at the Bight and Arthur's Town airports, but be warned that fares can be expensive, starting at about $20 for the 10-minute trip from the Bight Airport to the community of New Bight. Most inns and resorts will make arrangements for airport transfers, often complimentary.

## ARTHUR'S TOWN AND BENNETT'S HARBOUR

Arthur's Town's claim to fame is that it was the boyhood home of actor Sidney Poitier, who wrote about growing up here in his autobiography. His parents and relatives were farmers. The village has a BaTelCo station, a few stores, and Pat Rolle's **Cookie House Bakery** (☎ *242/354–2027*)—an island institution that serves lunch and dinner by the order, so call ahead. Or just stop by to say hello, as Pat is a wealth of island knowledge and more than happy to bend your ear.

When you drive south from Arthur's Town, which is nearly at the island's northernmost tip, you'll wind along a road that passes through small villages and past bays where fishing boats are tied up. Fifteen miles south of Arthur's Town is Bennett's Harbour, one of the island's oldest settlements. Fresh-baked breads and fruit are sometimes sold at makeshift stands at the government dock, and there is good bonefishing in the creek.

### WHERE TO EAT

$ BAHAMIAN

🍴 **Da Smoke Pot.** Cold beer, Bahama Mama rum drinks, conch anyway you want it, and live Rake 'n' Scrape music—Da Smoke Pot is an authentic Bahamian experience, named for the old local tradition of lighting green brush in the evening to keep the bugs at bay. Julian and the band will even let you take a turn playing on the saw with a screwdriver, while they sing and play along with you. You can't help but leave with a smile on your face. [$] *Average main: $12* ✉ *Arthur's Town, Cat Island* ☎ *242/354–2094* ✍ *Reservations essential* 💳 *No credit cards.*

$$ EUROPEAN Fodor's Choice ★

🍴 **Shannas Cove Restaurant.** This resort restaurant boasts a beautiful towering view above the sea and the rest of the island. The lunch menu features large fresh salads and homemade 12-inch pizzas. At dinner, choose from a selection of fresh vegetable soups and an array of international dishes including rack of lamb, pork tenderloin, steaks, and grilled fish. Unlike other restaurants, this kitchen is open all day. [$] *Average main: $35* ✉ *Shannas Cove, North of Orange Creek, Cat Island* ☎ *242/354–4250* 🌐 *www.shannas-cove.com* 🕓 *Closed Sept.*

$$ BAHAMIAN

🍴 **Sammy T's Restaurant and Bar.** Before sitting down to dinner on the wooden deck outside, grab a drink and take a stroll down the boardwalk bridge to the beach—a great place to see the sunset. The outside deck also has a pool table and darts for added entertainment. The setting far outweighs the food, but each meal is served with a warm and friendly smile. Breakfast includes omelets and fresh fruits. For lunch the salads are fresh and served with Sammy T's secret dressing, and the burgers are big and tasty. The evening menu includes fish, shrimp, lobster, or conch prepared anyway you want it, with traditional Bahamaian sides like peas 'n' rice, fried plantains, and coleslaw. Call ahead because the restaurant closes if business is slow. The bar stays open after dinner as demand indicates. [$] *Average main: $32* ✉ *Sammy T's Beach Resort, Bennett's Harbour, Cat Island* ☎ *242/354–6009* ✍ *Reservations essential* 🕓 *Closed Sept.*

$ JAMAICAN

🍴 **Yardie's Restaurant, Bar & Conch Stand.** Yardie's serves up genuine Jamaican and Bahamian dishes like Jerk chicken, steamed pork chops, curry mutton, barbecue ribs, and fresh conch salad. If you really want an island meal, try the breakfast grits with tuna or corned beef. A fun fact

The Hermitage on Mt. Alvernia in Cat Island's most iconic sight.

for the kids is that Yardie's is the only stop on the island for ice cream. This place is no frills, but a great shady spot to stop for lunch, a snack, or just a cold drink and a game of dominoes. $ *Average main: $12* ✉ *Bennet's Harbor, Cat Island* ☎ *242/354–6076.*

## WHERE TO STAY

$$ · RESORT · FAMILY · **Halvorson House Villa Resort.** Opened in January 2012, this family-run resort has a warm and friendly B&B feel, with four chic yet eco-friendly beach cottages, a second-level club house with a spacious dining room and wraparound balcony, and a lower level recreation room called the "kids club," full of arts and crafts, books, and movies to keep young ones occupied while parents relax and unwind. **Pros:** kid-friendly; long stretch of private beach; complimentary shuttle to Arthur's Town Airport. **Cons:** limited Internet access; areas on property still under construction. $ *Rooms from: $129* ✉ *Bennett's Harbour, Cat Island* ☎ *242/359–9500, 242/354–6003* ⊕ *www.halvorsonhouse.com* ⤳ *4 Cottages* ⦿*No meals.*

$ · RESORT · **Pigeon Cay Beach Club.** In a wide bay a half mile off the main road just south of Alligator Point, this family-owned-and-operated resort has 10 deluxe cottages that are colorfully decorated and perched steps away from a secluded 3-mile stretch of pristine sugary white beach. **Pros:** fully equipped kitchens in rooms; Wi-Fi; bicycles, kayaks, and snorkel gear available; cars available for a small fee. **Cons:** no TV; surcharge for airport transfers; meals are served only a few times a week, so plan to cook for yourself; don't forget your insect repellent. $ *Rooms from: $140* ✉ *Rokers, 3 miles south of Bennetts Harbor, Cat Island* ☎ *242/354–5084* ⊕ *www.pigeoncaybahamas.com* ⤳ *10 cottages* ⦿*No meals.*

$ RESORT **Sammy T's Beach Resort.** Tucked away in a small cove on a dream beach, this tranquil, friendly resort has seven one- and two-bedroom villas. **Pros:** private beach is great for sunsets; staff will arrange daily fishing/snorkeling excursions and rental cars. **Cons:** villas are not on the beach; facilities and villas are worn; pool has been filled in with a rock garden. [$] *Rooms from: $160* ✉ *Bennett's Harbour, Cat Island* ☎ *242/354–6009* 🌐 *www.catislandbeachresort.com* 🛏 *7 villas* 🕒 *Closed Sept.* 🍴 *No meals.*

$$ RESORT **Shannas Cove Resort.** Opened in 2009, this quiet and secluded owner-run beach resort is perched high on the hill on the northern tip of Cat Island, granting sweeping views of the beautiful beach at Shannas Cove and the rest of the island. **Pros:** expansive beach; excellent onsite restaurant; roomy cottages; a real Out Island experience. **Cons:** no TVs; isolated from the rest of the island; rooms are not on the beach; no children under 18. [$] *Rooms from: $180* ✉ *North of Orange Creek, Cat Island* ☎ *242/354–4249* 🌐 *www.shannas-cove.com* 🛏 *5 villas* 🕒 *Closed Sept.*

## SPORTS AND THE OUTDOORS

### SCUBA DIVING

Coral Reefs teeming with fish and mysterious shipwrecks, make great diving off the north end of the island, where visibility ranges from 165 to 200 feet thanks to a natural filtering system of limestone and rich fauna.

**Diving with Shannas Cove Resort.** This is not a licensed dive shop, but the owners of Shannas Cove are master divers and will organize exclusive diving tours upon request—for beginners and experienced divers alike. They also offer individual reef diving, steep face diving, and more from their 22-foot Catamaran. Diving spots can be reached within 5 to 30 minutues. Well-maintained equipment is available for rent. ✉ *Shanna's Cove Resort, north of Orange Creek, Cat Island* ☎ *242/354–4249, 242/359–9668* 🌐 *www.shannas-cove.com* 🕒 *Closed Sept.*

### TOURS

**Cat Island Experience.** Get the inside scoop on Cat Island with native islander Danny King. He can show you everything North to South, stopping to tour caves, introduce you to locals, shop for handmade straw goods, view historical churches and plantation ruins, taste fresh conch salad, and even scrape salt from the lagoons if the season is right. And he does it all with a warm smile, lots of patience, and a free T-shirt for you. ✉ *New Bight, Cat Island* ☎ *242/464–6193, 242/225–6210, 242/342–3104.*

## NEW BIGHT

Yachts large and small anchor off the coast of Regatta Beach, and boaters dingy in to the Custom House, located in a small collection of government buildings, in this pretty little community, the largest town on the island. Houses face the Queen's Highway, which twists through green hills. Yachties and visitors stock up at the small grocery store and a bakery. The island's most iconic sight is **Mt. Alvernia**, which is crowned with a little abbey. There's also a colorful **Fish Fry**, a collection of fish shacks on Regatta Beach that's a lively hangout on weekends, lovely old churches, and eerie abandoned stone cottages many of which are plantation ruins. The town sits along the calm white beaches of the west coast and has peaceful saltwater estuaries that are nesting areas for great blue herons, egrets, and pelicans.

### EXPLORING

Fodor's Choice ★ **The Hermitage.** At the top of 206-foot Mt. Alvernia, the highest point in The Bahamas, The Hermitage is the final resting place of Father Jerome. Born John Hawes, he was an architect who traveled the world and eventually settled in the Bahamas. An Anglican who converted to Roman Catholicism, he built two churches, St. Paul's and St. Peter's, in Clarence Town, Long Island, as well as the St. Augustine Monastery in Nassau. He retired to Cat Island to live out his last dozen years as a hermit, and his final, supreme act of religious dedication was to carve the steps up to the top of Mt. Alvernia. Along the way, he also carved the Stations of the Cross. At the summit, he built an abbey with a small chapel, a conical bell tower, and living quarters comprising three closet-size rooms. He died in 1956 at the age of 80 and was supposedly buried with his arms outstretched, in a pose resembling that of the crucified Christ.

The pilgrimage to the Hermitage begins next to the commissioner's office at New Bight, at a dirt path that leads to the foot of Mt. Alvernia. Don't miss the slightly laborious climb to the top. The Hermitage provides a perfect place to pause for quiet contemplation. It also has glorious views of the ocean on both sides of the island. A caretaker clears the weeds around the tomb—which islanders regard as a shrine—and lights a candle in Father Jerome's memory. ⊠ *New Bight, Cat Island.*

### BEACHES

**Fernandez Bay Beach.** Imagine the perfect calm cove in the tropics—a 1-mile stretch of glistening, pristine white sand, inviting shade under coconut palms and sea grape trees, quaint resort cottages and verandahs facing the spectacular sand, and calm azure water. Two resorts (Fernandez Bay Village and Island HoppInn) have restaurants and bars built on decks overlooking the water and they each rent kayaks and paddleboards to guests. The beach is often deserted, so dinner for two might really mean just that. **Amenities:** food and drink; water sports. **Best for:** solitude; snorkeling; sunset; swimming; walking. ⊠ *Just north of New Bight Airport, Cat Island.*

---

**ISLAND SPECIALTIES**

Cat Island is known for its tasty dishes, most notably spicy grits and crab cakes, and grits and peas, both cooked with tomatoes, onions, lima beans, and okra, depending on the cook's preferences. The island's distinctive coarse yellow grits, made from guinea corn, was originally brought from Africa. Many visitors take a bag with them when they leave the island. Island cooks are also known for their "flour cakes," similar in taste to vanilla wafers.

Tiki Bar is the place to hang out at Fernandez Bay Village resort.

## WHERE TO EAT

**$$$$**
BAHAMIAN
FAMILY

✕ **Fernandez Bay Village Restaurant.** Buffet meals are served in the Clubhouse at Fernandez Bay Village, and outside on the beach terrace. The breakfast buffet is loaded; you can pile on sweet rolls, croissants, bacon, sausage, grits, pancakes, and fruit. Grilled cheese, tuna, turkey, and ham sandwiches, conch chowder, and conch burgers are just a sampling of lunch options. The sumptuous dinner buffet can include lobster in white sauce, grouper almandine, pork loin, filet mignon, and a grilled catch of the day along with scalloped potatoes, salads, and fresh baked breads. Stay for an after-dinner drink from the honor bar where you can play the ring toss game and socialize with other guests, or enjoy the nightly bonfire on the beach. They also have a kids' menu, but call ahead so children's meals can be served in time with the buffet. ⓢ *Average main: $48* ✉ *Fernandez Bay Village, 1 mile west of New Bight airport, New Bight, Cat Island* ☎ *242/342–3043, 954/474–4821, 800/940–1905* ⊕ *www.fernandezbayvillage.com* ⌛ *Reservations essential* ⊙ *Closed mid-Aug.–Oct.*

**$$$**
BAHAMIAN
FAMILY

✕ **Island HoppInn Tiki Bar and Restaurant.** This authentic, island-style, open-air restaurant and bar is right on the beach, just steps away from the tranquil lapping waters of Fernandez Bay. The 24-seat patio has a barbecue grill for cooking up fresh fish of the day, shrimp, lobster, steaks, and ribs. Owner–chef Cathy Perdok is renowned for her conch chowder, fish and vegetable stews, fresh-baked breads, and killer desserts. She will also cater to food allergies and vegetarian and vegan diets. Guests staying at the inn, which has a bed-and-breakfast casualness, mix in by cooking their own dinners at times. The service is good and very personal, the crowd (when there is one) a lot of fun, and the tropical rum drinks are a mellowing delight. $ *Average main: $30* ✉ *Island HoppInn, Fernandez Bay, New Bight, Cat Island* ☎ *234/542–4657, 216/337–8800, 740/777–4477* ⊕ *www.islandhoppinn.com* ✍ *Reservations essential.*

### WHERE TO STAY

**$$**
RESORT
Fodor's Choice
★

🏨 **Fernandez Bay Village.** This owner-run resort is one of the best kick-back retreats in the islands, boasting rustic but charming villas and cottages that are spread along a dazzling, horseshoe-shaped white-sand beach shaded by casuarina pines and coconut palms. **Pros:** a "wow" beachfront location; private spacious accommodations; friendly accommodating staff; main clubhouse has shelves of books and board games to borrow. **Cons:** no TV; Wi-Fi in the main clubhouse only; insect repellent needed for outside dining in the evening. $ *Rooms from: $280* ✉ *1 mile north of the Bight airport, New Bight, Cat Island* ☎ *242/342–3043, 800/940–1905* ⊕ *www.fernandezbayvillage.com* ✍ *6 villas, 9 cottages.*

**$$**
B&B/INN
FAMILY

🏨 **Island HoppInn.** This B&B-like resort has four suites, each with a private porch perched ocean-side overlooking magical Fernandez Bay. **Pros:** small private resort on the perfect white-sand beach; kid friendly; the crowd (when there is one) is fun and full of laughs. **Cons:** don't forget your insect repellent for evenings outside. $ *Rooms from: $250* ✉ *Fernandez Bay, New Bight, Cat Island* ☎ *242/342–2100, 216/337–8800* ⊕ *www.islandhoppinn.com* ✍ *4 suites.*

### NIGHTLIFE

**Regatta Beach Fish Fry.** For an authentic Bahamian experience, don't miss the Regatta Beach Fish Fry on Regatta Beach, just south of the government buildings in the town center. The half dozen fish shacks open late in the afternoon and stay lively on into the night. Duke's Deck offers the best conch salad on the island and you can watch him make it from start to finish, including cracking the conch from the shell. Cedell's gathers a regular crowd for her food. On weekends, Rake 'n' Scrape music performed by famed Bo Hog and the Rooters usually gets started around 8 pm. It's a great place for sunset watching and mingling with locals. ✉ *New Bight, Cat Island.*

### SHOPPING

**Pam's Boutique.** This little shop at Fernandez Bay Village has reasonably priced resort wear including sarongs, Haviana flip-flops, logo hats, and T-shirts. They also sell jewelry, bags, coffee cups, post cards, local art, and books. This is one of your few chances to get a Cat Island T-shirt. ✉ *Fernandez Bay Village, Cat Island* ☎ *242/342–3043, 800/940–1905, 954/474–4821.*

8

Fernandez Bay Beach is a perfect, calm cove for swimming.

### SPORTS AND THE OUTDOORS
#### FISHING

**Mark Keasler.** A resident fishing guide, Mark Keasler offers deep-sea fishing and bonefishing off the coast of New Bight, in addition to eco-tours through Pigeon Creek. Book trips through Fernandez Bay Village. ✉ *Fernandez Bay Village, Cat Island* ☎ *242/342–3043, 800/940–1905, 954/474–4821* ⊕ *www.fernandezbayvillage.com/fishing.html.*

## PORT HOWE

At the conch shell–lined traffic roundabout at the southernmost end of the Queen's Highway, you must turn either east or west; head east out toward Port Howe, believed by many to be Cat Island's oldest settlement. Nearby lie the ruins of the **Deveaux Mansion,** a stark two-story, whitewashed building overrun with vegetation and pretty much unexplorable. Once it was a grand house on a cotton plantation, owned by Captain Andrew Deveaux of the British Navy, who was given thousands of acres of Cat Island property as a reward for his daring raid that recaptured Nassau from the Spaniards in 1783. Just beyond the mansion ruin is the entrance road to the Greenwood Beach Resort, which sits on an 8-mile stretch of unblemished, velvet pink-sand beach.

**Greenwood Beach.** An 8-mile stretch of pink sand on the Atlantic Ocean makes this one of the most spectacular beaches on Cat Island. Hypnotized by the beauty, most visitors walk the entire beach, some even farther to an adjoining sandy cove accessible only by foot. After such a long walk, a dip in the shallows of the turquoise ocean is pure bliss. The beach is on the remote southeastern end of the island and is home to just one hotel, Greenwood Beach Resort, which has loungers, umbrellas, and water sports equipment for rent. **Amenities:** food and drink; water sports. **Best for:** solitude; snorkeling; swimming; walking. ✉ *Greenwood Beach Resort, just north of Port Howe, Cat Island* ⊕ *www.greenwoodbeachresort.com.*

### WHERE TO STAY

$ 　🏨 **Greenwood Beach Resort.** Set on an 8-mile stretch of pink shell-strewn
HOTEL 　sand, this remote resort is about 35 minutes from the Bight airport, but the peaceful solitude is what brings regulars back. **Pros:** private Atlantic beach location; swimming pool; continual ocean breeze keeps the bugs at bay. **Cons:** long drive to explore other parts of island; must reserve air-conditioned rooms in advance; rooms are dated; property is somewhat run-down. $ *Rooms from: $110* ✉ *Ocean Dr. off Queen's Hwy., Port Howe, Cat Island* ☏ *242/342–3053* ⊕ *www.greenwoodbeachresort.com* ↝ *16 rooms* ⦿*No meals.*

---

## DEVIL'S POINT

The small village of Devil's Point, with its pastel-color, thatch-roof houses, lies about 10 miles west of the Queen's Highway. Beach-combers will find great shelling on the pristine beach; keep an eye out for dolphins, which are common in these waters. From Devil's Point, drive north through the arid southwest corner of the island to **McQueens,** then west to the area's biggest resort, Hawk's Nest Resort, which has an airstrip, marina restaurant and bar. This resort is well known to serious anglers and divers, who often fly in to the resort's private airstrip and stay a week doing little else. The southwest end of the island also has good diving spots teeming with an abundance of marine life and coral heads.

### WHERE TO EAT

$$ 　✕ **Hawk's Nest Resort Restaurant and Bar.** High-beamed ceilings, tiled
BAHAMIAN 　floors, blue-and-lime-green walls, and blue ceramic-topped tables create a cheerful vibe to go with the Bahamian comfort-food menu. Start your day with fresh juices and a full breakfast. For lunch and dinner, there are burgers and Bahamian specialties such as cracked conch, lobster and fish, or the touted conch tacos. You can eat on the terrace by the pool or inside with ocean views. The bar runs on the honor system and the 60-inch TV can catch you up on news, sports, and everything else you're happy to miss while lounging in paradise. $ *Average main: $30* ✉ *Hawk's Nest Resort and Marina, turn right when Queen's Hwy. ends, Devil's Point, Cat Island* ☏ *242/342–7050, 954/376–3865* ⊕ *www.hawks-nest.com* ⬦ *Reservations essential* ⊙ *Closed mid-Sept.–Oct.*

### WHERE TO STAY

$ 　🏨 **Hawk's Nest Resort and Marina.** Catering to private pilots, yachters,
RESORT 　and serious fishermen, this small laid-back resort at Cat Island's southwestern tip has its own 3,100-foot runway and a 28-slip full-service marina with a dive shop. **Pros:** on-site restaurant serves three meals a

day; fully stocked honor bar; only PADI licensed diving on the island. **Cons:** if you want to explore the rest of Cat Island, it's a long drive; the beach is rocky and not good for swimming or strolling. $ *Rooms from: $165* ✉ *Turn right when Queen's Hwy. ends, Devil's Point, Cat Island* ☎ *242/342–7050, 954/376–3865* ⊕ *www.hawks-nest.com* ↩ *10 rooms* ⊙ *Clubhouse and hotel closed Sept.–Oct.* ¶ *Breakfast.*

### SPORTS AND THE OUTDOORS

#### FISHING

**Hawk's Nest Marina.** Blue-water angling boat owners make a point of using Hawk's Nest Marina to access the dynamite offshore fishing. Look for wahoo, yellowfin tuna, dolphin, and white and blue marlin along the Exuma Sound drop-offs, Devil's Point, Tartar Bank, and Columbus Point. March through July is prime time with multiple annual fishing tournaments on the books. Winter fishing, December through February, is also good for wahoo. You can arrange bonefishing through the marina with top guide Nathaniel Gilbert; just call him Top Cat. ✉ *Hawk's Nest Resort and Marina, Devil's Point, Cat Island* ☎ *242/342–7050, 954/376–3865* ⊕ *www.hawks-nest.com.*

#### SCUBA DIVING

**Hawk's Nest Marina Dive Shop.** Hawk's Nest has the only PADI certified diving on Cat Island and conducts guided diving adventures, rents diving and snorkeling gear, and has equipment and sundries for sale. The running time to dive sites off the southern tip of the island is 15 to 30 minutes in the shop's 43-foot custom dive boat, outfitted with VHF and GPS. Call ahead for bookings. ☎ *242/342–7050, 954/376–3865* ⊕ *www.hawks-nest.com.*

# SAN SALVADOR

On October 12, 1492, Christopher Columbus disrupted the lives of the peaceful Lucayan Indians when he landed on the island of Guanahani, which he renamed San Salvador. Apparently he knelt on the beach and claimed the land for Spain. (Skeptics of this story point to a study published in a 1986 *National Geographic* article in which Samana Cay, 60 miles southeast, is identified as the exact point of the weary explorer's landing.) Three monuments on the island commemorate Columbus's arrival, and the 500th anniversary of the event was officially celebrated here.

The island is 12 miles long—roughly the length of Manhattan—and about 5 miles wide, with a lake-filled interior. Some of the most dazzling deserted beaches in the country are here, and most visitors come for the peaceful isolation and the diving; there are about 1,200 residents and more than 50 dive sites. There's also world-renowned offshore fishing and good bonefishing.

### GETTING HERE AND AROUND

#### AIR TRAVEL

The island has one airport, in Cockburn Town (ZSA). Air Sunshine flies from Fort Lauderdale on demand. American Eagle flies from Miami on the weekends. Bahamasair flies from Nassau daily and also offers direct

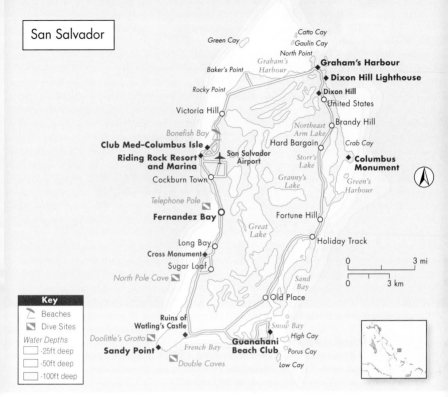

San Salvador

Green Cay
Catto Cay
Gaulin Cay
North Point
Graham's Harbour
**Graham's Harbour**
Baker's Point
**Dixon Hill Lighthouse**
Rocky Point
**Dixon Hill**
United States
Victoria Hill
Brandy Hill
Bonefish Bay
Northeast Arm Lake
**Club Med–Columbus Isle**
Hard Bargain
Crab Cay
**Riding Rock Resort and Marina**
San Salvador Airport
Storr's Lake
**Columbus Monument**
Cockburn Town
Granny's Lake
Green's Harbour
Telephone Pole
Fortune Hill
**Fernandez Bay**
Great Lake
Long Bay
Holiday Track
Cross Monument
Sugar Loaf
North Pole Cave
Sand Bay
Old Place
**Key**

2 Beaches
Dive Sites
*Water Depths*
-25ft deep
-50ft deep
-100ft deep

Ruins of Watling's Castle
Snow Bay
High Cay
Doolittle's Grotto
French Bay
**Guanahani Beach Club**
Porus Cay
**Sandy Point**
Double Caves
Low Cay

0 — 3 mi
0 — 3 km

service from Miami three days a week, though this is subject to change. Spirit Airlines flies from Fort Lauderdale on Saturday only. Club Med has packages that include air charters. Riding Rock Resort and Marina can arrange charters.

**Contacts San Salvador Cockburn Town Airport** ☎ 242/331–2131.

## BOAT TRAVEL

Mail boats that bring supplies to the island each week make an adventurous mode of transportation. You'll ride with groceries, large and small appliances, automobiles, and sometimes even livestock. All boats depart from Potter's Cay in Nassau. Schedules change frequently. M/V *Lady Francis* leaves Tuesday for San Salvador and Rum Cay, returning Friday (12 hours; $60 one-way).

**Contacts Mailboat Port/Dockmaster's Office in Nassau** ✉ *New Providence Island* ☎ 242/393–1064.

## BIKE TRAVEL

For a short visit to Columbus Cross or the lighthouse, a bike is a sufficient mode of transportation. Bike rentals are available at Club Med and Riding Rock Resort.

San Salvador has several popular diving sites.

### CAR TRAVEL

If you want to see the entire island, rent a car. Queen's Highway forms an oval that skirts the island's coastline, and road conditions are excellent. Car rentals are about $85 a day.

Contacts **D & W Car Rental** ⊠ *Cockburn Town, San Salvador Island* ☎ *242/331–2484, 242/331–2488.* **Riding Rock Resort and Marina** In addition to cars, Riding Rock Resort rents bicycles, minivans, and golf carts. ☎ *800/272–1492, 242/331–2631.*

### SCOOTER TRAVEL

Scooters are a convenient way to get around the entire island.

Contacts **K's Scooter Rentals.** Kate & Keith of K's Scooter Rentals rent 50cc, fully automatic, two-seater scooters hourly, daily, or weekly. Credit cards accepted, valid driver's license required. ⊠ *Cockburn Town Airport, San Salvador Island* ☎ *242/331–2125, 242/331–2651, 242/225–7392* ⊘ *Mon.–Sat. 9–7.*

### TAXI TRAVEL

Club Med meets all guests at the airport. Riding Rock, five minutes away, provides complimentary transportation for guests. If you want to take your own taxi, it's approximately $10 to either resort.

Contacts **Clifford Fernander** ☎ *242/331–2676, 242/427–8198.* **Nat Walker** ☎ *242/331–2111.*

## TOURS

**Fernander Tours.** In addition to being a taxi driver and island tour guide extraordinaire, Mr. Clifford Fernander is also The Bahamas Ministry of Tourism's representative for San Salvador Island, and is full of information for the inquisitive tourist. ✉ *San Salvador Island* ☎ *242/331–2676, 242/427–8198.*

FAMILY **Lagoon Tours.** Cruise through secluded Pigeon Creek in a flat-bottom boat that maxes at five people to view baby sharks, sea turtles, and starfish, and top off the trip shell hunting on High Cay. Lagoon Tours caters to all interests from nature walks and historical tours to bird-watching and excursions through the quiet waters of the lagoons. This family-run company is very proud of San Salvador island and they are happy to show you their favorite off-the-beaten-path spots, with a smile and a cooler full of refreshments. ✉ *San Salvador* ☎ *242/452–0101, 242/452–0506* ⊕ *www.lagoon-tours-bahamas.com.*

**Nat Walker's Island Adventures.** As the island's Warden for the Bahamas National Trust, Nat Walker has a unique understanding of the island's nature and history, and he will customize island tours to include visits to monuments, private beach picnics, native restaurants, shopping, and the like. ✉ *San Salvador Island* ☎ *242/331–2111, 242/464–9038.*

# FERNANDEZ BAY TO RIDING ROCK POINT

In 1492 the inspiring sight that greeted Christopher Columbus by moonlight at 2 am was a terrain of gleaming beaches and far-reaching forest. The peripatetic traveler and his crews—"men from Heaven," the locals called them—steered the *Niña, Pinta,* and *Santa María* warily among the coral reefs and anchored, so it's recorded, in **Fernandez Bay.** A cross erected in 1956 by Columbus scholar Ruth C. Durlacher Wolper Malvin stands at his approximate landing spot. An underwater monument marks the place where the *Santa María* anchored. Nearby, another monument commemorates the Olympic flame's passage on its journey from Greece to Mexico City in 1968.

Fernandez Bay is just south of what is now the main community of **Cockburn Town,** midisland on the western shore. This is where the airport is, and where the weekly mail boat docks. This small village's narrow streets contain two churches, a commissioner's office, a police station, a courthouse, a library, a clinic, a drugstore, and a telephone station.

From Cockburn Town to Club Med you'll pass **Riding Rock Point.** All fish excursions leave from the marina. Riding Rock Resort makes a good spot to stop for a drink, meet locals and divers, and buy a local T-shirt.

## BEACHES

**Bonefish Bay.** The 3-mile beach in front of Club Med has bright white sand as fine as talcum powder, and water that is such a bright neon shade of turquoise it seems to glow. It might possibly be the most gorgeous water you ever lay eyes on. There are activities, such as water-skiing, snorkeling, sailing, kayaking, and paddleboarding in front of Club Med, but the beach is long enough that you'll be able to find an isolated spot. **Amenities:** food and drink; showers; toilets; water sports. **Best for:** partiers; snorkeling; swimming; windsurfing. ✉ *Club Med, San Salvador Island.*

## WHERE TO EAT

$$$$ 🍴 **Christopher's at Club Med.** The dinner buffet at Christopher's changes themes nightly, so even after a week it doesn't get boring. Caribbean Night has local fare, such as conch and fresh fish, and other themes include Mexican and Mediterranean. Carving stations and European pastries and breads are impossible to skip, and simple pastas and pizzas are mainstays for the finicky eater. Don't forget the chocolate chip bread—so good you'll order some loaves to bring back with you. If you're not staying at Club Med, a dinner pass will cost you $60 and is good from 7:30 pm to 1 am, including an open bar and the night's scheduled entertainment. All-you-can-eat breakfast passes are $20 and good from 8 to 10 am; lunch passes are $35, 12:30 to 2:15 pm. [$] *Average main: $60* ✉ *Club Med, 3 miles north of Riding Rock Point, San Salvador Island* ☎ *242/331–2000* 🌐 *www.clubmed.com* ✍ *Reservations essential.*

$$ ITALIAN 🍴 **Guanahani Beach Club Restaurant.** At this resort restaurant, fresh fruit smoothies, panini on crusty French bread, fresh salads, and various authentic Italian dinners, based on fresh seasonal ingredients, are all made to order by owner-chef Elena Sparta. The outside patio is beautiful and overlooks Snow Bay; inside, you'll find an all-white contemporary dining room and bar complete with couches and coffee tables for lounging. [$] *Average main: $25* ✉ *Snow Bay, Sunrise Rd., San Salvador Island* ☎ *242/452–0438* 🌐 *www.guanahanibeachclub.com* ✍ *Reservations essential* 💳 *No credit cards.*

$ BAHAMIAN 🍴 **Paradis Restaurant and Bar.** A typical Bahamian restaurant, Paradis has a daily changing menu written on a chalkboard. Home-cooked food such as conch, ribs, and the fresh catch of the day are simply prepared. The restaurant is popular with both locals and visitors and offers complimentary Wi-Fi. [$] *Average main: $16* ✉ *Island Plaza, 3 miles from Cockburn Town, across the street from the airport, San Salvador Island* ☎ *242/331–2400* 🕒 *Daily 8 am–10 pm.*

$$ CARIBBEAN 🍴 **Riding Rock Seafront Restaurant.** Eat inside this 60-seat restaurant, take a table on the patio by the pool, or sit on the back patio overlooking the ocean. Androsia-print tablecloths add a colorful tropical flair. Fruit, fresh-baked breads, pancakes, and eggs any style with bacon and grits are a good way to start the day. Burgers, sandwiches, conch chowder, and cracked conch are lunch favorites. The just-off-the-boat catch of the day—wahoo, mahimahi, tuna, grouper, snapper—grilled with lemon and butter, or baked with tomatoes and spices, is the dinner specialty. Broiled or stuffed lobster (in season), barbecue shrimp, steaks, and chicken round out the choices, though all are not available each evening as the menu changes based on availability. During slower seasons or depending on resort guests, the restaurant is not always open, and each meal is set between certain hours—make sure to call ahead. [$] *Average main: $25* ✉ *Riding Rock Resort and Marina, San Salvador Island* ☎ *242/331–2631, 954/453–5031* 🌐 *www.ridingrock.com* ✍ *Reservations essential.*

$$$$ SEAFOOD 🍴 **Watling's at Club Med.** Watling's, the seafood restaurant at Club Med, offers table service and is open for late lunches and dinner on certain days each week; reservations must be made a day ahead. If you're not

staying at Club Med, a dinner pass will cost you $60 and is good from 7:30 pm to 1 am, including an open bar and the night's scheduled entertainment. [$] *Average main: $60* ✉ *Club Med–Columbus Isle, 3 miles north of Riding Rock Point, San Salvador Island* ☎ *242/331–2000* 🌐 *www.clubmed.com* ✍ *Reservations essential.*

## WHERE TO STAY

$$$$ ALL-INCLUSIVE FAMILY **Club Med–Columbus Isle.** This 89-acre oceanfront village is one of Club Med's most luxurious resorts, with state-of-the-art dive facilities and every water sport and activity imaginable. **Pros:** gorgeous beachfront location; revolving dinner themes; full service dive shop. **Cons:** no children under two; outlying rooms require a lot of walking; fee for in-room Wi-Fi. [$] *Rooms from: $500* ✉ *3 miles north of Riding Rock Point, San Salvador Island* ☎ *888/932–2582, 242/331–2000* 🌐 *www.clubmed.com* 🛏 *236 rooms* 🍴 *All-inclusive.*

$$$ RESORT Fodor's Choice ★ **Guanahani Beach Club.** Opened in 2011, this cozy, owner-operated resort is elegant and sophisticated, offering both quiet solitude on a stunning private beach and serious adventure for sports enthusiasts. **Pros:** excellent on-site restaurant; simple and chic villas; private beach adorned with loungers and hammocks. **Cons:** no children under 16; credit cards not accepted; far from other island amenities so you will probably want a rental car. [$] *Rooms from: $325* ✉ *Snow Bay, Sunrise Rd., San Salvador Island* ☎ *242/452–0438* 🌐 *www.guanahanibeachclub.com* 🛏 *3 villas* 💳 *No credit cards* 🍴 *Some meals.*

$ B&B/INN **Riding Rock Resort and Marina.** Good for serious divers, this modest motel-style resort is a long-standing property on San Salvador and has a restaurant on-site serving breakfast, lunch, and dinner. **Pros:** budget-friendly alternative to other resorts; friendly accommodating staff; rooms are standard but clean. **Cons:** food and fuel supplies can run low at times; boats are not always available during slow season; diving is not daily and dependent on resort guests; small, rocky beachfront. [$] *Rooms from: $150* ✉ *Cockburn Town, San Salvador Island* ☎ *800/272–1492, 242/331–2631* 🌐 *www.ridingrock.com* 🛏 *30 rooms* 🍴 *All meals.*

## NIGHTLIFE

**Club Med – Columbus Isle.** Evening passes to Club Med cost $60 and include themed dinners, nightly entertainment, and all you can drink from 7:30 pm to 1 am. ✉ *Club Med, San Salvador Island* ☎ *888/932–2582, 242/331–2000.*

**The Driftwood Bar at Riding Rock Resort.** Driftwood decorated with messages, stickers, and accolades from regular visitors covers the walls and hangs from the ceilings of this little bar, giving it real character. Fishermen and scuba divers from all over the world gather frequently to tell tall tales, making it a favorite evening hangout. Try your luck at the ring toss game, catch up on sports from home on the big-screen TV, or grab a cold Kalik or frozen piña colada (touted as the best on the island) and enjoy the sunset on the open-air back patio overlooking the sea. ✉ *Riding Rock Resort, San Salvador Island* ☎ *242/331–2631, 800/272–1492, 954/453–5031* 🌐 *www.ridingrock.com* 🕒 *Daily 4 pm–11 pm.*

8

## SHOPPING

**Club Med – Columbus Isle.** Club Med has a small boutique with souvenirs, Roxy brand clothes, Havaiana flip-flops, swimsuits, and sunglasses, along with Club Med apparel. ⊠ *Club Med, San Salvador Island* ☎ *242/331–2000* ⊘ *Daily 9 am–8 pm.*

**Simply Bahamiam.** A small local crafts and liquor store across the street from the airport sells locally made purses and sarongs featuring Andros batik. ⊠ *Cockburn Town, San Salvador Island.*

## SPORTS AND THE OUTDOORS

### KITE SAILING AND OTHER WATER SPORTS

**Club Med – Columbus Isle.** If you are not a guest at Club Med, you can buy a day pass for $50 which gives you access to water sports (including daily guided snorkeling trips, Hobie Cat sailing, paddleboards, kayaks, and windsurfing) and regular sports activities (including group power walks and jogging, beach volleyball, tennis, various aerobics classes, yoga, and tai chi). The day pass includes lunch and all you can drink and is good from 10:30 am to 6:30 pm. ⊠ *Club Med, San Salvador Island* ☎ *242/331–2000* ⊕ *www.clubmed.us.*

**Guanahani Surf & Sail Center.** San Salvador is one of the last "uncrowded kite surfing paradises," with ideal wind conditions and year-round warm waters. Licensed by IKO (International Kiteboarding Organization), the Guanahani Surf & Sail Center offers in-depth kiteboarding instruction for every level. Led by qualified trainers with Cabrinha kites and boards, courses last anywhere from 3 to 10 hours and are best done over the course of a few days. The flat, calm shallow waters in Snow Bay offer the perfect practice and play area. ⊠ *Snow Bay, Sunrise Rd., San Salvador Island* ☎ *242/452–0438* ⊕ *www.guanahanibeachclub.com.*

### SCUBA DIVING

San Salvador is famous for its vibrant wall dives and abundant marine life, including hammerhead sharks, sea turtles, Eagle rays, and more.

**Telephone Pole.** This is a stimulating wall dive where you can watch stingrays, grouper, snapper, and turtles in action.

Fodor'sChoice **Seafari Dive Center at Club Med Columbus Isle.** The diving operation at Club
★ Med is now run separately by Seafari International, and all dive trips and certifications (PADI and CMAS) are exclusive to Club Med guests only. If you are not staying at Club Med you must buy a Day Pass ($50), which is all-inclusive of meals and other resort activities, in addition to paying for any dives. This professional dive center consistently offers three dives a day, in addition to a weekly night dive, to over 35 dive sites with permanent moorings. Divers go out on one of two catamarans, 54 and 52 feet. A hyperbaric chamber is on-site, and the staff consists of 10 dive instructors and four dive masters. All necessary equipment is available for rent including underwater cameras, dive computers, and Nitrox. ⊠ *Club Med, San Salvador Island* ☎ *242/331–2000, 242/331–2195* ⊕ *www.clubmed.us.*

**Riding Rock Resort & Marina.** The dive operation here (both SSI and PADI recognized) uses mostly buoyed sites to avoid damaging the marine environment by dropping anchor. The 42- and 46-foot dive boats are spacious and comfortable. Resort and certification courses are offered, and all new computerized dive gear and camera gear are available for

Isolated French Bay is on the southern end of San Salvador.

rent. There's also a modern underwater photographic facility. Complete dive packages, including meals and accommodations, are available through Riding Rock Resort and Marina. However, dive trips are not offered daily so book well in advance. Riding Rock also rents bicycles and golf carts and can arrange half-day and full-day reef, inshore, and offshore fishing trips. The offshore waters hold tuna, blue marlin, dorado, and, in winter, wahoo. ⊠ *Riding Rock Resort & Marina, Riding Rock Point, San Salvador Island* ☎ *800/272–1492, 242/331–2631, 954/453–5031* ⊕ *www.ridingrock.com.*

## ELSEWHERE ON SAN SALVADOR

Sometimes you just don't want to stay put at the resort. San Salvador's off-the-beaten-path places require some work, but make interesting sightseeing. The Gerace Research Centre and the lighthouse are not difficult to get to, but the "other" Columbus monument requires a little more work and an adventurous spirit.

### EXPLORING

**Columbus Monuments.** Christopher Columbus has more than one monument on San Salvador Island commemorating his first landfall in the New World on October 12, 1492. The simple white cross erected in 1956 at Landfall Park in Long Bay is the easiest to find, on Queen's Highway just outside of Cockburn Town. (Also on the site is the Mexican Monument which housed the Olympic flame in 1968 on its journey from Greece to Mexico City. The flame has never been lit since, but this location is popular for weekend family picnics and local gatherings.) The older and more difficult to find is the Chicago Herald

Monument erected in 1891 to celebrate the 400th anniversary of the explorer's landing. No roads lead to this monument—a sphere hewn from native limestone—so you'll have to trek through East Beach on Crab Cay by foot, which is fun for the more adventurous. ⊠ *Queen's Hwy., Cockburn Town, San Salvador Island*.

**Dixon Hill Lighthouse.** A couple of miles south of Graham's Harbour stands Dixon Hill Lighthouse. Built around 1856, it's the last hand-operated lighthouse in The Bahamas. The lighthouse keeper must wind the apparatus that projects the light, which beams out to sea

> ### HISTORIC LIGHTHOUSES
>
> Since the 19th century, sailors' lives have depended on the lighthouse beacons that rotate over the southern islands and the treacherous reefs that surround them. But for landlubbers, these lighthouses also offer bird's-eye vantage points. Visit the 115-foot Bird Rock Lighthouse on Crooked Island, the Castle Island Lighthouse on Acklins Island, the Inagua Lighthouse, and San Salvador's Dixon Hill Lighthouse.

every 15 seconds to a maximum distance of 19 miles, depending on visibility. A climb to the top of the 160-foot landmark provides a fabulous view of the island, which includes a series of inland lakes. The keeper is present 24 hours a day. Knock on his door, and he'll take you up to the top and explain the machinery. Drop $1 in the box when you sign the guest book on the way out.

**Graham's Harbour and Gerace Research Centre.** Columbus describes Graham's Harbour in his diaries as large enough "to hold all the ships of Christendom." A former U.S. Naval Base near the harbor houses the Gerace Research Centre, previously known as the Bahamian Field Station. The GRC is a center for academic research in archaeology, biology, geology, and marine sciences, backed by The College of the Bahamas and affiliated with many U.S. universities. It provides accommodations, meals, and air transportation arrangements for students and researchers from all over the world who come to study in this unique environment. ⊠ *San Salvador Island* ⊕ *www.geraceresearchcentre.com*.

**Sandy Point.** Sandy Point anchors the island's southwestern end, overlooking French Bay. Here, on a hill, you'll find the ruins of Watling's Castle, named after the 17th-century pirate. The ruins are more likely the remains of a Loyalist plantation house than a castle from buccaneering days. A 5- to 10-minute walk from Queen's Highway will take you to see what's left of the ruins, which are now engulfed in vegetation. ⊠ *San Salvador Island*.

## SPORTS AND THE OUTDOORS
### SCUBA DIVING
*For more information about these and other sites, contact the Riding Rock Resort & Marina or Seafari at Club Med.*

**Doolittle's Grotto.** This is a popular site featuring a sandy slope down to 140 feet. There are lots of tunnels and crevices for exploring, and usually a large school of horse-eye jacks to keep you company.

**Double Caves.** As the name implies, Double Caves has two parallel caves leading out to a wall at 115 feet. There's typically quite a lot of fish activity along the top of the wall.

**North Pole Cave.** North Pole Cave has a wall that drops sharply from 40 feet to more than 150 feet. Coral growth is extensive, and you might see a hammerhead or two.

# LONG ISLAND

Long Island lives up to its name—80 gorgeous miles are available for you to explore. The Queen's Highway traverses its length, through the Tropic of Cancer and many diverse settlements and farming communities. The island is 4 miles at its widest, so at hilly vantage points you can view both the white cliffs and the raging Atlantic on the east side, and the gentle surf coming to you like a shy child on the Caribbean side. It is truly spectacular.

Long Island was the third island discovered by Christopher Columbus, and a monument to him stands on the north end. Loyalist families came to the island in support of the crown, and to this day there are crown properties all over the island, deeded by the king of England. Fleeing the Revolution, their attempt at re-creating life in America was short-lived. The soil and lack of rainfall did not support their crops, cotton being their mainstay. Today you can see wild cotton growing in patches up and down the island, along with the ruins of the plantations.

Fishing and tourism support the 3,000 residents of Long Island. Farms growing bananas, mangoes, papaya, and limes also dot the landscape. Boatbuilding is a natural art here, and in the south you can always see a boat in progress as you travel the Queen's Highway.

Progress has come to the island slowly. There is now high-speed Internet and cell-phone service, but shops and modern forms of entertainment are still limited. People who come to Long Island don't seem to mind; they're here for the beauty, tranquillity, and the friendly people. Deep-sea fishing and diving are readily available, and bonefishing flats attract sport fishermen from all over the world. The beaches provide breathtaking views, shelling, exploring, and magnificent pieces of sea glass. The laid-back lifestyle is reminiscent of a slower gentler time.

## GETTING HERE AND AROUND
### AIR TRAVEL
Long Island has two airports: Deadman's Cay (LGI) in the south and Stella Maris Airport (SML) in the north. Bahamas Air and Southern Air airlines provide daily service from Nassau to Stella Maris and Deadman's Cay airports. There are also charter services from Nassau, Fort Lauderdale, and the Exumas.

Guests staying at Cape Santa Maria or Stella Maris Resort should fly into Stella Maris airport. Chez Pierre Bahamas' guests can fly into either airport, although the Stella Maris airport is a bit closer. All others should fly into Deadman's Cay airport. Flying into the wrong airport will cost you not only an hour's drive, but also $100 or more in taxi fare. Listen carefully to the arrival announcement when you approach Long Island; most commercial airlines stop at both airports.

Contacts **Deadman's Cay Airport** ☎ *242/337–1777.*
**Stella Maris Airport** ☎ *242/338–2006.*

### BOAT TRAVEL

Mail boats that bring supplies to the island each week make an adventurous mode of transportation. You'll ride with groceries, large and small appliances, automobiles, and sometimes even livestock. All boats depart from Potter's Cay in Nassau. Schedules change frequently. M/V *Mia Dean* leaves Tuesday for Clarence Town and returns Thursday (18 hours; $60 one-way). The *Island Link*, a fast boat, leaves Tuesday with stops in Salt Pond, Deadman's Cay, and Seymour's, returning Thursday (eight hours; $70 one-way).

Contacts **Mailboat Port/Dockmaster's Office in Nassau** ✉ *New Providence Island* ☎ *242/393–1064.*

### CAR TRAVEL

A car is absolutely necessary to explore the island or visit any place outside your resort. The Queen's Highway curls like a ribbon from north to south, ending abruptly at the ocean in the north and at a stop sign in the south. It's narrow, with no marked center line, which makes bikes and scooters dangerous modes of transportation. The highway is easily traversed, but some off roads require four-wheel drive, such as the road to the Columbus Monument, which is treacherous. The roads to Adderley's Plantation and Chez Pierre's are rough, but passable.

Most hotels will arrange car rentals, and can have your car waiting on-site. Rentals range from $60 to $85. Some include gas; all have a limited number of vehicles.

Keep your gas tank full; although there are service stations along the highway, hours can be irregular and some take only cash. Gas stations are closed on Sunday, so if that's your departure day, be sure to fill up the night before so the tank will be full when you return the car.

Contacts **Mr. T's Car Rental** Come here for the cheapest rate on Long Island: $60/day plus gas. Three days or more is $50/day. ✉ *Deadman's Cay, Long Island* ☎ *242/337–1054, 242/357–1678.* **Omar's Rental Cars** Cars here are available for pickup/return on the north end of the island only. ✉ *Cape Santa Maria Resort, Long Island* ☎ *800/926–9704, 242/338–5273* ⊕ *www.omardaley. com.* **Williams Car Rental** ✉ *Glintons, Long Island* ☎ *242/338–5002.* **Unique Wheels Rental** In addition to cars and SUVs, this company also rents scooters, ATVs, and go-karts. Rentals are available for pickup/return on the south end of the island only. ✉ *Clarence Town, Long Island* ☎ *242/225–7720, 242/225–8630* ⊕ *www.uniquewheelsrental.net.*

### TAXI TRAVEL

Taxis meet incoming flights at both airports. From the Stella Maris airport, the fare to Stella Maris Resort is $10 per couple; to Cape Santa Maria, the fare is $30 per couple. Guests staying at Chez Pierre Bahamas pay $40 from the Stella Maris airport and $60 from Deadman's Cay. From the Deadman's Cay airport to Gems of Paradise, the fare is

$50. Ellen's Inn and Winter Haven provide free transportation from the DC airport. A full-day tour of the island by taxi would cost about $350, and a half-day tour would be about $120. However, all taxis are privately owned, so rates can be negotiated. It is generally cheaper to rent a car for the duration of your trip than it is to pay taxi fares every time you want to go somewhere.

**Contacts Jerry's Taxi Service** ⊠ *Long Island* 🕾 *242/338–8592, 242/472–8065.* **Leonard Darville** ⊠ *Long Island* 🕾 *242/472–0024.* **Omar Daley** ⊠ *Long Island* 🕾 *242/357–1043.* **Scoffield Miller** ⊠ *Long Island* 🕾 *242/338–8970.*

### TOURS

**Bahamas Discovery Quest.** Discover the beauty of Long Island in a variety of adventures on land and sea: deep sea, deep drop and reef fishing, snorkeling, sponging, crabbing for land crabs at night, sea life eco tours, hiking, beaching, shelling, and historical tours with Long Island native, Charles Knowles, who will take you off the beaten path to meet farmers and taste native dishes you wouldn't easily find on your own. These guys do it all! ⊠ *Long Island* 🕾 *242/472–2605, 242/337–6024* ⊕ *www.bahamasdiscoveryquest.com.*

**Omar's Long Island Guided Tours.** Omar is more than just a tour guide. Raised on Long Island, he's fun and friendly and full of knowledge about the land and the people, and he will cater tours to your interests—from showing you the best spots to jump into Dean's Blue Hole, to introductions to native straw and sea shell artisans. However, that's just the start of his long list of services: He's also a dive master and boat captain with Stella Maris Marina who will feed sharks and lead you through wrecks, a taxi driver who can transport you to and from the airport to your hotel, and the owner of Omar's Rental Cars if you want to explore the island on your own. ⊠ *Cape Santa Maria Resort, Long Island* 🕾 *242/338–5273, 242/357–1043, 242/357–1477, 800/926–9704* ⊕ *www.omardaley.com.*

## NORTH LONG ISLAND: CAPE SANTA MARIA TO GRAY'S

In the far north you will find two large resort communities: **Cape Santa Maria** and **Stella Maris**. Scattered between are the small settlements of **Seymour's, Glinton's,** and **Burnt Ground.** Columbus originally named the island's northern tip Cape Santa Maria after the largest of his three ships. The beach here is gorgeous, full of private homes and resort villas, and a restaurant, bar, and gift shop that are open to the public. North of the Cape Santa Maria Resort are the **Columbus Monument,** commemorating Columbus's landing on Long Island, and **Columbus Cove,** where he made landfall. Twelve miles south of the Cape, Stella Maris, which means Star of the Sea, is home to the so-named resort. The Stella Maris airport sits on the property, along with private homes, restaurants and bars, the magnificent **Love Beaches,** a full-service marina, and a tackle and gift shop; all open to the public. Just north of Stella Maris, off Queen's Highway, are the ruins of the 19th-century **Adderley's Plantation.**

8

The oceanfront deck of Cape Santa Maria Beach House Restaurant is always popular.

Traveling south about 8 miles, you'll come to **Simms**, one of Long Island's oldest settlements. The Tropic of Cancer cuts through the island close to here, dividing the subtropics from the tropics.

Farther south are the idyllic communities of **Thompson Bay** and **Salt Pond**; both providing safe harbors for those who visit by sailboat. Salt Pond, a hilly bustling settlement so named for its many salt ponds, hosts the annual Long Island Regatta. Continuing south, you will pass the settlements of **the Bight** and **Gray's** before reaching **Deadman's Cay**.

### EXPLORING

**Cape Santa Maria Beach.** Located on the leeward side of the island in the north at Cape Santa Maria Resort, the water colors here range from pale blue to aqua to shades of turquoise. The 4-mile stretch of soft white sand beckons you to stroll, build sand castles, sun worship, or wade into the calm shallow waters. In the early morning, you're likely to see a ray swimming along the shore. The resort has a beachside restaurant and lounge chairs for guests, in addition to kayak and paddleboard rentals, but there's also plenty of sand to find a secluded stretch all your own. **Amenities:** food and drink; water sports. **Best for:** solitude; snorkeling; sunset; swimming; walking. ⊠ *Cape Santa Maria Resort, Long Island.*

**Adderley's Plantation.** Just north of the Stella Maris Resort are the ruins of 19th-century Adderley's Plantation, a cotton plantation that once occupied all of Stella Maris. Clearly marked, the road is marginally passable by car. It is about a 1-mile drive and then a fairly long walk. The walking path is marked by conch shells, and leads to the cotton plantation ruins. Seven buildings are practically intact up to roof level, but it is overgrown with vegetation. For historians, it is well worth the time.

**Columbus Monument.** Two miles north of Cape Santa Maria is the Columbus Monument, commemorating Columbus's landing on Long Island. The road to the monument is off the Queen's Highway, and while the sign is often not visible, any Long Islander will gladly give you directions. The 3-mile treacherous road is too rough for vehicles without four-wheel drive, and most rental car companies won't let you drive it without an SUV, yet it is an extremely long hike. At the end of the road is a steep hill, called Columbus Point, and a climb to the summit affords a spectacular vista. This is the highest point on Long Island, and the second highest in the Bahamas. Farther north on Queen's Highway is Columbus Harbor, on Newton's Cay. Columbus made landfall in this cove, protected by limestone outcroppings. The more adventurous can follow the beach to the left, where a rough walking path leads to three other coves; each one a delight. Two coves up you will find sea glass scattered on the beach like sparkling jewels, and by climbing through limestone formations, you will discover another cove perfect for snorkeling.

## WHERE TO EAT

After a period of rain, the mosquitoes and no-see-ums come out, so bring mosquito repellant with you when dining outdoors.

$$ SEAFOOD FAMILY

🍴 **Cape Santa Maria Beach House Restaurant and Bar.** Upstairs in the Cape Santa Maria Beach House, guests enjoy sweeping vistas of the turquoise bay during the day, and bobbing boat lights in the evening along with the gentle sounds of the sea. Breakfast can be light with yogurt parfait and a seasonal fruit medley, or a splurge with banana bread French toast topped with carmelized plantains or Bahamian-style eggs Benedict. Sit under a colorful umbrella on the oceanfront deck for lunch with a burger or salad. For dinner, delight in Caribbean coconut shrimp, fresh grouper, or Bahamian lobster tail—just don't miss the chocolate drizzled rum cake! Full bar service is available in the open air, screened-in oceanfront bar and a lively happy hour takes place every evening from 5 to 7, with complimentary conch fritters. This is one of the best spots on the island to grab a drink and watch the sunset. [$] *Average main: $28* ✉ *Cape Santa Maria Beach Resort and Villas, Galliot Cay off Seymour's, Long Island* ☎ *242/338–5273, 800/926–9704* 🌐 *www.capesantamaria.com* ✍ *Reservations essential* 🕒 *Closed Sept. and Oct.*

$$ ECLECTIC Fodor's Choice ★

🍴 **Chez Pierre Bahamas.** At this airy oceanfront restaurant a few steps from the beach, Chef Pierre has spent the last 12 years creating his sumptuous cuisine. This curmudgeonly chef serves the best food on the island, hands down. Specialties include pasta dishes with shrimp and scallops, fresh fish, and pizzas that are to die for. Bahamian lobster, steaks, and chicken, along with vegetarian dishes, are also available, and the salads (big enough to share) are both fresh and beautiful. A full bar is available on the honor system and you're expected to get your own drinks, since Pierre runs the place almost single-handedly. The surly host greets you himself; make sure you are on time for your reservation or he'll be tempted not to serve you at all! But pay no mind, as the food is well worth it and there is a smile hidden deep beneath his brusque outer shell. To get here, watch for the sign on Queen's Highway

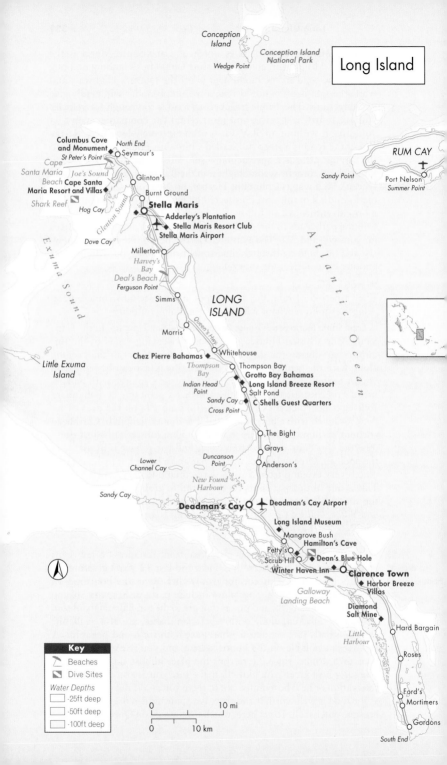

Conception
Island

Conception Island
National Park

Wedge Point

Long Island

RUM CAY

Columbus Cove
and Monument
North End
Seymour's
St Peter's Point
Cape
Santa Maria
Beach
Cape Santa
Maria Resort and Villas
Joe's Sound
Glinton's
Burnt Ground
Shark Reef
Hog Cay

Sandy Point

Port Nelson
Summer Point

Stella Maris
Adderley's Plantation
Stella Maris Resort Club
Stella Maris Airport

Glenton Sound

Dove Cay

Exuma
Sound

Millerton
Harvey's
Bay
Deal's Beach
Ferguson Point

Simms

LONG
ISLAND

Atlantic

Morris'

Queen's Hwy

Little Exuma
Island

Chez Pierre Bahamas
Whitehouse
Thompson
Bay
Indian Head
Point
Sandy Cay
Cross Point
Thompson Bay
Grotto Bay Bahamas
Long Island Breeze Resort
Salt Pond
C Shells Guest Quarters

Ocean

The Bight
Grays
Anderson's

Lower
Channel Cay

Sandy Cay

Duncanson
Point
New Found
Harbour

Deadman's Cay
Deadman's Cay Airport

Long Island Museum
Mangrove Bush
Hamilton's Cave
Petty's
Scrub Hill
Dean's Blue Hole
Winter Haven Inn
Clarence Town
Harbor Breeze
Villas
Galloway
Landing Beach

Diamond
Salt Mine
Hard Bargain

Little
Harbour

Roses

Ford's
Mortimers

Gordons
South End

**Key**

Beaches
Dive Sites
*Water Depths*
-25ft deep
-50ft deep
-100ft deep

0                    10 mi

0          10 km

between the settlements of Wemyss and Miller's. $ *Average main: $25* ⊠ *Miller's Bay, Long Island* ☎ *242/338–8809, 242/357–1374* ⊕ *www. chezpierrebahamas.com* ⌂ *Reservations essential.*

$ ✕ **Long Island Breeze Restaurant.** Overlooking the Salt Pond harbor, this
AMERICAN restaurant serves everything from native dishes to Continental cuisine, along with steaks, lamb chops, chicken, and the freshest of fish. You can dine inside or on the balcony overlooking the lovely harbor; both provide views of magnificent sunsets. The restaurant is only open for dinner, but the **Pool Patio Bar and Grill** is open Tuesday–Saturday for lunch, early dinner, and late snacks, and serves more casual fare. Full bar service is available and the evening happy hours are lively and full of regulars. Dinghy and motorboat dockage are available. $ *Average main: $20* ⊠ *Long Island Breeze Resort, Salt Pond, Long Island* ☎ *242/338–0170* ⌂ *Reservations essential* ▭ *No credit cards* ☉ *Closed July–Oct. and Sun. and Mon.*

$ ✕ **Moonshine Bar & Grill.** The views surrounding Stella Maris Resort
BAHAMIAN Club's new poolside bar are as beautiful as the frozen fresh fruit
FAMILY daiquiris they serve. Kids will be entertained on the playground or in the pool, and for a really special sight, take a walk along the winding boardwalk to the resort's "ocean lagoon," a natural pool cut into the rocks that ebbs and flows with the waves. The menu offers Bahamian and American favorites. $ *Average main: $12* ⊠ *On the beach at Stella Maris Resort Club, Stella Maris, Long Island* ⊕ *www. stellamarisresort.com.*

$$ ✕ **Stella Maris Resort Club Restaurant and Bar.** Fresh fruit and home-baked
SEAFOOD muffins highlight the breakfast buffet, or you can order a full breakfast from the menu. Lunch includes a choice of conch chowder, club sandwiches, burgers, and salads. You can have lunch in the dining room or out on the stone terrace, where you can relax under an umbrella and delight in the views of the Atlantic. For dinner, the kitchen prepares the freshest fish in a variety of ways, along with Bahamian lobster tail, a seafood platter, and cracked conch, an island favorite. Steaks, pasta, chicken, hamburgers, and vegetarian dishes are also available. Fresh fruit and ice cream make for a great hot-weather dessert. You can order from the bar menu until 9 pm or have pizza delivered to your room. $ *Average main: $25* ⊠ *Stella Maris Resort Club, Stella Maris, Long Island* ☎ *242/338–2050* ⌂ *Reservations essential* ☉ *Closed Sept.*

## WHERE TO STAY

$ ⌂ **C Shells Guest Quarters.** These quaint self-catering, full-kitchen suites
B&B/INN sit just steps away from a quiet private beach on Salt Pond, with a
FAMILY large grassy garden space perfect for family picnics, naps in the hammock, and a vacation without the hustle and bustle of a busy resort. **Pros:** centrally located; friendly, accommodating owners; Wi-Fi; affordable. **Cons:** no maid service; no on-site restaurant; rental car is essential to explore the island. $ *Rooms from: $85* ⊠ *Salt Pond, Long Island* ☎ *242/338–0103, 954/889–5075* ⊕ *www.cshellsguestquarters. com* ⤴ *4 suites.*

8

$$ RESORT FAMILY Fodor's Choice ★ **Cape Santa Maria Beach Resort and Villas.** This lovely resort consists of spacious one- or two-bedroom colonial-style cottages, each with a furnished screened porch, overlooking peaceful turquoise waters on a 4-mile gorgeous white-sand beach. **Pros:** only 15 minutes from Stella Maris Airport; friendly staff arranges dinner reservations and excursions; great swimming beach. **Cons:** isolated location means you'll need a rental car to explore. [$] *Rooms from: $235* ✉ *Galliot Cay off Seymour's, Long Island* ☎ *242/338–5273, 800/926–9704* 🌐 *www.capesantamaria.com* 🛏 *20 bungalows, 18 luxury villas* ⏲ *Closed Sept. and Oct.* 🍴 *Multiple meal plans.*

$ RESORT **Chez Pierre Bahamas.** Lining lovely Miller's Bay beach, this rustic and remote resort has six simple cabins on stilts right on the beach, making it a real "get-away-from-it-all" place (guests should be self-sufficient and adventurous). **Pros:** breezy porches are screened in and you literally wake up to the sounds of the sea; large private beach; excellent on-site restaurant serves three meals a day. **Cons:** must rent a car to explore the island; no air-conditioning; bathroom water is slightly salty. [$] *Rooms from: $155* ✉ *Miller's Bay, Long Island* ☎ *242/338–8809* 🌐 *www.chezpierrebahamas.com* 🛏 *6 cottages* 🍴 *Some meals.*

$ B&B/INN **Grotto Bay Bahamas.** In the settlement of Salt Pond is this small private hideaway, a labor of love for owners Kris and Jean who built three lovely guest rooms (with sweeping decks facing the ocean) on the lower level of their home. **Pros:** centrally located for exploring north and south; personalized service; beautiful lush landscaping. **Cons:** no in-house restaurant, bar, or meals; you need to rent a car to explore the island. [$] *Rooms from: $120* ✉ *Salt Pond, Long Island* ☎ *242/338–0011* 🌐 *www.grottobaybahamas.com* 🛏 *3 rooms* 💳 *No credit cards* 🍴 *No meals.*

$ HOTEL **Long Island Breeze Resort.** This owner-run hotel overlooking Salt Pond harbor has a variety of affordable accommodations including king and double suites and a one-bedroom apartment. **Pros:** great on-site restaurant; staff can arrange picnics, fishing, diving, snorkeling, bicycles, and car rental; free Wi-Fi. **Cons:** TVs in the rooms are for DVDs only (no reception); beach is small and not ideal for swimming or strolling. [$] *Rooms from: $125* ✉ *Salt Pond, Long Island* ☎ *242/338–0170* 🌐 *www.longislandbreezeresort.com* 🛏 *7 suites, 1 apartment* 💳 *No credit cards* ⏲ *Closed July–Oct.* 🍴 *No meals.*

$$ RESORT **Stella Maris Resort Club.** Stella Maris is more than a resort, it is a long-standing family-fun community that sits atop a hilly ridge offering many accommodation choices (including private homes), complemented by multiple pools, breathtaking views of the Atlantic, fun bars and restaurants, and activities for every interest. **Pros:** all accommodations have an ocean view or balcony; natural pool cut into the rock; great for events or big groups. **Cons:** the property is so vast that you will need a car or a bicycle to get around; room decor is dated and some in-room and property facilities are worn; on-property beach is rocky for swimming. [$] *Rooms from: $190* ✉ *Stella Maris, Long Island* ☎ *800/426–0466* 🌐 *www.stellamarisresort.com* 🛏 *16 rooms, 4 cottages, 6 houses* 🍴 *Multiple meal plans.*

Cape Santa Maria Beach Resort is the best on the island.

## NIGHTLIFE

**Long Island Breeze Resort.** This bar gathers a crowd for evening happy hours during the week. ✉ *Long Island Breeze Resort, Salt Pond, Long Island* ☎ *242/338–0170.*

**Stella Maris Resort.** This resort often has live music on the weekends, including Rake 'n' Scrape. Every Thursday night is their Rum Punch Party, which includes rum punch, conch fritters, and dinner. Cost is $55 for nonguests. Call ahead to make reservations. ✉ *Stella Maris Resort Club, Stella Maris, Long Island* ☎ *242/338–2050.*

## SHOPPING

**Bonafide Bonefishing Fly Shop.** This fly and tackle shop and souvenir boutique is located in Stella Maris on Queen's Highway. In addition to fishing gear, they sell cold drinks and snacks, and apparel and jewelry. James "Docky" Smith is the fishing guru behind Bonafide Bonefishing. A native to Long Island, he is a popular and knowledgeable bonefishing guide who "knows the flats." ✉ *Stella Maris, Queens Hwy., Long Island* ☎ *242/338–2035, 242/357–1417, 242/338–2025* ⊕ *www. bonafidebonefishing.com* ⊗ *Mon.–Sat. 9–5.*

**Cape Santa Maria Resort.** There is a small gift shop in the lobby with clothes, swimsuits, native straw works, island books, souvenirs, cold drinks, and sundries. ✉ *Cape Santa Maria Resort, Long Island* ☎ *242/ 338–5273, 800/926–9704* ⊕ *www.capesantamaria.com.*

**Harding's Supply Center.** This well-stocked shop sells food, toiletries, and supplies. ✉ *Salt Pond, Long Island* ☎ *242/338–0333.*

**Hillside Supply.** Here you can find fresh produce, dry foods, toiletries, and supplies. In the back of the store you will find just about anything, from snorkeling gear and ice chests to towels. ⊠ *Salt Pond, Long Island* ☎ *242/338–0022.*

**Tingums.** *Tingums* is Bahamian for "I don't know what to call it." This cute gift shop sells clothing, books, and toiletries. ⊠ *Stella Maris Resort Club, Stella Maris, Long Island* ☎ *242/338–2050.*

## SPORTS AND THE OUTDOORS

### DIVING AND SNORKELING

**Conception Island Wall** is an excellent wall dive, with hard and soft coral, plus interesting sponge formations. The **M/V Comberbach**, a 103-foot British freighter built in 1948, sank off Cape Santa Maria in 1984, and was scuttled by the Stella Maris Resort in 1986 to create an artificial reef and excellent dive site. Take a guided diving excursion to **Shark's Reef** and watch a scuba master safely feed dozens of sharks.

FAMILY  **Cape Santa Maria Resort.** This resort uses expert divers and guides for a myriad of diving and snorkeling trips to various reefs, walls, and wrecks around Long Island as well as trips to Conception Island; dive and snorkel equipment is available for rent. In addition, visitors can rent stand up paddleboards and Hobie Cat sail boats to explore the coast of Cape Santa Maria Beach and its surrounding bays. ⊠ *Cape Santa Maria Resort, Long Island* ☎ *242/338–5273, 800/926–9704* ⊕ *www. capesantamaria.com.*

**Stella Maris Marina & Stella Maris Water Sports.** Now under new ownership, Stella Maris Marina is the most southerly full-service marina in The Bahamas and home to the oldest dive shop, where shark dives originated. The owners (who live on-site) are reopening the original marina bar and restaurant with new handmade, painted tables, a rebuilt bar with authentic driftwood, and newly constructed walls adorned with 30 years of *National Geographic* magazines and original nautical art. As the only licensed full-dive shop on the island, they offer daily dive trips to reefs and wrecks, shark feeds, and certifications. They also offer fishing and snorkeling trips, and cater to all ages. ⊠ *Stella Maris, just south from Stella Maris Resort Club, Queen's Hwy., Long Island* ☎ *242/338–2055, 242/357–1130, 242/338–2033* ⊕ *www.stellamarismarina.com.*

### FISHING

**James "Docky" Smith's Bonafide Bonefishing.** James "Docky" Smith is highly regarded as one of the best bonefishing guides in the Bahamas. He does full- and half-day bonefishing excursions, as well as reef-fishing trips. He is also an expert fly-casting instructor. Book well in advance. His operation is based out of the Bonafide tackle shop in Stella Maris, which rents conventional and fly-fishing gear, prepares snacks and box lunches, and sells a range of tackle, clothing, and flies. ⊠ *Stella Maris, Long Island* ☎ *242/338–2025, 242/357–1417* ⊕ *www. bonafidebonefishing.com.*

A gray shark circles a boat off Long Island.

## SOUTH LONG ISLAND: DEADMAN'S CAY TO GORDON'S

The most populated area on the island is **Deadman's Cay**. This umbrella central settlement covers all the communities stretching from **Gray's** to the north to **Scrub Hill**, and is the social, economic, and educational center of the island. The Deadman's Cay airport is in Lower Deadman's Cay and the infamous Max's Conch Bar is only a short distance to the south. Shops, restaurants, and bars dot this area, along with amazing views of the Bahamas Banks.

Past Scrub Hill is **Dean's Blue Hole**, the deepest blue hole in the world. Free-diving contests, without use of any breathing apparatus, are held here each year, and divers come from all over the world to challenge the record. Fantastic snorkeling can be had around the blue hole's edges.

**Clarence Town** is the capital of Long Island and home to the Flying Fish Marina in one of the prettiest and safest harbors in the Out Islands. Situated at the top of the highest hills in town are the twin-towered Moorish style churches of **St. Paul's** and **St. Peter's**, designed by Father Jerome. Clarence Town is the last large settlement on the south end of the island.

South of Clarence Town you will find **Galloway Landing**, a long stretch of amazing beaches and saltwater canals dug into the limestone hills by the now defunct Diamond Salt Mine. From here to **Gordon's** is the most undeveloped stretch of the island. Plantation ruins are at **Dunmone's**, secluded beaches at **Ford's**, and the incredible pink flamingos at Gordon's along with the biggest assortment of sea glass.

## DID YOU KNOW?

"The sand is Bora-Bora soft. The water is so warm and so shallow, I can walk a hundred yards from the shore. It's gorgeous."
—DavefromCA

## EXPLORING

Fodor'sChoice   **Dean's Blue Hole.** Known as the deepest blue hole in the world with a
★   depth of 663 feet, Dean's Blue Hole is the most amazing sight on the
island. A blue hole is a term for a water-filled sinkhole with an entrance
below the water level. Free divers from around the world gather here
annually to take the plunge. In 2010 William Trubridge broke the world
record free-diving to 302 feet without fins. Dean's Blue Hole is surrounded by a pretty cliff and a superb beach. The shallows at the edge
of the hole are perfect for snorkeling and swimming, and the more
adventurous visitors can jump into the water from the cliffs above. To
find the blue hole, watch for the well-marked sign on your left (going
east on Queen's Highway) after passing through Scrub Hill. ⊠ *Just
south of Scrub Hill, North of Clarence Town, Long Island*

**Galloway Landing.** This remarkable beach on the South East coast of the
island, south of Clarence Town is relatively unknown and visited mostly
by the locals. Swim and sun at the first beach, or walk a short distance
south to an even more wonderful and secluded stretch of sand. Here,
canals carved into the limestone hills by the now defunct Diamond
Salt Mine are filled with the palest blue ocean water and are home to
small marine life. It's a wonderful area to kayak, snorkel and swim, and
collect sea glass. A bit farther south, a narrow bridge leads to beyond-
stunning lagoons and ocean flats. **Amenities:** none. **Best for:** solitude;
snorkeling; swimming; walking. ⊠ *2.4 miles southwest of Clarence
Town, Long Island.*

**Hamilton's Cave.** The largest cave system in The Bahamas, Hamilton's
Cave features stalactites and stalagmites, and passages over 15 meters
wide. Leonard Cartwright will take you on a guided tour, complete
with flashlights, as you explore inside the dark depths of his child-
hood playground where Lucayan drawings and ancient artifacts have
been found. For added excitement, plan to go closer to dusk when the
resident bats are most active! ⊠ *Queen's Hwy., Deadman's Cay, Long
Island* ☎ *242/337–0235, 242/472–1796* 🖾 *$10 adults, $5 children.*

**The Long Island Museum and Library.** The Long Island Museum and
Library is housed in a beautiful little pink cottage with native trees in
front. Patty will share the history of Long Island and show you artifacts collected by local Long Islanders in hopes of preserving cultural
heritage. You don't need to stay long, but it is worth a short stop.
Native wares, homemade jellies, and other island goods are for sale, in
addition to books on Long Island and a Bahamian calendar created by
locals. ⊠ *Buckley's, Long Island* ☎ *242/337–0500* 🖾 *$3* ⊗ *Mon.–Fri.
8–4, Sat. 9–1* ⊗ *Closed Sun.*

**St. Paul's & St. Peter's Churches.** The twin, towered Moorish churches of St.
Paul's (Anglican) and St. Peter's (Catholic) are two of the island's most
celebrated landmarks. Father Jerome, often referred to as the hermit of
Cat Island, built St. Paul's when he was Anglican; later, after converting
to Catholicism, he built St. Peter's. The architecture of the two churches
is similar to the Spanish missions in California. The churches are open
sporadically, but tours are available through the ministry of tourism.
⊠ *Clarence Town, Long Island.*

## WHERE TO EAT

$ BAHAMIAN 🍴 **Forest 2.** This family-owned-and-operated takeaway restaurant offers ribs, cracked conch, fish fingers, and the ever popular Forest Burger, a hamburger with boneless ribs and sautéed onions. Call ahead for your order or sit and wait with a cold beer. [$] *Average main: $12* ✉ *Just off Queen's Hwy., Deadman's Cay, Long Island* ☎ *242/337–3287, 242/337–1246* 💳 *No credit cards* ⏰ *Closed Sun.*

$ BAHAMIAN 🍴 **Max's Conch Bar and Grill.** This island treasure is known up and down the island by locals and visitors alike. You can sit all day on a stool at the colorful roadside gazebo or at a table on the garden patio, nursing beers and nibbling on conch salad prepared right in front of you. Become a veritable expert on Long Island and its people with Max and his staff. Such is the draw of this laid-back watering hole. Be sure to try the conch fritters, steamed snapper, and breadfruit chips, or any of the daily specials such as pot roast and crawfish stuffed potatoes. Max also offers complimentary Wi-Fi for those needing to stay connected. [$] *Average main: $15* ✉ *Deadman's Cay, Long Island* ☎ *242/337–0056* 🌐 *www.maxconchbar.com* ⏰ *Closed Sun.*

$ BAHAMIAN 🍴 **Outer Edge Grill at Flying Fish Marina.** Reopened with new management, Outer Edge Grill is what local Long Islanders call a "poop deck," meaning a restaurant on the water. Open daily for lunch and dinner, Outer Edge serves up Bahamian favorites like conch fritters and fish fingers, along with sweet potato french fries, mozzarella sticks, and homemade desserts. This is one of only a few restaurants open on Sunday. [$] *Average main: $12* ✉ *Flying Fish Marina, just down from Winter Haven Inn, Clarence Town, Long Island* ☎ *242/337–3430, 954/654–7084.*

$ AMERICAN 🍴 **Rowdy Boys Bar and Grill at Winter Haven Inn.** Don't let the name scare you—it's named after the Knowles family's well-known construction company and the owners' two sons. Breakfast, lunch, and dinner feature authentic Bahamian and American fare. The restaurant overlooks the roaring Atlantic, with a pool and bar on the large outside deck. This is one of the few restaurants open on Sunday. [$] *Average main: $20* ✉ *Winter Haven Inn, Clarence Town, Long Island* ☎ *242/337–3062* 🌐 *www.winterhavenbahamas.com* ✍ *Reservations essential.*

$ BAHAMIAN 🍴 **Seaside Village at Jerry Wells.** Located at the end of Jerry Wells road, this charming authentic conch shack on the water is truly local, offering friendly service, fun music, and good food. House favorites include fresh conch salad (watch Kenny pull the conch straight from the water), grilled lobster, and grouper made any way you want it—all go best with a cold Kalik. Seaside Village is one of the very few restaurants open on Sunday. [$] *Average main: $20* ✉ *Deadman's Cay, Long Island* ☎ *242/337–0119, 242/357–1080* 💳 *No credit cards.*

## WHERE TO STAY

$$ RENTAL Fodor's Choice ★ 🏨 **Harbor Breeze Villas.** Long Island's newest luxury villas are nestled among garden pathways atop a hillside, each with private balconies affording views of Clarence Town Harbour and the Atlantic Ocean. **Pros:** owner rents cars and will stock your villa with groceries ahead of your arrival; complimentary transfers to Arthur's Town Airport; laundry facilities on-site. **Cons:** no on-site restaurant; not on beach;

office can be hard to reach by phone. Ⓢ *Rooms from: $250* ✉ *Lochabar, just north of Clarence Town, Long Island* ☎ *242/225–3086* ⊕ *www. harborbreezevillas.com* ⤴ *14 villas* ⦿ *No meals.*

Ⓢ ⊞ **Winter Haven Inn.** This small, colorful inn has two-story houses with
HOTEL  rooms overlooking the dark-blue waters of the Atlantic right in the heart of Clarence Town. **Pros:** complimentary airport transfers to Deadman's Cay airport; on-site restaurant serves three meals a day; complimentary Wi-Fi. **Cons:** no kitchen facilities in-room; you must rent a car for exploring; rough, rocky beach not good for swimming. Ⓢ *Rooms from: $150* ✉ *Clarence Town, Long Island* ☎ *242/337– 3062, 866/348–5935* ⊕ *www.winterhavenbahamas.com* ⤴ *16 rooms* ⦿ *No meals.*

## NIGHTLIFE

**Midway Bar and Restaurant.** Stop by here on Friday for happy hour from 6 to 8 pm, or come on Saturday for karaoke that starts at 10 pm. Lunch and dinner are available with Caribbean choices like Jamaican jerk and various curries. Hours can be erratic, but the restaurant is generally open Tuesday through Saturday. ✉ *Off Queen's Hwy., The Bight, Long Island* ☎ *242/337–7345.*

## SHOPPING

**Sea Winds Super Mart and Supplies.** This is one of the largest grocery stores on the island and has everything you need for a picnic or to stock your vacation kitchen. Toiletries and other supplies are available. There are several other shops in this "strip mall," including Yukon Jack's Wholesale and Retail Liquor. ✉ *Off Queen's Hwy., Petty's, Long Island* ☎ *242/337–0212.*

**It's All Under the Sun.** As the name suggests, this "department store" has everything from a coffee café with used books and Wi-Fi to office supplies, toys, baby stuff, souvenirs, and fishing equipment. ✉ *Off Queen's Hwy., Mangrove Bush, Long Island* ☎ *242/337–0199* ⊙ *Closed Sun.*

## SPORTS AND THE OUTDOORS

### FISHING

**Samuel Knowles Bonefish Adventures.** For more than 10 years, Samuel Knowles Bonefish Adventures has drawn a loyal following of saltwater anglers from around the globe, and they have earned a reputation as one of the most popular bonefishing programs in the islands. The main attraction is their expert guides, who are Long Island natives, fourth- and fifth-generation bonefishermen, and champions of four of the five Bahamas bonefishing tournaments. Their location at the center of Long Island's pristine shoreline, with unique landlocked flats, creates an unforgettable fishing adventure for all ages and experience levels. ✉ *Deadman's Cay, Long Island* ☎ *242/337–0246, 242/357–1178* ⊕ *www.deadmansbones.com.*

**Winter Haven Inn.** Winter Haven Inn organizes fishing and boating adventures through various local guides. ✉ *Clarence Town, Long Island* ☎ *242/337–3062* ⊕ *www.winterhavenbahamas.com.*

### DIVING AND SNORKELING

FAMILY **Bahamas Discovery Quest.** This company offers full- and half-day snorkeling trips, along with many other unique island escapades including sponging, crabbing, beaching and shelling, and different types of fishing. ✉ *Long Island* ☎ *242/472–2605, 242/337–6024* ⊕ *www.bahamasdiscoveryquest.com.*

**Dean's Blue Hole.** Surrounded by a beautiful powder-beach cove, the area surrounding Dean's Hole offers a great place for a beach picnic if it's not too windy. Visitors can jump into the blue hole from various locations on the overhanging cliff above, some at 25 feet above the water. Snorkelers will see a variety of tropical fish and marine life, and Stella Maris Water Sports at Stella Maris Marina offers guided dive trips; flashlights included and necessary! Although Dean's Blue hole is safe for swimming, it is recommended that all swimmers be competent or wear life jackets.

# CROOKED AND ACKLINS ISLANDS

Crooked Island is 30 miles long and surrounded by 45 miles of barrier reefs that are ideal for diving and fishing. They slope from 4 feet to 50 feet, then plunge to 3,600 feet in the **Crooked Island Passage,** once one of the most important sea roads for ships following the southerly route from the West Indies to the Old World. If you drive up to **the Cove** settlement, you get an uninterrupted view of the region all the way to the narrow passage at **Lovely Bay** between Crooked Island and Acklins Island. Two lighthouses alert mariners that they are nearing the islands.

The tepid controversy continues today over whether Columbus actually set foot on Crooked Island and its southern neighbor, Acklins Island. What's known for sure is that Columbus sailed close enough to Crooked Island to get a whiff of its native herbs. Soon after, the two islands became known as the "Fragrant Islands." Today Crooked and Acklins islands are known as remote and unspoiled destinations for fishermen, divers, and sailors who value solitude. Here phone service can be intermittent, Internet connections can be hard to find, and some residents depend on generators for electricity. Even credit-card use is a relatively new development. The first known settlers didn't arrive until the late 18th century, when Loyalists brought slaves from the United States to work on cotton plantations. About 400 people, mostly fishermen and farmers, live on each island today. Two plantation-era sites, preserved by the Bahamas National Trust, are on Crooked Island's northern end, which overlooks Crooked Island Passage that separates the cay from Long Island. Spanish guns have been discovered at one ruin, **Marine Farm,** which may have been used as a fortification. An old structure, **Hope Great House,** has orchards and gardens.

## GETTING HERE AND AROUND
### AIR TRAVEL
Crooked and Acklins have one airport each: Colonel Hill Airport (CRI) on Crooked Island and Spring Point Airport (AXP) on Acklins Island. Bahamasair and Pineapple Air fly from Nassau to Crooked and Acklins islands twice a week. Crooked Island Lodge picks up its guests flying into Colonel Hill with prior arrangement. The private 3,500-foot airstrip at Crooked Island Lodge is complimentary for hotel guests. Non-guests pay landing and parking fees. This airstrip is most convenient for private and charter flights if you're staying in the area of Pittstown and Landrail Point. Ask your hotel to make arrangements for picking you up at the airport in case there are no taxis.

Hotels will arrange airport transportation. Generally someone from even the smallest hotel will meet you at the airport, but taxis are usually waiting on flights.

**Contacts Acklins Island Spring Point Airport** ☎ *242/344–3169.*
**Crooked Island Colonel Hill Airport** ☎ *242/344–2357.*

### BOAT TRAVEL
Mail boats that bring supplies to the island each week make an adventurous mode of transportation. You'll ride with groceries, large and small appliances, automobiles, and sometimes even livestock. All boats depart from Potter's Cay in Nassau. Schedules change frequently. M/V *Vi Nais* sails Wednesday to Acklins Island, Crooked Island, and Long Cay, returning Sunday (30 hours; $90 one-way).

Ferry service between Cove Landing, Crooked Island, and Lovely Bay, Acklins Island usually operates twice daily on varying schedules between 9 and 4.

**Contacts Mailboat Port/Dockmaster's Office in Nassau** ⊠ *New Providence Island* ☎ *242/393–1064.*

### CAR TRAVEL
Reserve a car through your hotel prior to your arrival, but even with a reservation be prepared for the possibility of not having one. Gas is also not always available on the island, as it's delivered by mail boat, which are sometimes delayed. Fortunately, it's easy to get a ride to most places with locals.

# EXPLORING

**Bird Rock Lighthouse.** The sparkling white Bird Rock Lighthouse (built in 1876) once guarded the Crooked Island Passage. The rotating flash from its 115-foot tower still welcomes pilots and sailors to the Crooked Island Lodge, currently the islands' best lodging facility. This lighthouse is located 1 mile offshore and can only be reached by boat. ⊠ *Crooked Island.*

**Castle Island Lighthouse.** The Castle Island Lighthouse (built in 1867), at Acklins Island's southern tip, formerly served as a beacon for pirates who used to retreat there after attacking ships.

Deep sea fishing in the Southern Out Islands.

## WHERE TO STAY

**$** — **RENTAL** — 🏠 **Casuarina Villas.** Five modern cottages sit on a ½-mi stretch of white-sand beach between Landrail Point and Pittstown Point Landings. **Pros:** beachfront location; spacious economical accommodations; great place to hang out, fish, and relax. **Cons:** you need to arrange transportation to do anything; take plenty of insect repellent. 💲 *Rooms from: $135* ✉ *Landrail Point, Crooked Island* ☎ *242/344–2197* ⤵ *5 cottages.*

**$$** — **RESORT** — 🏠 **Crooked Island Lodge.** A true anglers' paradise, this is one of the best flats, inshore, and offshore fishing destinations in the Bahamas and Caribbean. **Pros:** mind-bending ocean and beachfront location; good on-site restaurant and bar; private airstrip on the property for easy access. **Cons:** take a lot of insect repellent and have it on when you step out of the plane; don't go unless you want remote, private, and nothing to do but fish and relax. 💲 *Rooms from: $150* ✉ *Portland Harbour, Pittstown Point Landings, Crooked Island* ☎ *242/344–2507, 888/344–2507* 🌐 *www.crookedislandlodge.com* ⤵ *12 rooms* 🍽 *All meals.*

## SPORTS AND THE OUTDOORS

### FISHING

Crooked Island has a number of highly regarded bonefishing guides with quality boats and fly-fishing tackle. Most can be booked through the Crooked Island Lodge, but the guides also take direct bookings. Be aware that telephone service to and from Crooked and Acklins islands is not always operational.

You can stalk the elusive and swift bonefish in the shallows, or go deep-sea fishing for wahoo, sailfish, and amberjack.

**Michael Carroll** (☏ 242/344–2037), **Derrick Ingraham** (☏ 242/344–2023), **Elton "Bonefish Shakey" McKinney** (☏ 242/344–2038), **Randy McKinney** (☏ 242/344–2326), **Jeff Moss** (☏ 242/344–2029), and **Clinton** and **Kenneth "The Earlybird" Scavalla** (☏ 242/344–2011 or 242/422–3596) are all knowledgeable professional guides. **Captain Robbie Gibson** (☏ 242/344–2007) has a 30-foot Century boat and is the most experienced reef and offshore fishing captain on Crooked Island, where astounding fishing in virgin waters is the rule. Many wahoo weighing more than 100 pounds are landed each season with his assistance. Robbie's personal best wahoo is a whopping 180 pounds. He's also a skilled guide for anglers pursuing tuna, marlin, sharks, barracuda, jacks, snapper, and grouper.

### SCUBA DIVING

**The Wall.** The Wall starts at around 45 feet deep and goes down thousands more. It's about 50 yards off Crooked Island's coast and follows the shoreline for many miles.

**Captain Robbie Gibson.** In addition to fishing expeditions, Captain Robbie Gibson offers scuba diving, snorkeling, and day tours. ☏ 242/344–2007, 242/422–4737 ⊕ *www.thunderbirdoffshoreandscuba.com*.

# INAGUA

Inagua does indeed feel like the southernmost island in the Bahamas' 700 mile-long chain. Just 50 miles from Cuba, it's not easy to get to—there are only three flights a week from Nassau, and you must overnight there to catch the 9 am flight.

At night the lonely beacon of the **Inagua Lighthouse** sweeps the sky over the southern part of the island and the only community, **Matthew Town**, as it has since 1870. The coastline is rocky and rugged, with little coves of golden sand. The terrain is mostly flat and covered with palmetto palms, wind-stunted buttonwoods, and mangroves ringing ponds and a huge inland saltwater lake. Parts of it look very much like the Florida Everglades, only without the alligators and poisonous snakes.

Matthew Town feels like the Wild West, with sun-faded wooden buildings and vintage and modern trucks usually parked in front. It's obviously not a tourist mecca, but it's a shame that more people don't make it here. They are missing one of the great spectacles of the western hemisphere: the 70,000-some West Indian pink-scarlet flamingos that nest here alongside rare Bahama parrots and roseate spoonbills. If you're not a bird lover, there's extraordinary diving and fishing off the virgin reefs.

Although there are few tourists, this remote island is prosperous. An unusual climate of little rainfall and continual trade winds creates rich salt ponds. The Morton Salt Company harvests a million tons of salt annually at its Matthew Town factory, where most of the 1,000 Inaguans work.

8

### GETTING HERE AND AROUND

#### AIR TRAVEL

Inagua has one airport: Matthew Town Airport (IGA). Bahamasair has flights on Monday, Wednesday, and Friday from Nassau. Hotels will arrange airport transportation. Generally someone from even the smallest hotel will meet you at the airport, but taxis sometimes meet incoming flights.

**Contacts Inagua Matthew Town Airport** ☎ *242/339–1680, 242/339–1415.*

#### BOAT TRAVEL

Mail boats that bring supplies to the island each week make an adventurous mode of transportation. You'll ride with groceries, large and small appliances, automobiles, and sometimes even livestock. All boats depart from Potter's Cay in Nassau. Schedules change frequently. The *Lady Matilda,* which rotates with the *Rosalind,* leaves Tuesday and returns Sunday (36 hours; $100 one-way).

**Contacts Mailboat Port/Dockmaster's Office in Nassau** ⊠ *New Providence Island* ☎ *242/393–1064.*

#### CAR TRAVEL

You can rent a car for about $80 a day, but there are few rental cars on the island, so call in advance. If you are driving outside Matthew Town, you will need an SUV or truck to navigate dirt roads. If you plan to stay in Matthew Town, you can easily walk everywhere.

**Contacts Ingraham Rent-A-Car** ☎ *242/339–1677.*

### TOURS

**Great Inagua Tours.** Mr. Colin Ingraham has been a tour guide for over 20 years, specializing in birding and island sightseeing. He can also take you trawling for deep-sea fish including tuna or wahoo, or snorkeling on the reefs. A complete island tour includes a stop in the National Park to scout birds and wildlife (including flamingos and wild donkeys) and visits to natural caves, the Morton Salt facility, lighthouses, and the local museum. ⊠ *Southwest Inagua, Burnside St., Great Inagua Island* ☎ *242/453–0429.*

## EXPLORING

**Inagua National Park.** Nothing quite prepares you for your first glimpse of the West Indian flamingos that nest in Inagua National Park: brilliant crimson-pink, up to 5 feet tall, with black-tipped wings. A dozen flamingos suddenly fly across a pond, intermixed with fantastic pink roseate spoonbills.

It's a moving experience, and yet because of the island's remote location, only about 50 people witnessed it in 2009. In 1952, Inagua's flamingos dwindled to about 5,000. The gorgeous birds were hunted for their meat, especially the tongue, and for their feathers. The government established the 287-square-mile park in 1963, and today 70,000 flamingos nest on the island, the world's largest breeding colony of West Indian flamingos. The birds like the many salt ponds on Inagua that supply their favorite meal—brine shrimp.

You must contact the Bahamas National Trust's office (☎ *242/393-1317* 🌐 *www.bnt.bs*) or Warden Henry Nixon (☎ *242/225-0878*) to make reservations for your visit. All visits to the park are by special arrangement. ✉ *10 miles west of Matthew Town, Great Inagua Island* 🌐 *www.bnt.bs.*

**Erickson Museum and Library.** The Erickson Museum and Library is a welcome part of the community, particularly the surprisingly well-stocked, well-equipped library. The Morton Company built the complex in the former home of the Erickson family, who came to Inagua in 1934 to run the salt giant. The museum displays the island's history, to which the company is inextricably tied. The posted hours are not always that regular. The Bahamas National Trust office, and the office of the Inagua National Park, is also here, but hours are unpredictable. ✉ *Gregory St. on the northern edge of town across from the police station, Great Inagua Island* ☎ *242/339-1863* 🎟 *Free* 🕒 *Mon.-Fri. 9-5, Sat. 10-1* 🕒 *Closed Sun.*

**Inagua Lighthouse.** From Southwest Point, a mile or so south of Matthew Town, you can see Cuba's coast—slightly more than 50 miles west—on a clear day from atop Inagua Lighthouse, built in 1870 in response to the number of shipwrecks on offshore reefs. It's a grueling climb—the last 10 feet are on a ladder—but the view of the rugged coastline and Matthew Town is worth the effort. Look to the west to see the hazy mountains of Cuba. Be sure to sign the guest book, just inside the door to the lighthouse. ✉ *Gregory St., 1 mile south of Matthew Town, Great Inagua Island.*

**Morton Salt Company.** Marveling at the salt process lures few visitors to Inagua, but the Morton Salt Company is omnipresent on the island: it has more than 47 square miles of crystallizing ponds and reservoirs. More than a million tons of salt are produced every year for such industrial uses as salting icy streets. (More is produced when the northeastern United States has a bad winter.) Even if you decide not to tour the facility, you can see the mountains of salt, locally called the Salt Alps, glistening in the sun from the plane. In an unusual case of industry assisting its environment, the crystallizers provide a feeding ground for the flamingos. As the water evaporates, the concentration of brine shrimp in the ponds increases, and the flamingos feed on these animals. Free tours are available by reservation at the salt plant in Matthew Town. ☎ *242/339-1300, 242/457-6000* 🌐 *www.mortonsalt.com.*

8

## WHERE TO EAT

**$** BAHAMIAN 🍴 **Cozy Corner.** Cheerful and loud, this lunch spot—locals just call it Cozy's—is the best on the island. It has a pool table and a large seating area with a bar. Stop in for a chat with locals over a Kalik and a Bahamian conch burger. Cozy's also serves excellent island-style dinners on request—steamed crawfish, grilled snapper, baked chicken and fries, homemade slaw, macaroni and cheese, and fresh johnnycake. If it's not open when you stop by, you might still be able to get food and a drink if you ask. [$] *Average main: $8* ✉ *Matthew Town, Great Inagua Island* ☎ *242/339-1440* 💳 *No credit cards* 🕒 *Closed Sun.*

## WHERE TO STAY

$    **Enrica's Inn Guest House.** This affordable inn is a small complex of
RENTAL   three two-story Bahamian-colonial-style cottages with inviting verandahs leading to five guest rooms in each building. **Pros:** inexpensive;
efficient and friendly service; walking distance to town. **Cons:** no pool
or beach views. $ *Rooms from: $85* ✉ *Victoria St., Matthew Town,
Great Inagua Island* ☎ *242/339–2127* ⊕ *www.enricasinn.com* ⇌ *15
rooms* ⊟ *No credit cards* ⦿ *No meals.*

$    **The Main House.** The Morton Salt Company operates this small, afford-
HOTEL   able guesthouse. **Pros:** inexpensive; clean; walking distance to a couple
of bars and restaurants. **Cons:** no Internet service; power plant can be
noisy. $ *Rooms from: $60* ✉ *Kortwright St., Matthew Town, Great Inagua Island* ☎ *242/339–1267* ⊕ *www.inaguamainhouse.com* ⇌ *6 rooms.*

$    **Sunset Apartments.** This is your only option for a room with a water
RENTAL   view, and a great place to watch sunsets. **Pros:** great place for bonefishing; Ezzard is a wonderful host and a top fly-fishing guide. **Cons:** no
Internet service; nothing to do but fish and bird-watch; you need to pay
in cash. $ *Rooms from: $150* ✉ *Matthew Town, Great Inagua Island*
☎ *242/339–1362* ⇌ *2 apartments* ⊟ *No credit cards.*

## NIGHTLIFE

**Da After Work Bar.** This local bar on Gregory Street (the main street)
next to Kiwanis Park is the most popular hangout in town and a good
place to meet the mayor and other town notables. It's also a nice spot
for watching games of Whisk and Dominoes. Typically they close on
Sundays, but if you stop by they will still be happy to sell you a cold
drink! ✉ *Northwest Mayaguana, Gregory St., Great Inagua Island*
☎ *242/339–3001.*

**The Fish Fry.** A collection of fish shacks next to the water is open on
weekends, with DJs occasionally in the covered pavilion next door.

## SPORTS AND THE OUTDOORS

### FISHING

**Ezzard Cartwright.** One of Inagua's leading bonefishing and deep-sea fishing guides, Ezzard Cartwright has been featured in outdoors and fishing
magazines and on ESPN Outdoors shows. He is one of few locals with
access to Lake Windsor, home to Tarpon and snook as well as bonefish
that can only be reached by boat. Call him if you're a hard-core fisherman who wants to fish for eight hours a day. He's usually booked from
January to June for bonefishing, so reserve early. ☎ *242/339–1362.*

# TRAVEL SMART BAHAMAS

# GETTING HERE AND AROUND

## ▋ AIR TRAVEL

Most international flights to the Bahamas connect through airports in Florida, New York, Charlotte, or Atlanta. The busiest airport in the Bahamas is in Nassau, which has the most connections to the more remote Out Islands. If you're traveling to these more remote islands, you might have to make a connection in both Florida and Nassau—and you still may have to take a ferry or a water taxi to your final destination.

A direct flight from New York City to Nassau takes approximately three hours. The flight from Charlotte to Nassau is two hours, and the flight from Miami to Nassau takes about an hour. Most flights between the islands of the Bahamas take less than an hour. You'll probably spend more time on the ground waiting than in the air.

### AIRPORTS

The major gateways to the Bahamas include Lynden Pindling International Airport (NAS) on New Providence Island, and Freeport Grand Bahama International Airport (FPO) on Grand Bahama Island. There are no hotels near either airport. *For more airports, ⇨ see individual chapters.*

**Airport Information Grand Bahama International Airport** ⊠ *Bahamas* 🖷 *242/352–2205.* **Lynden Pindling International Airport** ⊠ *Bahamas* 🖷 *242/702–1000.*

### FLIGHTS

Air service to the Bahamas varies seasonally, with the biggest choice of flights usually available in the Christmas to Easter window.

Local carriers come and go, especially in the Out Islands, which are served mostly by smaller commuter and charter operations. Schedules change frequently. The smallest cays may have scheduled service only a few days a week. In the Out Islands, ask your hotel for flight recommendations, as they are likely to have the most up-to-date information on carriers and schedules; some can even help you book air travel.

**Major Airlines American Airlines** ⊠ *Bahamas* 🖷 *800/433–7300.* **Delta Airlines** ⊠ *Bahamas* 🖷 *800/221–1212.* **JetBlue** ⊠ *Bahamas* 🖷 *800/538–2583.* **Spirit Airlines** ⊠ *Bahamas* 🖷 *800/772–7117.* **United** ⊠ *Bahamas* 🖷 *800/864–8331.* **US Airways** ⊠ *Bahamas* 🖷 *800/428–4322.*

**Smaller Airlines Bahamasair** ⊠ *Bahamas* 🖷🖷 *242/342–4140* 🖷 *800/222–4262.* **Cherokee Air** ⊠ *Bahamas* 🖷 *242/367–1920* ⊕ *www.cherokeeair.com.* **Flamingo Air** ⊠ *Bahamas* 🖷 *242/225–1558* ⊕ *www.flamingoairbah.com.* **Florida Coastal Air** ⊠ *Bahamas* 🖷 *954/990–1700, 888/596–9247* ⊕ *www.flyfca.net.* **Golden Wings Charter** ⊠ *Bahamas* 🖷 *242/377–0039* ⊕ *www.goldenwingscharter.com.* **Island Air** ⊠ *Bahamas* 🖷 *800/444–9904* ⊕ *www.islandaircharters.com.* **LeAir** ⊠ *Bahamas* 🖷 *242/377–2356* ⊕ *www.flyleair.com.* **Locair** ⊠ *Bahamas* 🖷 *954/359–3001* ⊕ *www.locair.net.* **Performance Air** ⊠ *Bahamas* 🖷 *242/341–3281* ⊕ *www.performance-air.com.* **Pineapple Air** ⊠ *Bahamas* 🖷 *242/377–0412* ⊕ *www.pineappleair.com.* **Regional Air** ⊠ *Bahamas* 🖷 *800/598–8660* ⊕ *www.goregionalair.com.* **Sky Bahamas** ⊠ *Bahamas* 🖷 *242/377–8993, 954/357–0696* ⊕ *www.skybahamas.net.* **Southern Air** ⊠ *Bahamas* 🖷 *242/377–2014* ⊕ *www.southernaircharter.com.* **Twin Air Calypso** ⊠ *Bahamas* 🖷 *954/359–8266* ⊕ *www.flytwinair.com.* **Western Air** ⊠ *Bahamas* 🖷 *242/329–4000* ⊕ *www.westernairbahamas.com.*

# ▌ BOAT TRAVEL

## BOATS AND FERRIES

If you're adventurous and have time to spare, take a ferry or one of the traditional mail boats that regularly leave Nassau from Potter's Cay, under the Paradise Island Bridge. Although fast, modern, air-conditioned boats now make some of the trips, certain remote destinations are still served by slow, old-fashioned craft. Especially if you choose the mail-boat route, you may even find yourself sharing company with goats or chickens, and making your way on deck through piles of lumber and crates of cargo; on these lumbering mail boats, expect to spend five to 12 or more hours slowly making your way between island outposts. These boats operate on Bahamian time, which is a casual unpredictable measure, and the schedules can be thrown off by bad weather. Mail boats cannot generally be booked in advance, and services are limited. In Nassau, check details with the dockmaster's office at Potter's Cay. One-way trips can cost from $35 to $100.

Within the Bahamas, Bahamas Ferries has the most (and most comfortable) options for island-hopping, with air-conditioned boats that offer food and beverages served by cabin attendants. Schedules do change rather frequently; if you're planning to ferry back to an island to catch a flight, check and double-check the departure times, and build in extra time in case the weather's bad or the boat inexplicably doesn't make the trip you'd planned on. Ferries serve most of the major tourist destinations from Nassau, including Spanish Wells, Governor's Harbour, Harbour Island, Abaco, Exuma, and Andros. The high-speed ferry that runs between Nassau and Spanish Wells, Governor's Harbour, and Harbour Island costs $65 one-way, and takes about two hours each way.

Local ferries in the Out Islands transport islanders and visitors from the main island to smaller cays. Usually, these ferries make several round-trips daily, and keep a more punctual schedule than the longer-haul ferry.

It's possible to get to Grand Bahama by ferry from Florida. Balearia Bahamas Express sails from Fort Lauderdale's Port Everglades (Terminal 1) and provides fast-ferry service, making a day-trip possible, while Celebrations Cruise Line sails from Riviera Beach and is more like a small cruise ship, though hotel packages can include transportation to Grand Bahamas.

If you're setting sail yourself, note that cruising boats must clear customs at the nearest port of entry before beginning any diving or fishing. The fee is $150 for boats 35 feet and under and $300 for boats 36 feet and longer, which includes fishing permits and departure tax for up to four persons. Each additional person above the age of four will be charged the $15 departure tax. Stays of longer than 12 months must be arranged with Bahamas customs and immigration officials.

**Boat and Ferry Contacts Bahamas Ferries** ⊠ *Bahamas* ☎ *242/323–2166* ⊕ *www.bahamasferries.com.* **Balearia Bahamas Express** ⊠ *Port Everglades, Terminal 1, Fort Lauderdale, Florida, USA* ☎ *866/699–6988* ⊕ *www.ferryexpress.com.* **Celebration Cruise Line** ⊠ *1 E. 11th St., Riviera Beach, Florida, USA* ☎ *800/314–7735* ⊕ *www.bahamascelebration.com.*

**Potter's Cay Dockmaster** ⊠ *Bahamas* ☎ *242/393–1064.*

## CRUISES

A cruise can be one of the most pleasurable ways to see the islands. A multi-island excursion allows for plenty of land time because of the short travel times between destinations. Be sure to shop around before booking. Virtually all major cruise lines call in either Nassau or Freeport, and many of the major cruise lines offer "private island" experiences somewhere in the Bahamas.

From Florida, the Discovery Cruise Line departs for Grand Bahama Island at 9:30 am daily, except Wednesday, with its 1,100-passenger *Discovery Sun*, complete with swimming pool, casino, live entertainment, disco, and buffets. Passengers can make it a day trip, arriving in the Bahamas by 1:30 pm and departing at 5:15 pm, or they can stay on the island for a few days. Round-trip fares, including two buffets and drinks, start at about $80, plus a surcharge of $35 per person to cover fees and taxes.

# ▮ CAR TRAVEL

International rental agencies are generally in Nassau, and you will rent from privately owned companies on the small islands. Be warned that you might have to settle for a rusty heap that doesn't have working seat belts. Check it out thoroughly before you leave. And assume that companies won't have car seats—bring your own.

To rent a car, you must be 21 years of age or older.

It's common to hire a driver with a van, and prices are negotiable. Most drivers charge by the half day or full day, and prices depend on the stops and distance, although half-day tours are generally $50 to $100 for one to four people. Full-day tours are $100 to $200. It's customary to pay for the driver's lunch. All tour guides in the Bahamas are required to take a tourism course, pass a test to be a guide, and are required to get a special license to operate a taxi.

### GASOLINE
The cost of fuel in the Bahamas is usually at least twice that in the United States, and be prepared to pay in cash. Stations may be few and far between on the Out Islands. Keep the tank full. You can ask for a handwritten receipt if printed ones are not available. Gas stations may be closed Sunday.

### PARKING
There are few parking meters in the Bahamas, none in downtown Nassau. Police are lenient with visitors' rental cars parked illegally and will generally just ask the driver to move it. Parking spaces are hard to find in Nassau, so be prepared to park on a side street and walk. Most hotels offer off-street parking for guests. There are few parking lots not associated with hotels.

### ROADSIDE EMERGENCIES
In case of a road emergency, stay in your vehicle with your emergency flashers engaged and wait for help, especially after dark. If someone stops to help, relay information through a small opening in the window. If it's daylight and help does not arrive, walk to the nearest phone and call for help. In the Bahamas, motorists readily stop to help drivers in distress.

Ask for emergency numbers at the rental office when you pick up your car. These numbers vary from island to island. On smaller islands the owner of the company may want you to call him at his home.

### RULES OF THE ROAD
Remember, like the British, islanders drive on the left side of the road, which can be confusing because most cars are American with the steering wheel on the left. It is illegal, however, to make a left-hand turn on a red light. Many streets in downtown Nassau are one-way. Roundabouts pose further confusion to Americans. Remember to keep left and yield to oncoming traffic as you enter the roundabout and at "Give Way" signs.

# ▮ TAXI TRAVEL

There are taxis waiting at every airport and outside all of the main hotels and cruise-ship docks. Beware of "hackers"— drivers who don't display their license (and may not have one). Sometimes you can negotiate a fare, but you must do so before you enter the taxi.

You'll find that Bahamian taxi drivers are more talkative than their U.S. counterparts. When you take a taxi to dinner or to town, it's common for the driver to wait and take you back, which doesn't cost more. A 15% tip is suggested.

# ESSENTIALS

## ▌ ACCOMMODATIONS

The lodgings we list are the cream of the crop in each price category. We always list the facilities that are available—but we don't specify whether they cost extra: when pricing accommodations, always ask what's included.

### APARTMENT AND HOUSE RENTALS

**Contacts Bahamas Home Rentals**
⊠ *Bahamas* ☎ *888/881–2867*
⊕ *www.bahamasweb.com.* **Bahamas Vacation Homes** ⊠ *Bahamas* ☎☎ *242/333–4080* ⊕ *www.bahamasvacationhomes. com.* **Hope Town Hideaways** ⊠ *Bahamas* ☎ *242/366–0224* ⊕ *www.hopetown.com.* **Villas & Apartments Abroad** ⊠ *Bahamas* ☎ *212/213–6435* ⊕ *www.vaanyc.com.* **Villas of Distinction** ⊠ *Bahamas* ☎ *800/289–0900* ⊕ *www.villasofdistinction.com.* **Villas International** ⊠ *Bahamas* ☎ *800/221–2260* ⊕ *www.villasintl.com.* **Wimco** ⊠ *Bahamas* ☎ *800/449–1553* ⊕ *www.wimco.com.*

## ▌ COMMUNICATIONS

### INTERNET

Wireless Internet service is becoming more available throughout the islands, but there are still pockets where service is impossible or difficult to get, and it's likely to be slower than you may be accustomed to. If Internet is important, ask your hotel representative about service before traveling.

If you're carrying a laptop into the Bahamas, you must fill out a Declaration of Value form upon arrival, noting make, model, and serial number. The Bahamian electrical current is compatible with U.S. computers.

### PHONES

Bahamas Telecommunications Company (BTC) is the phone company in the Bahamas. Pay phones accept Bahamas Direct prepaid cards purchased from BTC at

> ### WORD OF MOUTH
>
> Did the resort look as good in real life as it did in the photos? Did you sleep like a baby, or were the walls paper-thin? Did you get your money's worth? Rate hotels and write your own reviews in Travel Ratings or start a discussion about your favorite places in Travel Talk on www.fodors.com. Your comments might even appear in our books. Yes, you, too, can be a correspondent!

vending machines, stores, and BTC offices. You can use these cards to call within the country or to the United States.

Check with your calling-card provider before traveling to see if your card will work in the islands (on the smaller cays it almost certainly won't) and to see about surcharges. Always ask at your hotel desk about what charges will apply when you make card calls from your room. There's usually a charge for making toll-free calls to the United States. To place a call from a public phone using your own calling card, dial 0 for the operator, who will then place the call using your card number.

When you're calling the Bahamas, the country code is 242. You can dial any Bahamas number from the United States as you would make an interstate call.

### CALLING WITHIN THE BAHAMAS

Within the Bahamas, to make a local call from your hotel room, dial 9, then the number. If your party doesn't answer before the fifth ring, hang up or you'll be charged for the call. Some 800 and 888 numbers—particularly airline and credit card numbers—can be called from the Bahamas. Others can be reached by substituting an 880 prefix and paying for the call.

Dial 916 for directory information and 0 for operator assistance.

## CALLING OUTSIDE THE BAHAMAS

In big resorts instructions are given by the room phones on how to make international calls and the costs, which differ from resort to resort. In small inns, especially those in the Out Islands, you may not be able to get an AT&T, Sprint, or other operator or international operator, but the hotel front desk can usually do it for you.

The country code is 1 for the United States.

**Access Codes AT&T USADirect** ✉ *Bahamas* ☎ *800/872–2881.* **MCI Call USA** ✉ *Bahamas* ☎ *800/888–8000.* **Sprint** ✉ *Bahamas* ☎ *800/389–2111.*

**Phone Company BTC** ✉ *Bahamas* ☎ *242/302–7000* ⊕ *www.btcbahamas.com.*

### MOBILE PHONES

Some U.S. cell phones work in the Bahamas; check with your provider before your trip. The BTC has roaming agreements with many U.S. companies, including AT&T, T-Mobile, and Sprint Nextel. Roaming rates are $3 per day and $1.19 per minute.

In Nassau you can rent phones from BTC on a variety of packages. Or purchase a SIM card for about $15 at any BTC office; this will allow you to use your own cell phone while in the Bahamas. (You'll also need a BTC prepaid minutes card, but these cards can be purchased for as little as $10.) You can rent GMS cellular phones from companies such as Cellular Abroad, which charges $1.14 to $1.32 a minute on calls to the United States plus the rental of the phone, starting at $69 for a week or less. Service is improving, but is still spotty, and on the Out Islands, cell phones may not work at all.

## ▮ CUSTOMS AND DUTIES

Customs allows you to bring in 1 liter of wine or liquor and five cartons of cigarettes in addition to personal effects, purchases up to $100, and all the money you wish.

Certain types of personal belongings may get a raised eyebrow—an extensive collection of DVDs, for instance—if they suspect you may be planning to sell them while in the country. However, real hassles at immigration are rare, since officials realize tourists are the lifeblood of the economy.

You would be well advised to leave pets at home, unless you're considering a prolonged stay in the islands. An import permit is required from the Ministry of Agriculture and Fisheries for all animals brought into the Bahamas. The animal must be more than six months old. You'll also need a veterinary health certificate issued by a licensed vet. The permit is good for one year from the date of issue, costs $10, and the process must be completed immediately before departure.

U.S. residents who have been out of the country for at least 48 hours may bring home $800 worth of foreign goods duty-free, as long as they have not used the $800 allowance or any part of it in the past 30 days.

**Contacts Ministry of Agriculture and Fisheries** ✉ *Bahamas* ☎ *242/325–7413.* **U.S. Customs and Border Protection** ✉ *Bahamas* ⊕ *www.cbp.gov.*

## ▮ EATING OUT

The restaurants we list are the cream of the crop in each price category. You'll find all types, from cosmopolitan to the most casual restaurants, serving all types of cuisine. Unless otherwise noted, the restaurants listed in this guide are open daily for lunch and dinner.

⇒ *For information on food-related health issues, see Health below. For dining price categories, consult the price charts found near the beginning of each chapter. For guidelines on tipping, see Tipping below.*

### PAYING

The U.S. dollar is on par with the Bahamian dollar and both currencies are accepted in restaurants. Most credit cards are also accepted in most restaurants. Typically, you will have to ask for your check when you are finished.

# LOCAL DO'S AND TABOOS

## CUSTOMS OF THE COUNTRY

Humor is a wonderful way to relate to the islanders, but don't force it. Don't try to talk their dialect unless you are adept at it. Though most Bahamians are too polite to show it, you may offend them if you make a bad attempt at local lingo. Church is central in the lives of the Bahamians. They dress up in their fanciest finery; it's a sight to behold on Saturday evening and Sunday morning. To show respect, dress accordingly if you plan to attend religious ceremonies. No doubt you'll be outdone, but do dress up regardless.

## GREETINGS

Bahamians greet people with a proper British "good morning," "good afternoon," or "good evening." When approaching an islander to ask directions or information, preface your request with such a greeting, and ask "how are you?" Smile, and don't rush into a conversation, even if you're running late.

## LANGUAGE

Islanders speak English with a lilt influenced by their British and/or African ancestry. When locals talk among themselves in local dialect, it's virtually impossible for the unaccustomed to understand them. They take all sorts of shortcuts and pepper the language with words all their own. When islanders speak to visitors, they will use standard English.

## OUT ON THE TOWN

When you hail a waiter, say Sir or Miss. Your check usually will not be brought until you ask for it. Bahamians do not like drunkenness, and, regrettably, frequently have to put up with drunken Americans. Bahamians generally are not smokers, so smokers should choose outdoor cafés and terraces at restaurants. And all you honeymooners, save the displays of affection for the hotel. PDAs are not accepted here—although Americans will blush at the way Bahamians dance, even the middle-aged, which is

pelvis to pelvis. Bahamians love to dress up and will wear Sunday suits and dresses to dinner at nice restaurants and clubs.

## SIGHTSEEING

Visitors should dress conservatively when going to houses of worship. Bahamians love hats, and you will see quite a parade of fancy hats at church even on small islands. You should not wear swimsuits into stores and restaurants, even those on the beach. There are very few homeless Bahamians, and on the few occasions when people ask for money, just shake your head and keep walking. Polite children in school uniforms will often have fund-raisers in tourist areas, and parents and teachers will be there. Donations are greatly appreciated and help local schools. A decade ago, drug dealers frequently approached visitors on Nassau's streets, but police have cracked down, especially in tourist areas. Most likely you'll only be asked if you want your hair braided. It's customary to address people by Mr., Miss, and Mrs. in business situations, and with taxi drivers, concierges, hotel managers, guides, and tour-desk operators. Bahamians are more formal than Americans, and they value good manners; always remember your pleases and thank-yous.

## TIME

Bahamians tend to have a more casual attitude about time than visitors may be used to, which islanders say is because they've long lived a good life in a land where nature provided just about every need for housing, food, and livelihood. Bahamians believe there is always time to worry about the bad things tomorrow. Don't take it personally; things DO get done, though perhaps not at the rate you'd expect. Asking a Bahamian to hurry, especially if done rudely, however, may just slow things down. Stay polite, keep your humor, and try to slow down yourself— you'll have a better island experience.

## RESERVATIONS AND DRESS

Reservations are sometimes necessary in Nassau and on the more remote islands, where restaurants may close early if no one shows up or says they're coming. We mention dress only when men are required to wear a jacket or a jacket and tie. Otherwise, you can assume that dining out is a casual affair.

## WINES, BEER, AND SPIRITS

Kalik and Sands beer are brewed in the Bahamas and are available at most restaurants for lunch and dinner.

# ▌ ELECTRICITY

Electricity is 120 volts/60 cycles AC, which is compatible with all U.S. appliances.

# ▌ EMERGENCIES

The emergency telephone number in the Bahamas is 919 or 911. Pharmacies usually close at 6 pm. Emergency medicine after hours is available only at hospitals, or, on remote Out Islands, at clinics.

⇨ *For health-care contacts, please see the numbers listed at the front of each chapter.*

**Emergency Contacts Bahamas Air Sea Rescue Association** ⊠ *Bahamas* ☎ *242/325–8864* ⊕ *www.basra.org.* **United States Embassy** ⊠ *Bahamas* ☎ *242/322–1181.*

# ▌ HEALTH

### FOOD AND WATER

The major health risk in the Bahamas is traveler's diarrhea. This is most often caused by ingesting fruits, shellfish, and drinks to which your body is unaccustomed. Go easy at first on new foods such as mangoes, conch, and rum punch. There are rare cases of contaminated fruit, vegetables, or drinking water.

If you're susceptible to digestive problems, avoid ice, uncooked food, and unpasteurized milk and milk products, and stick to bottled water, or water that has been boiled for several minutes, even when brushing your teeth.

Drink plenty of purified water or tea; chamomile is a good folk remedy. In severe cases, rehydrate yourself with a salt-sugar solution (½ teaspoon salt and 4 tablespoons sugar per quart of water).

### DIVING

Do not fly within 24 hours of scuba diving. Always know where your nearest decompression chamber is *before* you embark on a dive expedition, and how you would get there in an emergency. The only chambers in the Bahamas are in Nassau and San Salvador, and emergency cases are often sent to Miami.

**Decompression Chamber Bahamas Hyperbaric Centre** ⊠ *Bahamas* ☎ *242/362–5765.*

### INSECTS

No-see-ums (sand fleas) and mosquitoes can be bothersome. Some travelers have allergies to sand-flea bites, and the itching can be extremely annoying. To prevent the bites, use a recommended bug repellent. To ease the itching, rub alcohol on the bites. Some Out Island hotels provide sprays or repellents but it's a good idea to bring your own.

### SUNBURN

Basking in the sun is one of the great pleasures of a Bahamian vacation, but because the sun is closer to Earth the farther south you go, it will burn your skin more quickly, so take precautions against sunburn and sunstroke.

On a sunny day, even people who are not normally bothered by strong sun should cover up with a long-sleeve shirt, a hat, and pants or a beach wrap while on a boat or midday at the beach. Carry UVA/UVB sunblock (with an SPF of at least 15) for your face and other sensitive areas. If you're engaging in water sports, be sure the sunscreen is waterproof.

Wear sunglasses, because eyes are particularly vulnerable to direct sun and reflected rays. Drink enough liquids—water or fruit juice preferably—and avoid coffee, tea, and alcohol. Above all, limit your sun time for the first few days until you become accustomed to the rays. Do not be fooled by an overcast day. The safest hours for sunbathing are 4–6 pm, but even then it's wise to limit initial exposure.

## MEDICAL INSURANCE AND ASSISTANCE

The most serious accidents and illnesses may require an airlift to the United States—most likely to a hospital in Florida. The costs of a medical evacuation can quickly run into the thousands of dollars, and your personal health insurance may not cover such costs. If you plan to pursue inherently risky activities, such as scuba diving, or if you have an existing medical condition, check your policy to see what's covered.

Consider buying trip insurance with medical-only coverage. Neither Medicare nor some private insurers cover medical expenses anywhere outside the United States. Medical-only policies typically reimburse you for medical care (excluding that related to preexisting conditions) and hospitalization abroad, and provide for evacuation. You still have to pay the bills and await reimbursement from the insurer, though.

Another option is to sign up with a medical-evacuation assistance company. A membership in one of these companies gets you doctor referrals, emergency evacuation or repatriation, 24-hour hotlines for medical consultation, and other assistance. International SOS Assistance Emergency and AirMed International

provide evacuation services and medical referrals. MedjetAssist offers medical evacuation.

**Medical Assistance Companies AirMed International** ✉ *Bahamas* ⊕ *www.airmed.com.* **International SOS Assistance Emergency** ✉ *Bahamas* ⊕ *www.internationalsos.com.* **MedjetAssist** ✉ *Bahamas* ⊕ *www.medjetassist.com.*

**Medical-Only Insurers International Medical Group** ✉ *Bahamas* ☎ *800/628–4664* ⊕ *www.imglobal.com.* **International SOS** ✉ *Bahamas* ⊕ *www.internationalsos.com.* **Wallach & Company** ✉ *Bahamas* ☎ *800/237–6615* ⊕ *www.wallach.com.*

## ▌ HOLIDAYS

The grandest holiday of all is Junkanoo, a carnival that came from slaves who made elaborate costumes and instruments such as goatskin drums. Junkanoo is celebrated on Boxing Day, the day after Christmas, and New Year's Day (the bands compete in all-night parades that start in the wee hours). Don't expect to conduct any business the day after the festivities.

During other legal holidays, most offices close, and some may extend the holiday by keeping earlier (or no) hours the day before or after.

In the Bahamas official holidays include New Year's Day, Good Friday, Easter, Easter Monday, Whit Monday (last Mon. in May), Labour Day (1st Mon. in June), Independence Day (July 10), Emancipation Day (1st Mon. in Aug.), National Heroes Day (Oct. 12), Christmas Day, and Boxing Day (Dec. 26).

## ▌ HOURS OF OPERATION

Banks are generally open Monday–Thursday 9 or 9:30 to 3 or 4 and Friday 9 to 5. However, on the Out Islands banks may keep shorter hours—on the smallest cays, they may be open only a day or two each week. Most Bahamian offices observe bank hours.

Hours for attractions vary. Most open between 9 and 10 and close around 5.

Though most drugstores typically abide by normal store hours, some stay open 24 hours.

Most stores, with the exception of straw markets and malls, close on Sunday.

# ∎ MAIL

Regardless of whether the term "snail mail" was coined in the Bahamas, you're likely to arrive home long before your postcards do—it's not unheard of for letters to take two to four weeks to reach their destinations. No postal (zip) codes are used in the Bahamas—all mail is collected from local area post-office boxes.

First-class mail from the Bahamas to the United States is 65¢ per half ounce; you'll pay 50¢ to mail a postcard. Postcard stamps good for foreign destinations are usually sold at shops selling postcards, so you don't have to make a special trip.

From the United States a postcard or a letter sent to the Bahamas costs 98¢.

## SHIPPING PACKAGES

If you want to ship purchases home, take the same precautions you take in the United States—don't pack valuables or fragile items.

**Express Services Copimaxx** ⊠ *Bahamas* ☎ *242/328–2679.* **FedEx** ⊠ *Bahamas* ☎ *242/352–3402 Freeport, 242/322–5656 Nassau, 242/367–2817 Abaco, 242/368–2540 Andros, 242/332–2720 Eleuthera, 242/337–6786 Long Island, 649/946–2542 Grand Turk, 649/946–4682 Providenciales, 800/247–4747 U.S. international customer service.* **Mail Boxes Etc.** ⊠ *Bahamas* ☎ *242/394–1508.*

# ∎ MONEY

Generally, prices in the Bahamas are slightly higher than in the United States. Businesses usually don't care whether you pay in U.S. dollars or Bahamian dollars, since they're the same value. In the Out Islands you'll notice that meals and simple goods can be expensive; prices are high due to the remoteness of the islands and the costs of importing.

ATMs are widely available, except on the most remote islands, but often the currency dispensed is Bahamian. If you have any left at the end of your stay, you can exchange it at the airport.

Prices throughout this guide are given for adults. Substantially reduced fees are almost always available for children, students, and senior citizens.

## ATMS AND BANKS

There are ATMs at banks, malls, resorts, and shops throughout the major islands. For excursions to remote locations, bring plenty of cash; there are few or no ATMs on some small cays, and on weekends or holidays, those that exist may run out of cash.

Banks are generally open Monday–Thursday 9 or 9:30 to 3 or 4 and Friday 9 to 5. However, on the Out Islands, banks may keep shorter hours—on the smallest cays, they may be open only a day or two each week.

∎TIP➔ PINs with more than four digits are not recognized at ATMs in the Bahamas. If yours has five or more, remember to change it before you leave.

## CREDIT CARDS

When you book your hotel accommodations, be sure to ask if credit cards are accepted; some smaller hotels in the islands do not take plastic.

It's a good idea to inform your credit-card company before you travel, especially if you don't travel internationally very often. Otherwise, the credit-card company might put a hold on your card owing to unusual activity—not a good thing halfway through your trip.

Although it's usually cheaper (and safer) to use a credit card abroad for large purchases (so you can cancel payments or be reimbursed if there's a problem), note that some credit-card companies *and* the banks that issue them add substantial percentages to all foreign transactions, whether they're in a foreign currency or not. Check on these fees before leaving home, so there won't be any surprises when you get the bill.

**CURRENCY AND EXCHANGE**

The U.S. dollar is on par with the Bahamian dollar and is accepted all over the Bahamas. Bahamian money runs in bills of $1, $5, $10, $20, $50, and $100. Since U.S. currency is accepted everywhere, there really is no need to change to Bahamian. Also, you won't incur any transaction fees for currency exchange, or worry about getting stuck with unspent Bahamian dollars. Carry small bills when bargaining at straw markets.

# ▌ PACKING

Aside from your bathing suit, which will be your favorite uniform, take lightweight clothing (short-sleeve shirts, T-shirts, cotton slacks, lightweight jackets for evening wear for men; light dresses, shorts, and T-shirts for women). If you're going during high season, between mid-December and April, toss in a sweater for the occasional cool evening. Cover up in public places and downtown shopping expeditions, and save that skimpy bathing suit for the beach at your hotel.

Some of the more sophisticated hotels require jackets for men and dresses for women at dinner. The Bahamas' casinos do not have dress codes.

# ▌ PASSPORTS AND VISAS

U.S. citizens need a valid passport when entering and returning from the Bahamas, but do not need a visa.

# ▌ SAFETY

Since 2009 there has been a significant spike in violent crime in Nassau, especially near the cruise-ship dock and in off-the-beaten-path locations. Exercise caution in these areas: be aware of your wallet or handbag at all times, and keep your jewelry in the hotel safe. Be especially wary in remote areas, always lock your rental vehicle, and don't keep any valuables in the car, even in the locked trunk.

Women traveling alone should not go out walking unescorted at night in Nassau or in remote areas. To avoid unwanted attention, dress conservatively and cover up swimsuits off the beach.

**U.S. Department of State** ✉ *Bahamas* ⊕ *www.travel.state.gov/travel.*

# ▌ TAXES

There's no sales tax in the Bahamas; the $15 departure tax is usually included in the price of commercial airline tickets.

Tax on your hotel room is 6%–12%, depending on the island visited; at some resorts, a small service charge of up to 5% may be added to cover housekeeping and bellman service.

# ▌ TIME

The Bahamas lie within the Eastern Standard Time (EST) Zone, which means that it's 7 am in the Bahamas (or New York) when it's noon in London and 10 pm in Sydney. In summer the islands switch to Eastern Daylight Time (EDT).

# ▌ TIPPING

In the Bahamas, service staff and hotel workers expect to be tipped. The usual tip for service from a taxi driver or waiter is 15% and $1–$2 a bag for porters. Most travelers leave $1 to $3 per day for their hotel maid, usually every morning since the maid may have a day off. Many hotels and restaurants automatically add a 15% gratuity to your bill; if not, a 15% to 20% tip at a restaurant is appropriate (more for a high-end establishment). Bartenders generally get $1 to $2 per drink.

# ▌TRIP INSURANCE

Comprehensive trip insurance is valuable if you're booking a considerably expensive or complicated trip (particularly to an isolated region) or if you're booking far in advance. Comprehensive policies typically cover trip cancellation and interruption, letting you cancel or cut your trip short because of illness, or, in some cases, acts of terrorism in your destination. Such policies might also cover evacuation and medical care. (For trips abroad you should have at least medical-only coverage. ⇨ *See Medical Insurance and Assistance under Health.*) Some also cover you for trip delays because of bad weather or mechanical problems as well as for lost or delayed luggage.

Another type of coverage to consider is financial default—that is, when your trip is disrupted because a tour operator, airline, or cruise line goes out of business. Generally you must buy this when you book your trip or shortly thereafter, and it's available to you only if your operator isn't on a list of excluded companies.

Always read the fine print of your policy to make sure that you're covered for the risks that most concern you. Compare several polices to be sure you're getting the best price and range of coverage available.

Insurance Comparison Info **Insure My Trip** ⊠ *Bahamas* ☎ *800/487–4722* ⊕ *www. insuremytrip.com.* **Square Mouth** ⊠ *Bahamas* ☎ *800/240–0369* ⊕ *www.squaremouth.com.*

Comprehensive Insurers **AIG Travel Guard** ⊠ *Bahamas* ☎ *800/826–4919* ⊕ *www.travelguard.com.* **Allianz Global Assistance** ⊠ *Bahamas* ☎ *866/884–3556* ⊕ *www.allianztravelinsurance.com.* **CSA Travel Protection** ⊠ *Bahamas* ☎ *240/330–1529* ⊕ *www.csatravelprotection.com.* **HTH Worldwide** ⊠ *Bahamas* ☎ *610/254–8700* ⊕ *www.hthworldwide.com.* **Travel Insured International** ⊠ *Bahamas* ☎ *800/243–3174* ⊕ *www.travelinsured.com.* **Travelex Insurance** ⊠ *Bahamas* ☎ *800/228–9792* ⊕ *www. travelex-insurance.com.*

# ▌VISITOR INFORMATION

Contacts **Bahamas Ministry of Tourism** ⊠ *Bahamas* ☎ *800/224–2627* ⊕ *www.bahamas.com.* **Bahamas Out Islands Promotion Board** ⊠ *Bahamas* ☎ *954/475–8315* ⊕ *www.myoutislands.com.* **Caribbean Tourism Organization** ⊠ *Bahamas* ⊕ *www. doitcaribbean.com.* **Grand Bahama Island Tourism Board** ⊠ *Bahamas* ☎ *800/545–1300* ⊕ *www.grandbahamavacations.com.* **Harbour Island Tourism** ⊠ *Bahamas* ⊕ *www. harbourislandguide.com.* **Nassau/Paradise Island Promotion Board** ⊠ *Bahamas* ⊕ *www.nassauparadiseisland.com.*

**BahamasGateway.com** ⊠ *Bahamas* ⊕ *www.bahamasgateway.com.* **BahamasIslands.com** ⊠ *Bahamas* ⊕ *www. the-bahamas-islands.com.* **Bahamasnet. com** ⊠ *Bahamas* ⊕ *www.bahamasnet.com.* **Bahamas Visitors Guide** ⊠ *Bahamas* ⊕ *www. bahamasvisitorsguide.com.* **FishingtheBahamian.com** ⊠ *Bahamas* ⊕ *www.fishing. thebahamian.com.* **Friends of the Bahamas** ⊠ *Bahamas* ⊕ *www.friendsofthebahamas. com.* **Nassau Guardian** ⊠ *Bahamas* ⊕ *www. thenassauguardian.com.*

# INDEX

## A

**Abaco Beach Resort and Boat Harbour** ⌂ , *159*
**Abaco Club on Winding Bay,** *167*
**Abaco Inn Restaurant** ✕ , *169*
**Abaco National Park,** *146–147, 167*
**Abacos,** *10, 38, 144–186*
*beaches, 163, 168, 169*
*emergencies, 152*
*festivals, 149–150*
*itineraries, 151*
*lodging, 152, 159, 165, 168, 172–173, 176, 178, 182–184*
*mail and shipping, 152–153*
*nightlife and the arts, 159, 165, 173, 178, 184–185*
*prices, 152*
*restaurants, 152, 155–157, 163–164, 168, 169–172, 176, 177–178, 180–182*
*shopping, 159–160, 165, 168, 173–174, 176, 178, 185*
*sports and outdoor activities, 160–163, 165–166, 173, 174–175, 177, 178, 185–186*
*tours, 147, 162–163*
*transportation, 150–152*
*visitor information, 153*
**Acklins Island,** *298, 344–347*
**Adderley's Plantation,** *329, 330*
**Adelaide Beach,** *62–63*
**Adelaide Village,** *60*
**Air travel,** *352*
*Abacos, 150*
*Andros, Bimini, and the Berry Islands, 192*
*Eleuthera and Harbour Island, 232*
*Exumas, 274*
*Grand Bahama Island, 106*
*New Providence and Paradise Islands, 48*
*Southern Out Islands, 305*
**Albert Lowe Museum,** *179*
**Alice Town,** *210, 211*
**Allan's Cay,** *291*
**Andros,** *10, 188–209*
*beaches, 199–200, 203*
*emergencies, 193*
*festivals, 191*
*lodging, 193, 200, 203–204, 207, 209*
*nightlife, 200, 204, 209*

*prices, 194*
*restaurants, 193, 203, 207*
*shopping, 204*
*sports and outdoor activities, 205–206, 208, 209*
*transportation, 192*
**Andros Barrier Reef,** *194*
**Andros Lighthouse,** *201*
**Andros Town,** *201*
**Androsia Batik Works Factory,** *201–202*
**Angler's Restaurant** ✕ , *155*
**Apartment and house rentals,** *355.* ⇨ *See also* Lodging
**Arawak Cay,** *58*
**Ardastra Gardens, Zoo, and Conservation Centre,** *22, 58*
**Arthur's Town,** *310–312*
**Atlantis, Paradise Island** ⌂ , *22, 74*
**ATMs,** *360*
**Augusta Bay Bahamas** ⌂ , *283*

## B

**Bahamas National Trust Rand Nature Centre,** *108*
**Bahamian Brewery,** *108*
**Bailey Town,** *211, 213*
**Balcony House,** *52*
**Banana Bay Restaurant** ✕ , *122*
**Banks,** *360.* ⇨ *See also* Money matters
**Bannerman Town,** *249*
**Beach House Tapas Restaurant, The** ✕ , *243*
**Beach parties,** *19*
**Beaches,** *14, 18–20*
*Abacos, 163, 168, 169*
*Andros, 199–200, 203*
*Berry Islands, 221–222*
*Bimini, 213–214, 219*
*Eleuthera and Harbour Island, 237, 242–243, 244, 249, 254*
*Exumas, 279, 289–290, 294*
*Grand Bahama Island, 114, 116, 118*
*Long Island, 329, 330, 337, 340*
*New Providence and Paradise Islands, 61–63*
*pink sand beaches, 14, 18, 254*
*Southern Out Islands, 313, 316–317, 321, 329, 330, 337, 340*
**Behring Point,** *201*

**Bennett's Harbour,** *310–312*
**Berry Islands,** *10, 188–194, 220–224*
*beaches, 221–222*
*emergencies, 193*
*festivals, 191*
*lodging, 193, 223*
*prices, 194*
*restaurants, 193, 222*
*sports and outdoor activities, 223–224*
*transportation, 192*
**Bicycling**
*Exuma Cays, 295*
*Grand Bahama Island, 135*
*Great Abaco Island, 160*
*Harbour Island, 263*
*San Salvador, 319*
*Treasure Cay, 165*
**Big and Little Saddleback Cay,** *203*
**Big Farmer's Cay,** *291*
**Big Major's Cay,** *291*
**Bimini,** *10, 188–194, 210–220*
*beaches, 213–214, 219*
*emergencies, 193*
*festivals, 191*
*lodging, 193, 215–216, 219–220*
*nightlife, 216, 220*
*prices, 194*
*restaurants, 193, 215, 219*
*shopping, 216*
*sports and outdoor activities, 216–218, 220*
*transportation, 192*
**Bimini Biological Field Station Sharklab,** *218*
**Bimini Museum,** *213*
**Bimini Nature Trail,** *218–219*
**Bimini Road,** *213*
**Bimini Sands Beach,** *219*
**Bimini Sands Resort and Marina** ⌂ , *219–220*
**Bimini Twist** ✕ , *219*
**Bird Rock Lighthouse,** *345*
**Birdwatching,** *24–25, 279, 301*
**Blight, The,** *330*
**Blue Bar at Pink Sands, The** ✕ , *255*
**Blue Lagoon Island,** *61*
**Blue Lagoon Island Dolphin Encounter,** *22*
**Boat and ferry travel,** *353–354*
*Abacos, 150*
*Andros, Bimini, and the Berry Islands, 192*

## PHOTO CREDITS

# NOTES

# NOTES

# NOTES

# NOTES

# NOTES

# ABOUT OUR WRITERS

A born and bred Tar Heel with roots in North Carolina, **Julianne Hoell** began her love affair with the Bahamas after visiting New Providence in 1994. Following completion of a journalism degree from UNC-Chapel Hill, she moved to Eleuthera and began traveling to neighboring islands in search of the perfect conch salad and sunset view. Her answer is forthcoming as she continues to write about the Caribbean's best restaurants and hotels.

Born in England and raised in the Bahamas, **Jessica Robertson** has traveled the world for work and play but calls Nassau home. She has visited just about all of the populated islands in the Bahamas, as well as some occupied only by hermit crabs and seagulls, and works as the online editor for *The Tribune,* the country's daily newspaper.

**Paul Rubio**'s insatiable quest to discover and learn has taken him to the far corners of the world—more than 80 countries and counting. A Harvard-trained economist with a double masters degree, he took on his passion for travel writing full time in 2008 and hasn't looked back. Paul currently contributes to *Ocean Home Magazine, Palm Beach Illustrated,* and *Weddings Illustrated* as well as other Fodor's guides, jetsetter.com, and various outlets of Modern Luxury Media.

**Jamie Werner** is a freelance writer and photographer who lives on Grand Bahama Island. Prior to her arrival in Freeport, she lived throughout the Caribbean with her husband and young children, including Aruba, Trinidad, Barbados, and the Dominican Republic, where she taught writing and high school literature. She studied at Sydney University in Australia and the University of Arizona, earning degrees in journalism and photography. Raised in Wyoming and Colorado, her roots are well planted in the mountain ranges of the western U.S., but her heart is happiest on the beach with a book and a paddleboard.